ROUTLEDGE LIBRARY EDITIONS: EMPLOYEE OWNERSHIP AND ECONOMIC DEMOCRACY

Volume 3

NEW FORMS OF OWNERSHIP

NEW FORMS OF OWNERSHIP

Management and Employment

Edited by
GLENVILLE JENKINS AND
MICHAEL POOLE

Routledge
Taylor & Francis Group

LONDON AND NEW YORK

First published in 1990 by Routledge

This edition first published in 2018
by Routledge
2 Park Square, Milton Park, Abingdon, Oxon OX14 4RN

and by Routledge
711 Third Avenue, New York, NY 10017

Routledge is an imprint of the Taylor & Francis Group, an informa business

British Library Cataloguing in Publication Data
A catalogue record for this book is available from the British Library

ISBN: 978-1-138-29962-7 (Set)
ISBN: 978-1-315-12163-5 (Set) (ebk)
ISBN: 978-1-138-30641-7 (Volume 3) (hbk)
ISBN: 978-1-138-30645-5 (Volume 3) (pbk)
ISBN: 978-1-315-14177-0 (Volume 3) (ebk)

Publisher's Note
The publisher has gone to great lengths to ensure the quality of this reprint but points out that some imperfections in the original copies may be apparent.

Disclaimer
The publisher has made every effort to trace copyright holders and would welcome correspondence from those they have been unable to trace.

New Forms of Ownership
Management and Employment

Edited by Glenville Jenkins
and
Michael Poole

London and New York

First published 1990
by Routledge
11 New Fetter Lane, London EC4P 4EE

Simultaneously published in the USA and Canada
by Routledge
a division of Routledge, Chapman and Hall, Inc.
29 West 35th Street, New York, NY 10001

Phototypeset in 10pt Times by
Mews Photosetting, Beckenham, Kent
Printed and bound in Great Britain by
Mackays of Chatham PLC, Chatham, Kent

British Library Cataloguing in Publication Data

New Forms of Ownership: management and employment.
  1. Industries. Ownership. Rights of personnel
  I. Jenkins, Glenville, *1951–* II. Poole, Michael, *1943–*
338.6

ISBN 0-415-03637-2

Library of Congress Cataloging in Publication Data

New Forms of Ownership: Management and Employment / edited by
Glenville Jenkins and Michael Poole.
    p. cm.
  Includes bibliographical references.
  ISBN 0-415-03637-2
  1. Employee ownership – Great Britain. 2. Corporate reorganizations
  – Great Britain. 3. Privatization – Great Britain. 4. Management buyouts –
  Great Britain. 5. Profit-sharing – Great Britain. 6. Franchises (Retail trade)
  – Great Britain. I. Jenkins, Glenville, 1951– . II. Poole, Michael.
  HD5660.G7N48   1990
  338.6–dc20   90-31656
                                                                      CIP

Contents

Contents

Figures

Tables

Contributors

Peter Abell,
University of Surrey

Lesley Baddon,
University of Strathclyde

Paul Banfield,
Sheffield City Polytechnic

Robert J. Bennett,
London School of Economics

Alistair Bruce,
University of Nottingham

Trevor Buck,
University of Nottingham

Neil Carter,
University of York

Laurence J. Clarke,
University of Stirling

Christine Cousins,
Hatfield Polytechnic

John Coyne,
University of Nottingham

Ray Donnelly,
Heriot-Watt University

Alan Felstead,
Nuffield College, Oxford

Margaret Grieco,
University of Oxford

David Hague,
Sheffield City Council

Richard Hallett,
Consultant, Faircroft College

Charles Hanson,
University of Newcastle-upon-Tyne

Phil Hobbs,
Bristol University

Len Holmes,
Polytechnic of North London

Li Hong,
People's University of China

Laurie Hunter,
University of Strathclyde

Jeff Hyman,
University of Strathclyde

Keith Jefferis,
Kingston Polytechnic

John Leopold,
University of Strathclyde

Nick Oliver,
University of Wales College
of Cardiff

Mike Peel,
University of Wales College
of Cardiff

Contributors

Harvie Ramsay,
University of Strathclyde

John Sellgren,
London School of Economics

Alan Thomas,
Open University

Robert Watson,
University of Manchester
Institute of Science and
Technology

Richard Welford,
University of Bradford

Nick Wilson,
University of Bradford

Jonathan Winterton,
University of Bradford

Mike Wright,
University of Nottingham

Preface

The contributions to this volume arise from the Employment Research Unit's annual conference held at Cardiff Business School on 14 and 15 September 1988. The central theme of the conference was the changing nature of ownership in British industry and its impact on management and development. The events which have brought ownership to a focal point of attention include the major changes brought about by economic restructuring; privatization; the growth of employee profit-sharing and share-ownership schemes; the increased number of successful management buy-outs; the growth of co-operative ventures; and the existence of private tender arrangements particularly in the Health Service and in local government.

The annual conference of the Employment Research Unit has become an integral part of the expanding programme of research and scholarship in the Cardiff Business School. Previous conferences have covered the themes of new technology and labour-market changes, and the Japanization of British industry. The financial assistance of the Economic and Research Council in staging the 1988 Conference is greatly appreciated. At Routledge, Mary Ann Kernan and Rosemary Nixon deserve credit for their encouragement of this project. And Karen Owen played a valuable role, not only in typing, but also in other activities associated with bringing this book to fruition.

Introduction

Ownership has become an increasingly consequential theme in modern political, economic, and management thought. It is central to the furtherance of a property-owning democracy and the reduction of the role of government in economic management. And it is basic to attempts to stimulate managers and employees to commit themselves to their respective organizations and to create viable and dynamic enterprises which can compete successfully in an increasingly complex and open global economy.

This quickening of attention in the concept of ownership demands explanation and analysis. After all, for much of the twentieth century, the growing scale and complexity of industry, coupled with public ownership of the means of production and distribution, appeared to have heralded an inexorable separation of ownership and control in the enterprise. Moreover, control was viewed as the dominant force in modern societies. Admittedly rather different debates were conducted in the private and public sectors respectively. In the private sector the rise of the joint-stock company appeared to be linked with one of two distinctive departures. Either it was seen to be extending profit maximization by guaranteeing security for capital accumulation in a way which was inconceivable in the entrepreneurial firm with full liability. Or, more familiarly, it was underpinning the emergence of a new managerial elite with long-term company growth being its primary objective. Above all, a transformation in business behaviour and ideology appeared to have been effected, with the claims of various stakeholders (employees, consumers, the public, shareholders, and the managers themselves) all being accommodated. By contrast, in the public sector, the main concern was that a managerial elite was exploiting a position of control to further sectional interests and, by so doing, was occasioning the spread of an impersonal bureaucracy which had lost touch with its original constituency.

More latterly, however, it has become clear that these debates have been conducted in too conventional a guise. Indeed it is now recognized

1

that the prospects of a substantial change in patterns of ownership (with capital being widely, if unequally, distributed amongst modern working populations) are far more realistic than any stage since the rise of industry itself.

Most of the forms of ownership examined in this volume are actually rooted in practices which have an earlier ancestry. But what is novel about the current movement is a breadth and vigour which, arguably have no obvious historical parallel. Thus, encompassed in the recent movement have been phenomena as diverse as the upsurge of entrepreneuralism, restructuring and privatisation, profit-sharing and share-ownership schemes, management and employee buy-outs, and the resurgence of the producer co-operative.

Yet why, it may be reasonably asked, have such changes occurred and what, more specifically, are the prospects of these and similar trends continuing throughout the 1990s and into the twenty-first century? Underlying the modern movement would appear to be at least six partly divergent and partly intertwined forces. These are:

1 Dislocations in the political economies of the post-1970s brought about by the 'oil shocks', the dramatic and turbulent currency movements, inflation, and unemployment.
2 A transformation in ascendant ideologies and values in which new forms of ownership have been sought as counterpoints to the traditional capitalist firm, the managerially dominated corporation, and the impersonal state bureaucracy.
3 Legislative changes (reflecting these ascendant values) which have given a fiscal stimulus to profit-sharing and share-ownership and to similar departures.
4 New technologies which have placed a heavy premium on the retention of a core labour force which requires constant retraining in modern operational and production techniques, and which is encouraged to identify with the company as a whole.
5 Changing organizational cultures with an emphasis on unitary values and relationships. This phenomenon has been partly occasioned by a reduction in the power and influence of labour unions associated with high levels of unemployment and trade-union legislation.
6 The long-term movement towards greater organizational democracy in which employee participation in decision-making and involvement in ownership have been interrelated departures.

For nearly thirty years, the post-war economic order had been characterized by low levels of unemployment, governmental intervention in the macro-economy, and currency stability. The Keynesian precepts which underpinned the era were widely endorsed and 'the consensus' generally prevailed against the strictures of market-oriented classical economists and those committed to a root-and-branch transformation to a socialist system. But the 'oil shocks' of the 1970s, currency instability, rampant inflation, and an acceleration of unemployment to levels hitherto regarded as politically untenable, were to occasion a radical change in economic objectives and priorities. The rise of monetarism and an increasing reliance on markets for resource allocation became the dominant forces of the post-Keynesian world. Accompanying these changes, an emphasis on entrepreneurialism became increasingly ascendant, while experimentation in new forms of ownership occurred and proved to be a major fillip to the producer co-operative movement.

But changes in dominant ideologies and values were also encouraging new analyses of ownership and control in the business firm. Above all, the case was being articulated that neo-corporatist structures and institutions should be superseded by market-driven, adaptable firms which were far more sensitive to the consumer. Restructuring and privatization stemmed directly from these policies, with managers and employees being encouraged to take an equity stake in the emergent enterprises and to become fully committed to the market economy.

From the 1970s onwards there were also important legislative innovations on both sides of the Atlantic that were specifically to encourage profit-sharing and share-ownership schemes for employees. In the USA, the rise of Employee Stock Ownership Plans (ESOPs) is thus directly linked with the passage of a series of laws in the 1970s that give a substantial stimulus to employee financial participation. Moreover, in Britain, the Finance Acts of 1978, 1980, and 1984 have undoubtedly encouraged an appreciable expansion of profit-sharing in the 1980s. But the efficacy of this legislation may, in turn, be interpreted as a reflection of changing values on the nature of ownership which were to be a signal feature of the era.

The recent past has also witnessed a technological revolution which may well prove to be no less consequential than the emergence of industrial activities themselves for social structures and institutions. The implications for labour markets have been fundamental. Above all, it is increasingly necessary for managements to retain a core, adaptable labour force which requires constant retraining to meet the demands of advanced operational and production techniques. And, in such circumstances, it is especially important to secure the commitment of employees to their organizations and to further employee share-holding as part of this emergent strategy.

During the past decade there have also been dramatic changes in the culture of organizations. The most important single development here has been the re-emphasis on unitary approaches to organizational decision-making. Attempts to emulate the Japanese method of human-resource management has been part of this change in attitudes. But, in practice, managements have always preferred to operate on the basis of a conception of the organization as a unitary rather than pluralistic system.

During the 1960s and 1970s the power and influence of trade unions made such conceptions difficult to sustain. Nevertheless the weakening of unions by unemployment and labour law has changed this situation. Managements now have far more confidence in their own values and, in consequence, have sought to generate a climate or culture within the organization in which the integration of all employees is once again a recognizable feature. And, apart from developing improved communications, employee involvement and profit-sharing have become progressively more central to management policy.

A confident management has also sought new ownership arrangements (and particularly through the management buy-out) in which its own role in financial proprietorship has become progressively more dominant.

Furthermore, there does appear to be a long-term movement towards greater organizational democracy with its two main aspects (participation in ownership and in decision-making) becoming progressively more fused. The post-war conception of an industrial democracy had centred on the role of trade unions as oppositional bodies with the function of acting as a check to the power of management and state. This conception owed much to the recognition that the highly integrated corporatist societies of the inter-war years (Germany, Italy, and Japan) had significant negative consequences for social systems. However, the highly competitive economic era of the 1970s onwards occasioned a radical change in political thinking. The oppositional power of trade unions was becoming increasingly viewed as a brake upon efficiency and economic development. The argument ran: if organizational democracy could develop in a unitarist direction (by giving *employees* a voice in decision-making and a stake in ownership), it could ensure cohesive organizations, a motivated workforce, and a check on the powers of management. Moreover, the concern for greater employee involvement was encouraging an extension of this principle to worker participation in equity as well as in decision-making within the firm.

But what are the prospects of these trends continuing into the future? The best answer to this question is provided by the various contributors to the current volume. The first section looks at some of the issues of social and economic restructuring that have arisen in the wake of the 1980s recession. In the main, local initiatives of economic regeneration are examined in their attempts to ameliorate the conditions of unemployment and social deprivation. Such attempts have led to a number of novel and not so novel organizational forms developing particularly at a community level. The section begins, however, with Abell's contribution which provides, within the context of East–West relations, a much broader view of the impact of many of the developments considered in the following sections.

Abell highlights specific changes in the political economies of capitalist and socialist countries in the 1980s from which a thesis of the labour–capital partnership is developed. This type of partnership starts from the premise that both liberal-capitalist and socialist societies are seeking a way of bringing together the factors of production in a manner which is both *just* and *efficient*. Several attempts have been made to find a third way between socialist and liberal-capitalist pure conceptions of political economy. And Abell argues that, if a third way is to be found, then we will have to draw on both these conceptions of political economy and transcend them. Some recent and not so recent attempts are examined including people's capitalism, Weitzman's share economy, Langian market socialism, and labour-managed market socialism. In an insightful analysis of these propositions Abell finds them wanting but predicts and advocates a convergence toward labour-capital partnerships, i.e. partnerships based on the risks of income variation between the providers of capital and labour.

The second contribution by Bennett and Sellgren examines the ownership and management of organizations in relation to the economic development needs of local communities. Here the importance of the role of the state and the legislative constraints under which local authorities attempt to develop a policy of local economic development in the restructuring of their communities are clearly salient issues. In this context, they present an analysis of the form and structure of local economic development. As Bennett and Sellgren emphasize, ownership in the context of local economic policy is a complex phenomenon leading to a wide range of possible 'ownership vehicles' incorporating traditional and radical alternatives. The success of such initiatives lies in part in the relationships developed between local and central government, the private sector, and the needs of the local community.

Such relationships form the central thrust of both Holmes and Grieco's contribution and that of Banfield and Hague. Within a radical structuralist framework, Holmes and Grieco examine the development and construction of alternative forms of organization arising from radical initiatives in a community centre in a predominatly black community and in a training centre for unemployed adults. These organizations offered, initially at least, alternative decision-making structures, a pattern of distributed leadership, and flexible communication links. However, inter-organizational relationships, particularly with supporting funding agencies operating under a more conventional organizational structure, impinge upon the initial organizational form, so much so that the long-term consequence is that radical beginnings are overrun by the dominant organization's rationale. As Holmes and Grieco emphasize, the sponsorship of radical organizations 'permits radical initiatives to be encompassed and controlled by transforming their organizational forms, and thus permitting conflict to be defused in respect of the wider society yet intensified within the radical organization itself'.

This pattern is also reflected in Banfield and Hague's examination of the development of the Manor Employment Project; a project which had radical beginnings aimed at improving the employment opportunities in a deprived area of Sheffield. Here the initial support of the local authority became the source of the project's problems. There developed a movement from ideological support for the initiative to an increasingly calculative one which again influenced the decision-making process with the Manor Employment Project itself.

Obviously the lack of control is an important aspect of these cases and is particularly apparent when one considers the organizational successes outlined by Donnelly in his examination of co-operative ventures in Scotland and Northern Ireland. His analysis of the role of credit unions, consumer co-operatives, and housing co-operatives provides an insight into other alternative forms of restructuring taking place on the 'Celtic fringe'. In his view, democratic control in such initiatives is clearly vital in maintaining an ability to create jobs and regenerate local communities. Furthermore, Donnelly stresses the importance of the role of universities in sustaining such developments.

A major role in the restructuring of the economy has, of course, been played by the state, particularly in the attempts to privatize the public sector and to introduce wider share-ownership amongst the general public. Past privatization measures have radically changed the nature of the mixed economy and this is likely to continue. The programme has also made significant inroads into public-sector organization and management, particularly in the case of public-tender arrangements in health and local government. In some cases these developments have radically altered the employment relationship and modified contractual relationships for employees.

Part 2 is thus primarily concerned with the analysis of this strategy of Conservative economic policy. Consideration of some of the major elements in this strategy begins with Cousins' examination of the contracting-out of services in the National Health Service. The focus of her contribution is the impact of a mandatory programme of contracting-out of domestic, laundry, and catering services on the restructuring of ancillary work in two district authorities in the South-east of England. Unlike many privatization proposals, such as that considered by Hallett at British Telecom, the contracting-out of ancillary services was a policy few health managers would have adopted without government pressure. Cousins argues that, since privatization, management of such services has moved from managing and providing a service to monitoring, supervising, and evaluating contractual obligations. Moreover, following such changes, there is a fall in the level of direct management control over the quality and flexibility of services, low trust relations between manager and managed, and a decline in the ancillary worker's contribution to patient care and commitment to work. More broadly, the contracting-out system has led to a greater polarization and segmentation of health-service workers.

The second contribution by Hallett examines the impact of privatization on the corporate and management structure in British Telecom (BT). He points to the complete reorganization of the management structure and organization at BT on a divisional 'task'-oriented basis which commenced before privatization. However, he feels that the process of liberalization of BT in the international telecommunications market has had a greater impact than privatization *per se* in directing management thinking.

The future of the strategy depends in part on the continued privatization of the energy industries following the flotations of oil and gas. In this context Winterton examines the run-up to privatization of British Coal and its relation to the privatization of the electricity industry. The privatization of the electricity industry is seen as a prerequisite for the privatization of British Coal and, together with the pressures of supply from international coal production, electricity privatization will effectively liberalize the coal industry. This could be further enhanced by the expansion of private mining operations and the offer to miners of collieries earmarked for closure of the opportunity to form co-operative ventures. Once exposed to the increased competition in the domestic and international markets, British Coal is likely to change radically its production standards. Winterton examines these and other issues in relation to the miners' strike of 1984 and management's role at colliery level in the Yorkshire coalfield.

Finally, Hong's review of industrial reform in China through the Enterprise Responsibility System (ERS) provides an interesting contrast to developments in developed economies. While not changing the nature of state ownership of industry, the ERS makes way for the separation of ownership from management by releasing management from some of the major constraints of central planning. The ERS has stimulated competition and orientated managerial practice to both production and market needs. In aiding economic development and reform, the system is viewed as the forerunner of the establishment of a socialist market system.

However, no theme in the 'new ownership' debate has captured the imagination of scholars and practitioners more than the spread of equity rights to employees. The rise of profit-sharing and share-ownership has been particularly characteristic of this development; but of no less importance has been the growth of management buy-outs and the franchise movement. Hence in Part 3 of this volume these issues are addressed in depth and detail.

There are three main contributions on profit-sharing and share-ownership schemes for employees. The first by Hanson and Watson details empirical evidence on the effects of profit-sharing on company performance with special reference to 382 UK listed companies, 107 of which had profit-sharing arrangements. They are able to demonstrate that companies with all-employee profit-sharing schemes outperform similar non-profit sharing companies and that this applies especially to growth in sales. But they do add a cautionary note that a certain management style may be at the root of both profit-sharing and a good company performance.

In the second contribution, Ramsay and his colleagues cast doubt on the notion that major changes in employee attitudes and behaviour stem from the introduction of schemes. Based on the data from their 'Glasgow study' of 356 surveyed firms and 35 case-studies, their contribution focuses particularly on Save As You Earn share-option schemes. And, above all, they conclude that low contributions and the small 'bonus' element contained in these schemes are unlikely to produce a transformation in workplace attitudes and may, indeed, promote instrumental orientations to company and work.

However, Wilson and Peel, in their study of 52 UK engineering firms, provide evidence of a stronger effect of profit-sharing and share-ownership schemes. They assume that, alongside other forms of participation, there is a 'voice' mechanism here which may reduce labour turnover and absenteeism. Moreover, they are able to demonstrate that firms which have adopted profit-sharing and/or share-ownership schemes exhibit significantly lower absenteeism and labour-turnover rates than firms without schemes, though evidence relating to the effects of participation on temporary labour withdrawal is found to be more mixed.

But the spread of share-ownership in the 1980s and into the 1990s would appear to be as much a management as an all-employee phenomenon. As Bruce and his colleagues point out, in the UK Executive Share Option (ESO) schemes apply to senior managers in virtually every large company. Indeed the importance of motivating senior managers is widely recognized and, of course, the ESO is an obvious mechanism. Bruce and his colleagues also detail the phenomenon of management buy-outs (MBOs) which are, in many respects, a reflection of the strategies of an increasingly pro-active and confident management in the modern world. And what is particularly important here is the substantial variety in practices (with different implications for ownership and motivation) that have recently developed.

Moreover, the franchise movement has been especially important in linking ownership and control. In a detailed analysis of this phenomenon, Felstead provides many original insights and findings from his own researches and concludes that:

> Franchisees . . . occupy an intermediate position between wage workers and the truly self-employed (and *independent* small employers) who own their own means of production and reap the full rewards of their own (and others) labour. . . . While the slogan 'be your own boss in franchising' provides an appealing catch-phrase, it is prone to conceal much more than it reveals – it is of this that researchers, policy-makers, bankers, and would-be franchisees should be well aware.

But in any examination of new ownership patterns in the 1980s consideration would have to be given to the continual growth of co-operative ventures as alternative forms of ownership. In some of the contributions in Part 4 the ongoing debates on the extent and nature of this growth are examined. The section begins with Clarke's contribution which provides an interesting link between co-operative development and the preceding discussion. Indeed the recent experience of share-ownership co-operatives is examined in the context of members' perceptions, the value of shares, and the distribution of profits. Within this framework Clarke proposes a long-term solution to one of the major constraints on co-operative growth, that of capital shortfall.

Hobbs and Jefferis's contribution provides an up-to-date and rigorous statistical analysis of co-operative ventures in the UK. They confront the problems of definition, data collection, and methodology as well as presenting their own findings which point to an over-optimistic picture of the extent and growth of co-operation in the UK. And this pessimistic view is given some support from Welford's empirical analysis which emphasizes two distinct categories of co-operative organization. The one adopts the principles and practices of common ownership and democratic decision-making structures, whereas the other cannot in many respects be distinguished from its capitalist counterpart. Again the importance of financial support from local authorities and the Co-operative Development Agency (Holmes and Grieco) has particular relevance to the growth of the latter type. Further analysis points to a diverse co-operative sector in the UK, reflecting a varied number of objectives of coalitions between organizational members.

The tensions evident in Welford's survey between democratic organization and efficiency are again evident in Carter's examination of a firm of office-equipment suppliers in the London area. This firm represents an interesting transformation from a traditionally owned private company to an employee-owned co-operative that was subsequently taken over by a management buy-out. He provides an insightful analysis of the meanings actors placed on the co-operative organization, while stressing the continued saliency of control rather than ownership and the importance of organizational culture. He concludes that, on the basis of his case study, the transfer of ownership neither produces a radical change in the distribution of organizational power nor alters the way that people experience and give meaning to the organization of work.

The importance of organizational control also forms the central thrust of Oliver and Thomas's contribution concerning member behaviour in producer co-operatives. Here the importance of normative and cultural mechanisms of control are considered in three distinct organizational settings. They argue that the ownership structure in itself does not mean that normative control will be successful in co-operative organization and that co-operatives may indeed be run by more traditional hierarchical control mechanisms. In short, being a co-operative does not necessarily mean that conventional hierarchical control structures are absent, but that these will be supplemented by cultural control mechanisms which may be more appropriate to co-operative organization.

In sum, the various contributions to this study cover a rich range of issues within the broad debate on the development and impact of new forms of ownership. There are undoubtedly interesting changes in the structure of social relationships being occasioned by these transformations, but their precise effects are highly complex and, in some areas, more fundamental than in others. It is hoped that this volume will highlight the principal manifestations of a phenomenon which may well prove to be of far-reaching consequence in the 1990s and in the twenty-first century.

Part 1

Restructuring

Chapter one

Labour–capital partnership: a political economy of the third way

Peter Abell

On 8 March 1988 *Pravda* published a draft law on Soviet co-operatives. It allowed for the establishment of producer or worker co-operatives, by at least three persons, based upon principles of self-management, income-sharing, and members' ownership rights. Co-operatives are construed as an element in *Perestroika*, permitting effort-related rewards and encouraging worker entrepreneurship.

Similar and related events have recently occurred in a number of state-command socialist countries; the Chinese authorities are experimenting with a variety of economic arrangements, Hungarians can now purchase bonds in their employing enterprises, and some scholars are predicting the rapid emergence of a stock exchange in Budapest. Meanwhile the most prosperous region in Yugoslavia – Slovenia – is exhibiting a marked reluctance to remain under the aegis of the quasi-centralist federal Yugoslav state and planning system. There is talk of extending the spheres of influence of both co-operatives and private enterprises in Poland and other East European countries. Indeed we are witnessing the emerging contours of something quite significant in the 'socialist' countries. Some are predicting the eventual re-emergence of capitalist economic relations, others, mindful of the deep ideological and institutional opposition to private capital, look to a worker-managed Yugoslav-style economy as the path to salvation, although recent political and economic turmoil there has stripped much of the lustre away from worker-managed market socialism. Yet others feel we might expect something completely new – a third way – where property rights are adjusted in ways hitherto undreamed of. The intellectual ferment surrounding the demise of state-command socialism (for I am sure that is what it is) is complex and involves ideas not only about the proper disposition of property rights but also about the virtues and vices of competitive markets as against the planned allocation of resources and the acceptable levels of inequality in incomes.

Although things in the West are not moving as rapidly, there are incipient signs here also that arguments about the possibility of a third way will come to occupy more of the centre stage in the forthcoming decades. A wide commitment to co-operatives (often embracing both the political right and left) is a small but significant part of this argument, as are the proclaimed virtues of worker–management buy-outs, employee stock options, profit- and revenue-sharing and the slow but relentless advance towards worker participation in management[1] (Abell 1985). It admittedly takes rather a leap of the imagination to see these as threatening capitalism in the way that developments in the state-command economies undermine their particular brand of socialism; it, none the less, seems worthwhile speculating about the possibility of and nature of a third way.

Advocates both of competitive market capitalism and of socialism (in any one of its many varieties) are agreed upon at least one thing, namely that the objective must be to find a way of bringing together the factors of production in a manner which is both *just and efficient*. Further, if, as seems likely, these objectives collide one with the other, then some way of balancing their competing claims must be found. The advocates differ, however, in both their estimates of the prerequisites for efficiency and in their conceptions of justice in production and in consumption. I will argue that, if it is reasonable to assume a third way is to be found, it will in some significant sense draw upon both socialist and capitalist conceptions and, in so doing, transcend both.

As far as efficiency goes, all agree that capital and labour should be put together in a way that is allocatively and technically/productively efficient. So both should be put to their best possible use. In addition few would want to deny that any recommended arrangement should be X-efficient in Leibenstein's (1980) sense of the term.[2] That is, we need to find a way of organizing and motivating the factors within the enterprise which puts them to optimal use. It would be pointless to allocate capital and labour efficiently to enterprises which were not reaping all possible internal economies. Leibenstein argues forcibly, and to my mind convincingly, that the diseconomies of misallocation are, in practice, dwarfed by the diseconomies of X-inefficiency.

Justice is a more complex matter and in a paper of this length I cannot hope – even if I were capable – to cover all the issues involved adequately. I would like to suggest, however, that a political economy of the third way must provide cogent answers to the following questions:

1 How 'freedom' in both production and consumption should (a) be defined, (b), when defined, be guaranteed, and to what degree, and (c) distributed?
2 How productive resources (alienable and unalienable) should be allocated and income distributed?
3 How, if issues of freedom, resource allocation, and income distribution come into conflict, these should be resolved?

I will now, with a view to assembling the essentials of a third way, sketch how liberal-capitalist and socialist theories address these issues. In so doing I will mention four possible candidates for the third way, but only to dismiss each. They are: people's capitalism, Weitzman's share economy, Langian market socialism, and labour-managed market socialism. This accomplished, I will outline a system, based upon labour–capital partnerships which I regard both as more acceptable and more likely to prove attractive to the rationally free in search of economic efficiency.

Liberal-capitalist solutions

From a liberal-capitalist perspective the general equilibrium of competitive market exchanges amongst individuals exogenously endowed with alienable and unalienable[3] productive assets, to which they have full property rights, provides the intellectual bridge between issues of efficiency and justice. By property rights I shall mean throughout:

The right to possess, i.e. exclusive physical control of the thing owned.
The right to use, i.e. to enjoyment and use of the thing owned distinct from the rights to manage and receive income.
The right to manage, i.e. to decide how and by whom the thing owned shall be used.
The right to residual income (and liability of negative income), i.e. the benefits or costs from use or management of the thing owned.
The right to capital, i.e. the power to alienate, consume, modify, or destroy the thing owned.
The right to security, i.e. immunity from expropriation.
The right to transfer, i.e. to bequeath the thing owned.
The absence of term, i.e. no time limits on other rights and liabilities.
Prohibition of harmful use.
Liability to execution, i.e. the possibility of being deprived of the thing owned for repayment of debt.
Residuary character, i.e. rules governing the reversion of lapsed ownerhship rights (Honoré 1961; Abell 1983).

Individuals, with vested property rights to their capital and their labour, and as consumers, are deemed to be (economically) free to the degree that, legally, their property rights are protected and they are effectively[4] afforded the opportunity to enter into voluntary contracts within the framework of competitive markets (labour, capital, and commodity). It is the (effective) right to enter into such contracts which is deemed to confer the freedoms, not, according to the prevailing orthodoxy, the actual possession of resources which in practice would enable an individual to enter into contracts. This is the doctrine of *negative freedom* which enjoins a definition of the concept which is independent of the resources individuals happen to hold. It is further argued – at least according to the most persuasive account (Rawls 1971) – that freedoms should be available to the maximum degree which is compatible with their equal availability to all. Equality should have priority over total volume. Since freedoms are defined independently of the ownership of resources, this priority carries no implications whatsoever for resource distribution. Thus, Rawls can promote the separation of his first and second principles, putting matters of resource allocation and income distribution beyond the reach of matters of freedom. Socialists, of course, reject all of this.

Theories of the just allocation of resources and distribution of income divide along right and left lines.

On the right (or libertarian) wing Nozick (1974) is the best modern representative. He argues that any distribution of resources which comes about from either voluntary exchange or transfer, starting from a distribution which was generated in similar fashion, is to be regarded as just. Voluntary exchanges will then take place to a point of Paretian optimality. This argument is also used to justify the acquisition of alienable assets which heretofore were unowned.[5] Thus for the libertarian right market exchanges (and gifts) procure allocations of productive resources and income distributions which are wholly just.

On the liberal-capitalist left things are looked at rather differently; Rawls (1971) is perhaps the doyen. His second principle urges a distribution of 'primary goods' which maximizes the welfare of those found to be least well off in society, i.e. the so-called maximin criterion. Rawls, of course, reaches this conclusion by suggesting that this criterion would be chosen by rational individuals from behind 'the veil of ignorance' where they would not know their own endowments.[6] This procedure, in effect, calls into question the individual's entitlement to the full property rights of such endowments. Indeed the left liberal wing in general feel that unfettered rights to income from one's 'morally arbitrary' human capital is highly questionable.[7] Although it is not entirely clear from Rawls' second principle whether a maximin in 'primary goods' should be contrived by income transfers or by a reallocation of productive capital,[8] what is clear is that the Nozickian assumption which finds a right to income from unalienable human capital is robustly rejected.[9]

It is worth noting here what I think is a further implication of the maximin criterion. It would amount to a recommendation of equality of 'primary goods' if there were in society no incentive problem. To put it another way, the reason the position of the worst off cannot at any particular juncture be improved even further is that the need for incentives makes it impossible without a loss in collective income.

16

Turning now to matters of efficiency. It is here Pareto efficiency looms large, providing an intellectual bridge with the concepts of justice outlined above. Under standard assumptions,[10] perfectly competitive markets with private property rights lead to a Paretian optimum (efficiency) which is a necessary condition for welfare maximization.[11] Thus, a legal framework which supports property rights and competitive markets guarantees negative freedoms and provides the basis for allocative efficiency – at least under restrictive assumptions. The income differentials, generated because individuals bring different endowments (alienable and unalienable) to capital and labour markets are justified in Nozickian terms, though need to be taxed or reduced by reallocation to a maximin from a Rawlsian perspective. Indeed, any desired income distribution can in theory be attained by some suitable reallocation of alienable assets and the unfettered operation of competitive markets.[12] Thus, at least in theory, a Rawlsian minimax is attainable by this route. Intra-enterprise X-efficiency is also guaranteed by competitive markets, according to authors like Alchian and Demsetz (1972), if the property right to residual remuneration is in the hands of capital or its agents who, it is averred, are then motivated to organize production and labour appropriately.[13] This conclusion may, however, be rather hasty; X-efficiency is likely to depend upon a sense of common purpose amongst those party to productive effort and is unlikely to occur if residual remuneration is entirely at the disposal of capital.

So competitive markets with vested property rights to alienable assets resting with the providers of capital bring Nozickian justice, Paretian allocative efficiency, and X-efficiency. Rawlsian justice requires reallocation of resources or redistribution of income but the second theorem of welfare economics gives us a clear angle on this.

In reality, of course, capitalist economies are beset by various selective transfers and monopoly rents, and thus vast inequalities. The advocates of 'people's capitalism', in recognition of this, have proposed a significant redistribution of capital assets. Current policies in Britain which promote Employee Stock Ownership Plans (ESOP), etc., are rather modest genuflections in this direction. The theory here seems to be that, if income distributions are unjustifiable, then, rather than making direct tax-based income transfers, one should improve the asset position of individuals. If such could be equalized, of course, then in a competitive environment any income inequalities would be attributable only to luck or uncertainty or differences in unalienable assets. A thoroughgoing approach to 'equality of opportunity' (a concept that has always proved attractice to liberal capitalists – see Rawls' second principle) would presumably take as a policy objective greater equality in both alienable and unalienable assets (Abell 1989). More egalitarian people's capitalism is clearly a possible candidate for the third way, though with its

17

assumption that property rights (post any reallocation or redistribution) should rest entirely with capital, it is unlikely to prove attractive to socialists or to find X-efficiencies.

Recently, Martin Weitzman (1984) has actively promoted the idea of a share economy where labour and capital negotiate a share in net revenues rather than either a fixed wage rate (capitalist enterprises) or a fixed return to capital (labour co-operatives). The appealing feature of a share arrangement is that, since there is no fixed wage rate, an incentive always exists for capital (or their agents) to take on new employees as long as the revenues generated for the enterprise are positive. By contrast, of course, the capitalist enterprise will take on employees only if the net revenues are greater than the negotiated wage rate and the co-operative only if they are going to boost the average income of the existing members. This means that the share enterprise is by comparison labour hungry.

If the revenues of a share enterprise drop, then, unless the marginal net revenue of an employee becomes negative, the share enterprise will still wish to maintain its level of employment, albeit at a reduced rate of remuneration. If there were other booming sectors in the market economy, then employers would be attracted to these and this is, of course, desirable from the point of view of allocative efficiency. But even in a general recession, share enterprises will maintain high levels of employment at reduced levels of remuneration. The share enterprise, in effect, shifts the risk of unemployment for labour to a risk of a reduction in its income.

Established employees within a share enterprise will, however, eventually face a situation where, if the enterprise takes on new employees, the average income will fall. Then, it is not in the interest of the established employees to welcome new ones, unless a reduced share contract is negotiated for them, introducing differentials depending upon the time at which a worker joined the enterprise. Thus, although there is an incentive for capital to take on new employees who in turn wish to join the enterprise, the established employers have no such incentive. Indeed, unless the employment decision is securely in the hands of capital, then the desirable employment characteristics of a share enterprise are unlikely to materialize.

Weitzman's much applauded 'employment effect' will, as he fully recognizes, become apparent only in an enterprise controlled by capital – an arrangement which, I argued above, is not likely to secure the enhanced productivity characteristics attributable to a community of interest and thus X-efficiency.

Similar reasoning applies to the capital-investment decision also. In this case, with a fixed share ratio in net revenues, labour will always be keen to take on new capital as long as its productivity is positive.

Again, with eventual declining productivity of capital, unless capital can strike a flexible share-ratio contract with labour, there will be a disincentive for capital to invest in the share enterprise. Arrangements which allow flexibility so that labour and capital share the costs of new investment in the same ratio as their yields are a possibility; but this once again introduces a conflict of interests into the very heart of the enterprise.

Our conclusions must inevitably be that share enterprises are not what we are searching for. In general, they do not generate a community of interests between capital and labour: to put it succinctly, labour wants more capital and less labour; capital wants more labour and less capital and there is a conflict of interests between the established employees and those wishing to join the enterprise. We are thus not going to encounter enhanced X-efficiency. Nevertheless the idea of sharing not only the rights to income but wider property rights is an appealing one which I will return to.

Socialist solutions

We may conveniently distinguish between state-command and market-socialist solutions to the problems of justice and efficiency.

State-command theories of the just access to capital are usually predicated upon the labour theory of value and the consequent unacceptability of returns to capital. The labour contract whereby capital hires labour (at a market clearing rate) is deemed unjust (exploitative) to labour. Rather the planned allocation of socially owned capital is recommended where, if goods and services do not circulate at prices reflecting their labour content, the 'surplus' can be disposed of with social ends in view. The just allocation of collectively owned capital is one which guarantees access by all in proportion to ability or skill, i.e. unalienable capital.[14] Likewise the income distribution should also reflect unalienable capital. Thus 'from everybody according to their ability, to everybody according to their ability'.[15] Individuals have property rights to their own labour.[16] In practice, this amounts to guaranteed employment – something the state-command economies have by and large sought, though it is arguable, with a large efficiency cost.[17]

On matters of freedom there is significant agreement amongst all schools of socialist thought that it should not be conceived in purely negative terms. Though a legal framework which secures labour's access to productive capital (i.e. negative freedom) is necessary, this would be entirely empty without actual access. Thus, freedom must also be defined in positive terms. Similarly, in consumption, it is deemed that legal protections of consumers' rights are only part of the story – they are, without real disposable income, an empty abstraction. Access to capital, however, guarantees an income.

If we now turn to efficiency, Paretian sensibilities are not part and parcel of the state-command armoury, for obvious reasons. Using resources to maximize the growth in national product is the normal yardstick and the above-described allocation of state-owned capital is deemed to attain this. So, as with market capitalism, there is a happy coincidence of justice and efficiency.

As far as X-efficiency goes, it is assumed that state-appointed managers are motivated and informed sufficiently to find these benefits. Needless to say, it is precisely the malfunctioning of this integrated theory of justice and efficiency which Perestroika addresses. The arguments are so well known, they need not be repeated here.

Market socialists are critical of the possibility of both the efficient allocation and the generation of X-efficiency through centrally planned procedures. Their arguments are often identical to those coming from a liberal-capitalist direction[18] (Nove 1983). There are two rather different theories of market socialism; Langian (1936) and labour-managed market socialism (Vanek 1975). They judge the issues about attaining efficiency rather differently, though both in practice seek to mimic the competitive capitalist economy. They are attempts at a political economy of the third way coming from a socialist direction.

Lange's intellectual purpose was in fact to demonstrate the possibility of an efficient socialist economy (largely in response to Von Mises' arguments to the contrary). He advocated ordinary competitive markets for labour and consumer goods. A central planning board, however, was to be responsible for investment decisions[19] and industry managers for decisions about the entry and exit of enterprises. He claims to establish that a quasi-market system of this sort can attain Paretian efficiency[20] as long as the managers of enterprises and industries follow certain rules.[21] Although Lange offers us no theory of X-efficiency, it is clear that, if the managers do not have incentives to follow these rules, such efficiencies will not be forthcoming; nor will the planners know whether enterprises are operating efficiently.

Under the standard assumptions (see note 20) it is possible to devise an optimal incentive scheme without the centre's surrendering control of the profit/surplus (Hildebrandt and Tyson 1979). But in the face of non-competitive conditions and/or uncertainties, the central planning agency will have to offer incentives which begin to undermine the *raison d'être* of the socialist economy. It would seem that there is a particular problem with risk- and uncertainty-bearing. How is risk to be shared between the centre and the periphery without the centre offering incentives and surrendering some control over the surplus?

On matters of justice, Lange offers us no explicit theory but it is most likely that he endorsed a positive conception of freedom. In terms of a just access to capital and a just income distribution, his system, at least under standard assumptions, permits the operation of the second theorem of welfare economics, since it mimics competitive capitalism. So any just income distribution could be achieved by some initial distribution of assets and the operation of a Langian quasi-market system.

Let us now turn to labour-managed socialism: this is the system which, in several significant respects, the Yugoslavs have sought to establish. An appreciation of its intellectual foundations can be gained from the observation that all the general equilibrium-efficiency characteristics of the competitive capitalist market economy can be preserved whilst inverting the relationship between capital and labour.[22] That is to say, where labour hires capital and is residually remunerated rather than the reverse (Dreze 1976). There is nothing particularly socialist in this observation; it in fact licenses competitively place labour-owned and -run co-operatives. The socialist content enters with a proviso that capital is hired by the state (*de facto, de jure* by 'society') to competitively placed worker-managed enterprises which seek to maximize income per number net of a rental for capital.[23] If these rentals reflect the market clearing rate, then the economy will reach efficiency. However, exacting the appropriate rental is by no means a trivial matter, the information requirements are strong especially in an innovating economy (Horvat 1982). If the assumption of perfect certainty is relaxed, then, as with the Langian system, the question arises as to the optimal risk/uncertainty-sharing between the state and the enterprises. If the sysem is to mimic market-capitalist efficiency characteristics, then it is essential that proportionate gains and losses accrue to the risk bearer.

Finding a third way

People's capitalism, the Weitzman share economy, and Langian and labour-managed socialisms are all proposals for a third way between state-command socialism and liberal capitalism. Each introduces, from a state-command point of view, some market forces. Although all four can, under suitable assumptions, attain allocative and technical efficiency, they respond rather differently to real-world imperfections and uncertainties. Furthermore, none is likely to reap the full benefits of X-efficiency. People's capitalism and the Weitzman share economy are unjust from a socialist perspective, and Langian and labour-managed socialisms are inefficient from a liberal-capitalist standpoint.

State-command socialism is frequently, and not without some justification, castigated for its advocacy of large bureaucratic structures which inevitably fail to respond to people's needs and which restrict their choices. The identification of socialism with both bureaucratic sloth and restrictions upon choice has arisen as a consequence of the left's distrust of markets. This is not without foundation. Markets can be both inefficient and unfair, generating great inequalities and concentrations of wealth. But it is important to distinguish between the unjust consequences of markets *per se* and those consequences which arise as a result of the different assets which people bring to production.

It is salutory to emphasize once again that the inequalities which markets almost invariably generate are attributable to one or more of three factors: unequal endowments in production; lack of competitive conditions; and inescapable market uncertainties. To put it another way, in that perhaps ultimately unattainable world with perfectly equal productive endowments and certain and perfectly competitive markets, all incomes would be equalized. One should capitalize on this observation.

Let me set out the rough contours of a more acceptable solution to the problems I introduced earlier. As I opined in my opening remarks, any solution will draw upon both capitalist and socialist conceptions. What follows is in fact an amalgam of positive predictions (rooted I hope in some understanding of the intellectual debates taking place in the state-command socialist countries) and normative stipulation. I make no apology for breaking the canon by running the two together for, after all, the future, whilst shaped by the past and present, is still partly open. Recall also that I am speaking about a future for both the liberal-capitalist and socialist systems. Indeed I am predicting/advocating a form of convergence upon the third way.

1 The third way will endorse the allocative efficiency characteristics of markets, given just starting points. Labour, capital, and commodity markets will be favoured. The introduction of capital markets will obviously prove most difficult in the state-command countries, though the reduction in property rights of capital implied by labour/capital partnership will help. In one respect capitalism and state-command socialism are identically placed: they both rely upon capital hiring labour (albeit in the name of labour in the latter case) rather than the reverse and consequently both need to attenuate the property rights of capital.

2 X-efficiency will be sought by sharing arrangements between labour and capital at the enterprise level; enterprises will be labour-capital partnerships. The property rights of the enterprise will thus be divided between capital and labour. In the face of the just redistribution of capital (see the next point) there is no reason to favour exclusive labour or capital ownership and control of enterprises.

3 A positive concept of freedom will be endorsed alongside a negative one. Rectifying inequalities in positive freedoms will favour the redistribution of productive assets rather than income transfers.

4 Something like a Rawlsian minimax will be sought in connection with redistributive policies. That is to say, equality of positive freedoms

in production will be pursued to the point that the least well off in consumption is as well off as possible (given an assumed incentive problem).

5 The minimax consumption pattern can be progressively transformed into an equal distribution to the degree that value systems are promoted to overcome the incentive problem. Thus the Rawlsian ideal of equal freedoms at a maximum volume is now transformed to positive freedoms and ultimately realized.

A key issue is to align incentives such that X-efficiency is maximized. So incentives should be such that labour and capital find common interests in conducting the affairs of the enterprise, in particular, in sharing risk and fixing the levels of capital and labour employed. Also the incentives internal to the enterprise should be such as to attract labour and capital in an optimal fashion without indue inflationary pressures.

Meade (1986), in recognition of these objectives, has promoted the idea of discriminating labour/capital partnerships. This is not the place to explore his conception in detail, but such partnerships do appear to achieve the characteristics we are after.

A labour/capital partnership is essentially a form of enterprise which spreads the risks of variations in income between both the providers of captial and labour. Both possess share certificates which entitle the holder to a dividend in net income. Capital shares are tradable on the market, though labour shares are not. Labour shares are relinquished only at retirement or upon voluntary acquisition of alternative employment. The ultimate control of the enterprise is in the hands of the board of directors elected in equal numbers by labour and capital. New shareholders – capital or labour – enter the enterprise with an entitlement to a share in net income which appropriately discriminates in favour of the existing shareholders. This arrangement effectively overcomes many of the problems encountered in the Weitzman-type share enterprise. The existing capital and labour shareholders have an incentive to invite new shareholders (of either type) as long as their net contribution is positive. The labour/capital partnership is both capital and labour hungry. Since such partnerships discriminate an individual's income on the basis of seniority, strongly established norms to the contrary will prove troublesome. However, Japanese capitalism, at least in its core enterprises, seems to have moved some considerable distance in this direction. Western trade unions will offer resistance, but even here there are signs that they are coming to recognize that their future role will increasingly be one of supervising individual contracts.

Many variations on this basic theme are possible, in particular, both capital and labour may seek to strike a contract which makes only a proportion of their income variable and open to risk. There is thus within the framework of labour/capital partnerships a range of opportunities to share risks in a variety of ways, whilst building convergent incentives. It would be unwise to legislate for one particular enterprise type. Rather the third way will work from the premise that those forms of enterprise will occur which rationally free and equally endowed individuals will choose to construct.

In a society where the positive freedoms in the relations of production are step by step made more equal, income differentials will decline. The introduction of various forms of labour/capital partnership is likely to reduce the spread of intra-organizational income. Greater equality of consumption is thus already guaranteed.

An economy built around these ideas would be allocatively efficient, X-efficient, take both a positive and negative view of freedom, and be much more equal in production and consumption. It would draw upon theories of both socialism and liberal capitalism – it would be a just and efficient third way.

Notes

1 Recent evidence from the Industrial Democracy in Europe research group suggests that even in the 1980s there has been a European-wide move in this direction.
2 X-efficiency and technical efficiency are clearly interrelated. Theories of technical efficiency assume that the production function is known, and it is feasible to put production on the possibility frontier. Theories of X-efficiency assume that the production function isn't perfectly known or easily attainable.
3 For unalienable resources read human capital or skill. Enhancing genetically unherited skills through resource-absorbing activities like education is part of the exchange mechanism (Abell 1988).
4 'Effectively' in the sense that the legal framework is enforceable, not in the sense of necessarily possessing resources which command a price in the market-place.
5 Nozick believes that private property rights to alienable assets could have emerged according to his principles of just exchange where alienable assets were initially unowned, but where individuals owned themselves. If, by virtue of the latter, the better endowed use the heretofore unowned resources so as to render nobody worse off (i.e. a Pareto move), then the private appropriation of unowned assets is justified.
6 This conclusion has been much contested as has the whole artifice of the veil of ignorance, but nevertheless the maximin principle still has wide appeal.
7 If skills are ultimately rooted in our genes and the lottery of inheritance, then it is averred there should be no supposition about entitlement to income which is the fruit of our efforts.

8 Presumably the one that is least costly in gaining the minimax.
9 Cohen has questioned Nozick's justification of property rights.
10 Notably, of course, full information, absence of externalities, and economies of scale.
11 Welfare maximization requires interpersonal comparison of utility, e.g. a social-welfare function.
12 The so-called second theorem of neo-classical welfare economics.
13 Alchian and Demsetz assume teamwork where marginal value products cannot easily be measured. A monitor, assumed to be capital or its agents, is therefore needed to prevent free-riding.
14 This statement is ambiguous with respect to the interaction of innate and acquired human capital.
15 Marx, of course, never explicitly wrote this, though it can be argued, he implied it. It has become a standard socialist epithet.
16 Not complete, since labour can be directed.
17 It could still be argued that negative freedoms are equally available in the sense that the law should provide equal access to those of the same ability.
18 They are also the ones being used to support Perestroika, though they go, of course, much further than the Soviet authorities are prepared to contemplate at the moment.
19 The board acts as a Walrasian auctioneer in markets for intermediate goods also.
20 Again, under standard assumptions.
21 That is: (a) take prices as parameters, (b) operate on the lowest short-run marginal-cost curve, and (c) equate marginal cost with price.
22 Again, under standard assumptions.
23 The short-run problems of income-per-unit-of-labour maximizing are well known.

References

Abell, P. (1983) 'The viability of industrial producer co-operation' in Crouch, C. and Heller, F.A. (eds.) *International Year Book of Organizational Democracy*, vol. I. Chichester: Wiley.

Abell, P. (1985) 'Industrial democracy, has it a future?', *Journal of General Management*, 10, 50–62.

Abell, P. (1989) 'An equitarian market socialism' in Estrin, S. and Le Grand, J. (eds.) *Market Socialism*, Oxford: Oxford University Press.

Alchian, A. and Demsetz, H. (1972) 'Production information costs and economic organization', *American Economics Review*, 62, 777–95.

Drèze, J. (1976) 'Some theory of labour management and participation', *Econometrica*, 44, 1125–40.

Hildebrandt, G. and Tyson, L.D. (1979) 'Performance incentives and planning under uncertainty', *Journal of Comparative Economics*, 3.

Honoré, A.M. (1961) 'Ownership', *Oxford Essays in Jurisprudence*, Oxford: Oxford University Press.

Horvat, B. (1982) *The Political Economy of Socialism*, Oxford: Martin Robertson.

Lange, O. and Taylor, F.M. (1964) *On the Economic Theory of Socialism*, New York: McGraw-Hill.

Leibenstein, H. (1980) *Beyond Economic Man*, Cambridge, Mass.: Harvard University Press.

Meade, J.E. (1986) *Alternative systems of Business Organization and of Workers' Remuneration*, London: Allen & Unwin.

Mises, L. Von (1978) *Liberalism: Associo-economic Exposition*, Kansas City: Steed, Andrews, & McMeel.

Nordhaus, W. and John, A. (1986) 'The share economy: a symposium', *Journal of Comparative Economics*, 10: 414–75.

Nove, A. (1983) *The Economics of Feasible Socialism*, London: Allen & Unwin.

Nozick, R. (1974) *Anarchy, State and Utopia*, New York: Basic Books.

Rawls, J. (1971) *A Theory of Justice*, Oxford: Oxford University Press.

Vanek, J. (1975) *The Labour-managed Economy*, Ithaca, NY: Cornell University Press.

Weitzman, M. (1984) *The Share Economy*, Cambridge, Mass.: Harvard University Press.

Chapter two

Ownership and economic development: the partnership of business and local government[1]

Robert Bennett and John Sellgren

Economic development and local-government companies

This paper focuses on the question of ownership and management of business in relation to the economic-development needs of local communities. Ownership is approached through two primary agencies: private-sector independent businesses and local government. We do not raise the general issue of business ownership but discuss the conditions under which individual businesses may wish to exercise wider social responsibilities, act collectively with each other, and join with local government, local economic initiatives, local-government companies, or other institutions. This discussion leads in turn to seeking a definition of the relationship between individual business action and the role of the different sectors in undertaking economic development within local communities.

A major current debate focuses on two aspects of local-government powers: first, the role of Section 137/83 powers (this is the power to incur expenditure in the interests of local inhabitants up to the product of a 2p-levy); and second, the most appropriate legal framework for local-authority involvement in companies. At present the activities of local government in Britain are circumscribed by the *ultra vires* doctrine which has been developed to ensure that public authorities act only in an authorized manner bound by the rule of law. Even where statutory authorization is available, it is still possible for a decision to be declared *ultra vires* where the authority has contravened some principle of common law. Thus authorities may exceed their powers in a manner which the courts maintain Parliament did not intend. Economic development is an activity for which local authorities have no specific powers. However, they may undertake such activity under a variety of statutory powers. A study by the Joint Unit for Research on the Urban Environment (JURUE 1980) classified four types of power that may be used for economic development activity:

Statutory duties for employment services.

Statutory duties for other services which are not primarily concerned with employment objectives but may have an incidental effect upon them.

Permissive powers given to local authorities which may be used in certain circumstances to undertake employment initiatives.

Local powers arising either from local acts or from special acts which apply only to some local authorities or within specified areas.

In addition to the statutory provisions, local authorities are also able to draw upon their common-law powers to do anything which is reasonably incidental to their statutory functions.

Local authorities also have permissive powers which allow them, if they wish, to undertake a variety of additional activities. The most important of which are as follows: Sections 2, 3, and 4 of the Local Authorities (Land) Act 1963 which enables authorities to undertake or support the provision of land, buildings, and infrastructure and to provide advance factories, warehouses, or small units. Under the Local Authority Superannuation Regulations 1974 and 1984, authorities are empowered to invest up to 10 per cent of their superannuation funds in unquoted securities and thus may include local firms. The Local Government Act 1972 and Local Government (Scotland) Act 1973 provide a variety of powers which local authorities may be able to utilize for economic-development work and these include: appointing staff (Section 112/64) and thus they are able to appoint persons to industrial development posts; publishing information, arranging lectures, holding discussions or mounting displays on matters relating to local government (Section 142/88). Further, the authority can engage in a variety of activities to collect and circulate information relating to the area and thus to promote it. Sections 111/69 of these Acts make a general provision which empowers local authorities to do anything conducive or incidental to the discharge of any of their functions and this may include setting up economic/industrial-development units. Local authorities are also empowered to engage in some limited municipal enterprises; these include powers to establish and maintain municipal restaurants, markets, and slaughterhouses, and also to provide a varied range of goods and services which may be used by other local authorities or public bodies.

The most widely publicized permissive power which may be used to undertake economic development is Section 137 of the Local Government Act 1972 (in England and Wales, and its equivalent Section 83 of the Local Government (Scotland) Act 1973); under these provisions local authorities are able to incur expenditure in the interest of their area or its inhabitants up to a maximum of a 2p product of the rates. However, this power has been reviewed on a number of occasions, most recently by the Widdicombe Committee (Widdicombe 1986). This concluded that the existing position relating to Section 137/83 could be clarified by maintaining the notion of ensuring that benefits accrue to the local area, but 'defining more precisely the degree of benefits which must be achieved' (Widdicombe 1986, para. 8.85). They also felt that the yield from any discretionary power needed to be regulated. The most important recommendations were:

Para. 56: 'to have a financially limited discretionary power to spend in the interests of their area'.

Para. 57: to review 'the proper role of local authorities in economic development, taking account of the role of other governmental agencies, with a view to identifying any area in which additional local authority statutory powers should be introduced'. This review should include enterprise boards and arm's-length companies (recommendation 69).

Para. 59: that the expenditure limit under Section 137/83 should be set in future in relation to the population of an area.

Para. 60: that this limit should be regularly reviewed, by Order.

Para. 61: that the limit be set at £5 per head of population.

Para. 62: that 'the limit for single tier authorities should be double' that applying to two-tier authorities.

Para. 63: that the 2p limit for expenditure under Section 137/83 be increased to 4p as an interim measure before a population base is introduced.

Para. 64: that Section 137 for England and Wales be amended to be comparable to Section 83 for Scotland to the effect that the local authority may only use, with the consent of another local authority, its power for a purpose for which that other local authority has statutory responsibility.

Para. 70: that the law as 'local authority controlled companies should be amended (i) to make clear that they may be set up only where there is specific enabling legislation; (ii) to incorporate safeguards' on articles of association, membership, audit, and reporting.

The main government response to these proposals is contained in a white paper (UK Government 1988a). In this they argue that, whilst affirming that authorities should continue to exercise a general power of discretion to spend in the interests of their area, the government should seek to limit this financially and to legislate for a new specific power outside Section 137/83 for the case of local economic-development policy. The new financial limit is to be set at £5 per head of adult population (divided into £2.50 each for two-tier authorities), but with no interim increase in financial powers. The effect of the new limit, in comparison with the previous 2p-rate product, varies between areas dependent on the relationship between population size and rateable value. Whilst significant, the increase does not keep up with the value of the 2p-rate product defined originally in 1972.

On the question of local-authority companies a decision by the government will depend upon its response to a consultation paper issued in June 1988 (UK Government 1988b). However, the shape of the government's position is already clear. First, they reject the first of the Widdicombe Committee's recommendations; namely, to allow local-authority companies to be set up only where there is specific enabling legislation. The government propose instead that local authorities should have a controlling interest in only those companies whose activities are within the local authorities' powers and duties, and that a minority interest can be held only in specific circumstances. They define permitted classes of minority interest to include:

public transport companies.
public airport companies.
companies related to further education.
housing associations.
enterprise agencies.
management companies of land, buildings, and structures.
land development companies.
statutory companies.
professional associations.

Within these constraints the government proposes to follow the second Widdicombe Committee recommendation to incorporate safeguards into the means by which companies are run. They consider it to be an anomaly that local authorities' interest in companies is outside the rules which govern the conduct, scope, financial procedures, and propriety of local-authority business. In particular the government seeks to ensure that a local-authority company should not do anything that the controlling authority could not do, i.e. to act *ultra vires* (except in the provision of services between the authority and its company, or under the Transport Act, or in preparation for privatization). Thus the government has sought to stop local authorities circumventing restrictions on their powers: particularly restrictions on their capital account imposed by central government; or restrictions on membership which apply to local authorities but which have not affected companies.

As a result the capital transactions of local-authority-controlled companies are to be brought within the framework applying to local authorities generally; there are to be new requirements for presentation of accounts and audit; imposition of statutory rules on personnel involved; a code of practice; and a prohibition on local authorities' holding interests in companies outside the European Community. Politically most significant is the bringing of local-authority companies within the net of capital controls and the restrictions on personnel.

It is clear from these developments that the government has accepted a role for local-government control of companies, but only with very specific guidelines related to economic development and underpinning private-sector interest. We analyse this position further on page 38.

We define local economic development as a sub-national action, taking place within the context of a local labour market, with focus on the specific problems of locations requiring development or regeneration. Economic development is concerned with both wealth creation and questions of employment and distribution of economic activities. The actors involved often include local government, but also include the extensive network of private-sector bodies, corporate social responsibility units, venture capital funds, enterprise agencies, and enterprise boards. The field is, therefore, one characterized by a pluralism of agencies and approaches. We focus attention here on three main questions:

What are the forms and structures of projects which are being developed?
What does current experience tell us about future policy actions in this field?
What is the appropriate structure for businesses and local government in local economies?

Forms and structures

Both business collective action and local-government economic-development activities are growing rapidly in Britain, albeit (in both cases) from a very low initial base. These developments are exhibited in the analysis of a sample of local economic-development initiatives drawn from the Local Economic Development Information Service (LEDIS) in which Sellgren (1987) identified a wide range of actions; a large proportion of which were initiatives taking a legal identity separate from their founders (see table 2.1). One quarter took company status and this may be indicative of the manner of their operation, first, that they are in a position to register and to trade as a company; second, it may be significant when raising finance; third, it may be inferred that rather than being *ad hoc* responses to local economic crises, these initiatives were planned and co-ordinated and run along business lines,

Table 2.1 Ownership (legal) structures adopted by initiatives broken-down by initiating agency (percentage of agencies with different legal structures)

Initiating agencies	Company	Local authority	Educational body	Central-govt dept	Manpower Services Commission	Voluntary	Other
Council/board (elected)	5.1	1.5	0.0	7.7	0.0	2.8	12.3
Council/board (non-elected)	2.6	7.4	0.0	23.1	0.0	11.1	14.3
Company (charitable status)	15.4	11.8	0.0	7.7	0.0	44.4	36.7
Company	41.0	23.5	10.0	23.1	25.0	16.7	24.5
Subsidiary company	15.4	0.0	0.0	0.0	0.0	0.0	0.0
Co-operative	7.7	0.0	0.0	0.0	0.0	2.8	2.0
Voluntary	5.1	2.9	20.0	0.0	0.0	19.4	6.1
Other	2.6	5.9	70.0	38.5	75.0	2.8	4.1
Local authority	5.1	47.1	0.0	0.0	0.0	0.0	0.0

Source: Sellgren 1987 from LEDIS data

although the pursuit of profit may not have been their sole or major objective. A further 22.5 per cent were also registered companies but with charitable status, providing certain tax benefits for non-profit-orientated initiatives. The remaining half took a variety of legal forms. Almost half of these (a quarter of the sample) were in-house initiatives of the agencies by which they had been founded, of which 15.5 per cent were local authority, 7 per cent voluntary, and 3 per cent subsidiary companies. Of the rest, 9.1 per cent were managed by unelected councils or boards and a further 5 per cent by elected councils or boards. Table 2.1 shows the types of ownership (legal) constitutions adopted by initiatives set up by the range of agencies and demonstrates the propensity for initiatives to take a legal form similar to that of the agency responsible for setting it up. For example, it is notable that over half (56.4 per cent) of the initiatives set up by companies themselves took company status, almost 20 per cent of initiatives created by voluntary agencies had themselves a voluntary status. In addition, it is very common for initiatives to be run as in-house activities of the agency which set them up. This is the case for both the 15.4 per cent of initiatives run as subsidiary companies of initiating corporations, and almost all the 50 per cent of initiatives set up by local authorities. To some extent this figure is an over-representation since LEDIS contains a number of examples of the work of whole economic-development units, but it is clear that many of the projects with which local authorities are involved remain under their own umbrella. The legal-status section 'other' encompasses a number of the in-house activities of educational bodies and central-government departments. Seventy per cent of initiatives set up by educational bodies remain in-house, largely because the type of services provided, normally business-support schemes, form an extension to the educational facilities of the institution. Four of the initiatives set up by government departments (30.8 per cent) remained within their founding agency or department; the equivalent figure for Manpower Services Commission (MSC) projects was 25 per cent (one project).

The importance of the corporate sector in setting up local economic initiatives is readily apparent. However, it is argued by Mason (1987) that the level of corporate involvement in collaborative projects has often been somewhat limited and in many cases this has led to corporations' developing an individualistic approach to such initiatives. It is suggested that this has arisen as a consequence of a lack of suitable partners with which to develop projects; and a desire on the part of some companies to act unilaterally in order to maintain control over the funds which they have allocated, and also to maintain operational freedom. It is also pointed out that in acting unilaterally a company is able to gain maximum visibility for its efforts, although this must also operate where projects are less successful. Despite this, however, over 30 per cent of the initiatives in the LEDIS sample were supported financially by companies (Sellgren 1987) and many companies provide considerable in-kind support through the various means discussed above.

The importance of local authorities in setting up such local economic-development initiatives can be seen from the above. It was found by Sellgren (1987) that almost a third of the initiatives in the LEDIS sample were set up by a local authority. It has been argued that involvement with economic initiatives is one way in which local authorities have sought to develop their local economic-development activities. Their very close involvement in such schemes therefore merits closer examination. A survey of local authorities' involvement in industrial development and economic management was undertaken in 1987 and, whilst this sought detailed information on local authorities' economic-development activities, it also enabled an analysis of local authorities' involvement in economic-development initiatives, thus extending and enhancing the overview provided in the review of LEDIS (Sellgren 1987). The results of this survey provided detailed information on the work of over four hundred individual initiatives being supported in the 1986/7 financial year. Table 2.2 shows the legal status of the local-authority initiatives identified by this survey. Over 60 per cent of the initiatives which were surveyed were under the direct control of the local authority. Thus it appears that there is a strong tendency for local authorities to maintain control of economic initiatives which they have set up and thus must cast some doubt on the theory that initiatives are necessarily set up at arm's length as a means of circumventing statutory limitations on local-authority activities. Indeed, the fact that such a large proportion of initiatives remain under direct local-authority control may reflect a rejection of arm's-length approaches and a desire to maintain control over projects set up, managed, or supported by the authority.

The remaining 177 initiatives were structured under a variety of legal forms reflecting a similar range to those identified by the LEDIS sample. As with the LEDIS analysis, initiatives which had company status were well represented with 21.6 per cent of those analysed having some form of company status. The reasons for and possible advantages of the various forms of company registration have already been discussed above. One of the slight problems which arose in the case of local-authority initiatives was in identifying the precise nature of the company status, particularly in terms of those which had charitable status; this is due in large part to the difficulty of maintaining detailed knowledge of those projects which have developed independently from the authority. Where the precise company status was indicated, there appeared to be a more or less equal division between those of commercial and charitable status, very similar in proportion to the equivalent division within the LEDIS sample. Perhaps not surprisingly none of the initiatives identified in this survey were run as subsidiary companies. Examples of these were found in the LEDIS analysis where large companies had set up subsidiary operations to assist economic development; however, the local-authority survey did not reveal any examples of collaborative working with such projects.

In the LEDIS analysis 14.1 per cent of initiatives were constituted and run by councils and boards; the incidence of these in the local-authority survey was very much lower with a total of only ten (2.4 per cent) initiatives being organized in this manner. The survey of local-authority involvement with economic initiatives identified a small but significant number of co-operative ventures (three, comprising 0.7 per cent) and also a number (five, 1.2 per cent) being run on a voluntary basis. The survey also identified eight schemes (1.9 per cent) which had trust status. Since the LEDIS analysis had identified a series of linkages (particularly financial) between local and national government in the operation of local initiatives, it may have been considered a priori that local authorities may indicate involvement in initiatives for which government departments or agencies were primarily responsible. The results of the local-authority survey showed a very low level of such involvement however, with no authorities being involved with government projects and only a few examples of collaboration in schemes run by the MSC (1 per cent). However, rather more significant were the eleven examples (2.7 per cent) of schemes which had been developed through local- and central-government partnerships. The more general survey

Table 2.2 Legal structure of local-authority initiatives

Legal structure	%
Council/board (elected)	2.2
Council/board (non-elected)	0.2
Company (charitable status)	4.4
Company (status not stated)	12.1
Company	5.1
In-house to another initiative	0.2
Co-operative	0.7
Voluntary	1.2
Local authority alone	61.7
Local authority and government department	2.7
Local authority and private sector	4.6
Manpower Services Commission	1.0
Educational body	0.2
Trust	1.9
Management agreement	0.2
Other	1.5

Source: Survey of local authorities

analysis did, however, reveal considerable local-authority collaboration in the MSC training programmes, particularly the Community Programme and Youth Training Scheme (YTS). The survey also identified a significant number of schemes (nineteen, 4.6 per cent) which were operated as partnerships between the local authority and the private sector. It has already been suggested that initiatives are characterized by the collaborative nature of their operation and thus it is not surprising to find schemes which are set up with a collaborative partnership status.

The analysis of LEDIS (Sellgren 1987) found that almost 80 per cent of the initiatives had associated with them some form of advisory facility. The survey of local-authority economic initiatives found the largest category of activities to be those concerned with business support (35.6 per cent). It has also been seen that the survey of Mills and Young (1986) found that the most common economic development activity for local authorities was business development. Perhaps the best-known business support projects are enterprise agencies and enterprise trusts (see, e.g. Deloitte, Haskins, and Sells 1984: McCreadie 1985). Local authorities play an important role in sponsoring enterprise agencies, in 1987 accounting on average for 11.6 per cent of the total number of agency sponsors. More than half of all agencies will tend to be supported at least by their local district (or borough) council, and a considerable number will also be supported by the county authority. In some measure the number of authorities sponsoring an agency will be indicative of the size of the catchment area covered by the individual agency. The principal activity common to all enterprise agencies is the provision of free advice and counselling support for the setting up and development of viable small business. In addition to this, a large proportion of agencies have begun to develop a wider range of services to complement the advisory role; these include the provision of managed workshops, organizing skills training courses, and the provision of loans and grant funds.

Table 2.3 Proportion of enterprise agencies engaged in particular activities in 1986 and 1987

	1986	1987
	%	%
Counselling	100.0	100.0
Training courses/seminars	41.2	79.4
Exhibitions	35.1	59.2
Newsletters	35.1	51.8
Educational links	37.1	69.1
Small business club	29.0	46.1
Access to loan/grant funds	31.8	58.6
Property register	25.3	39.7
Meet the buyer	19.2	22.0
Trade directory	20.8	30.1
Workspaces	22.0	46.1
Business to business	13.9	20.2
Business competition	16.3	19.1
Youth enterprise	19.2	43.6
Resource-matching bureau	9.4	14.9

Source: Analysis of data in Business in the Community *Directory of Enterprise Agencies* 1986 and 1987

Enterprise agencies are often, but not exclusively, companies limited by guarantee. Table 2.3 shows the principal activities of enterprise agencies in 1986 and 1987. The figures are based on 245 enterprise agencies listed in the Business in the Community *Directory of Enterprise Agencies* in 1986, and 282 in the equivalent publication for 1987. The central importance of counselling services is illustrated very clearly, for this activity is a cornerstone of the enterprise agencies' activities. In discussing the role of Glasgow Opportunities (one of the Glasgow agencies) Paterson (1985: 13) argues that the one-stop-shop approach to providing free and confidential advice in a non-bureaucratic manner has proved to be the model for most enterprise agencies in the country. In addition, it is suggested that agencies' own business contacts have also been an important factor in their performance. It has been pointed out, for example, by Deloitte, Haskins, and Sells (1984), that in providing a counselling serviee an enterprise agency does not necessarily have to possess a large full-time staff. Indeed a recent survey (BiC undated) found 90 per cent of agencies surveyed had 5 or fewer full-time staff, with an average per agency being 3.2 full-timers and 2 part-timers. Many agencies have developed extensive networks of contacts to whom they may direct a client for specialist advice or support. These may be drawn from the agencies' sponsors, central and local government, development agencies, or financial and educational institutions. It is evident that enterprise agencies appear to have increasingly supported their counselling activities through other services, notably through training courses and seminars; these are also notable for having been expanded very rapidly in recent years. In addition, however, such other activities as producing newsletters, organizing business clubs, as well as developing business liaison, inter-trading, and promotion, have been offered by an increasing proportion of agencies. It is also notable that significant numbers of agencies are also active in assisting firms in respect of land and premises, either indirectly through the production of property registers, or directly through the provision or management of workspaces. Increasing direct financial involvement with firms to which enterprise agencies have offered their services is evident in the growing availability of loan and grant funds from almost 60 per cent of agencies in 1987. This is another area of activity which has seen very rapid growth in the extent of its availability. It is also apparent that enterprise agencies have sought to involve themselves increasingly with potential entrepreneurs of the future through seeking to assist youth enterprise and also by educational liaison schemes.

In seeking to ascertain the contribution of enterprise agencies to small-firm survival and job creation, a report by Enterprise Dynamics for Business in the Community (BiC undated) were able to be quite positive about the performance of the agencies which they had studied. It was found that businesses assisted by enterprise agencies had a superior survival rate when compared with other small firms (for example, those assisted under the Enterprise Allowance Scheme), since it was noted that the failure rate was of the order of 1 in 6 compared with a national figure of 1 in 3. It was also found that firms assisted by enterprise agencies also appeared to be contributing to job creation. A sample of 285 surviving firms which had been assisted showed that they had an average net gain of one job per business in the previous twelve-month period. In terms of the facilities and services offered by enterprise agencies, it was found that general and start-up advice was rated as the single most valuable form of agency assistance by 43 per cent of surviving firms surveyed. Where agencies offered workshop facilities, these ranked third behind general information and financial advice. A study carried out by the Centre for Employment Initiatives on behalf of the Community Initiatives Research Trust (Centre for Employment Initiatives 1985) took a random sample of enterprise-agency clients and found that 10 per cent of respondents would not have started in business without the involvement of the agency or felt that their enterprise would have folded. A further 44 per cent stated that without the agency it would have taken longer for them to have achieved what they had achieved or that they would have found it more difficult. Finally, 45 per cent of respondents felt that the assistance which they had from the agency did not have an effect on what they had done. This survey also asked the clients to make an assessment of the agency's role in helping to create or save jobs (within their own enterprise). The results found that 19 per cent of respondents felt that the help they had received from the agency was crucial; 38 per cent rated the agency's help as useful; 14 per cent felt the agency's help had been marginal; and 29 per cent of respondents regarded the agency's role as irrelevant in helping to create or save jobs.

Future possibilities

Businesses have an interest in local economic development internal and external to their firms, both from the perspective of their own 'self-interest', altruism, and social responsibility, and also from wider social goals. However, it is clear that there are very definite limits to voluntary collective action which are set by the need for firms to remain competitive and to prevent their being undercut by non-altruistic free-riders (see Bennett 1989). Thus it has been argued that a level of governmental action is required which sets, for all firms, a comparable local framework for social or collective action. Such a framework is subject to severe constraints. Compliance costs of governmental action must be minimized as well as offering minimum distortions to factor combinations and economic efficiency. Governmental regulatory policy, therefore, provides only limited scope for extending the range of business collective action. This leads to the need for governmental action to organize a level of public provision supplied as externalities to firms and supported by administrative, fiscal, expenditure, and debt policies.

The policies of government which are most likely to succeed relate to expenditure policy, chiefly through selective advisory services, general local public goods, and through facilitative and regulatory administrative policy. Public-choice theory has been used to define a possible classification of public-good activities of central and local government. In the most difficult situations requiring substantial economic regeneration, only central government can play the most effective role, but local government in conjunction with the private sector and private institutions can also be effective. There is a legitimate interest in restricting pure promotion and advertising activities by local areas, since these are deadweight burdens with zero-sum outcomes. Beyond such activities, however, local-government policies can be most effective if linked with the appropriate management skills and understanding provided by business. Although businesses have limited expertise, time, or resources to understand and act on issues of 'social responsibility', in most countries, but particularly in Britain, more support for these activities could be made than at present. The model of enterprise agencies may be particularly useful in this regard, since it suggests a means not only of providing cost-effective support, but also of overcoming business suspicions. This suggests that prime emphasis should be on 'partnership' approaches to local economic developments. This draws us to a number of conclusions on the most appropriate policy instruments (see also Bennett and Plowden 1988).

Facilitative and supportive actions by government, business 'social responsibility', and enterprise agencies suggest that the primary instruments should be providing counselling and advice, particularly in start-up and expansion of small businesses, and providing limited financial support, particularly equity. This in turn requires widening the access to risk and venture capital and widening the supporting environment of local and other actors (including government), particularly by the use of pump-priming, and other broad support, which seeks to get the local pre-conditions right. In this, central government's role, because of its larger and broader-based resources, is likely to be most important. This leads us to think of a specification of *roles* for the different actors in local economic development. These range from the firm's internal business policy, through its collective action, to governmental activity.

The role of internal business policy and 'social responsibility' The chief motive for internal action by businesses, and the main contribution a firm can make to economic development, is to remain competitive, retain and expand business, and to continue growing. In this way a business makes a major contribution to the creation of wealth in the local economy through wages, direct and indirect employment, local and central taxes as well as the production and sale of its goods and services. Internal action therefore emphasizes effective management, investment, and marketing.

Many businesses, however, widen their internal view beyond pure investment and marketing objectives towards a broader set of policies of 'social responsibility' or even 'altruism' in employment, trading, and local 'neighbourhood' relations, primarily, therefore, performing as a 'good corporate citizen'. They see it in their long-term interest to be involved with local communities, to be seen to be taking action, and to be 'progressive' and socially responsible. Self-interest remains a key aspect within this: fear of anti-industrial attitudes, a desire to improve the image of the firm or of business as a whole, good public and employee relations, or fear that if business does not take a lead government will.

The role of external business policy and collective requirements Beyond internal action many businesses act either independently or participate in collective activities, external to their main requirements.

Individual activities involve a widening of the 'good citizenship' policies internal to the firm so that a wider and stronger link to the local community is developed (see e.g. BiC 1986; Davies 1988). Key examples are:

Donations of cash and gifts in kind (often transport vehicles and facilities); education, employment and training; welfare, cultural, heritage and environmental activities. Sometimes this support may be set as a percentage of profits (as in per cent clubs).

Location and investment: sound investment projects are supported in more disadvantaged areas (such as inner cities or declining regions) rather than on green-field sites in order to provide employment and other benefits. Financial institutions may make available services at a preferential cost in order to help disadvantaged groups or localities, sometimes as 'soft loans'.

Employment and training: recruitment policy can be targeted to disadvantaged groups or localities; this can be combined with or separate from training and work experience programmes; this may extend to making available surplus training capacity, premises, or facilities for local community use.

Purchasing policy: sub-contracting and purchasing can be a major stimulus to the local economy, particularly if supplemented by early warning of requirements to new businesses and community business ventures, etc. 'Meet the buyer' events, counselling and advice, expansion of tender lists, and diffusion of information can all be used to stimulate local business activity.

Involvement in public affairs: staff and management can play important roles in community and local life, e.g. membership of school governing bodies and curriculum support groups, area health boards, voluntary organizations, etc., to provide business expertise and perhaps some financial support; secondment of staff to other local businesses (particularly start-ups and small firms), community projects, training schemes, specialist investment agencies, etc., to provide specialist skills.

Public-choice theory provides one approach to understanding business collective action in the economic development field. This suggests that collective action by firms will form 'clubs' where their service demands can be satisfied by joint action (Buchanan 1965). Such clubs may be sectoral or formed by other special interests, but frequently they are local clubs within a small group of sites, or within a local labour market. The objectives are therefore maximization of benefits and minimization of costs by collective as opposed to individual action. Benefits are to be gained in proportion to the level of joint externalities of each business and the level of spillovers. Costs will derive chiefly from the direct costs of collaboration (administrative, management, etc.), and the extent to which collective programmes involve support for actions which would be individually inappropriate but are necessary to obtain gains elsewhere. An optimal size of group for collective action will then derive from the accumulate costs: a so-called 'calculus of consent' (Buchanan and Tullock 1969). Clearly collective actions based on this approach will differ in scale depending upon the form of jointness and costs involved and there may be different levels of involvement for different collective objectives (cf. Buchanan, 1971, 1975). This may also embrace different geographical scales: neighbourhood, local-government unit, region, national. As the geographical scale of collective needs increases, and as the scale of the requirements also increases, it is likely that businesses by their individual actions will not be able to provide for collective needs. It is at this point enterprise bodies and local government, as well as other actors, assume importance.

Collective activities go beyond the individual links of single businesses to community agents or actors and involve several businesses acting in conjunction with each other. Collective action is commonly based on individual interests and may represent an attempt to overcome market failure without public-sector involvements. It is natural for businesses to find an appropriate agency to manage the larger resources and the collective range of priorities that arise when firms act together. The major potential management vehicles are:

trade associations: sectoral collective action.
chambers of commerce, local employer networks and business clubs: collective action at the local community level.
community business schemes: collective organization of donated cash resources.
Enterprise boards: collective action of businesses with other private-sector actors (particularly finance institutions) and usually governmental bodies. A particular form of this are private industry councils (PICs).
Enterprise agencies: government-led vehicles to stimulate collective action between businesses and to draw in other private-sector interests.

These vehicles are not mutually exclusive. The traditional forms have usually been trade associations, chambers of commerce, and business clubs. However, these have usually had limited impact, have been dominated by narrow interests, and are rarely geared to economic development, but their role is now rapidly expanding. Of greater significance have been community business schemes, such as community development partnerships, Business in the Community, PICs, and enterprise boards and agencies. These vehicles involve business with the wider group of actors who are important in providing the conditions for success of economic development, notably, financial institutions and sources of venture capital, provision of management expertise, support from local government and voluntary organizations. In the USA PICs have now become an important form of such agencies, and the PIC model is being actively considered by the government in Britain. Frequently the term 'partnership' is used to denote such arrangements. This reflects the emphasis on the need to combine individual actions in order to ensure success.

The marked growth and success of these collective vehicles have emphasized *endogenous* and *collaborative* action. However, the schemes that have been most successful in the most difficult circumstances have usually involved the introduction of external investment funds, either from private-sector financial institutions or government. Thus, although the emphasis is endogenous and collective, external support is also often required. The extent of external support required, and its form, draws us to the wider effects of market failures and the necessary role of governments.

The role of governmental action The case for governmental action is founded on the same criteria as private sector individual or collective actions; of providing the right circumstances for investment and economic growth. Like non-governmental actions the focus of attention can be internal or external to the firm and can encompass narrow business perspectives or wider social objectives. Governmental action is to be distinguished from collective action, however, by its scale, form, and its ability to enforce.

The traditional and technical definition of the requirements for governmentally provided goods (public goods) is constructed for the case where the market will fail. Such goods normally should have the following three characteristics (Musgrave and Musgrave 1986): *joint supply*: supply to one individual or firm allows identical supply to all at no extra cost; *impossibility of exclusion*: supply to one prevents the good being withheld from another; and *impossibility of rejection*: once supplied a good must be consumed equally by all. A pure collective good possesses all three of these characteristics; most collective goods do not but satisfy enough of each of these conditions to justify public action.

These collective-good characteristics lead to market failure which normally means that it is not in the interests of any one firm to supply the good since this would allow free supply to other firms for no return. An example would be one firm's bearing the cost of building a road connecting its factory on an industrial estate to a major highway; or one firm's bearing the cost of expensive labour training in a highly mobile employment sector subject to high risks of 'poaching'; or one firm's embarking on a high level of pollution control which disadvantages it in comparison with competitors. However, despite the economic disincentives to the action of individual firms, there are major benefits to all firms or to the community as a whole from undertaking such expenditures. A means has to be found therefore of encouraging all (or most) firms to this kind of provision so that the required benefits are obtained. This is akin to the 'prisoner's dilemma' in game theory where individually rational action results in higher costs than collective action (see, e.g. Davis and Whinston 1961). The necessary agency to overcome this problem cannot usually be provided by voluntary collective action, as discussed earlier, but requires a government acting on behalf of a wider community (either locally or nationally).

There are a number of other limits to business collective action. Strong local commitments are undermined by the *mobility* of employees, executives, skills, and the location of firms; uncertainty and imperfect information about weakly perceived benefits undermine voluntary action and social pressures; also it is not appropriate for the business to be 'an all-purpose institution that should right all social wrongs' – instead this is 'the job of the politician working in a democratic process. The businessman . . . should not be making essential social decisions' (Diebold 1972, quoted in Baumol 1975: 46–7). Most of all, however, there is the free-rider problem, that competition between firms and their trading environment precludes large-scale voluntary activity since a firm so engaged can be undercut and put out of business by other firms lacking the same degree of social responsibility.

Many economic development needs have strong public good attributes either at national, regional, or local level. This is often particularly true of large-scale local economic regeneration. For example, in an extreme case of urban dereliction the economic incentives to an individual business are not to reinvest, not to upgrade the quality of its premises, nor to invest in local labour skills; rather the local disincentives are so great as to encourage movement elsewhere or closure. This has been referred to as the Samaritan's dilemma by Buchanan (1975). However, a large number of businesses acting together in a run-down area, and businesses acting collectively with those other institutions which possess the ability to affect education, labour skills, crime levels, environmental quality, communications, access, and infrastructure, can make the fortunes of an area change and stimulate regeneration. The leadership and resources required in this extreme case will normally far exceed the ability of non-governmental action, particularly if it is sought to make these changes over a reasonably short period of time.

The case for governmental action in *local* economic development arises from local collective-good characteristics. Indeed many business requirements which have the highest degree of jointness, non-excludability, and non-rejectability are characteristics of the community in which the business is located; infrastructure, transport areas, environments, labour-market characteristics, education facilities, crime levels are all goods dominated by local characteristics. Other collective goods are regional or national public goods, because they spill over between localities or are subject to tapering off of access, e.g. general education, skill level, overall economic climate, monetary and fiscal incentives, and economic stability, etc. It is possible, therefore, to define a hierarchy of collective economic-development goods ranging from pure individual, to pure local, to pure national goods, with various mixed collective–individual goods in between. This hierarchy is a straight-forward extension of the collective-good concepts of Buchanan and Tullock (1969) to the case of local economic development but with properties depending upon the form and extent of geographical exter-nalities to each business.

Taking the case of geographical jointness and combining it with joint-ness to collectives of business irrespective of their location yield one possible classification:

Pure collective goods are those to which the Musgrave-Samuelson conditions apply (jointness, non-excludability, non-rejectability) with no geographical bounds within a given country. These should be the main objectives of national economic policy.

Pure individual goods are restricted in supply and demand to individual businesses. These goods should be held outside collective action except in so far that there is a collective benefit by collaborations.

Pure local goods are those which are joint within a given area but restricted to those businesses in that locality. It is these which are the prime focus of local government's economic-development policy. However, there is a wide range of goods which are partially joint either between businesses or between areas. These form the nexus of debate as to the most appropriate form of action (public or private). They also present the greatest difficulty in reaching the best combination of local- and central-government activities.

It is clear that ownership in this context becomes a complex phenomenon since the roles for local and central government, the private sector, and attention to the needs of the local community require an interlocking. It may be, therefore, that ownership as such is not the relevant focus for debate. Instead the focus should be on objectives and outcomes of economic development. From this then will derive the appropriate actors and the roles they should play. This in turn leads us to the range of possible 'ownership vehicles' which range across private companies, local-authority companies, enterprise agencies, and other forms. It will often be the case that a variety of alternative ownership vehicles will satisfy the objectives of local economic development. The key question to be resolved in a local context will then be to find the vehicle which provides the best guarantee of success in drawing actors together in the most appropriate roles.

Note

1 This research derives from projects supported by the Economic and Social Research Council, the Leverhulme Trust, the University of London Central Research Fund, and the Anglo-German Foundation.

References

Baumol, W.J. (1975) 'Business responsibility and economic behaviour', in E.S. Phelps (ed.) *Altruism, Morality and Economic Theory*, New York: Russell Sage Foundation: 45–6.

Bennett, R.J. (1989) 'Local economic development: the possibilities and the limitations of decentralized policy', in R.J. Bennett (ed.) *Decentralization: setting the new intergovernmental agendas*, Oxford: Oxford University Press.

Bennett, R.J. and Plowden, W. (eds.) (1988) *Local Economic Development: Defining the Research Priorities*, London: Economic and Social Research Council.

BiC (1986) *Business and the Inner City*, London: Business in the Community.

BiC (undated) *Small Firms: Survival and Job Creation: The Contribution of Enterprise Agencies*, London: Business in the Community.

Buchanan, J.M. (1965) 'An economic theory of clubs', *Economica*, 32, 1–14.

Buchanan, J.M. (1971) 'Principles of urban fiscal strategy', *Public Choice*, 11, 1–16.

Buchanan, J.M. (1975) 'The Samaritan's dilemma', in E.S. Phelps (ed.) *Altruism, Morality and Economic Theory*, New York: Russell Sage Foundation: 71–85.

Buchanan, J.M. and Tullock, G. (1969) *The Calculus of Consent*, Ann Arbor: University of Michigan Press.

Centre for Employment Initiatives (1985) *The Impact of Local Enterprise*

Agencies in Great Britain: Operational Lessons and Policy Implications, London: Centre for Employment Initiatives/Business in the Community.

Davies, R. (1988) 'Approaches from the private sector', in R.J. Bennett and W. Plowden (eds.) *Local Economic Development: Identifying the Research Priorities*, London: Economic and Social Research Council: 40–2.

Davis, O.H. and Whinston, A.B. (1961) 'The economics of urban renewal', *Law and Contemporary Problems*, 26: 105–17.

Deloitte, Haskins, and Sells (1984) *Local Enterprise Agencies: A New and Growing Feature of the Economy* London: Deloitte, Haskins & Sells.

Diebold, J. (1972) 'The social responsibility of business', conference address, cited in W.J. Baumol (1975) 'Business responsibility and economic behavior', in E.S. Phelps (ed.) *Altruism, Morality and Economic Theory*, New York: Russell Sage Foundation: 45–6.

JURUE (1980) *Local Authority Employment Initiatives*, Birmingham: Birmingham-Joint Unit for Research on the Urban Environment.

McCreadie, J. (ed.) (1985) 'Enterprise agencies and local economic development', *Planning Exchange: Occasional Paper no. 17*, Glasgow: Planning Exchange.

Mason, C. (1987) 'Job creation initiatives in the UK: the large company role', *Industrial Relations Journal*, 18: 298–311.

Mills, L. and Young, K. (1986) 'Local authorities and economic development: a preliminary analysis', in Hausner, V.A. (ed.) (1986) *Critical Issues in Urban Economic Development*, vol. 1, Oxford: Clarendon.

Musgrave, R.A. and Musgrave, P.B. (1986) *Public Finance in Theory and Practice*, 3rd edn, New York: McGraw-Hill.

Paterson, G. (1985) 'Developing counselling and advisory services', in J. McCreadie (ed.) 'Enterprise agencies and local economic developments', *Planning Exchange: Occasional Paper no. 17*, Glasgow: Planning Exchange.

Sellgren, J. (1987) 'Local economic development and local initiatives in the mid-1980s: an analysis of the Local Economic Development Information Service', *Local Government Studies*, 13 (6): 51–68.

Sellgren, J. (1989) 'Assisting local economies: an assessment of emerging patterns of local authority economic development activities', in Gibbs, D.C. (ed.) *Government Policy and Industrial Change*, London: Routledge.

UK Government (1988a) *The Conduct of Local Authority Business: The Government Response to the Report of the Widdicombe Committee of Inquiry*, Cm 433, London: HMSO.

UK Government (1988b) *Local Authorities' Interest in Companies: A Consultation Paper*, London: Department of Environment.

Widdicombe, D. (1986) *The Conduct of Local Authority Business: Report of the Committee of Inquiry into the Conduct of Local Authority Business*, Cmnd 9797, 1985–6, chaired by David Widdicombe QC, London: HMSO.

Chapter three

Radical beginnings, conventional ends? Organizational transformation – a problem in the development of radical organizations[1]

Margaret Grieco and Len Holmes

Every democracy needs a dictator.

> (Greater London Council liaison official at
> meeting called to discuss the management
> structure of the Charlton Training Centre)

The dynamics of transformation

The major purpose of this chapter is to draw attention to the problems experienced by radical agents and agencies in their attempts to develop and construct alternative forms of organization. The chapter indicates the character and nature of the problems of interaction between poorly resourced groups (the social base from which radical initiatives are typically drawn) and the more powerful and better-resourced funding agencies on which such 'popular' initiatives are typically dependent.

The structural disadvantages which generate the impetus or need for radical organization as a corrective mechanism, in the first instance, dictate that typically external funding will be necessary for the development of the new form. Radical organizations, initially at least, exist at the discretion of, and with the consent of, the powerful inside that same structure that disadvantages them and the effects of which they seek to combat. Hence the discussion of radical organizational forms cannot take place without reference to the controls and constraints placed upon them by the general funding structures within which they operate.

Our main argument here is that radical aims and forms of organization are frequently subverted or changed as a consequence of this interaction. This process is aptly characterized by the term 'organizational transformation'. Changes take place in the fundamental organizational structure without any accompanying change in organizational language, a situation which serves to disguise the extent to which fundamental changes have taken place. Put simply, our thesis is that radical intention and initial organizational form typically give way to radical rhetoric accompanied by a conventional management form; rather than treating such diversions of organizational goals and purpose as deviations from normality or as pathological, this chapter attempts to trace the dynamic and structural base on which such value slippage takes place.

It does so by using two particular radical organization case histories (the Charlton Training Centre and the Stonebridge Bus Garage Project), in which the authors were involved as either action researchers or managerial personnel, to illustrate properties which are deemed to be general. Each of the two organizations analysed have a central place in terms of radical approaches to the question of the relationship between vocational training and ethnicity in the UK. Similarly the funding agencies examined were the major funders of organizational experiments, i.e. radical organizations, within the UK during this period (radical labour-party-controlled local authorities such as the Borough of Brent and the Greater London Council and the European Economic Community Social Fund). Both these organizations were subject to fundamental changes in organizational purpose and form. That subversion or transformation into conventional forms occurred in these particular institutions provides strong ground for a deeper examination of this process. Our argument here is that the dynamics observed should not be viewed as maverick but rather viewed as typical. The analysis we provide here should in this respect be classified as lying within the radical structuralist paradigm (as identified by Burrell and Morgan 1979).

Our object, however, is not to produce a detailed case history of organizational change, though this may be a valuable task in itself (Pettigrew 1979), but rather to identify some general properties of the transformation of radical organizations into their conventional counterparts. The case study is used as a mechanism for illustrating processes which we perceive and believe to be general.

The attempt to develop organizational forms with alternative participative decision-making structures, which often represents the initial rationale for organizational birth, is typically, as in both these cases (see also Banfield and Hague, Chapter 4), hi-jacked; for the processes of interaction between funding agencies and popular organizational forms give rise to the construction of conventional leaders and leadership forms.

To use terms developed in the social psychology of leadership (Hosking and Brown 1986; Hosking and Morley, 1988), the early stages of organizational formation evidence a pattern of distributed leadership, that is prior to the interaction with the funding agency; the later stages of organizational development exhibit a pattern of hierarchical or focused leadership. For whereas the earlier stages of organizational formation exhibit patterns of internal communication in which the initiating role moves easily amongst the interested membership (itself a very open and flexible structure), i.e. distributed leadership (Clarricoates 1985; Cain 1986), later organizational stages evidence patterns of strongly hierarchical and entrenched leadership, with little or no shift in the incumbency of powerful structural locations (Holmes 1987).

Power relations within the radical organization are affected and altered by the imperatives imposed by the need to service stronger and more established organizations in order to raise the finance necessary for survival. This process of organizational transformation is not confined to the post-funding stage or period, though clearly the ability of other agencies to steer the direction of organizational development (Child 1985) – both directly and indirectly – is accentuated by the actuality of funding and the implied threat of its withdrawal, but commences with the process of bidding and negotiating for external funds. For not only do goals have to be framed in a way which is compatible, consistent, or congruent with the dominant agency requirements but sets of pressures for the continuity and authoritativeness of personnel involved in the negotiating process are generated (Grieco and Holmes 1989).

Participative forms are time expensive and the bureaucratic imperative is to streamline the negotiations between popular planning forms and the funding agency. The work practices and organization of the dominant organization come to determine the work practices and organization of the radical institution. The 'inefficiency of democracy or participation', generated as a slogan in these formational stages, comes to be adopted as a slogan within the internal processes of the organization as its own physical development becomes more concrete. Even in these early stages, the language of technical efficiency is already operating to screen or force out those considerations of participation, justice, and social rebalancing which were the initiating rationale of the movement. The demands, or perceived demands, of the funding agency legitimate the initial organizational movement away from fully participative structures. External communication requirements come to dominate internal preferences for collective forms of operation (Mantle 1985).

As these practices of focused leadership develop, so incumbents have the organizational opportunity for the development of particular stakes, and in the absence of an earlier establishment of codes and practices to ensure that practices of leadership alternation and succession are consistent with a distributed leadership format, we should expect that Michels (1915) iron law of oligarchy will come into play.

In the same way that decision-making forms and processes are structured through the negotiating process into compliance, so the goals which are expressed, and the terms in which they can be expressed, have important and constraining impacts for radical organization. In order to obtain resources, objectives and aims have to be stated in terms consistent with the dominant view, that is to say, such organizations receive funding on the basis of goal descriptions which view the correction of problems as technical rather than political matters. The acceptance of these descriptions by the disadvantaged in their bid for resources has a confirmatory or legitimatory aspect.

In the case of the organizations we study here, this dynamic is clear. In order to obtain resources, the black community and indeed women collude in the skill-led and skill-deficiency models of labour-market change and practice. In the bid for resources, they are 'compelled' to acceptance of the understanding that their position in the labour market is explained in terms of their lack of possession of such skills. In this way, the attempt to set up training centres to serve these fractions of the labour market can be viewed as confirmatory at the level of the system. The deeper processes which structure the dimensions that are deemed relevant to situations of exclusion and inclusion, i.e. selection and recruitment, within the labour market are not addressed (Grieco, Pickup, and Whipp 1989; Grieco 1987; Lee and Wrench 1981; Manwaring 1982). The analysis remains at the surface; the discourse is shaped and orchestrated by the dominant interest. Furthermore, the adoption of skill-led strategies, where skill deficiency is not the actual principle of exclusion, forces the organization into failure. Its success, if one continues along this logic, is being measured in terms of the non-achievement of an impossible goal.

Two points are evident here: first, the establishment of radical organizations is functional for the system to the extent that, in order to obtain resources, radical agents and agencies are obliged to provide rationales in terms of the dominant understanding and, thereby, both embrace and are seen to embrace those explanations of social failure which place the blame on the disadvantaged themselves. Second, radical organizations are labouring under intensified difficulties; necessarily they are running marginal candidates in the context of mainstream or non-marginal competition which characterized the problem in the first instance.

In order to justify their existence, radical training centres, for instance, have to generate placement rates which better those of the conventional institutions. Indeed, claims that this is possible have to be constructed in order to obtain the desired resources. Yet typically such radical institutions operate in situations of severe funding uncertainty. Such funding uncertainties have important and serious side-effects, for, typically, these are associated with complex sets of arrangements designed to measure organizational performance which absorb disproportional amounts of the organization's energy and resources.

Massaging performance evaluations becomes a major organizational activity which heavily detracts from both the expressed and 'concealed' founding organizational goals. Radical or marginal organizations are more likely to experience these pressures than those with more conventional and congruent operational bases. In this respect radical organizations are frequently operating with their hands tied behind their backs.

Processes of power domination are not confined to the control of physical and financial resources but are also intellectual in character. The extent to which the structuring of research is determined by dominant power agencies mirrors and feeds in to the way in which the structuring of organizational forms is determined by dominant conventional organization (for a related point, see Burrell and Morgan 1979: 105).

Research commissioned by the sponsor of radical organizational structure and performance frequently takes the form of monitoring, or contains within it this potential. Sponsorship of the radical organization by the mainstream provides the institutional equipment for generating a greater number of organizational tasks than is necessary to the operation of the radical agency. Task proliferation can be viewed as an instrument for exhausting the energies and resources of radical agencies. It is not necessary to apply a conspiracy understanding to this situation of central/dependent organizational interaction; it is sufficient to note the self-evidence of the proposition that sponsorship should be accompanied by and provides an entitlement to stronger patterns of accountancy control over the subject or client within modern industrial society and that the consequence of this understanding, for the radical organization, is the dynamic of task proliferation.

An additional and related matter for consideration at this point is the consequences of narrow technical problem descriptions for the operation of radical organizations which such bureaucratic controls herald. The consequence is to close off other development options which are possible and better directed as either irrelevant or in conflict with the primary goal set through the funding process. Flexibility (and, therefore, the ability to respond to popular need and action) is reduced.

The thrust of this set of arguments is that the sponsorship of radical organizations and groups by dominant agencies can operate as a controlling device, serving to constrain popular pressure and conflict into more readily directable channels and institutions. Sponsorship permits radical initiatives to be encompassed and controlled by transforming their organizational forms, and thus permitting conflict to be defused in respect of the wider society, yet intensified within the radical organization itself. Conflict over resources which was previously directed at outside agencies is now internal to the black community itself. Conflict shifts from an inter-community to an intra-community domain. This analysis as to the institutionalization of conflict necessarily presents a problem for activist and researcher. The dynamics of cultural pluralism are less straightforward than contemporary discussion suggests.

The goal of this chapter is then to indicate the structural basis of the process of goal displacement experienced by alternative organizations (Etzioni 1961). Radical organizations exist by and with the consent of established conventional organizations; their weaker financial and resource basis determines their directability. They exist in a situation of structural dependency. Inevitably they experience a set of organizational dilemmas as a consequence of the tension between continued survival and adherence to founding values. Despite a radical organization's role as a response to existing structures of advantage/disadvantage, its basis for challenge is not independent. Those very properties of structural weakness which inform its birth carry through into all subsequent levels of organizational interaction and operation. To summarize, the implicit question posed by the chapter is that of the possibility of truly radical organization within capitalist society.

Micro-politics and the transforming organization: radical goal slippage

In order to provide a more grounded description of the shifts in organizational goals and practices, we provide an event history from each organisation as illustration. A fuller analysis of these events has been provided elsewhere.

Stonebridge 1: From community initiative to state enterprise

The Stonebridge Bus Garage Project was established in 1982 to convert a disused London Transport bus depot into a multi-purpose community centre. The centre was intended to provide facilities to the local community for arts, sports, and recreation, for social and welfare services, for education, training, and employment, and for establishing small enterprises. The local, 1960s-built high-rise Stonebridge housing estate has a large black population, over 70 per cent Afro-Caribbean, with a large proportion being young (under 25). Unemployment is very high, especially among young black males; crime rates in the local area are high, and there is a high rate of custodial sentences passed on young males convicted of crime. The area lies in the London Borough of Brent which has the highest proportion of ethnic-minority residents and is one of the poorest in the UK.

Much of the initiative for establishing the project came from an informally organized group of local young black people, the Harlesden Peoples Community Council (HPCC). They had formed in early 1981 and converted the disused basement of a local health centre for their own use. In the autumn, when the bus depot was closed, they were key figures in the calls made by local community representatives for Brent Council to buy the site for conversion to community use, rather than allow its redevelopment for commercial gain. After a joint group of local councillors and community representatives produced a report making proposals for redevelopment of the site for community use, Brent Council bought the site. The site was given over (under licence) to a steering group consisting of seven members of HPCC, three other community representatives, and two councillors, one each from the two main political parties. The phrase 'community co-operative' was applied to the organization to be developed to run the centre. The report drew attention, with apparent approval, to the fact that 'the Community Council had no written constitution, no written rules, no formal system of membership and (had) not adopted many of the bureaucratic forms of administration which prevail in Britain today.'

The capital funding envisaged was just over £2 million. Of this £1.5 million was anticipated through the Urban Programme, a scheme for funding projects to combat inner-city deprivation. This funding was to be provided in equal instalments over *three years*. A further half million pounds was expected from the Greater London Council (GLC), the rest to come from a variety of smaller funding schemes (e.g. the Sports Council).

The steering group took over the site in May 1982. Funding was obtained from a variety of local and national government sources and the European Social Fund to employ a number of people ('co-ordinators') who had professional qualifications and experience in key areas: finance, architecture, business development, training. These were recruited and in post by January 1983, along with an overall project co-ordinator. Each co-ordinator was supported by one or two assistants, recruited from HPCC itself. Funding was also obtained through the Manpower Services Commission (MSC) to employ other staff. Clerical and administrative support staff were recruited along with building workers who rehabilitated semi-derelict areas of the site for temporary use until full-scale redevelopment took place.

In March 1983 the firm of architects appointed began to develop detailed redevelopment plans. Steering group meetings soon became dominated by issues about finance. The capital funding needed was uncertain until the architect had developed an initial scheme design. As the architect began producing outlines of a scheme design, in consultation with the steering group, the expected capital cost began to rise. By autumn 1983 the expected cost was about £3.5 million, and steering-group meetings became confused affairs as the complexities of 'promised', 'anticipated', and 'possible' sources of funding were discussed. By December 1983 the plans for a three-stage conversion had been agreed by the steering group to match the phased funding. However, the lowest tender received for stage A was half a million pounds more than anticipated, and over twice the funding which had been formally agreed. Moreover various officers at Brent Council and GLC expressed doubts about the projections made about the income the centre could expect. In March 1984, after representatives of Brent Council, GLC, and the Department of the Environment (DoE) had met to discuss this crisis, the steering group was aksed to agree to an appraisal of the project by an 'independent consultant'.

The steering group agreed, expressing confidence that the plans would be proven feasible, with consequent increase in funding. The draft terms of reference from the DoE referred to the consultant's undertaking a 'financial appraisal' of the project and indicated that an examination of possible partnership with the private sector be made. The steering group replied by asking that the appraisal should be an economic and social one as well as financial, and that the reference to partnership with the private sector should take account of the objective of ensuring direction and control by the local community. These changes were not accepted by the DoE, but the steering group did not object to this and a consultant started some weeks later. The person appointed was, in fact, already working with the DoE on secondment from an international firm of accountants.

The consultant was provided with office accommodation but was rarely on site and postponed indefinitely a number of meetings with the key project staff. In an informal discussion with the finance co-ordinator he stated that he was attempting to develop a set of proposals which took the existing level of assumed funding as the basis for the cost of the centre. The consultant met with the steering group on 4 July 1984 to present his initial findings. The co-ordinators were excluded from the meeting, but Brent Council's link officer was present. The consultant then made a number of points including that, in his view, the project had been badly served by its professional advisers. He stated that he could not justify the cost of the proposed scheme (now estimated to be about £5.8 million). He criticized income projections as being unrealistic. The steering group agreed to consider his views and respond to them before he submitted his final report.

Following this, Brent Council's link officer proposed that the steering group produce a new report indicating its proposals in the light of recent events. An alternative scheme design was produced, the cost of which was likely to be between £2.3 and £3.6 million. A new, more conservative set of income projections was prepared, under which continuing funding from public sources were required. The new report was produced under the direction of the link officer and presented to all funding bodies. The report was accepted by Brent Council and there followed a period of frequent meetings between public officials and a small group of HPCC members, during which attempts were made to produce a proposal which was nearer to the existing level of funding. Eventually agreement was reached under which the architect was dismissed, Brent Council's Development Department took over, a new scheme design was produced and funding was approved. The DoE insisted that in future it would deal only with Brent Council rather than directly with the steering group.

The organizational structure and management of the project also came under criticism. There had never been formal agreement on the authority relationships between various key parties: project co-ordinator, co-ordinators, their assistants, steering group, HPCC, and especially those assistants to co-ordinators who were members of HPCC. There was an informal agreement of some form of collective management, but this was never formalized. The role of the chairman of the steering group was further confused because he was also the chairman of the HPCC, was not employed by the project but spent considerable time at the project. The project co-ordinator left the project in May and his post was formally taken over by his assistant pending the outcome of the negotiations.

In January 1985 Brent Council's link officer proposed that a review of project management be undertaken, a key element of which was that the steering group appoint someone as overall manager to whom all staff were ultimately responsible, who would implement steering-group decisions. This, it was argued, would enable the steering group to concentrate on policy matters. By now most of the original co-ordinators had left or were due to leave soon. The steering group agreed to the link officer's proposals, and the details of these were accepted by Brent Council in April 1985, as part of the process of reconstructing the funding package. The report indicated that the project would have a hierarchical rather than a co-operative structure, with the creation of a project-manager post and the development of a senior management team reporting to the Manager. The posts which were to replace the co-ordinators who had left or were leaving were in future to carry salaries at about 10 per cent below those which the co-ordinators had been paid.

The active membership of the steering group became less as the negotiations continued. At first some members wanted to engage in high-profile publicity about the threat to funding, particularly by arousing local interest and support which had waned. Those were were mainly involved in the detailed negotiations preferred to continue to try to work with the funding agencies. Increasingly this latter group became the *de facto* management, especially as they were also the key members of the HPCC Committee. In fact, they had earlier closed down the small youth centre (The Annexe) in which HPCC had started, because they wished to overcome the problem of drug-taking about which local police had complained. Apart from the Bus Garage Project, HPCC had no significant activities. Yet in all the publicity emerging from the project, and in all the descriptions of the project's progress presented to the funding agencies, the language of 'community initiative' was utilized. By now this was rhetoric, as the project took on the characteristics of a component of the local-authority bureaucracy.

Charlton 1: From participative organization to chair's action

The Charlton Training Centre was established by GLC funding on the site of a former MSC Skills Centre retraining unemployed adults. After MSC announced the planned closure in 1982, Greenwich Employment Resource Unit (GERU), a local voluntary-sector body, persuaded the local council, London Borough of Greenwich, and the GLC to call a meeting of interested parties in the community to examine issues arising from the loss of local training facilities. At that meeting it was agreed to form the Charlton Training Consortium to develop alternative provision. The consortium developed over the next two years a set of proposals leading to the GLC's providing funding for the consortium's reopening the site as the Charlton Training Centre.

At first the consortium had been concerned to examine what kind of training arrangements might be appropriate for the local community. The GERU representative was also involved in a campaign to improve the opportunities for women to obtain SkillCentre training, especially in non-traditional areas of manual skills. The black (mainly Afro-Caribbean) community groups involved wanted greater training opportunities for black people, especially as they were disproportionately affected by unemployment. There was discussion about establishing a number of smaller training facilities around the local area, rather than reopening the Charlton site. However, by November 1982, the consortium had decided that one major training centre was needed, probably on the Charlton site. GLC representatives had indicated that the GLC would be willing to fund a major adult-training establishment in line with the policy of the controlling Labour party group, elected in 1981 on a radical manifesto. In the absence of any other identifiable source of major funding, the consortium quickly tied itself to a single major project, funded mainly through one agency.

A further main element of the consortium's proposal was that the centre should be managed in a co-operative manner and involve the local community. This emerged in part from the influence of GERU, which was mainly a co-operative development agency, and partly from the policy of GLC which promoted the notion of popular planning, a policy largely developed out of the movement which emerged from the Lucas Aerospace trade unions' alternative corporate plan (e.g. see Wainwright and Elliott 1982). By March 1983 the consortium had agreed a constitution which stated among its objectives: 'To agree a democratic management structure for the Charlton Skills Centre which ensures full participation by all those concerned with the operation of the Centre.'

The absence of a formal constitution resulted in GLC Legal Department's objecting to an application for funding for outreach workers to examine how the centre could meet specific needs in the local community. A company limited by guarantee was established with three members of the consortium as the original members and directors. Most other members then also became members of the company, by providing the notional £1 guarantee. Greenwich Council decided not to join on the advice of the Council's solicitor. By now the original representative of Greenwich Council had left, and his successor was instructed to withdraw from the consortium.

The consortium agreed that on a day-to-day basis the centre should be managed by four co-ordinators, with different areas of responsibilities, but working as a team. Other staff would report as appropriate to one or other of the co-ordinators. In response to the GERU representative's proposal that a policy of pay parity should be examined in line with the general philosophy, the consortium decided that this was something 'they might like to see happen but it was impractical'.

During 1983 attendance at consortium meetings declined, and the detailed work was being undertaken by only a few members, with the work mainly focused on the technicalities of the funding. The application was agreed in principle by the GLC's Greater London Training Board, and the link officer from the Training Board's Support Unit was the GLC's representative on the Consortium. The first 'permanent' staff were appointed in April 1984, and problems of management of the centre were soon being articulated, in particular that the consortium was operating line management under the guise of community participation. A paper from the GERU representative was accepted, by which the consortium agreed to develop a structure whereby the consortium would become 'part of a radical new management structure attempting to operate collective ways of working, and worker participation in management of a large institution, and in implementing some of the ideas of popular planning.' It was agreed that centre co-ordinators would be ex-officio members of the board of directors, that staff would elect two representatives who would be board members, and that any member of staff could attend board meetings as an observer. It was also agreed to set up nine sub-groups which would be the basis for overseeing the work of the centre co-ordinators.

By September 1984 the staff were articulating complaints about the way the board was managing the centre. They complained particularly that they had to justify everything they asked for, no matter how trivial, made recommendations in sub-groups which did not get on to the board's meetings' agendas and did not know how much power was vested at each level of structure. The meeting with the board which they called had little outcome, apart from ratifying that the staff representatives were voting members of the board. Despite these problems, the centre was being publicized by the GLC as a major initiative, an 'exemplary project', and the major funding application was approved. The first training courses were started in December 1984, but the staff continued to experience practical difficulties and the formal procedures for handling day-to-day matters remained confused.

In April 1985 the board reviewed again the management structure to clarify lines of responsibility and authority and established three groups of staff, each responsible to a designated co-ordinator. The place of the Women's Unit was left undecided. The matter had been raised by the trainee support Co-ordinator, whose proposals were in the main formally accepted. However, she left shortly afterwards.

In June the chair appointed an administrative worker as personnel officer. The chair was abroad when the board met next. Staff representatives objected that the equal-opportunities procedures had been breached, and the meeting decided that the appointment was invalid. At the subsequent meeting the chair defended her decision on the grounds that, as chair, she had responsibility to ensure that the centre ran smoothly. Because she was about to go on her trip, she had decided to take 'chair's action'. The voting on the matter was split and the issue was not raised again.

Immediately prior to this meeting the chair, vice-chair, secretary, and GLC link officer held a meeting, later referred to as an 'officers' meeting'. Other members of the board, including staff representatives and co-ordinators who arrived for the board meeting were asked to wait outside the room until this prior meeting was ended. When, during the board meeting, one of these officers had complained that staff tended to regard the board as consisting only of the officers, a staff representative responded that by their actions the officers had 'made it crystal clear that there is a division'.

Problems over financial and administrative issues continued, and the finance/administrative co-ordinator was dismissed. No staff representative was present for the board meeting at which he was dismissed, and the one trainee representative was asked to leave the meeting since it concerned a staff matter. The training co-ordinator, the only other co-ordinator was also absent. The treasurer was appointed to work at the centre, for an honorarium, to deal with financial matters. A member of the education team (also a staff representative) was appointed as acting administrative co-ordinator.

As these events unfolded many other key staff had left, including the women's unit co-ordinator and the co-operative education worker. A number of planned courses did not start, and the Women's Unit ceased activity pending a review of its role and activities. No disabled trainees were recruited, partly because, it was stated, of the problems of building alterations. At a meeting called by the chair of the Greater London Training Board to which all staff and trainees were invited, he declared that GLC supported the centre, was concerned to try to ensure that it continued after abolition of the GLC and invited views of those present on how to proceed. Although, sòme members of the staff raised complaints about the move away from the collaborative structure originally planned, there was no coherent and co-ordinated opposition to the existing structure. The GLC later agreed to fund the centre until August 1986, i.e. after the abolition of the GLC. The centre failed to obtain the funding to continue after August and so closed.

Supporting radical organization: the need for participative codes and practices and supporting structures

This final section is concerned with providing a first approach to the problem of combating slippage in organizational goals and discussing the potential role of explicit codes and procedures in modifying this situation. Although, in the main, the approach taken in this chapter is radical structuralist in orientation, that is to say, the position is taken that there are dominant power structures and that these determine the form and direction of other activity, our analysis is that such control is never complete. Because control is never complete, we see the possibility for radical organizations to strategize their links to one another, and for the formation of a strategized network of radical organizations and support agencies. The naïve assumption of organizational autonomy can have no place in any theory or practice of radical organizational formation; the delineation of strong boundaries, i.e. purely local initiative, around any particular radical organization is liable to lead to its failure. Looking towards the industrial-democracy literature, a good example is given by the developments which have taken place at Mondragon in the Basque province of Spain (Oakeshott 1979).

Given such structural constraints, it is easy to be pessimistic about the possibilities and prospects for the development of radical organization. Rather than end in total pessimism, we would like to offer some suggestions, arising out of our analysis, as to how attempts at radical organizing by disadvantaged groups might be better supported.

First, we suggest that attempts be made to overcome the fragmentation of such efforts, and the experiences gained. Second, in forming the organization, attention should be paid to the establishment of clear codes in those areas which experience shows to be at the centre of the processes of transformation from radical to conventional organizational form. Third, the activities in auditing the organization's performance in the social and political areas which formed the core of founding values should take an equal if not greater place in the explicit monitoring of the organization.

Our first suggestion envisages that greater support should be provided to the founders of the radical organizations in the form of explicit links with others similarly engaged. We have seen how the members of radical groups who attempt to retain founding values typically limit their articulation of dissent because of the need to maintain funding. It is difficult for them to develop a clear perspective of what is happening and to make specific proposals on what action should be taken. If the organization were to involve members of other radical groups similarly engaged there would be a greater likelihood that the subtle processes of transformation would be perceived and that such partial outsiders would be in a position to raise issues in an explicit manner denied to the fully internal membership. The problem experienced would be contextualized, identified as structural in origin rather than being interpreted as individual and therefore culpable failure.

Our second suggestion emphasizes the need to make explicit the founding values of the organization, and to state these in a form in which actual practice can be audited. The fact that organizations continue to be described as radical, even when they more closely resemble conventional rather than radical organizational forms, indicates clearly that founding values are quite easily used as rhetorical instruments. To prevent this, the organizational and social meaning of such statements of founding values needs to be made more explicit and be embodied in the form of codes of practice. These should be based on some consideration of how the organization is likely to operate, so that a form of 'rehearsal' may be undertaken rather than allowing individual, casually arising incidents to dictate policy formation. Such codes should focus on those areas in which significant moves away from founding values may be anticipated. These include the issues of working relationships between staff of the organization, procedures for handling disputes, authority given to certain persons, and the boundaries to this authority, resources required by those assigned responsibility for certain actions particularly in terms of time and practical facilities.

One particular area in which such codes may be of significant value is with regard to the claims to and rights of leadership within the organization. In order to resist the pressures for the 'popular' form of leadership, with its distributed pattern, to move to conventional management-leadership with its focused form, clear limits should be placed upon the time span allowed for the holding of formally recognized leadership positions. These would include positions which typically carry such titles as 'co-ordinator', 'company secretary', and 'treasurer', as well as 'chair'. Interestingly, the Greater London Training Board included such a provision within its general funding criteria but this was not implemented in the case of the Charlton Training Centre.

A further area in which explicit codes of practice are important is in connection with the relationship between the funding agency and its representatives. In order to weaken the subtle, and possibly unintended, influence which the funding agency has in interaction with the radical organization, the possible effects of this influence in transforming the organization should be considered at an early stage. As a carrier of important information between funder and organization, the funder's representative should be subject to agreed disciplines concerning what types of information should be made available to whom, in what circumstances, and in what form.

The third suggestion is that the monitoring process should include some form of 'social auditing' (Geddes 1988), so that the founding values take on a significant role in examining the degree to which the organization is succeeding. This would include an examination using socio-political criteria such as the rate of participation by particular social groups, degree of popular support both within and outside the organization, relative dispersion of power and authority, and the extent to which energy and enthusiasm are harnessed for collective benefit. The technical and administrative monitoring required by the funder should be placed alongside or within this social-auditing frame, to ensure that the former does not tend to marginalize and discount the latter. Moreover, such social auditing should take into account the tendency for organizational transformation over time and so should be undertaken in a manner which shows the history of the organization. In this way, movement towards or away from strategic political and social goals can be plotted, making the use of rhetoric to obscure transformation more difficult. The recontextualization of organizational experience has utility as an instrument for learning as well as an instrument of auditing (Moore 1988).

To summarize, our concern in this chapter has been with the organizational transformation of radical institutions into conventional forms rather than with the more simplistic question of organizational success or failure. We have indicated the structural basis on which such transformation takes place and have drawn attention to a number of dilemmas confronting radical agencies in their attempts to retain their original values. In the cases analysed here, our title 'Radical beginnings, conventional ends' has a definite applicability. A more symmetric outcome for radical organizational performance remains unlikely whilst radical initiatives remain at the level of localized, untheorized, isolated experiments. Radical beginnings require maintenance by radical support and auditing agencies to achieve the prospect of radical ends.

Note

1   This chapter is a highly condensed version of an earlier paper. The research and preliminary drafting were undertaken at the London Economic Policy Unit, Polytechnic of the South Bank.

References

Banfield, P. and Hague, D. (1990) 'The Manor Employment Project' in Poole, M. and Jenkins, G. (eds.) *New forms of ownership*. London: Routledge.

Burrell, G. and Morgan, G. (1979) *Sociological paradigms and Organizational Analysis*, Aldershot: Gower.

Cain, H. (1986) Working paper, Charlton Training Centre research project, London: Thames Polytechnic.

Child, J.C. (1985) 'Managerial strategies, new technology and the labour process', in Knights, D., Wilmott, H. and Collinson, D. (eds.) *Job Redesign*, Gower: Aldershot.

Clarricoates, K. (1985) Working paper, Charlton Training Centre research project, London: Thames Polytechnic.

Etzioni, E. (1961) *A comparative analysis of Complex Organizations*, Glencoe, Illinois: Free Press.

Geddes, M. (1988) 'Social audits and social accounting in the U.K.: a review', *Regional Studies*, 22, 1: 60–5.

Grieco, M.S. (1987) *Keeping It in the Family: Social Networks and Employment Chance*, London: Tavistock.

Grieco, M.S., Pickup, L. and Whipp, R. (1989) *Gender, Transport and Employment*, Aldershot: Gower.

Grieco, M.S. and Holmes, L. (1989) 'Overt funding, buried goals and moral turnover: the organizational transformation of radical experiments', paper presented to the EGOS Colloquium on Organizational Transformation, Berlin, July 1989.

Holmes, L. (1987) 'Management: a radical critique', unpublished MPhil thesis, University of Lancaster.

Hosking, D.M. and Brown, H. (1986) 'Distributed leadership and skilled performance as successful organization in social movements', *Human Relations*, 39 (1).

Hosking, D.M. and Morley, I. (1988) 'The skills of leadership' in Hunt, J.L. (ed.) *Emerging Leadership Vistas*, Lexington: Wiley.

Lee, G. and Wrench, J. (1981) *In Search of a Skill*, London: Commission for Racial Equality.

Mantle, A. (1985) *Popular Planning not in Practice*, London: Greenwich Employment Resources Unit.

Manwaring, T. (1982) *The Extended Internal Labour Market*, Berlin: E.I.I.M.

Michels, R. (1915) *Political Parties: A Sociological Study of Oligarchical Tendencies in Modern Democracy*, translated by Eden and Cedar Paul (1959), New York: Dover.

Moore, R. (1988), personal communication.

Oakeshott, R. (1979) *The Case for Worker Co-operatives*, London: Routledge & Kegan Paul.

Pettigrew, A. (1979) 'On studying organisational cultures', *Administrative Science Quarterly*, 24, December.

Wainwright, H. and Elliott, D. (1982) *The Lucas Plan: A New Trade Unionism in the Making?*, London: Allison and Busby.

Chapter four

The Manor Employment Project: the conception, development, and transition of a community-based employment initiative

Paul Banfield and David Hague

Introduction

The subject of this paper is the Manor Employment Project (MEP), and tracing various aspects of its evolution has occupied myself and four colleagues from the Department of Organization and Management Studies for the last two years. Our objective was to try to capture and record as much information as we could about a significant experiment in social and economic organization. We hoped to produce the story of the MEP.

I suppose the realization that the more one becomes involved in this kind of activity, the more complex and multi-faceted the phenomenon appears, is a quite normal and an almost inevitable aspect of social research. What started off, therefore, as an apparently straightforward – we thought – recording process rather quickly became a much more difficult and involved challenge. Perhaps the most obvious illustration of this, was the problem we faced in deciding whose story we should tell. We also had to decide what should be included and excluded, what should be given prominence rather than a passing reference, and, of particular importance to us as researchers, how far we could impose our own mark on the events we were trying to present through our perceptions, interpretations, and conceptualizations, without this leading to an unacceptable level of distortion. We were at all times aware of the dangers inherent in 'outsiders' telling someone else's story, and as far as we could, we have tried to minimize this effect, but I have to say that, for those who were directly involved in the MEP, parts of what we have written are bound to be controversial.

Less obvious to us, at the time we embarked on the research, were the difficulties that five academics would have in not only answering important methodological and theoretical questions, but in arriving at an acceptable consensus. On a more practical plane, we had to decide on the allocation of responsibilities and find a way of taking what eventually became individualistic contributions and moulding them into a reasonably coherent and integrated whole.

The first of these problems did not, and realistically cannot, have any objective solution. Our influence on the final account, both deliberate and unintentional, was an inevitability, but this would have occurred even if a group much closer to the project had undertaken the task. In fact, those that were, in this respect, better qualified to write the story admitted that being too close to what had happened represented an obstacle to earlier and individual efforts.

Responses from those who have read the draft manuscript suggest that we managed to produce something that has a general level of acceptability. Two factors have had a bearing on this. One is that the initiating and integrating member of the research team was closely involved in the MEP from its conception to its transition in 1986. Notwithstanding the point made in the previous paragraph, his dual role as researcher and participant proved to be an invaluable help in organizing and checking a wealth of historical material, and in getting the rest of the team accepted by those whose co-operation we depended upon.[1]

Second, the team made an initial and fundamental commitment to include as many individual contributions from MEP members and other involved parties, as we could. The result of our work (Pedler *et al.* 1988) therefore contains fifteen separate 'tales', some presented as verbatim interview transcripts which allow a representative cross-section of the participants to give their version of events. Our attempt to explore key project themes, we believe, complements rather than dominates these personal recollections.

I owe a great deal to Mike Pedler, for it is undoubtedly the case that without his initial commitment and subsequent determination to produce a permanent record of the life of the MEP, this paper would not have been written. Recognition also needs to be given to my co-researchers from the Department of Management and Organization Studies who made important contributions to our original work: John Gill, Ian Boraston, and John Shipton. Of the many people whose time and co-operation were freely given over a long period, I would like to make particular reference to my co-presenter, David Hague, from the Department of Employment and Economic Development (DEED) at Sheffield City Council, Dave Clarson, who began as project co-ordinator in 1981 and is still working on the Manor, and Ursula Edmonds who provided a valuable insight into the role of the local authority.

The origins, development and transition of the Manor Employment Project

Let me begin this section by trying to answer certain questions that relate to the organizational, ideological, and physical features of the MEP. These are critical to an understanding of its evolution, and whatever lessons are there to be learned about community development, depend very much on recognizing the importance these features played in the project's successes and failures.

The Manor is a well-known part of the city of Sheffield. The area today, located to the east of the city centre and adjacent to the Don Valley industrial complex, is dominated by a council housing estate. Historically the estate has been amongst the most deprived in the city, with employment linked to, and heavily dependent on, traditional steel and engineering sectors.

Without going into the details of the effects on the city generally, and the Manor in particular, of the economic recession of the early 1980s, which is probably familiar to those who witnessed similar processes of de-industrialization, the social and economic consequences were profound. Structural rather than cyclical changes in the city's industrial base triggered off a rapid and apparently permanent increase in the level of unemployment, followed by a recognition and acceptance that traditional solutions and sources of assistance were unlikely to be available or effective on the scale required.

To understand the origins of the MEP is to understand the human and social costs of concentrated unemployment. But the project itself was an expression of the determination of a group of people from diverse backgrounds to take the initiative in the fight against the worst effects of unemployment, albeit on a small localized scale. Moreover, it represents very clearly, a commitment by these people to take responsibility for themselves in the creation of new employment opportunities on the Manor.

This positive perspective was closely related to a politicization process which affected those directly touched by unemployment, and others whose social conscience was influenced by the growing material inequality that separated the more affluent parts of the city from working-class areas. Some were influenced by radical political ideas which seemed increasingly appropriate and applicable in the early 1980s. Others had been exposed to alternative forms of economic and social organization as a result of visiting the Mondragon Co-operative in Spain, and some, of more pragmatic persuasion, were committed to any form of positive action which would alleviate the apparently inexorable rise in unemployment.

This politicization was widespread throughout Sheffield. It embraced local residents, middle-class activities, unemployed workers, trade unionists, and local politicians. The MEP was but one expression of this phenomenon. All were born out of the material conditions that existed in the city at that time, the significance of which was enhanced by the feeling that capitalist solutions in the form of private investment or demand management strategies, were, for different reasons, inappropriate.[2] This led to the realization that the people of Sheffield, the local authority and other interested groups must necessarily assume responsibility for the regeneration of the city's economic base and community revitalization. The MEP has to be seen in the context of the beginning of a new era of self-help, community action, and an emerging and influential municipal role.

The transformation from the MEP to the Manor Training and Resource Centre in 1987 must be seen, therefore, in part as reflecting the changing material and ideological situation that the city experienced through the 1980s, in addition to the outcome of the project's own internal dynamics.

Translating the commitment to act into a tangible and functioning expression of the underlying idea began with a series of discussions between a group of 'outsiders',[3] Manor residents, and community workers in the spring of 1981. During the summer of that year contacts were made with representatives of the local authority and the Gulbenkian and Rowntree Trusts, to establish external sources of support and funding. At the same time, the debate about the organizational and ideological structure the project should take continued.

The linkage and integration between the two parts of the project, the community focus and employment creation, were made early and explicit and were expressed in one of many papers that were circulating at that time. 'The MEP had from its earliest beginnings one basic aim – a concern to involve Manor people in the whole process of employment; enquiring into employment possibilities, shaping an actual employment project, and being employed by that project.'[4]

As the process of deciding what the project should actually provide in the way of employment opportunities continued, two particularly important developments occurred which had an unforeseen but pervasive effect on the projects evolution. First, the formative group began to articulate and make explicit their ideology which would largely determine the social organization of the MEP and identify to the external environment what the project represented in political terms. The rejection of conventional solutions and capitalist employment relations, with a corresponding emphasis on self-help and alternative work structures, were clearly expressed in one of the project's earliest reports to the city council. In it one of the founder members introduced the project in the following terms:

> Manor Employment Project is an experiment based on the fundamental belief that the traditional entrepreneurs are only able, at best, to offer the majority of working people a living wage, and at worst as now will exploit, reject and degrade the people who create their wealth. We consider that there is a need to show that with the right kind of

assistance, working class, so-called unskilled people can take control of the means of production and can through mutual aid create real alternatives to being someone else's wage slave or living on the meagre state benefits.[5]

This unequivocal statement was not empty rhetoric, nor did it claim to represent a solution to the city's unemployment problems. What it meant for the project's early members was a kind of statement of intent: a belief that something could be done on and for the Manor and that, whatever could and might be achieved, it ought to be through the efforts of the people on the Manor, with the help and support of the professional group.

No ideology is either completely accepted or fully consistent; nor is it unchanging. However, there is no doubt that in many important respects, members of the project (without implying unanimity) continued to act and reflect these sentiments for most of the duration of project's first phase. They created a legal entity, based on friendly-society principles and rules, and formulated a constitution and a decision-making structure that reflected their belief in co-operation, equality, and mutual support. The belief in and commitment to individual worth and development, through the provision of the experience of work and employment in the widest sense, were restated in a report to one of the Council's committees in 1984. It was stated that

> MEP has spent three years testing the notion that every person in our society has value and talent that can be usefully developed both for the benefit of the individual and the wider community. Since arriving on the estate with a set of ideas on how this might be achieved a great many lessons have been learnt. The fifty or so people actively involved in MEP are challenging the whole idea that people can ever be considered redundant[6]

In addition to the crystallization of its ideological character, the second major development that had a lasting impact on the project was the acquisition of the means by which these ideas could be given a concrete and physical form. What the MEP consisted of, by the end of 1980, was its founding members, the numbers of which were gradually increasing, its ideology and objectives, and an energy that needed an expression and a focus. Questions about what form the project should take, and how they would achieve their objectives had, of course, been the subject of considerable debate, but no agreement had been reached. The opportunity, therefore, of acquiring the tenancy of an old works-department site on the edge of the Manor Estate, provided an almost ready-made solution.

The use of this four-acre site, for an initial two-year period at a peppercorn rent, together with a revenue grant of £23,000 over the same period, was in the words of one of the members, 'too good an opportunity to miss'.[7] Not only did the workshops (albeit run down) and other site facilities offer obvious possibilities for embryonic businesses, but it gave the project the physical existence and visibility that meant that the vital step between having a vision and translating this into something tangible had been taken.

The advantages of taking over the site were obvious, but the consequences of so doing were not all positive, and potential problems associated with equating the project with the site were understood. One of these was that the site might suck in resources and creativity from the wider environment, resulting in the project's becoming, at least in the physical sense, separate from the community it was originally created to serve, resulting in the worksite developing *instead* of other project work, rather than in parallel to it. Another was that if, for whatever reason, the site might at some future date become unavailable, or economically unattractive, the very project itself might become threatened.

However, the site was acquired, the project grew through individuals and groups setting up businesses, permanent staff were recruited, and a crucial relationship between the MEP and the city council was forged. During the peak of its development the project consisted of twelve separate businesses, all operating within the shared organization and social structure. Turnover reached £250,000 per annum, and almost the same amount had by mid-1986 been received in revenue expenditure from the Trusts and local authority.

That period represented, for many of the people involved in the MEP, an important personal experience which is difficult to express and quantify and is a part of the MEP story that is often subordinated to the interest in the project's economic achievements, the number of jobs it created, and the attempts to quantify the effects of its activities. The more we, as researchers, explored the project from different analytical perspectives and encouraged those who were involved to re-live their experiences, the more we realized how rich and complex a vein of social life we were tapping.

Our original work focused on four particular aspects which we felt at the time offered particularly interesting insights, ones moreover that might have policy implications of value to those with similar interests and ideas. One involved the experience of creating and developing small businesses, another concentrated on what was described as the project's 'social glue' which involved trying to identify the forces that held the project together for five years. A third dealt with the organization and management issues, and the last explored the relationship between the project and the local authority which was to assume a significant, if not deterministic, influence on the way the MEP evolved.

These aspects of the MEP are documented in detail in the manuscript (Pedler *et al.* 1988); what I would like to develop in the rest of this paper is first, an account of the transition from MEP Mark I, based on the worksite and consisting of small businesses, to the Manor Training and Resource Centre (MaTReC), with its quite different approach to community development, and, second, the way in which the changing external environment and tensions that were building up *within* the project affected its decision-making and control structures.

Evolution and transition

One of the difficulties inherent in trying to explain change is the choice of a theoretical model which somehow seems to fit reasonably comfortably into the available empirical data. In addition, deciding which particular aspects of the project's development should be part of this kind of analysis inevitably involves choices, often omissions and uneven treatment. Mike Pedler's chapter dealing with developmental issues and processes, applied three different models to the MEP, one of which, the life cycle model, is perhaps the most useful as far as this paper is concerned.

The concept of a life cycle has been frequently applied to organizational analysis. One of its central hypotheses is that organizational change can be understood in terms of a series of stages or phases. One writer in this field has gone so far as to suggest the existence of certain 'laws of development' (Lievegoed 1973). Without necessarily validating his ideas, almost everyone who contributed to the research, whether consciously or not, made some reference to stages in the project's life, and to critical incidences which either led to the temporary resolution of a crisis or precipitated one.

We have tried to represent the growth of the MEP, and the transition to MaTReC, in terms of time, critical incidents, and level of activity. Figure 4.1 is a diagrammatical representation of its life cycle. In addition to the familiar terminology used to describe the different stages, it is also possible to speculate, with some justification, on the changing psychological states associated with each stage, and on the level of individual and collective energy that was fed into the project.

The first two stages, for example, were characterized by a high level of optimism and creative energy; a belief that problems, whatever they were, could be solved. Moving into the middle period of relative maturity, the apparent and real success of many of the enterprises and the realization that the project was still in existence were linked to a feeling of confidence and self-assurance, whilst the latter peiod of decline and rebirth led many members to experience apprehension, suspicion, and

Figure 4.1 Life-cycle model of MEP

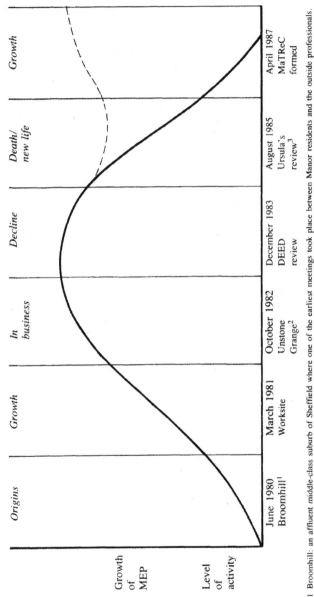

Origins	Growth	In business	Decline	Death/ new life	Growth

Growth of MEP

Level of activity

June 1980 Broomhill[1]	March 1981 Worksite	October 1982 Unstone Grange[2]	December 1983 DEED review	August 1985 Ursula's review[3]	April 1987 MaTReC formed

1 Broomhill: an affluent middle-class suburb of Sheffield where one of the earliest meetings took place between Manor residents and the outside professionals.
2 Unstone Grange: the location of a strategically important meeting at which the future structure and organization of the project was discussed.
3 Ursula's review: the final local-authority review which led ultimately to the end of the MEP in its original form.

dejection with, for those who could see beyond the present and immediate future, the re-emergence of optimism and the recharging of batteries.

However, whilst it might well be possible to predict in general terms an organization's evolutionary process, it would be profoundly misleading to suggest that all share the same time-scale or experience the same outcome. There are many important variables associated with original objectives, organizational structure, member motivations, and the continuing appropriateness of resources and means which give each organization/project its own individual identity and destiny.

As far as the MEP is concerned, the reasons behind its decline and break-up and its replacement by a new and, in certain important respects, different expression of the original ideas are partly located within the project itself and, to a significant extent, relate to changes within the parts of the local authority that were involved in funding and resourcing the project. Let me consider the internal factors first.

It has already been stated that the project's overriding objective was the creation of jobs, in response to the rapidly rising level of unemployment. The way in which these were to be provided was to encourage unemployed people on the Manor to use their existing productive skills, or to develop latent abilities through the setting-up of small-scale businesses. Moreover, these would operate within a social structure and organizational framework that reflected unequivocally democratic and social (some would say Socialist) principles and values.

However, it became clear to certain members of the project that these fundamental and defining characteristics were the source of inconsistencies and contradictions which at least contributed to the difficulties the project faced from 1984 onwards. One of these arose from the nature of the activity the project was trying to foster and the backgrounds and experience of the people who joined the project. The emphasis on starting a business, which for almost all those who joined the project meant from scratch, had implications few at that time fully appreciated. At best their previous lives and work experience had given them certain practical skills, but in the role of employee, and in hierarchically structured organizations. They were now expected to acquire urgently needed business skills in addition to establishing the basic production or service activity that was for them the heart of the business. It quickly became apparent that the absence of such skills would inhibit the prospect of expansion – and therefore the creation of further employment opportunities – and could also threaten the survival of the businesses. Project staff and outside experts seconded to work with the project provided valuable assistance, but the low starting-point meant that deficiencies in finance, marketing, and organization continued to be a source of concern.

A second problem that was to have an even more fundamental impact, was indentified by the project co-ordinator as stemming from 'a basic

71

misconception in its foundation'.[8] Whereas limitations in the knowledge and experience of running businesses and other practical difficulties could over time be remedied or at least managed, this second one could not. It is significant that this comment was made in 1986, during a period in which the project's social fabric began to decay, and when the cumulative effect of pressures and weaknesses could no longer be contained or ignored.

In the search for explanations for the project's imminent collapse, reference was made to the project's constitution, weaknesses in the management structure, inadequate resources, and other operational difficulties, but these in the words of the co-ordinator, 'contributed to MEP's downfall, but they only hastened what was an inevitable end'. In identifying what he considered to be the source of the project's inherent weakness, he argued that

> MEP was founded on the belief that the unemployed could build a future for themselves through the creation of a socially conscious and mutually supportive organization. It set out to do this through the creation of traditional businesses. If you like, it sought to build socialism through capitalism, an impossible dream.[9]

This contradiction is, of course, impossible to ignore in any attempt to explore the project's internal structure and logic. The crucial question that helps us to understand arguments over the project's failures and achievements is whether, and for whom, the successes of the businesses and the creation of employment rather than, or in addition to, its success as an experiment in social organization was the chosen perspective.

If the latter dominates or is exclusive, then the importance of the 'contradiction' is clear. On the other hand, if the former is emphasized, then one is faced with the possibility of interpreting the end of MEP Mark 1 as not only likely and even inevitable, but as desirable and necessary. The reason for this is to be found in the very success of those businesses that survived and became permanent. In retrospect, their continuation and growth – providing security and additional employment – depended on becoming independent of the project and becoming integrated within the wider economic environment. Although at the time this prospect was not viewed with any great alacrity, it does seem as though the project's forced break-up benefited rather than compromised their interests.

The defence of sectional rather than the interests of the whole, particularly under pressure for more economic accountability from the local authority, severely tested the project's social structure and personal relationships. The review document previously referred to, provides an insight into what must have been the project's most depressing and demoralizing time.

The sense of failure as a social experiment is clearly expressed in the following extract.

When it came down to the test of our commitment to acountability and our stated aims of mutual support we failed. Some groups and individuals simply cracked under the pressure and left. Others buried their heads in the sand and hoped that it would all go away. Others cynically believed that they could fool the reviewers and deliberately withhold information. The project's management was found to be seriously lacking in its response to the review. Staff were left to deal with the situation. The project had no united front to offer, it lost control of the situation, failed to respond to problems, simply reacting to information passed on by staff. MEP was exposed as a collection of individuals not a community. Self interest divided the groups, self preservation motivated the staff.[10]

It is interesting to consider the relationship between the survivability of a particular social structure, linked to an underlying ideology, in the face of human motivation and economic imperatives, without denying the value of personal experience.

In attempting to identify the major issues that were largely internal to the project and had a bearing on the transitionary period, one final point needs to be made. It had increasingly become apparent to some of the project's members, and to certain officers within the local authority, that what had begun as an avowardly community initiative had, through the occupancy of the worksite, become excessively introspective and isolated. Although up to half of the MEP's members were connected in one way or another to the estate, there was a clear feeling that the project had failed to develop outwardly into the community in the way that was originally envisaged.

It would be unfair and unrealistic to translate this observation into a major criticism. The limited resources and scale of the project could, irrespective of what form the project took, have made only a marginal impact on the social and material disadvantages many Manor residents faced. Nor could it be argued that contacts with Manor residents not involved were ignored. The reality was, however, that these were difficult to maintain and develop, partly due to the immediacy of the problems in organizing and running the worksite, and also because of an understandable feeling amongst certain residents that only a priviliged few had benefited from the project's resources and opportunities.

The interaction and effects of these problems played a large but not conclusive part in the decision to terminate the MEP in April 1986, and to begin the process of creating the second organizational expression of the largely retained aims and objectives. The Manor Training and Resource Centre was formally established in March 1987 and has been functioning for about fifteen months.

The essential differences are, first, that its legal structure, as a company limited by guarantee, offers the possibility of an almost unlimited number of directors, thereby increasing access and influence to a wider community of interests. Second, instead of being directly involved in developing businesses, MaTReC acts more as a facilitator, helping to identify economic and social needs, and in conjunction with others working towards the provision of facilities and opportunities. It also provides direct employment through the development and renovation of properties.

Its major activities to date, include establishing a job-search and - placement scheme, linking available skills to employer requirements; setting up education and training programmes, and providing access for Manor residents to city-wide college and adult education courses; encouraging economic development through the collaborative research into the economics of community investment; and generating a wide range of contacts with regional and national bodies that have an interest in, and a commitment to community projects.

Decision-making and control structures

Questions relating to those aspects of the MEP which had a bearing on the location, exercise, and pattern of control and influence are amongst the most interesting and illuminating of those we sought to answer. In exploring the issues that seemed to us to represent the most promising lines of enquiry, it became apparent that we were faced with a particularly complex situation which had internal and external dimensions, different levels of expression and both personal and structural forms. Within the constraints of this paper only a very limited indication of our findings can be given.

Implicit in the concept of community development is the notion that control should be located within the community. This does not mean, and realistically cannot mean, total community independence, but rather that the people involved in this type of development need to be given or can acquire for themselves a significant degree of control over key elements of any project, and that this is permanent rather than temporary. If these two preconditions are not met or become compromised, then some redefintion of what began at the grass roots or community level may be necessary.

The original founders of the MEP always made it clear that the project should develop along certain well-defined lines and be run in accordance with agreed rights and procedures that would establish how decisions were to be made, and what rights individual members would have in influencing the decision-making process. In many respects those early principles and commitments continued to be adhered to through to the creation of MaTReC, but not without challenge or some reformulation.

Figure 4.2 Some themes of MEP

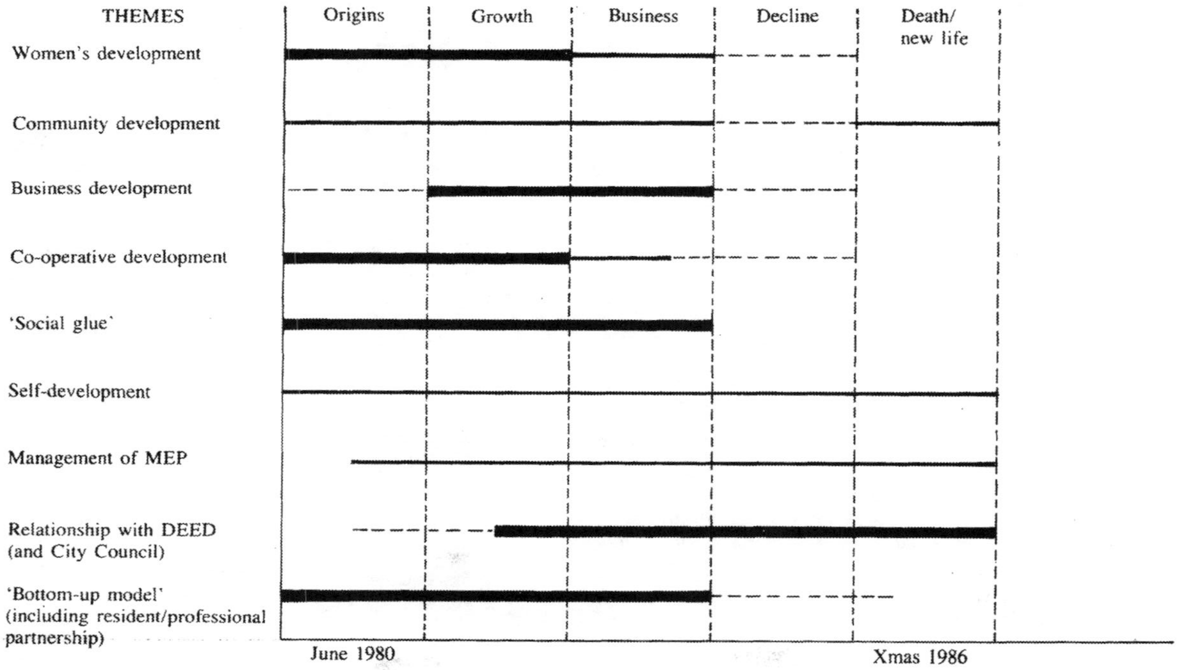

THEMES	Origins	Growth	Business	Decline	Death/new life

Women's development

Community development

Business development

Co-operative development

'Social glue'

Self-development

Management of MEP

Relationship with DEED
(and City Council)

'Bottom-up model'
(including resident/professional
partnership)

June 1980   Xmas 1986

The MEP was originally registered as a friendly society, and run as a co-operative in which each member enjoyed the same status and rights as any other. Membership was based on three main categories: the people who sat up businesses and those they employed; staff employed by the project, e.g. the co-ordinator and the development worker; and supporters who came from the early group of professionals, community workers, and Manor residents.

Decisions on all matters relating to the project were based on general meetings at which all members were entitled to participate. They were taken on the basis of discussion, argument, and peer-group pressure, and it was almost always the case that a decision was based on a consensus rather than through voting. The general meeting also created sub-committees which were responsible for recruitment and liaising with outside bodies, but whose decision or recommendations had to be approved and ratified by the next general meeting.

At its most developed, the project employed five staff. In addition to the two mentioned, a site manager, administrative worker, and office junior represented the permanent support group. As well as the whole project being run on co-operative lines, the staff group also operated as a co-operative in the sense that they agreed to be paid the same, have equal rights in decision-making, and avoid creating a hierarchical structure. Their function was defined as advisory rather than managerial; they had the responsibility of implementing project decisions but without any formal power to enforce them.

One of the most interesting indications of the concern to avoid traditional forms of control was the comment made by one of the staff that, 'in the early days, the word management was not viewed with approval'.[11] The attempt, however, to operate the staff co-operative was not successful in practice, largely because of the functional differences in the five jobs. In particular, the role of co-ordinator and the expectations held by project members of the occupant's contributions were not consistent with the absence of formal authority. Operating on the basis of responsibility without power was not sustainable in the light of the increasing pressure to manage in a functional sense, and the position of co-ordinator was changed by the general meeting to allow greater discretionary powers within the framework of agreed policy.

As far as the individual businesses were concerned, whilst a co-operative structure was encouraged, and in fact about half were run on these lines, partnerships and sole traders were also accepted and established. Decision-making by those running the businesses had to reflect their particular needs and requirements and at the same time reflect the interests, policies, and pressures affecting the project as a whole. The relationship between the project staff and the groups on site was formally an advisory one with no powers to require action or to issue instructions. Although enjoying equality as individual project members, the staff were also employees and at the same time were required to play an important functional role which was potentially compromised by the absence of formal powers and their subordinate status.

The concentration of formal control within the general meetings was felt to be problematical in terms of the technical requirements of running the project. The lack of clarity in the organization structure, and the absence or enforcement problems of rules regulating social and business activities was seen as a weakness and a contributory factor in the project's inability to cope with increasing external pressure in the 1984–6 period. Some businesses were more open than others, and the need for greater financial accountability met an uneven response. It was suggested that, as certain businesses became economically secure and successful, there was a tendency for the balance of commitment to swing towards the specific rather than the general interest, thus weakening the project's social cohesion and co-operative structure.

The interests of staff, project leadership, and the individuals and groups constituting the businesses were in many respects crucial variables in the MEP story and subject to a wide range of pressures and influences. The potentially destabilizing effects of these interests' diverging in certain circumstances was probably understood by some but not all of those involved. Trying effectively to contain this potential within the decision-making framework established by the project's founders was a task that eventually became impossible to complete.

Perhaps the most important of these external pressures came from the local authority which had initially been perceived in a very positive way, because of its early financial support and through the provision of the worksite, but eventually became to be seen by some as the source of the project's problems. The relationship between the various interests within the authority and the project was complicated and became increasingly ambivalent as a consequence of two particularly significant factors.

First, the city council had, during the 1980s, formulated a response to economic change which led to a series of policy initiatives and resource allocations to its own and other local projects. Its vision of a municipal-led economic revival, based on co-operative and self-managed enterprises, helped to inform its responses to requests for assistance from local groups. Over the years, however, there has been an ideological shift in the council's position, partly linked to the outcome of the early learning process and the experience gained in the context of economic regeneration, and also as a consequence of the national government's economic and political initiatives.

Attitudes within the authority to the project's development and needs did change, and continuation of the council's support increasingly reflected calculative rather than ideological considerations. A result of this, was that decision-making within the MEP appeared to be dominated by the pressure that was perceived to be building up outside.

Second, despite political statements supporting the concept of community development, the city council was never able to translate this into an effective and enduring community policy. One consequence of this was that the MEP felt unsure of precisely what the authority was expecting in terms of the project's development and use of resources. This uncertainty was compounded as a result of different departments, committees and liaison officers' expressing what often seemed to be different views on what the project should be doing and applying divergent criteria in the evaluation of progress. Attempting to respond to what was perceived to be an unstable and, at times, unknown set of requirements, increasingly determined by the authority, contributed to the feeling that the project's members had lost control of their own destiny.

Being able to retain control is, I believe an important characteristic of community development, but whether the success of such initiatives, in terms of visible outputs is dependent on the maintenance of member control, or whether this in itself is seen as the indicator of achievement, is a controversial issue (McArthur 1986). Mike Pedler, in making his position clear, provides an insight into the delicate and sensitive balance between this and the necessary level of external support. He argued that 'it requires selective resourcing from outside but only when people in the Manor are ready and able to make use of them and, therefore, control the pace and direction of development; it requires protection and subsidy from outside but just enough to maintain and sustain development' (Pedler 1983).

As far as the local authority was concerned, whilst there was a residue of continued support for the MEP, as a co-operative and community-based venture – support which was crucial to the transition to, and viability of, MaTReC – the ambivalence in its position comes through clearly in the following statement contained in an internal policy statement: 'in general, officers prefer to work closely with groups developing such initiatives to ensure that policies and practices conform as closely as possible with the policy of the City Council'.[12]

Conclusions

The Manor Employment Project represented an ideology and a practical working expression of peoples' desire to make something more of their lives than simply being unemployed and dependent on others. The application of one to the other led initially to the development of the worksite, and out of this to the establishment of the new resource centre. In itself and for what was born out of its collapse the MEP meant something. It certainly meant something very important to many of its members whose lives were enriched and changed by their experiences there. Moreover, it contributed and is still contributing to providing work and training for the people it set out to help.

Trying to quantify and measure its achievements is fraught with difficulties and is unlikely to lead to any complete expression of the project's significance. What is deemed to be measurable and the means used to achieve it are not only controversial in themselves, but tend to detract from the realization that so much of what took place on the Manor defies measurement and quantification. It is no less important for that.

Perhaps it is appropriate to end this paper with a comment made by one of the project's original members, and chosen by Mike to provide a conclusion for our research. He said:

> the real output is the experience of grappling with and defining problems and trying to stitch together solutions in an atmosphere where people felt a great deal of responsibility to each other and to what they were doing . . . and I think a lot of people developed the ability to make decisions about their lives through the process of working through the project in ways which didn't result in the apparent objective of setting up small businesses or whatever, but are nevertheless part of that devlopment process . . . so it's a more intangible outcome which can't be expressed in balance sheets and so on . . . you're talking about the capability to act on one's behalf really, and in the end I'm persuaded that creating that capability is the most important objective that one should be aiming at, because such capability then allows people access to a lot of other things . . .

(Pedler 1988)

Notes

1 Dr Mike Pedler, Founder Member and Senior Lecturer in the Department of Management and Organization Studies, Sheffield City Polytechnic.
2 Large-scale private investment is the dominant, current theme in Sheffield's regeneration, part of which is in partnership with the city council.
3 The so-called 'Cosmopolitans' who conceived the idea consisted of a group of professional people from education, community development, and social work. Their early work in producing briefing papers, lobbying councillors, and submitting grant applications was a vital part in the creation of the project.
4 Extract from document explaining role of project development worker, May 1981.

5   Pete Sacker, Community Worker, writing in a MEP progress report, June 1981.
6   Extract from MEP progress report submitted to the Council's Employment Committee, October 1984.
7   Pete Sacker, MEP Member and Community Worker.
8   D Clarson, MEP Coordinator, in a report to Special General Meeting, 4 March 1986.
9   ibid.
10 ibid.
11 Dave Clarson, interview comment.
12 Internal Department of Employment and Economic Development paper, 1986.

References

Lievegoed, B.C.J. (1973) *The Developing Organization*, Millbrea, CA: Celestial Arts.
McArthur, A.A. (1986) 'An unconventional approach to economic development: the role of community business', in *Town Planning Review*, 57, 1.
Pedler, M. (1983) 'Action learning and economic and social regeneration in Sheffield', unpublished paper, November.
Pedler, M. (1988) 'The Founder's Tale' in Pedler, M., Banfield,
P., Boraston, I., Gill, J., and Shipton, J. (1988) 'MEP: a story of the Manor Employment Project in Sheffield 1980–87', an unpublished manuscript.
Pedler, M., Banfield, P., Boraston, I., Gill, J., and Shipton, J. (1988) 'MEP: a story of the Manor Employment Project in Sheffield 1980–87', unpublished manuscript.

Chapter five

Employment creation through community co-operation: Celtic lessons

Ray Donnelly

Job creation through co-operatives is almost always understood to mean worker co-operatives. Indeed some 10,000 jobs have been created by the roughly 1,000 worker co-operatives established during the last decade. There is still great potential for changes in employment and ownership from that source, but that is not the only part of the co-operative movement which can create jobs. Other, less heralded, but equally valid forms of co-operatives can do that and generally facilitate regeneration of communities.

While worker co-operatives will always be a small part of the industrial base and will require special skills and commitment from their members, thus reducing the number of people who will be able to be involved, other forms of co-operation, linked to people's basic needs have a more universal application as forerunners of urban or rural renewal. These forms of co-operatives include:

credit unions
consumer co-operation
housing co-operatives

and their beneficial effects on many communities can be seen on the Celtic fringe of Scotland and Northern Ireland.

There are fine examples of job creation from all these categories, which can be found in many towns and villages throughout the regions mentioned; those described here are used purely as examples. Their potential for job creation is great and their capacity to aid regeneration of communities almost limitless.

The purpose of this paper is to examine several examples of successful co-operatives operating on the Celtic fringe and to try to establish why they have been successful, what lessons they hold for other communities, and, lastly, what can universities do to facilitate their development.

The first example is from the area of credit co-operatives or credit unions as they are known in Britain and Ireland.

Derry Credit Union

The Derry Credit Union was founded in 1960 by a group of local inhabitants including a certain John Hume, later to come to prominence in another area. The savings and loans co-operative – for that is what a credit union is – has now been in existence for twenty-eight years. During that time it has built up its full-time staff to eighteen, while lending out over £20 million pounds to its members, all local residents. Today the credit union has some 13,000 members. They have between them £6 million in savings, and loans stand at over £5 million per year, and a new and larger building is presently under construction. Derry Credit Union is believed to be the biggest non-industrial credit union in the world.

In growing to its present size, Derry Credit Union has conferred not just the benefit of eighteen jobs per annum over the last ten years or more, but many other benefits on its community. This in a locality which has not had its problems to seek over the last twenty years. These benefits arise from the nature of the operation and the nature and principles of co-operation.

Credit unions exist to pool the savings of members of a community and to lend those savings to each other in times of need. The members of the Derry Credit Union belong to the group most affected by recent unemployment and so the need for help has been great. By law the maximum credit unions can charge in interest is an annual percentage rate (APR) of 12.68 per cent (or 1 per cent per month on the declining balance). This is charged to members who borrow. These members would normally use hire purchase or the Provident Cheque system to finance their credit requirements, paying at least 35 per cent APR and at other times 106 per cent APR or 156 per cent APR or indeed higher. These rates are all legal. They are the normal charges of finance companies and of the Provident Cheque Company Ltd. The difference in cost between such forms of borrowing and the credit union is illustrated by the example in table 5.1.

Table 5.1 Cost of borrowing £100 (repaid over one year)

Institutions	APR
	%
Credit union	12.68
Bank	18 to 20
Visa	26.2
Trade credit (e.g. House of Fraser)	39
Government – electricity board	39 to 44
Chequing company	up to 130
Finance company	up to 156

It is one of the nastier aspects of capitalism that the poorer you are, the more you pay to obtain credit. The members of Derry Credit Union, coming from a troubled area with a male unemployment rate in excess of 40 per cent in an area of multiple deprivation, would surely be forced to the upper end of the borrowing scale. Thus, by pooling their savings in the credit union, members are able to finance their borrowings and those of the other members at a much lower cost than would be possible without the credit union.

This in turn brings two further benefits to the local community: first, the people have a higher disposable income after debt repayments than would otherwise be the case and, second, what interest is paid is paid to a local co-operative employing local people and not to a London-based finance company acting as a leak to the local economy. These two benefits act together to reinforce the beneficial effects upon employment within the local environment. First, the directly created jobs in the credit union, averaging eighteen full-time equivalents over the last ten years, though with the benefit widely spread as more part-time staff are employed, and, second, the jobs located throughout Derry itself as a result of a policy of staunching the flow of the funds out of the area. How many jobs this has helped save or create is hard to tell, but, if Derry Credit Union has lent out over £20 million since its inception, and if we assume the alternative cost of credit to be 40 per cent APR as against the 12.68 per cent APR of the credit union, then £5,464,000 has been injected into the pockets of local residents rather than into the accounts of a finance house or the government through its agencies such as the electricity board. This figure of over £5 million is almost certainly an understatement of the true contribution to the local community, as borrowers would almost certainly have to pay more for credit than the 40-per-cent figure used.

The contribution to the local community is further enhanced by the fact that the money which is paid in interest is paid out to local residents as a dividend on their savings, thus completing the circle which keeps these vast amounts of money (by the standards of local communities) operating within the local economy and not leaking away from it.

If it is remembered that the city of Derry has not just this one, but two other credit unions, then the importance of their contribution to the local economy and job retention and creation cannot be understated.

Yet such is not the prime goal of a credit union. A credit union exists to serve its members, 'not for profit, not for charity, but for service' being its motto. Indeed the financial and economic benefits of the credit union are only one side of the coin. To a community without Derry's problems to seek a credit union brings pride, a chance to serve, and a valuable socially owned asset. There are many who would say that these were the real achievements of the credit unions and that any help they provided in creating or sustaining jobs was welcome, but a bonus.

How has this important contribution to the local economy come about? The answer lies in the nature and philosophy of co-operation as practised in all credit unions. Co-operatives are about democracy and credit unions are the most democratic form of co-operative. The board of directors are in complete control. The manager and staff of a credit union never refer to 'customers' but always to 'members'. As such, the power of the community is enhanced, control stays in the hands of local people and does not pass to so-called professionals from outside, as has happened in other areas of co-operative activity. In the specific case of Derry Credit Union the loyalty of the members of the credit union is seen by many as the outstanding feature. A bad debt ratio of only 2.77 per cent on loans is testimony to the close feelings members of the local community have for their credit union. From John Hume and the other founders down to the present day, with people like Philip O'Doherty who gladly gives up at least six nights out of seven to work as a board member, the quality of leadership has been inspirational. This is enhanced through the selection of the staff and their total loyalty to the credit union. The manager, Sean Drummond has been the only manager they have had, and his deputy, Carmel Toye, has worked there for twenty years, and their total support for board members makes success more certain.

Credit unions now exist in other parts of the United Kingdom. In Dalmuir in Scotland a group of women heard about the Irish experience in these matters and formed their own credit union. Now eight years later, they have 2,500 members and almost half-a-million pounds in savings. They have already lent out over £1 million and again this is in an area of high unemployment and social deprivation. This credit union, the largest community credit union in Great Britain, has its own premises and is now in a position to start employing staff. Thus, while the rest of Britain is behind Ireland in this area, it will probably catch up, provided the government is prepared to treat credit unions as fairly as it treats other financial institutions. At present in Britain there are ninety-eight credit unions, having 29,000 members, with total savings of £6.6 million and total loans of £6.3 million. The figures are supplied by the Association of British Credit Unions Limited – the central body for British credit unions. At present these credit unions employ only twenty people, but that will increase rapidly over the next decade, and with their ability to keep money within local communities credit co-operatives will play their part in helping to create and sustain employment in many local communities.

Credit co-operatives are not, however, the only area in which Derry City can give a lead to employment creation or social ownership. Derry also exhibits a fine example of consumers' co-operation.

Consumers' co-operation in Britain has been in decline since 1945. At that time it was possible to claim that one pound out of eight was spent in a co-operative society. Today the figure would be more like one out of twenty-five and it is still falling.

Against this backdrop of slow contraction the Galliagh (Derry) Co-operative Society was formed in 1981 by the residents of the Galliagh housing estate, Derry, to replace a service which had been withdrawn by a private trader.

Galliagh Co-operative

The Galliagh housing estate is a fairly modern, reasonably well-designed public-housing complex on the west side of Derry. The unemployment rate for males is in excess of 60 per cent. In common with many other post-war housing developments little thought was given to the provision of services for the community. Thus shopping facilities were minimal. People were forced to rely on mobile shops or walk a minimum of a mile to a chain store situated in the road between Galliagh and the neighbouring estate. The alternative to this was to journey into Derry by bus. This is costly and not a favoured option. In 1980 when the chain supermarket closed due to continual harassment by paramilitary forces, the people of the Galliagh had to rely totally on mobile shops which were very expensive. It was against this background that the idea of developing a community-based retail co-operative was formed.

Here it has to be said that, like Derry Credit Union, the idea was not to create jobs, but to provide a service. In 1981 the Northern Ireland housing executive decided to auction a piece of ground for retail development in a central part of the Galliagh estate.

This provided the spark which brought to life the Galliagh society. Several local people started to argue the case for a community-owned shop. There can be little doubt that, if it had not been for the work of this group, little or nothing would have happened. Of prime importance in this area was the involvement and commitment to the co-operative ideal of the local priest, Father Kevin Mullen.

This group worked hard throughout 1981 to raise the money necessary to enable the community to purchase the land from the housing executive. Some £80,000 was raised in selling shares in the proposed co-operative society. Such an achievement cannot be underestimated. This sum was raised in an area of multiple deprivation where there was no history of retail co-operation, with the nearest retail co-op being eighty-two miles away in Belfast. However, there were mistakes made during this exercise which were to have lasting effects on the society's future. The collectors going round the doors tended to oversell the idea and the potential members were in some cases left with false ideas as to what the co-op could provide and at what price. Assumptions about people's motives in joining the co-op tended to be naïve. In an area of very high unemployment it is not surprising, or it should not have been surprising, that many people joined in the hope that they, or at least a member of their family, would get employment out of the venture. Some of the leaders tended to see the development of membership in a more philosophical light, believing that the bulk of the new members shared their ideological commitment to democratic socialism and retail co-operation.

This problem is, of course, not unique to Galliagh. There are many such examples in the history of retail societies throughout the United Kingdom.

Despite these problems, unseen at the time, the plot of ground was purchased on behalf of the community by the society and work commenced on building a suite of shops. Many people in Galliagh attended the auction for the land and great were celebrations when the society's bid was the only one lodged and accepted.

The Galliagh Co-operative Society opened its premises in December 1981. The first day of trading was a tremendous learning experience. More money was taken on that first day than in any full week since. On the other side of the coin, the members learned that having their own co-op shop did not mean goods being sold at cost price, or something just above cost price. This came as a shock to many of them who, having little knowledge about co-operation or retailing, were unable to interpret correctly the prevailing expectations about the benefits of co-operation. Their expectations were totally unrealistic. The result of this was serious both to the society and the community. There immediately developed a group of residents within the estate who became implacably opposed to the society. They felt they had been 'conned'. Over 400 people applied for the ten full-time and fourteen part-time jobs created. Any unbiased reporter could commend Galliagh's community spirit in providing twenty-four jobs where only eight full-time equivalents could be justified. This, of course, did not placate the applicants who were unsuccessful. Further, the families of those rejected felt aggrieved and misled. All of a sudden it seemed as though only those with relatives on the management committee had got jobs. This was nonsense but was believed by certain people. These unfortunate people, over-ambitious in the hopes either for cheap food or jobs, or both, did not return to the society, withdrew their share capital and did their best to poison the estate against the society, and it was only one day old. As one director said of the first day: 'The people came, they saw and they went home disappointed and told their neighbours why.' To make matters worse, no dividend stamps were available at the checkouts and some members had been relying on the anticipated dividend to finance 'a small family holiday in Spain'.

What had been provided was a fine suite of three shops, a supermarket, a post office, and a corner shop, all owned and operated by the co-operative. The buildings stand comparison with any others in the north-west of Ireland and provide a valuable selection of services which were not available previously: giro cashing, cigarette sales, newspapers, as well as groceries. Notwithstanding these factors, the general feeling of the community after the first day was hostile to the society. The next six months saw things go from bad to worse.

By the end of the first six months trading at a loss of some £6,000 was being recorded. This was against the projected profit for the same peiod of £10,000. Attention was now focused on personnel and management. As the expectations of the community had been pitched too high for the society to fulfil, so the expectations of the directors towards the commitment of the staff were likewise misplaced. It was assumed by the managing committee that staff would need 'minimal supervision of punctuality, work performance, tea breaks, etc'. That all staff would share the ideology of the co-operative was taken to be axiomatic. It was simplistic to believe, as the directors did, that employees would become committed co-operators overnight. Further, despite the loss of members and the hostility of many residents to the society, it was still likely to take over £1 million in its first year, if, that is, it survived that long. This volume of trade demands a management expertise which the initial management of the society did not, at that time, possess.

Two separate but related problems arose because of the serious nature of the society's financial position. First, the quality of the management of the society and, second, the role of the management committee in the day-to-day running of the society.

To take the role of the committee first, a problem had developed whereby members of the committee adopted too high a profile in the store. They became identified with the society to such an extent that some customers believed that the society was a family business. Further, the staff did not know to whom they were responsible. Was it the manager, was it a member of the management committee who was in the store all day, or was it to the member/shoppers, some of whom were very quick to remind the members of staff who it was who ultimately owned the store? This problem of the relationship between directors and a manager is, of course, not unique to the Galliagh, but it was intruding into the performance of staff and thus into the performance of the society.

The larger problem of the management of the society on a day-to-day basis depends upon the resolution of the problem outlined above. Once the directors decided that their role was *not* to manage on a day-to-day basis, then it became possible to construct a management system capable of providing a professional manager with the information necessary to the operation of a million-pound business. In May 1982 a thorough review of the society and its operation was carried out by the development officer for the community who also happened to be a director of the society. Over a period of eight weeks the complete operation was put under a microscope. Every single activity performed in the course of co-operative business was examined to estimate its contribution to the viability of the enterprise. The skills, talents, and contributions of each employee were monitored, and a 'team effort approach' was evolved which required each employee to work on his/her own intiative to ensure their future employment and the success of the venture. Responsibilities and roles were clearly delegated to each employee. The workload of the organization was broken into five main functions and one senior member of staff made responsible for the management of each particular function. The sales-management function was differentiated from the administration-management function. The bookkeeping and administration function was completely reviewed. The merchandising, purchasing, pricing, marketing, cash-flow, and stock-control functions were reviewed and improved upon to complement the efficiency of the whole operation.

A further result of this survey was a change of management personnel. The manager, assistant manager, and two other persons left. With the help and advice of the Belfast branch of the Co-operative Wholesale Society (CWS) retail-operations group, the store was redesigned and a new manager appointed. The help given by the CWS is important and is worthy of note for three reasons. First, the aid given by CWS personnel is a fine example of co-operation between co-operators and gives the lie to the mistaken belief that CWS is only interested in taking over independent societies. Second, the aid built up a strong sense of loyalty to the British retail movement among the Galliagh directors, a loyalty exhibited by their deliberate policy of promoting co-op 'own label' products. Third, the aid is in marked contrast to the defunct Belfast Society which refused similar aid when in 1958 a group of people in Derry asked for assistance in the establishment of a retail society. The men of 1982 were true co-operators.

Since that time the Galliagh society has gone from strength to strength. At the end of the first year a modest profit of £21,131 was reported. In each subsequent year a similar profit has been recorded and in 1985 the members were given a 10-per-cent rate of interest on share capital.

The importance of Galliagh's community base, which it has been trying to re-establish, is shown in the attitude of the members to dividend. At the AGM in February 1984, attended by well over 100 members, a decision was recorded that no individual payments of dividend or dividend stamps would be allowed. Instead any surplus that remained after proper reinvestment and placing to reserves would be put into a separate fund to create a social dividend. This fund is to be used for the development of projects which will benefit the community as a whole, such as the provision of an adventure playground for local children, and the erection of lock-ups to enable local people to start their own enterprises.

By 1986 the future of the Galliagh society seemed assured. There was still little opposition within the estate. As expectations became more realistic, more householders on the estate started using the society. The usual retail-society problem of member apathy has, however, begun. During the troubled period of the first year and for a time thereafter members attended meetings in large numbers. The 1984 AGM started at 8 p.m. and in excess of 100 people were still there after midnight. Now there is much less interest as things get much better. In 1988 the society was making modest profits of just over £33,565 on a turnover of £1 million. The modest profit is a result of employing thirty-five people when ten could do the job.

Despite the difficulties of the first years, and the dangers that might lie ahead, it would be foolish to underestimate their achievement. The people of the estate, or at least many of them, have developed a self-help approach which is spreading into other areas such as production. The Galliagh society showed that retail co-operation was not a purely nineteenth-century phenonemon as some have suggested. In Galliagh it is a lively thriving activity which others in areas of deprivation can follow. To all who believe in retail co-operation it gave a real shot in the arm. Above all, a socially owned enterprise is meeting the needs of the local community where it is most needed, in the community itself.

Although the Galliagh society has never set out to be a job-creation exercise, the directors are, of course, happy that so many jobs have been created. As long as the society remains profitable, they will continue to be more than generous in the provision of jobs.

Recent developments for the society include plans to build a new, much bigger supermarket on the estate and discussion with residents of the neighbouring housing scheme – the Kreggan – as to whether the residents of that estate should form a co-operative of their own or whether Galliagh should expand its activities to take in the neighbouring estate. Opinions are divided, but a separate society is the more likely outcome. Other ideas under consideration include construction of a social club for the community and a fast-food outlet to provide another necessary service for the community. In other areas, such as the Highlands and Islands, co-operatives such as Galliagh with its community base and concept of service would be called community co-operatives.

Calvey Road Housing Co-operative

Similar developments are shown by another type of co-operative in Glasgow, the Calvey Road Housing Co-operative, Glasgow is justly famous for its housing co-operatives. Since the formation of the first tenant-managed co-operative at Summerston some ten years ago, many housing officials have made the journey to Glasgow to study co-operation – Calvey is, however, something special. Unlike Summerston, it is not a new-built co-operative. Calvey is part of Easterhouse, one of post-war Britain's greatest disaster areas. In the mid-1980s the residents decided to form a co-operative with the help of Glasgow's housing department. The housing stock in that area could only be described as poor and rehabilitation was the carrot which enticed the local people to opt for the co-operative.

Today Calvey Road is a picture of clean, bright, well-decorated houses and well-kept gardens and common grounds. What made the difference to the buildings is obvious – the rehabilitation money – but what made the change in attitude is more important, and that was participation. It was a condition of the contract that builders wishing to get the contract for work had to employ local labour. Architects wishing to get the contract had to undertake to listen to the local people who have to live there long after the architects had departed. This meant that the local residents were involved at every stage of the development and many got paid employment out of it. Apart from the creation of these temporary jobs, several other benefits accrued to the local community. First, people began to feel that they were having a part in the redesign of their community, and this led to a development of a much stronger community feeling than had been there previously. Second, two full-time jobs were created by the co-op in the administrative field. Third, after the completion of the work, the community turned its attention towards facilities, or rather the lack of them, within the area. Plans are now being drawn up to turn closed business premises into a community café, a community pub, and workshop for people wishing to start their own businesses. Calvey Road co-op has shown what talent, skills and energies can be released for the benefit of all when local communities are involved enough and feel proud enough about community developments. All the plans above will create jobs in an area of persistent high unemployment, at present over 70 per cent among males.

All the examples above brought great benefits to the communities they serve. All have helped regenerate the local economy, they provide much needed services to their communities, they provide a source of activity in which local people can participate, they allow local people to have their voices heard in areas that are of great importance to them, money, shopping and housing. All of them act as a source of pride to those involved and attract fierce loyalty from their members. Above all, they promote involvement among a population which might well have been expected to be apathetic to everything, so much of their lives being controlled by the state or its agencies. These are manifold blessings in themselves, but in addition all have created real jobs, kept purchasing power within the area, and provided greatly needed services to local community. All are forms of ownership which are social, non-capitalist, and democratic. They are all outstanding examples of what people acting in co-operation can do for themselves and for each other.

Conclusions

What lessons can be learned from their success which can be used to aid other communities who wish to regenerate their environment?

There are six areas from which others might learn. First is the community itself. All the communities cited had strong community ties. They were not large enough to be amorphous and had all started from strong key groups. The quality of the early leadership is vital to the growth of community feeling and mistakes at the early stage can prove dangerous. The Galliagh found to its cost that over-expectation among prospective members, can lead to resentment when expectations are not met. The lesson was that the starting group must keep everyone informed about developments, not allow expectations to arise, and keep everyone going towards the chosen goal. Further, the involvement of key local figures, opinion formers, is very helpful. Father Kevin Mullen, a curate in the local church, a fine and brave man, was and still is deeply involved with the Galliagh Society.

Second is local control. The directors of Derry Credit Union are very much in control of the affairs of the union. There has been a tendency over recent years for democratic control to be reduced in value certainly within more established retail and agricultural co-ops. In the credit unions this is not the case. The directors are in complete control. Management has not supplanted the directors as it has in many other co-operatives. The Galliagh has the same tight control exercised by the board, as with Dalmuir Credit Union and to the greatest possible extent in the Calvey Road. When directors are supplanted by managers, local control is impaired, the feeling of ownership by the community is reduced, and apathy will eventually appear.

Third is having local staff recruited from the membership. It is not always possible to recruit a manager and staff from among the membership, but it is more often possible than is imagined and far too many organizations rely on so-called professional advice and appoint from outside before considering any of their own people. There are, of course, problems in appointing from within and the Galliagh Society suffered from this. However, they fared no better appointing from outside the members. When they chose a member to be their fourth manager, they secured the services of a very good leader. The Derry Credit Union has only ever had one manager in over twenty years, Sean Drummond, and he was recruited as a member. His skills and ability are reflected in the performance of the credit union. Indeed, while the staff of Derry Credit Union give all credit to the members of the union in guaranteeing its success, no one can doubt that the members have been loyally, capably, and faithfully supported by the staff over the years. Staff recruited from members, particularly active members, do much more to support local control than others might from a so-called professional background. Certainly in the case of Paul Whorisky, now manager of Galliagh co-op and previously an active member, he is a real managerial find, recognized as such by Mr Graham Melmoth, secretary of the CWS who recommended his appointment to the local society. Local active members prefer democracy even when they are managers.

Fourth, it is vital that the group has a clear idea of what it is in business to achieve. What is its goal? Groups with one clear concept and who stick to pursuing it have a far better chance of succeeding than groups with vague general ideas about doing several things. 'Stick to the knitting' is as vital for community group as it is for large capitalist concerns, especially in the initial or in difficult stages. This combines with the fifth point. All the above examples, particularly the ones from Northern Ireland, have created lasting employment in an area of high unemployment. They did not, however, set out to do so. Here is the real lesson for those seeking to promote new forms of ownership, management, and employment. No matter what business form or organization is employed, its success or failure will depend on finding a gap in the market, on satisfying demand for goods or services; if that is done, then real and lasting jobs will follow as in Derry. Job creation through community co-operation is a result of the community's being able to supply goods and services which people are prepared to buy.

This paper has mentioned only three examples out of many from the co-operative sector which have led to new forms of employment and management under democratic control. There are many more. The community co-operatives of the Western Highlands established by the Highlands and Islands development board are one glaring omission and worthy of a paper on their own. Further, the work of the CWS in helping co-ops like the Galliagh and in spreading co-operative principles and membership throughout Northern Ireland and Scotland, something no independent retail society seems able to do, deserves the highest praise. Retail co-operatives still employ over 80,000 full-time equivalent people throughout the UK and despite their obvious faults they are still far and away the largest employers in the co-operative sector. All these and many more are worthy of mention, but time and space prohibit. Their omission does not imply that their role in the creation of new forms of control management and employment is any less important than those mentioned here – they all have a vital role to play.

The universities' contribution

One last point does deserve consideration. What, if anything, can universities do to help ventures such as those outlined above or, indeed, can they do anything to help people create new forms of employment, management, or control? Here again the role model must come from Derry.

Magee College is one of the oldest institutions of higher education in Ireland. In 1964 it became the Institute of Continuing Education of the New University of Ulster. In this role Magee's staff became more and more involved with community activities in Derry. One of the staff, Paul Sweeney, was a major force in establishing the Galliagh Co-operative Society. Paul Sweeney is currently Director of the Northern Ireland Council of Voluntary Services.

In 1983 the College established a Co-operative Education Research and Training Unit offering a Certificate in Co-operative Studies. This course was well supported by the Derry Credit Union, Galliagh Society, and the CWS among others. This unit has now been subsumed into the larger community studies unit, but it still provides help and advice to those in the north-west of Ireland who wish to establish co-operatives. At present the staff of the unit are working with six groups who are hoping to form various worker and community co-operatives.

Perhaps this is a most important lesson for academics. It is not enough to talk about alternative forms of employment or ownership; sometimes it is necessary to be proactive and get out into the community in the way Magee staff have done and offer help, remembering always that co-operatives can never be imposed from above. They can grow only from the bottom up if they are to survive and provide employment. The academic can act as a facilitator, preparing the soil, raising awareness about co-operation, providing information, giving support, but he must then let the group get on with their own co-operative, because that is the best way to ensure success.

Part 2

Privatization

Chapter six

The contracting-out of ancillary services in the NHS[1]

Christine Cousins

In 1983 the government imposed a mandatory programme of contracting out domestic, laundry, and catering services in the National Health Service (NHS). This paper considers the implications of these policies for the restructuring of ancillary work through a case study of the implementation of a programme of contracting out in two district health authorities.

The study was part of a larger research project conducted by the author in two district health authorities in a county in south-east England. NHS managers and staff were interviewed in acute hospitals, psychiatric and mentally handicapped hospitals, and in community services in the two districts in a ten-month period during 1985-6. Some preliminary findings with respect to the contracts two years later are also included in the paper.

The research drew on recent discussions of the labour process in the state sector (Batstone *et al.* 1984; Ferner 1985; and Cousins 1986, 1987). These writers have argued that the restructuring of public-sector work has to be understood in the context of the structural role of the state in contemporary capitalist societies as well as specific political and ideological policies and practices. Thus, the state's productive activities in the post-war period exacerbated the financial problems of governments and opened up the state to political and social conflicts over state resources themselves (Offe 1975a, 1975b; O'Connor 1973).

These fiscal and social crises and government responses to them contributed to the conditions in the late 1970s under which the ideological shift to the right took place. In the 1980s Conservative administrations have sought to restructure the welfare state by the recommodification of certain public services, the reduction of public expenditure and employment, and by weakening the role of the public-sector trade unions.

The formulation of state management policies, however, takes place in the absence of market criteria and in a context of a diffusion of objectives in public policy-making, political pressures, and interest group demands as well as budgetary constraints. Moreover, the different economic and political demands may be non-commensurate and have

contradictory effects. State managers, therefore, face particular difficulties in devising appropriate structures of control which make
compatible these conflicting pressures. A few studies, for example,
Batstone *et al.* (1984) on the Post Office, Ferner (1985) on British Rail,
and Cousins (1986, 1987) on the NHS have used this theoretical approach
to demonstrate that this different mode of rationality (or to use Batstone's
term 'political contingencies') in the public sector, has consequences for
the strategies adopted by management, trade unions, and workers.

The research carried out by the author, therefore, focused on the extent
to which the particular economic and political context of health-service
work had an impact on the strategies pursued by management and
employees within the NHS. For example, political strategies and the
mobilization of public support are important forms of resistance for
health-service workers and community groups at both local and national
levels. An earlier paper by the author noted that health managers faced
considerable difficulties in legitimating their practices and found
themselves faced with political pressures and opposition from the diverse
groups in the NHS. Trade union, professional, and community groups
were therefore able to deny the validity of health managers' policies by
reference to the social-welfare aims of the health service (Cousins 1988).

The propositions discussed above may though underestimate the
government's capacity to impose more direct forms of control on public-
sector organizations. Techniques applied in private-sector organizations
have been introduced in the public sector throughout the post-war period
and have led to the increased bureaucratization of work. More recently
private-sector styles of management, compulsory contracting out of
services, and the use of efficiency criteria have all rationalized and
intensified work processes in welfare organizations. Some workgroups
too are more vunerable to management control strategies than others and
ancillary workers in particular have, as a result of the contracting-out
programme, been subject to a lowering of their wages, increased
workloads, and increased job insecurity or redundancies. Ancillary
workers have also found it difficult to oppose the effects of the
contracting-out programme. This paper examines a number of reasons
why ancillary work has been more vunerable in this respect than other
sections of the health service.

Contracting-out continues to be an attractive policy for the Conservative government for it is considered to subject state agencies to the discipline of the market, provide profitable markets for private companies,
and weaken the strength of the public-service unions. The paper discusses
the political influences on the government which led them to impose this
policy and also examines the conflicting pressures on health managers
and trade-union leaders when faced with the requirement to implement
a policy which they perceived as inappropriate or illegitimate. Evidence

from the case study also indicates that the introduction of contracting-out into ancillary work has begun to change the terms, conditions, and security of employment of the ancillary workers. It is argued that the introduction of market rationality in the NHS has generated social costs, has obscured the purposes of state welfare work and has generated a number of problems and tensions for managers which have further to be resolved.

The background to contracting-out

In 1983 the government issued a circular requiring all health authorities to contract out their catering, laundry, and domestic services (DHSS 1983b). A few weeks later the government abolished the Fair Wages Resolution of the House of Commons 1946;[2] this meant that private contractors did not have to pay their employees Whitley Council rates of pay. Since then health authorities have been instructed by ministers not to include fair-wages clauses in their contracts.

In its first term of office the government issued draft circulars on contracting-out, but the slow progress of health authorities in this direction brought the government under increasing pressure from a number of groups. First, the UK proponents of the free market, the Adam Smith Institute, Aims of Industry, and the CBI, urged the government to privatize, claiming that this was a superior form of service provision (for example, Forsyth 1982; CBI 1981). Second, in 1982, the Institute of Directors published a paper which advocated privatization as 'the obvious and most desirable' strategy of breaking the strength of the public-sector unions, by reducing union membership, and making bargaining arrangements more localized (Institute of Directors 1982). Third, the contracting companies themselves considered that contracting-out in the NHS would provide them with ready and profitable markets, around £175 million a year according to the public relations firm of Forsyth (*Guardian*, 5 July 1984). Fourth, pressure also came from a parliamentary lobby consisting of some thirty MPs who had shares in the private companies or who were directors or consultants to the firms (*Tribune* 1985). Fifth, contracting-out was an attractive policy to a government committed to reducing public expenditure and public employment and weakening the strength of the public-sector unions which were considered to be outside the market discipline which by then had affected the private-sector unions. Finally, professional legitimation had also come earlier from public-administration associations (Dunleavy 1986).

Hence there was political compulsion for health authorities to contract out, despite the lack of evidence that contracting-out is cheaper in the long term than the direct production of services. In some cases health authorities have been instructed to award contracts to private companies, even when their own in-house bids have been lower (Labour Research 1984).

The government claim that the policy of contracting-out leads to 'savings which can then be spent on improvements in services to patients'. By March 1988 the Department of Health and Social Security (DHSS) estimated that 96 per cent of domestic and laundry services and 76 per cent of catering services had been put out to tender at a saving of £106 million (*Hansard*, 6 July 1988). The National Audit Office, in assessing the savings generated at September 1986, reported that the savings at this time (£73 million) represented about 20 per cent of previous costs for those services put to contract (National Audit Office 1987). The cost savings have been substantially higher where services are carried out by private contractors, although the high savings associated with early tenders are likely to have been loss making to the companies concerned and involved reductions in staff and standards of service. As we discuss below, private companies have experienced great difficulties in winning later contracts and the majority of contracts have been won by in-house teams.

The reality of the savings generated by contracting-out can, however, be questioned. There are a number of factors which are difficult to quantify but must be taken into account, and these suggest that the savings are much lower than is claimed by health authorities. For example, the National Audit Office found that there was inconsistency in the way savings had been reported; some included the cost of redundancies, whilst others did not. Moreover, cash 'savings' achieved through contracting-out do not take into account the amount of management time and effort involved in implementing the policy. The National Audit Office conservatively estimated that this cost might be of the order of £15m. Further costs are also generated through increased monitoring and evaluation costs, through contractors' failures and cost overruns, as well as increased costs to other public agencies through redundancies and increased unemployment. As we discuss below, social costs are also generated which are borne by health workers, whose pay and conditions are reduced, and by patients through reduced levels and quality of service. Women in particular bear the brunt of these costs as ancillary workers and as the main users of the services (Radical Statistics Health Group 1987).

Management strategies

The contracting-out of ancillary services took place in the context of changing management arrangements following the recommendations of the *Griffiths Report*. A team of businessmen led by Griffiths, the managing director of Sainsbury's, was appointed in 1983 by the government to give advice on the 'effective use and management of manpower' in the NHS. Their report focused on the creation of a new management culture and ethos, namely the introduction of a commercial-style management into the health service.

Consensus management teams, which had been introduced in the 1974 reorganization and consisted of a medical representative, a nursing officer, an administrator, and a treasurer, were replaced with a general line manager at every tier in the health service. General managers were to have individual managerial responsibility and were to be responsible for 'major cost improvement programmes'. The appointments were to be on a fixed-term contract for three years and their pay was to be performance related to 'the extent to which they achieve change' (DHSS 1983, 1986). The Griffiths Report proposals were central to the government's attempts to implement tighter management and financial controls and general managers were seen as the key to ensuring the effectiveness of centrally initiated policies.

In the author's study it was noted that the introduction of general management challenged the medical professionals in particular. There was, however, evidence of the assertion of managerial prerogatives in a number of other areas, including the pushing through of contracting-out and 'efficiency' savings. A report written by the accounting firm of Coopers and Lybrand, appointed by the government to find ways of making contracting-out more attractive for the contractors, considered that the initial phase of the tendering process was constrained by the former consensus-management teams who handled the process on a committee-type basis. General managers, however, have brought a much more 'incisive approach' which the report considers has greater potential for the contractors in the second round of contracting out (Coopers and Lybrand 1985).

General managers interviewed in the two districts thought that the contracting-out of ancillary services was one area where they could make savings without affecting front-line staff or closing hospitals. Ancillary workers tend to be an 'invisible' element of hospital workers; unlike nurses they are not 'public figures', so that the contracting-out of ancillary services was less likely to become a local public issue than closing hospitals, wards, or beds.

Managers and work-study officers in this study welcomed contracting-out as a better test of efficiency than bonus schemes. Bonus schemes covered about half the ancillary services in the two districts and, since they had been introduced in the 1970s, highly formalized procedures had been instigated for controlling hours of work, costs, performance, and quality of work. The schemes were negotiated through the unions and had given them considerable degrees of relative autonomy within the procedures.[3] Managers and work-study officers regarded the schemes, however, as 'giving bonuses regardless of performance', of leading to 'slippage' in the hours of work, and being inadequately supervised. By removing the bonus schemes it was felt that contracting-out would enable managers to exert more managerial controls over workers, increase managers' discretion, increase supervision and productivity, and remove the relative autonomy of the unions.

Nevertheless, the managers disliked the political compulsion and dogma behind the tendering process, they disliked the loss of control over their own staff, the loss of trust and commitment of ancillary managers and workers, and the breakup of the ancillary team. As the tendering programme progressed, it also became clear that there were associated problems of maintaining standards and monitoring the contracts, especially when contractors failed to provide an adequate service.

These conflicting pressures on management could, however, be reconciled by winning the in-house tender, but to win management had to undercut the unknown bids of the contractors. By the end of the research period all the ancillary services which had been tendered in the two districts had been won by the in-house teams. Manager and union interviewees commented that when awarding a contract there was a tendency to favour the in-house tenders. For example, private companies whose bids were lower than the in-house team were in some cases disqualified because their conditions of service and rota patterns did not take account of the difficulties of recruiting staff in the local labour market. At a national level too there has been a trend for more and more contracts to be won by the in-house tenders. By March 1988 the majority of contracts had been awarded to the in-house teams, accounting for 80, 85, and 97 per cent of domestic, laundry, and catering services respectively (*Hansard* 6 July 1988).[4]

Union strategies

The trade unions were also caught in a dilemma for, if they negotiated with management during the preparation of the in-house tender, they were agreeing to a deterioration of pay and conditions of work for their members, which, if the in-house tender won, might be worse than the conditions of private contractors. If the contractors won, the unions were likely to lose members and negotiating rights and their members could lose jobs or suffer loss of pay and reduced terms and conditions of work.

The fragmented and decentralized nature of contracting-out, management control of the tendering process, and the inexperience of branch officials in negotiating tenders, meant that union leaders were at a loss to know how to deal directly with privatization. Union officers in the study were initially reluctant to co-operate with the tendering process but eventually became involved in the hope of winning the in-house tender and thereby retaining Whitley conditions and pay rather than losing their members' jobs altogether.

Local officials felt that the lack of support from other health workers and the sectionalism between the multiplicity of professional groups and unions within the NHS had hindered the ability of the unions to resist the contracting-out process. A further problem was the low public visibility of ancillary workers, for privatization of ancillary work generated, as mentioned above, little local attention in the press or in public debate.

Although, in some districts, there has been local action by unions which has prevented the lowering of wages and conditions, the most successful strategies have been those at a national level which have focused on contractors' failures and reductions in quality of service. These campaigns have been part of the unions' anti-privatization publicity which has built on and mobilized the popular public support for the NHS. Union leaders claimed, for example, that these campaigns had helped to prevent the widespread privatization of the NHS which was promised in the earlier years of the Conservative administration.

Labour relations during the tendering process

In both health authorities the preparation of the specifications[5] and in-house tender was perceived as a managerial activity with a dominant influence from work-study officers. In one district, however, management adopted a strategy of non-confrontation with the unions. In this case the unions were characterized by strong inter-union co-operation and organization, high union density, and 'traditional' understandings with management established during the 1970s. The union officials were therefore able to participate in the preparation of the specifications and in-house tender, they were given full information, were able to use delaying tactics, and to assess the contractors invited to tender. For management it was a successful strategy because union branch officers persuaded their members to relinquish their bonuses and accept a reduction in pay and conditions. The in-house tender won and union officers felt that at least they had preserved jobs and NHS negotiating procedures.

In the other district, unions (who did not have inter-union organization) were consulted in the preparation of the in-house tender, but they and their members wished to keep their bonus payments and Whitley conditions of work and pay. Management considered they were under pressure from the health minister to exclude fair-wages clauses from the contracts and ignored the preferences of the unions and the workforce. The in-house tender won but employees and branch officials were demoralized and lack of trust in district management became a characteristic of subsequent labour relations. As one union official explained:

No matter how reasonable one's arguments are, or how fair, you are fundamentally demoralized by what happens. The difficulty is how to fight when you are demoralized and by that time you are tired as well.

In this district labour relations became more acrimonious and adversarial, as general managers used contracting-out as a means of confronting the unions and tackling other contentious issues.

The contract in operation

If an in-house tender wins a contract, the service has been subjected to the discipline of competition and, although labour is still not conducted for profit, the labour process is organized as if it were. Ancillary services in the districts were reorganized prior to and during the tendering period by introducing more labour-saving equipment, employing casual and part-time staff, leaving vacancies unfilled, and reviewing and tightening bonus schemes. In the latter case, new work-study data were used for the specifications of the tender, but this could be competitive only if staff then relinquished their bonus pay. Moreover, it was felt by service managers that competition must be continuous and must extend through the life of the contract. The contractor cannot become complacent, managers and workers are now under an obligation to keep to the terms of the contract, which must be continuously monitored and evaluated.

Since ancillary services are labour intensive, costs can only be reduced by intensifying work and lowering the wages and working conditions of staff. It is noticeable that the tendering programmes have proceeded more rapidly for cleaning services, for, as they are more labour intensive than either laundry or catering, there is a greater margin of cost reductions for health authorities or profits for private contractors. The National Audit Office Report found that 78 per cent of cost savings had been achieved on domestic services.

In the in-house contracts in this study, workers' conditions of work and pay were reduced, as they suffered increased workloads, reduced pay through cuts in their hours and lost bonus and overtime payments. At a national level many contracts have involved excessive use of part-time work and reduced access to union protection, although grave abuses of these are more prevalent in the private companies (NUPE 1985). Contract work also removes security of employment, a traditional feature of public-service work, as the contracts are only for a short duration. Contract workers and their managers reported that they felt continuously insecure and under threat, since they did not know if they would win the next contract.

Ancillary work is predominantly work carried out by women and ethnic-minority workers. Women ancillary workers are concentrated on the lowest pay grades in the NHS, full-time workers earning between £72-5 a week in 1985-6. The trade unions argue that 80 per cent of female ancillary workers earn less than the 'official' (supplementary benefit level) of poverty (Ancillary Staffs Council Trade Union Side 1985). Even before services were contracted out then, ancillary workers were amongst the lowest-paid groups in the country. The effect of contracting out was to devalue further the worth of labour of the most vunerable groups in the health labour force.

Once a contract was in operation, it became socially divisive, for ancillary workers were no longer part of the health-care team but became isolated and separated by the 'factorylike' regime of work which conflicted with the patient-care values and priorities of other health-care workers. Patients often have more contact with ancillary workers than nurses. For example, one ancillary worker in a hospital for mentally handicapped patients commented: 'I've been here much longer than most nurses. I know the patients better and they come to me, not the nurses.' But the intensification of work meant that ancillary workers could no longer make the traditional caring contribution to patient care which the work process of direct labour allowed. The workloads of nurses were also intensified as they had to take on patient-orientated tasks previously carried out by ancillaries and through the additional domestic work which the ancillary workers could not do in the times allowed.[6]

The different regime of work imposed by the contract was also incompatible with other welfare policies; for example, the routinized and intensified nature of contract ancillary work reduced the effectiveness of the flexibility of domestic work required by the rehabilitation programmes of community care. Nurses working on the rehabilitation of mentally ill or mentally handicapped patients used to teach patients everyday domestic activities such as cooking, cleaning, and washing before they left to live in community homes. The flexibility of domestic, catering, and laundry work required by this rehabilitation programme conflicted, however, with the rigid and specific schedules of contract work. One ancillary manager emphasized the difference between the two regimes of work:

> Nurses don't realize that wards are a workplace, with workplace regulations, health and safety requirements and people working to a contract – they are not a home.

Staff motivation and morale

In those services that have been contracted out, however, local managers have been faced with a number of problems. The process of tendering itself had the effect of lowering the trust and morale of staff. One domestic manager said:

> The way that the tender was carried out was in a very wishy-washy, negative way. Nobody knew what they were doing, there was a lack of communication, the whole process was protracted, everyone was very demoralized by it and many staff left.

Ancillary managers themselves were particularly bitter about the mandatory nature of contracting-out for, if a private contractor won the contract, they could be made redundant or be taken on as monitoring officers, with no career prospects or pay progression. Even when the in-house team won the contract, however, this bitterness was still evident, as the following comment by a domestic manager demonstrates: 'Competitive tendering has killed our profession. It's like watching everything you have worked for for years taken away, and everything you do treated as second best.'

Managers were sometimes able to use the pride of the in-house team in winning the contract as a way of motivating their staff. For example, a district catering manager made the following comment when the in-house catering team won the contract in one hospital: 'At present they don't have a pride in the company [the NHS] but they do have a pride in themselves. Their attitude is "we'll show them".' But in a recent interview with a domestic manager, after two years of working to a contract, he said with reference to the second round of tendering:

> We would be thankful if we lost the tender. We would welcome a private contractor taking over the next contract. This was not the case before. Then there was a pride in winning the contract, but not now. We would all rather have the redundancy money. You would be surprised how many managers feel like that now. It is probably better that a private contractor with his harsh methods ran the contract as it is now, rather than the in-house team.

Recruitment of staff

The insecurity of the tendering process, the low wages of contract work, and the intensification of workloads meant that the health authorities had difficulties in recruiting and retaining staff.[7] One NUPE official commented 'Many staff left to take jobs at a local factory – they said "who would work at hospital wages under that pressure?" ' Workers who were previously predisposed to accept low wages when the job offered security of employment, accomodation, and non-pecuniary benefits such as a contribution to patient care, were no longer willing to accept the new terms and conditions.

Preliminary findings from interviews with domestic managers, two years after the contract had been in operation, suggest that recruitment of staff was still a major problem. In one hospital most of the older, more experienced staff had left and the ancillary workforce was composed almost entirely of 16-year-olds or people with employment difficulties. The manager said 'the workers get a hell of a little for a massive input and the word has got around that work in this hospital is just not worth doing'. The constant understaffing meant there was no flexibility for cover during absence of staff or for any kinds of training of staff.

Monitoring and maintaining standards

Managers also had difficulties in maintaining and monitoring standards for, in order to make savings, the specifications were reduced below the previous standards. The specifications state the inputs to the service, that is the individual tasks to be performed, and not the required outputs. This means that monitoring compliance with the contract is difficult as there will be some uncertainty with respect to expected performance. Some staff were able to use the contract as a set of rules which stipulated minimum performance. Since workloads were intensified and times for work tasks reduced, these ancillary workers felt that 'if standards are not achieved in the time set, that's a management problem'. Nevertheless, this attitude was not expressed by all workers. Women cleaners often bring their own personal standards of cleaning from home and their own expectations may conflict with the lowered contract standards, leading to a lack of job satisfaction.

The nature of health-care work also means that it is difficult to include all contingencies of ancillary work in the specifications of the tender. Ancillary managers recognized that for certain patients there would always be additional but unpredictable amounts of work, but as these were outside routine work they could not be costed or included in work-study data. Even the in-house contracts then were more inflexible than direct labour and overruns on budgets increased costs to the health authorities.

Conclusion

Contracting-out of ancillary services was a policy few health managers would have adopted without government pressure. In this respect contracting-out in the health service is unlike that in the private sector where management may decide to contract out on the basis of advantages to the company. In the health services, although a few managers perceived some advantages in contracting-out, for example, tightening hours and supervision of ancillary work, or the assertion of managerial prerogatives in labour relations, most considered that it had led to a loss of their direct control over quality and flexibility of service.

Managers also recognized that contracting-out had brought a loss of trust between manager and the managed and the loss of ancillary workers' traditional contribution to patient care. Managers now had to find new ways of increasing the commitment and efforts of staff and they faced difficulties in recruiting, retaining, and training staff for their in-house contracts. Moreover, contracting-out had shifted the problems of managing and providing a service to that of monitoring, supervising, and evaluating the contract.

Ancillary workers have always been marginal within the health labour force, their peripheral status enhanced by low wages, a low social status, and a lack of bargaining power in the labour market. Contracting-out ancillary work, however, has not only reinforced this peripheral status by reducing the terms, conditions, and security of work, but ancillary workers have become separated from other health-care workers by the different regime of work imposed by the contract. Contracting-out too has reinforced pre-existing gender relations by specifying work, which is seen to be appropriate for women, as even more low waged, insecure, and dispensable.

In this respect then the impact of contracting-out on ancillary workers does support the thesis of the Institute of Manpower Studies of an increased polarization and segmentation of the labour force (Institute of Manpower Studies 1986), although there is little evidence that the government is pursuing policies which secure the long service and commitment of its core workers. As this study has shown the introduction of contracting-out has caused considerable disruption, undermining and damaging the morale of health service staff. It is difficult to disagree with Brown's comment that 'the public sector trauma of the 1980s is thus not just one of financial crisis but of a challenge to a whole system of labour control and motivation' [1986: 167].

Notes

1 The author wishes to thank the Editor of *Work, Employment and Society* for his kind permission to use material from C. Cousins, 'The restructuring of welfare work: the introduction of general management and the contracting out of ancillary services', *Work, Employment and Society*, 2, 2: 210–28.

2 The House of Commons Fair Wages Resolution of 1946 'instructed government departments to require contractors to provide their workers with terms and conditions "not less favourable than those established for the trade or industry in the district where the work is carried out"' (Heald and Morris 1984: 31).

3 At a national level, bonus schemes enhanced the membership, strength, and organization of the health unions when they were introduced in the 1970s (Manson 1976).

4 Private contractors have experienced a number of problems in the tendering programme (lack of success in winning tenders and therefore fewer profits than initially anticipated, termination of some contracts in mid-term, financial difficulties of some companies) and others have withdrawn from the tendering programme altogether (London Health Emergency 1986). Although there were initially some forty companies tendering for NHS services, this number is now down to about sixteen, as a number of companies have withdrawn from tendering for NHS services and others have been subject to takeovers. It is now difficult to apply the term 'competition' to the domestic tendering process, since two companies, BET and Hawley, dominate the contract cleaning market, holding about half of all government and NHS cleaning contracts and two-thirds of local-government cleaning contracts.

These difficulties led the contractors' association, the Contract Cleaning and Maintenance Association, to put pressure on the government to change the rules of contracting-out in their favour. Accordingly, in January 1986, new instructions which do favour the contractors were issued to health authorities by the DHSS. The rules include advice to health districts not to investigate the projected workloads or the terms and conditions of service for employees, nor the expected profit margins of contractors; the rules have also made it more difficult for districts to terminate a contract when companies fail to provide an adequate service (DHSS 1985).

5 The specifications stipulated the levels, frequencies, and standards of service required; although they could not specify employment levels, they did determine numbers of staff, wage levels, conditions of work, hours of work, and work routines.

6 A National Audit Office *Control of Nursing Manpower* found that nurses now spend a considerable proportion (21 per cent) of their time on catering and domestic duties (House of Commons 1985/6).

7 Experience elsewhere has shown that health authorities and private contractors have had considerable difficulties in recruiting and retaining staff, and turnover of staff has been high, especially in areas such as London and the South-east of England where there are similar but higher-paid jobs and high costs of living. In Croydon DHA, for example, in the first five months of a cleaning contract by Crothalls, 87 people held 25 jobs (*Guardian*, 13 March 1986). In some cases this has affected the continuity and quality of the ancillary services which in turn have affected the quality and provision of health care. Recruitment difficulties have been further exacerbated by a Rayner efficiency scrutiny which recommended that NHS accommodation be sold, so that ancillary workers who live in tied hospital accommodation have lost their right to that accommodation.

References

Ancillary Staffs Council Trade Union Side (1985) *Health Workers Pay: Time for Action Now*, London: Ancillary Staffs Council.

Batstone, E., Ferner, A., and Terry, M. (1984) *Consent and Efficiency: Labour Relations and Management Strategy in the State Enterprise*, Oxford: Blackwell.

Brown, W. (1986) 'The changing role of trade unions in the management of labour', *British Journal of Industrial Relations*, 24, 2, 161–8.

Coopers and Lybrand (1986) *Health Management Update File*, London: Coopers & Lybrand Associates.

CBI (1981) *Report of CBI Working Party on Government Expenditure*, London: Confederation of British Industries.

Cousins, C. (1986) 'The labour process in the state welfare sector' in D. Knights and H. Willmott (eds.) *Managing the Labour Process*, Aldershot: Gower.

Cousins, C. (1987) *Controlling Social Welfare: A Sociology of State Welfare Work and Organization*, Brighton: Wheatsheaf.

Cousins, C. (1988) 'The restructuring of welfare work: the introduction of general management and the contracting out of ancillary services in the NHS, *Work, Employment and Society*, June, 2: 210–28.

DHSS (1983a) *NHS Management Inquiry*, Department of Health and Social Security, London: HMSO.

DHSS (1983b) Circular HS (83) 18, Department of Health and Social Security, London: HMSO.

DHSS (1985) *Competitive Tendering: Further Advice for Health Authorities*, Department of Health and Social Security, London: HMSO.

DHSS (1986) *General Managers: Arrangements for Remuneration and Conditions of Service*, Department of Health and Social Security, London: HMSO.

Dunleavy, P. (1986) 'Explaining the privatization boom: public choice versus radical approaches', *Public Administration*, 64, 1, 13–34.

Ferner, A. (1985) 'Political constraints and management strategies: the case of working practices in British Rail', *British Journal of Industrial Relations*, XXIII, 1, 47–70.

Forsyth, M. (1982) *Reservicing Health*, London: Adam Smith Institute.

Heald, D. and Morris, G. (1984) 'Why the public sector unions are on the defensive', *Personnel Management*, 16, 5, 30–4.

House of Commons, (1985/6) *Control of Nursing Manpower*, Committee of Public Accounts 14th Report, London: HMSO.

Institute of Directors (1982) *Some Thoughts on the Tasks Ahead*, London: Institute of Directors.

Institute of Manpower Studies (1986) *Changing Working Patterns: How Companies Achieve Flexibility to Meet New Needs*, London: NEDO Books.

Labour Research (1984) 'Privatization: NHS and laundries', *Labour Research*, May, 113–15.

London Health Emergency (1986) *Patients or Profits*, London: London Health Emergency.

Manson, T. (1976) 'Management, the professions and the unions' in Stacey, M. *et al.* (eds.) *Health and the Division of Labour*, London: Croom Helm.

National Audit Office (1987) *Competitive Tendering for Support Services in the NHS*, HC 318, London: HMSO.

NUPE (1985) *Privatization Fact Sheets Series E*, London: National Union of Public Employees.

O'Connor, J. (1973) *The Fiscal Crisis of the State*, New York: St Martin's Press.

Offe, C. (1975a), 'The theory of the capitalist state and the problem of policy formation' in Lindberg, L., Alford, R.R., Crouch, C., and Offe, C. (eds.) (1975) *Stress and Contradiction in Modern Capitalism*, Lexington, Mass.: D. Heath.

Offe, C. (1975b) 'Legitimacy versus efficiency: introduction to Part 111', in Lindberg, L., Alford, R.R., Crouch, C., and Offe, C. (eds.) (1975), *Stress and Contradiction in Modern Capitalism*, Lexington, Mass.: D. Heath.

Radical Statistics Health Group (1987) *Facing the Figures: What is Really Happening to the NHS*, London: Radical Statistics Health Group.

The Tribune Group (1985) *The Welfare State Under the Tories: A Skeleton Service*, London: Tribune Publications.

Chapter seven

Privatization and the restructuring of a public utility: a case study of British Telecom's corporate strategy and structure

Richard Hallett

Introduction

There can be no dispute that the last decade has seen fundamental changes in the structure and nature of the telecommunications industry in this country. During this time the telephone company has not only changed its name but has been transformed from a publicly owned corporation to an aggressive multi-national company. Telecommunications has become the site of rapid technological change and now provides many of the communications needs demanded by the international restructuring of capital; it has become a major factor in economic development. The major computing and electronics corporations have entered the industry partly because of their desire to exploit and control telecommunication services and facilities but also because this industry has become a highly profitable area of activity. The service has been reconstructed to exploit the opportunities presented by these demands.

With a government actively committed to the needs of private capital, it is not surprising, given its central position in the economy, that telecommunications has become a focus for much political debate and legislation. For its part the government has opened up the service market to competition and handed the service-providing company over to private ownership. Faced with competition and in its eagerness to become an international force in the international telecommunications market, British Telecom (BT) has overhauled its corporate structure through a process of divisionalization.

The period has seen a shift of focus for BT away from the provision of a service for the domestic market, its traditional area of operation, towards an increased range of facilities for industry. This has resulted in a reduced commitment to the public service, increased costs to domestic subscribers, and created a confused and much more antagonistic set of industrial relations within the industry.

It has become common for trade unions and other analysts of the industry to attribute these changes to the policy of privatization and have in turn demanded the renationalization of the industry in order to preserve the public telephone network. This chapter argues that this is a simplistic analysis, and that one has to look at the interaction of all the pressures on the industry to identify any possible benefits from a policy of social ownership of the telecommunications service industry.

History and development

BT, and before it the Post Office, was held in public ownership from 1912 until privatization in 1984. It was originally nationalized to ensure that a uniform and integrated telegraphic and telephonic service was provided (Batstone, *et al.* 1984: 22). The industry was built on the principle of universal access developed by Rowland Hill with the Penny Post which enabled anyone in the country to send a letter to anyone else at unit cost. This commitment to public service has meant that the telephone network has become an essential part of everyone's life, whether it be the ability to make immediate connection to the emergency services, to call home from a public kiosk, or to make sure that Grandma is OK.

The Post Office was a part of the civil service until 1969 when it was given more independence from the government and a more commercial approach by being converted into a public corporation (Batstone *et al.* 1984: 11). The same Act of Parliament started the process of separating the postal and telecommunications sides of the corporation and also introduced tighter financial controls (Solomon 1986: 186). It was not until 1981, when the separation was completed, that British Telecom was created, only to be turned into a private company and have 50.2 per cent of its shares sold on the stock market in October 1984.

An essential characteristic of the universally accessible telephone network is that it is a natural monopoly and has to be organized through a single, coherent corporate structure. The service's utility is increased with each and every extra subscriber (BTUC 1984: 4). Even in countries where the telephone network has not been publicly owned, this characteristic has been adhered to. AT&T (Bell Telephone) in the United States, which provided the model for the British Post Office back in 1912 (GLC 1984: 21), had a virtual monopoly until it was deregulated by the American government in 1982, when the industry was split between a myriad of smaller companies.

As a part of the trade-union campaign against the privatization of British Telecom, the British Telecom Union Council (BTUC) researched the effects of this deregulation (BTUC 1983a and b). It identified three distinct phases that led to the break-up of the monopoly. First, other operators were allowed to provide competing long-distance or trunk services without having any responsibility for the less profitable local and public-service networks. Second, competition for trunk services led to a price war which could not be controlled by the government's regulatory body. Third, this led AT&T to divest itself of its local, low-profit networks which were purchased by other companies who had to pay for the interconnection with the trunk network. Originally AT&T was meant to pay to be linked to them but, when the regulatory body tried to insist on this arrangement, Bell threatened to construct alternative local networks using satellite technology.

There are distinct parallels between the US and UK experiences. Although British Telecom has not yet sold off any local networks, it is certainly constructing units of operation that would make this possible. The liberalization that licensed Mercury Communications as a competing operator has forced British Telecom to adjust its tariffs in order to remain competitive with Mercury.

When a single operator controls both the local and trunk telecommunications network, it allows for the cross-subsidization of the more expensive services by the highly profitable ones. Local and public service networks are relatively expensive since they demand both extensive cable networks to subscribers' homes and dedicated equipment in the exchange. Facilities like the 999 service and the network of telephone kiosks are high in public utility, but generate low cash returns. These networks and services are used mostly by the domestic subscriber, whilst the long-distance and international lines, which generate disproportionate profits, are used more by business subscribers, who often need to transmit digitized data. The effect of this process has had serious consequences for domestic subscribers in the United States where local phone rates rose by between 200 and 300 per cent in the year after deregulation (GLC 1984: 22). In this country long-distance tariffs were the lowest of anywhere in the world, whilst local calls cost the most (GLC 1985: 8).

The range of services provided by the network has been rapidly increasing during the last twenty years. These are developments that have been made possible by the interaction of technological developments and the demands of business users. Figure 7.1 shows this developmental burst over the last few years and predicts that the process will continue into the next century.

A major influence of these developments has been the convergence of telecommunications and computing technologies which has served to widen the concept of the industry. In particular the new breed of telephone exchanges are little more than dedicated computers that have made the transmission of digitized data possible. As more companies, like IBM and Honeywell, have entered this market, it is becoming increasingly difficult to maintain an integrated approach to the industry (Communications Campaign 1985b: 8).

Figure 7.1 Growth of telecommunications services

					Telemail
					Home-
					Newspapers
					Colour Fax
				Radiopaging	Radiopaging
				Confravision	Confravision
				Viewphone	Viewphone
				Viewdata	Viewdata
				Low-cost Fax	Low-cost Fax
				Telemetry	Telemetry
				Telecommand	Telecommand
				Super Telex	Super Telex
				Enhanced-data	Enhanced-data
			Radiophone	Radiophone	Radiophone
			Datel	Datel	Datel
		Telex	Telex	Telex	Telex
		Facsimile	Facsimile	Facsimile	Facsimile
	Telephony	Telephony	Telephony	Telephony	Telephony
Telegraphy	Telegraphy	Telegraphy	Telegraphy	Telegraphy	Telegraphy
1870			1970		2000

Source: Coventry Workshop 1979: 2

Legislation and technology

These technological and market changes in the telecommunications industry were in their early days when the first Thatcher Government was elected in 1979. The Post Office had already committed itself to exploiting the new markets. It had recognized that the domestic market was finite and was beginning a process of structural change, despite the severe cash limits imposed by the last Labour administration that had left the industry severely undercapitalized. The switching system was old fashioned and there were long delays for new connections (Solomon 1986: 186).

It is not then surprising that a new government, committed to opening up the public-sector markets to private capital, should put through legislation to restructure the telecommunications industry very quickly. Solomon identifies six imperatives that underpin what he calls 'an unusually clear-cut policy' (1986: 186) that was applied to the telecommunications industry. First, customer choice will provide a measure of efficiency and should be applied to markets that have state-monopoly control. This is a theme that can be seen to run through much recent legislation, but particularly the Education Reform and the Housing Acts. Second, he cites the government's commitment to allow managers to manage in these markets, whilst workers may decide their own destinies and investors are free to invest according to their assessment of company

115

performance. Third, that the government was convinced that the infrastructure demanded by private capital would be best provided by the private sector itself.

His fourth and fifth points relate to the internal operation and philosophy of public utilities. In order to compete in the market-place the nationalized industries are going to have to undertake a radical cultural change, and that without this British industry will not be able to regain its dominance of world markets. Sixth, Solomon sees privatization as the tool to be used to achieve the above.

The government has introduced two significant pieces of telecommunications legislation in the last ten years. First, liberalization in 1981 opened up the telecommunications network to competition. It removed BT's monopoly on subscribers' terminal equipment, allowed subscribers to sell spare capacity on their leased lines and licensed Mercury communications to operate an alternative private network.

Second, through the Telecommunications Act, 1984, BT was turned into a private limited company. It was released from the constraints of the public-sector borrowing requirement (PSBR), and BT management started the process of turning BT into a 'Top Telco' through diversification and operating in the international markets.

The government had to construct a regulatory framework so that the new BT did not either abuse its subscribers or crush its new competitor. The Office of Telecommunications (OFTEL) monitors performance to ensure that BT adheres to the conditions of its licence and only makes price increases in accordance with a statutory formula.

The telecommunications industry has been the site of a disproportional number of new technological developments. New technology has enabled the production of new services as well as overhauling the production process itself. Hi-tech services have been developed to meet the demands of the trans-national corporations to transmit digitized data, whilst sophisticated systems are to be introduced to unify the service offered by telephone operators. The new digitized System X exchanges and other developments have serious implications for trade unions both in terms of substantial changes in job design and content and staffing levels.

Two earlier papers contain a more detailed analysis of the interaction of government policy and new technological developments, 'Privatization and industrial relations' (Hallett 1987) and 'Privatization and the Re-Structuring of A Public Utility' (Hallett 1988 [the September 1988 conference paper] are available from the author.

Corporate strategy and structure

In response to the combined pressures of commercial demand, finite markets, technological change, and the twin government policies of liberalization and privatization, BT has completely overhauled its corporate structure. The company has been completely reorganized on a divisional task-oriented basis, and this process of change was well under way by the time that the 1981 Telecommunications Act received the royal assent. Batstone *et al.* noted the first steps of the reorganization when they carried out their research in 1979 (1984: 68). They describe the way in which the management of the national telephone company responded to a finite and reducing domestic market by seeking to move into the more commercial markets of information technology and data transmission.

In 1980 a new chairman, Sir George Jefferson, who came from British Aerospace Dynamics where he had undertaken a major rationalization and prepared the way for privatization (CIS 1982: 3), recruited senior management and board members from the private sector in order to further the principles that had been laid down in a new-style business plan that had first been published in 1979; this was the first step in changing the ethos of the industry, directing it away from the principles of public service and towards the more competitive commercial markets.

The strategy employed by the board had three major elements. First, there was a commitment to develop BT's sales, marketing approach, and facilities in order to be able to penetrate the new information-technology markets. Second, capital investment was to be targeted towards that part of the industry designed to provide high-profit and innovative services for business users and thus directly linking capital investment to areas of high-profit generation. The third commitment was to reducing costs by 25 per cent in three years (CIS 1982: 4), and since labour costs account for two-thirds of these, this represented a determination to reduce the size of the workforce. The new breed of managers recognized that commercialization and competition bring with them higher levels of financial risk and that these must be quantified wherever possible (Batstone *et al.* 1984: 67). Financial appraisal systems were developed so that costs could be allocated to each and every service and area of operation independently.

Construction of a new corporate structure has been a constant process of evolution, during which three main periods are identifiable. An initial divisional structure was in place before liberalization in 1981. A second structure operated over the following two years up to privatization in 1984. Since then there have been further significant adjustments of corporate organization culminating with the present configuration that is a far cry from that of the national telephone company of the 1960s and 1970s.

The major elements of the shape of organization during each of these three periods demonstrate this process of change and draw a picture of the complicated interrelation of the product and service divisions and

117

geographical organizations. These structures determine the intricate and sometimes confusing set of interwoven command structures.

The divisional structure

British Telecom is a huge industry and its remodelling has been a process of incremental change determined by corporate policy implemented over a number of years. The underlying principle, as identified by Batstone *et al.* (1984) was to develop a task orientation that maximized the opportunities to exploit and, in some cases, like Cellnet radio telephones, create new markets. The divisional structure, which was largely in place by liberalization in 1981 (described in figure 7.2), grew on a piecemeal basis, producing a set of four divisions with specific tasks.

Figure 7.2 BT Divisional Structure I

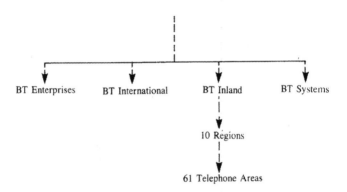

This is an essentially straightforward organization with BT Enterprises (BTE), formed in 1981 in preparation for the marketing of the services, systems, and equipment, opened up to competition in the 1981 Telecommunications act. In less than a year the new division had recruited 950 sales and marketing staff. BT International (BTI) was responsible for all overseas services and, according to Counter Information Services (CIS), accounted for half of BT's profits in the year ending on 31 March 1982 (1982: 6), although it employed less than 6 per cent of the total BT staff. BT Inland was by far the largest of the four, employing 85 per cent of the total workforce and being responsible for the whole of the domestic telephone network. It was charged with the task of implementing the huge capital investment programme to digitalize the network. BT Systems (BTS) was largely the research and development arm of the company with over half of its complement of 4,000 staff being employed at

118

the Martlesham research centre where significant developments like optic-fibre cables and the digital System X exchange equipment had been pioneered.

Detailed information of the management structure and the responsibilities of these early divisions was not available; in particular, it is not known whether any industrial relations functions had been specifically decentralized at this time. The CIS document speculates that the purpose of the process was to push responsibility for the generation of profit as far down the managerial line as possible (1982: 4). In the case of BTI and BTE this responsibility landed on the desk of the divisional general manager as these two divisions were declared 'profit centres', or distinct units that had to generate profits in their own right.

The situation in BT Inland was much more complicated where responsibility for profit was pushed down to a much lower level. The division was split up into ten telephone regions and sixty-one telephone areas. Each of the areas was designated a 'profit centre'. This arrangement created anomalies between areas like those covering Westminster or the City of London where huge profits were made, and areas with a predominance of domestic and small business subscribers where profits were much harder to generate. In the latter cases it was more difficult for area managers to invest in upgrading and developing the network and hence the service to domestic subscribers. Since area managers had increased autonomy over costs and their allocation, it is reasonable to assume that they had more scope to determine the nature and scope of industrial relations.

The internal organization of telephone areas had not yet followed the move towards 'task orientation'; figure 7.3 shows how they were still organized around engineering functions. In this structure the workforce was organized on a job or skill basis, installation engineers being responsible for installing the complete range of equipment to the complete range of subscribers, internal workers working only in telephone exchanges, and those on external duties being responsible for the physical network of telephone cables. Workers did move from one area of work to another as they progressed through the company career structure, but there was no practice of moving people between functions on a day-to-day basis; internal workers would never be asked, or expected, to work on external duties and vice versa.

The concept of the 'profit centre' relies upon the ability of accounting structures and marketing forecasts to allocate costs and speculate on profits from each part of the service and operation. In order to achieve these new evaluation and accounting facilities, there was a dramatic rise in the employment of accountants in all areas of the company (CIS, 1982: 4), at national, divisional, regional, and area levels. The manager of each profit centre needed to be able to see at a glance whether the

Figure 7.3 BT Inland area structure

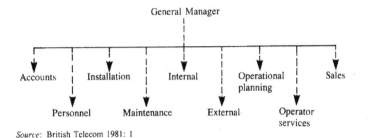

Source: British Telecom 1981: 1

profit target had been reached and identify where any problems might lie. This information was required by BT headquarters which was building up the ability to monitor performance centrally.

In a sense, it could be argued that, this form of decentralization actually provided the tools for increased centralized managerial and financial controls.

There were a number of teething problems with this new structure. In particular, the new marketing division, BTE, seen by the chairman as the strong arm of the new competitive BT, did not live up to his initial hopes. BTE very quickly ran into competitive tension with the Inland Division. A small national and divisional staff was employed early in 1981, with a further 850 sales staff being employed at area level within the Inland Division. Once area general managers discovered the advantage of having their own sales facilities, they were reluctant to hand the sales staff over to BTE.

Preparing for privatization

In order to present a coherent structure to potential shareholders, and to respond to the challenge of competition from Mercury Communications Ltd for trunk traffic, the divisional structure of the company had been refined by 1983. The major change from the previous arrangement was the splitting of the Inland Division into two, one having responsibility for the local telephone networks, Local Communications Services, and the other having control of the trunk network, called National Networks.

Figure 7.4 represents Local Communications Services and National Networks as two distinct divisions, just as they are in the Kleinwort Benson Ltd publication. This does not tie in with some later BT internal publications that describe these as separate parts under the umbrella of

Figure 7.4 BT Divisional Structure II

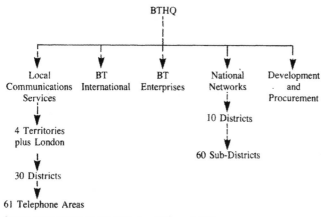

Source: Kleinwort Benson Ltd 1983: 7, and Haywood 1987

Inland Communications. Since these two units of the company have very different sub-structures, as well as their own managing directors and administrations, they are clearly independent organizations.

By the time this structure was in place, divisional, territorial, district, and area heads now had a very clear responsibility for a wide range of industrial-relations issues. The set of agreements that had been negotiated nationally and contained in a set of documents called Technical Instructions were to be renegotiated at a local level. The key management grade for this process would be district general managers, reflecting an increase in divisional autonomy in the ways in which financial and service provision targets were met.

Local Communication Services was by far the largest of the divisions; it employed 200,000 of the total 1983 BT workforce of 251,647 (NCU 1986a: 1), it was responsible for the company's 6,000 telephone exchanges and managed more than 80 per cent of BT's fixed assets. It was undertaking a massive modernization programme designed to improve all aspects of the service, with more than £300 million being spent on new telephone exchanges in 1983 alone (Kleinwort Benson 1983: 8).

Figure 7.4 shows that Local Communications Services had started to develop its own internal structure. The reduction of 10 Regions to 5 Territories and the creation of the districts was a continuation of the policy of pushing managerial responsibility further down the hierarchy. It was during this time that the internal organization of the areas was remodelled in line with the task orientation of the corporate structure

121

as laid out in figure 7.5. The structure described there allows district managers to allocate both financial and human resources according to the type of service being produced and the consumer being served rather than the type of work being carried out by various groups of personnel. This point was clearly made by engineers giving evidence to the GLC's public enquiry into the effects of privatization. They pointed out that both installation and maintenance teams had been split into those servicing business subscribers and those who work only on domestic services. Even before privatization there was a tendency for resources to be concentrated on the business services (GLC 1984: 18).

This period of district reorganization is the clearest possible example of the reorientation of the company and clearly shows how the concentration on the 'task' is the method used to allocate costs. This is a view that was clearly expressed by management:

> So the key to the re-organization was to look at how each member of staff in an Area was doing his or her job from the customer viewpoint. The result brings together staff into different groups, each dealing with particular types of customer requirements and each group being able to see directly how its results are contributing to the Area's overall results.
>
> (British Telecom 1983: 3)

Figure 7.5 Local Communications Services – area organization

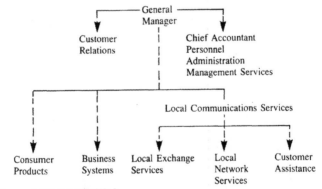

Source: British Telecom 1983: 2

The other significance of this development is that it laid the foundation for enabling local management to require workers to cross skill boundaries. By working in teams to provide service to particular classifications of customers in multi-disciplinary teams, it was only a matter of time before management would be asking external workers to undertake internal exchange work. The true impact of this built-in flexibility was not realized until 1987 when it became the source of the conflict that instigated the bitter strike by engineers.

Comparing the area structure of Inland Communications (figure 7.3) and Local Communications Services (figure 7.5) shows the fundamental changes that were beginning to take hold of the shape of the industry. Similar, although less comlex, arrangements were being developed in the other divisions, with BTE establishing Merlin (responsible for office telephone and office automation systems), Consumer Products (the new range of modern telephones), Information Systems (Yellow Pages and Prestel services), and Spectrum (electronic message and other modern services made possible by new systems). BTI had also reorganised into groups concentrating on particular services.

National Networks, on the other hand, also had a geographical structure, but this corresponded to the old regional structure for Inland Communications described in figure 7.2. Each of the districts, areas, and divisional groups was declared a profit centre 'not because the name of the game is simply profit but because we need to know how much we spend and how much we earn from providing each service and whether we are running it efficiently' (British Telecom 1983: 2).

All the changes in corporate structure, so far described, were in place and operating before BT was privatized. It is unclear whether they would have been implemented if privatization had not been in the wind, but the pressure from the government and its commitment to competition meant that the restructuring that took place during this period was quite independent of BT's being declared a private company. It was the 1981 Telecommunications Act and liberalization in particular that were the key factors in changing the ethos of the company and with it the nature of industrial relations.

Corporate structure and the international market

During the period leading up to privatization the process of divisionalization involved all parts of BT, creating many new forms of organization to meet the demands of an expanding market. Many of the new units that were created during this period were designed to market and provide a new range of services for business subscribers in this country. Indeed the Development and Procurement division was actually responsible for designing and developing many of these new systems. The market focus was essentially on the needs of subscribers in this country. Once privatized, however, BT moved its commercial activity into the international field. The telecommunications industry is fiercely competitive and has become one of the major arenas for the restructuring of international capital. Senior management within BT were, and indeed still are, eager to rise to this challenge and have coined the catch phrase that BT has to be turned into a 'Top Telco', this has been a theme used by BT's chief executive, now chairman, Iain Vallance in attempting to gain the commitment of BT staff to make the company the best in the world (British Telecom 1987f: 4).

The present corporate structure, described in figure 7.6, shows how the process of internationalization of the compnay is reflected in the new form of organization where three of the five operational divisions have an international focus. The Overseas Division, although the smallest with about 2,500 staff, is an important arm of the international BT. It provides consultancy, training, and advisory facilities to overseas telecommunications operators and has taken up the lead in the diversification of BT's activities (British Telecom 1987h: 14). The range of these activities is quite broad and includes the ownership of companies like International Air Radio that provides air traffic-control facilities and personnel at a number of major international airports around the world. The division also owns the Isle of Man telecommunications company as well as having controlling interests in the networks of other countries, but perhaps the most surprising undertakings are those that run the fire services at Manchester airport and the ownership of a hospital in Saudi Arabia. The secretary of the BTUC saw this set of developments as a significant statement of the intention of BT to become a major transnational corporation that is not wedded to any particular set of products or services, but is prepared to operate wherever it is financially advantageous.

The purchase of non-UK companies has been the hallmark of the early operations of the International Products Division (IPD) which was formed by the amalgamation of more than ten separate operations in July 1986. By 31 March 1987 the Division employed 8,300 people (British Telecom 1987h: 25) and was on target to make a contribution of half a billion pounds to BT revenue (British Telecom 1987b: 4), of which 60 per cent is generated from international markets. There are currently about a dozen IPD businesses producing the 160 products and systems marketed by the division (1987b: 4). Some of these businesses, like Fulcrum, a one-time BT-owned repair factory in Birmingham, and Consumer Electronics based on yet another old BT Factory in Cwmcarn, are now subsidiaries of the parent company, charged with the production of new products such as a video mapping system in Birmingham and a labelling system in South Wales. As wholly owned subsidiaries they are also obliged to generate profits independently of any other BT division or subsidiary.

Other IPD businesses, in particular MITEL producing PABXs and telephone exchange switches, are companies that have been acquired by BT since this was made possible after privatization. MITEL is based,

Figure 7.6 BT Corporate Structure – June 1987

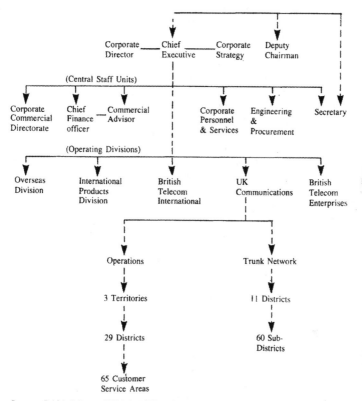

Sources: British Telecom 1987d: 1, 1987b: 14, and Haywood 1987: 8a

and has a factory, in Canada with other plants in South Wales and Florida and is active in the PABX markets in the United States, Germany, Italy, Scandinavia, and Australasia (1987b: 4). In its 1987 annual report to shareholders BT lists seventeen subsidiary and related companies, eleven of which it wholly owns, and has a controlling interest in a further four. Seven of these companies are telecommunications-equipment manufacturers, and four are cable-television services providers. Whilst most of the subsidiaries are based in the UK (eleven), three have their head offices in Canada and two in the United States (1987g: 46).

IPD also controls BT's military and defence activities through GAP (Government Advanced Products), designing and selling equipment for this specialized market. London is the major international switching centre for military telecommunications. Although this highly sensitive work is now controlled and run by a private company, the business is expanding and the contradictions of the arrangement are meant to be controlled by the requirements of the BT licence and monitored by OFTEL.

British Telecom International, employing 9,500 staff (British Telecom 1987h: 25), is essentially unchanged from the previous structures, being responsible for all international networks and having a three-part internal organization to undertake specific tasks. Despite its commitment to divisionalization, BT found it necessary to set up a unit to co-ordinate activities between BTI and the districts within UK Communications. BTI management has realized that there are substantial areas of overlap in operations and that these need to be co-ordinated in order to exploit marketing opportunities (British Telecom 1987e: 2). Whether this is the first step in recentralizing the organization is open to debate, but what this example does show is that, in this case at least, the divisional structure has created operational problems and internal competition. It is quite likely that the need for central co-ordination runs throughout the company. This was one of the vigorous points made by the BTUC, whose secretary felt that the divisional structure was not only making life more complicated for trade unions but was wasting other resources on a large scale through the duplication of activities.

The new division, UK Communications, which has been constructed by merging Local Network Services, National Network Services and Business Services, employs over 85 per cent (199,900 people) of the total BT workforce. In announcing the formation of the new division, its managing director stated that the express intention of the reorganisation was to ensure greater teamwork between all parts of the service offered to subscribers in this country (British Telecom 1987d: 3). Although there has been an adjustment of the local network structure, with the number of territories being reduced from five to three, the number of districts being whittled down to twenty-nine and an increase in areas to sixty-five, the major impact of the latest round of changes is at divisional headquarters. The task orientation of area activities has been maintained in a similar form to that (shown in figure 7.4) in the pre-privatization period. The co-ordination between districts and other operating units will be controlled from the centre of the division, a process that must to some extent challenge the autonomy of district general managers, the hallmark of the previous structure.

Figure 7.7 describes the new arrangements at UKC divisional headquarters and shows that there has been the construction of a complex set of command structures to provide central monitoring of district and area operations through an enlarged directorate.

When addressing the effects and implications of the new divisional

Figure 7.7 UK Communications – Divisional Management Structure

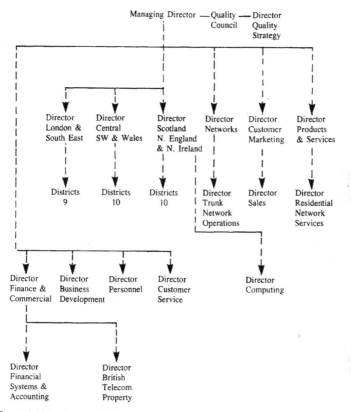

Source: British Telecom 1987d: 3.

structure, trade union representatives, and in particular the BTUC, pointed to the number and range of changes that had taken place in recent years as presenting very real problems for bargaining processes. Since personnel and industrial relations departments exist at all levels within the structure of the company, it is very often unclear what is the appropriate level for negotiation on a particular issue. There was a general view amongst national representatives that this was used as a device to frustrate union negotiators. At the local level, National Communications Union (NCU) branches found that the local line management said that they were not in a position to strike an agreement and that the issue had to be referred to the next rung up the managerial and corporate structure.

We are always told that we are looking at the wrong manager whenever we try to negotiate a solution to a particular manpower problem or even merely to ask for information. Never before has the 'three card trick' been played more frequently than in BT since reorganization, as District Managers supposedly freer than ever before in the age of devolution complain of now being more tightly restricted by budgets imposed from above on which they claim less influence. (NCU 1986b: 3)

There are a number of inconsistencies within the new structure, for example, figure 7.6 shows that two sections within UKC have different forms of geographical structure, that of UKC Operations with its territories, districts and areas described earlier, whilst, on the other hand the Trunk Network is organized on a completely different basis: in fact, it is almost identical to that which was in operation prior to the first phase of divisionalization. The eleven trunk districts correspond to the old regions, with the sub-districts taking the place of the old telephone areas. Little detailed information was available about the internal organization of the trunk network, but it does appear that it relies very heavily on the old structures. It is not at all clear why this distinction exists: there seems to be no good logical reason, other than a suggestion from the NCU research officer that the managerial structure was designed to mirror the physical structure of the trunk network. If this is the case, then the principle of task, and not function, orientation within BT does not appear to operate in this part of the company. This is the more surprising when one remembers that the trunk network and its services to private capital are the site of intense competition with Mercury Communications Ltd.

Total quality management

In a letter to the Chief Executive, for discussion at the September 1987 meeting of the General Purposes committee of the National BT Joint Consultative Committee, the National Secretary of the British Telecom Union Council (BTUC) asked for details of future staff requirements. He pointed to devolution of power and decision-making to the divisions as frustrating the unions' ability to draw an accurate picture of employment trends within the company. A constantly changing structure meant that there was now little or no co-ordination from BTHQ. The National Secretary also blamed the new process of 'Total quality management' as greatly increasing the uncertainty for BT workers and their organizations by fundamentally changing the ways in which management decisions are made. Figure 7.6 shows that UKC had employed a director of quality strategy and set up a quality council at the most senior divisional management level. A combination of the changes of structure and the methods of management was working to make the analysis of future developments within the company increasingly difficult.

Total quality management (TQM) is the system used by BT to maintain the quality of the service provided in relation to the available resources. It is a direct development from the concept of 'quality circles' and is designed to make sure that all managers' ideas for greater efficiency and tighter control on finances can be utilized. According to the document produced by the NCU research department (Downing 1987) TQM is being introduced to BT by the 'quality director' as a follow-up to various experiments with quality circles and participation programmes.

The principles of TQM to be employed by BT are laid down in a booklet by Dr Steve Smith entitled *Take Part in the Quality Revolution: A Management Guide* and quoted extensively in the Downing paper (1987: 11). In brief, the philosophy of TQM is to eradicate internal waste by making sure that all production processes are completely predictable, and that the elimination of errors and unnecessary activities through innovation will reduce labour, energy, and material costs, while maintaining or increasing the volume of output (1987: 12). The General Motors Saturn project is cited as the foremost example of TQM where the company stands to save nearly $5 billion a year through staff reductions, in a programme that has been developed jointly with the motor workers' union, the UAW. Hazel Downing draws the conclusion that, in this context, quality means the reduction of staff in all areas of BT.

In essence the process involves the setting up of a hierarchy of management working groups, workshops, and seminars, all designed to put the notion of quality management at the top of every managers' agenda. Quality councils, made up of senior managers, meet on a regular basis to review the progress of the various quality programmes, and quality co-ordinators are employed to advise line managers on what quality improvements they may make in their department. An initial step in establishing TQM is to hold intensive two-day-long 'Top Team' workshops to gain the commitment of senior management to the process before involving more junior levels. Total-quality seminars are three-day events involving managers from a range of functions and are held to introduce the techniques of TQM. Small teams of managers meet in improvement action teams to monitor and review quality improvements within single departments, whilst task forces are established to iron out any interdepartmental problems that may arise from quality management programmes, with the express intention of ensuring customer satisfaction. The bottom tier in the hierarchy is the quality circle itself, which is a voluntary meeting of peer groups to focus on quality problems in their own immediate area of work. They are specifically designed to encourage workers to apply their creativity to solving quality problems and then to implementing their suggestions. It is recognized that the circles will only work if the proposals they make are backed by efficient management systems, and machinery and systems that enable people to do a quality job (1987: 15).

Conclusion

The interaction of the interests of international capital and the present government has worked to restructure the national telephone company. The period has seen the company develop from an underfinanced public service to a major multi-national corporation. The realization by the Post Office and then BT management that there was only a finite market for domestic telephone services coincided with the growth of information technology as an instrument in the process of the international restructuring of capital, presenting the industry with the challenge of developing services to meet the growing demands of industry.

New technological systems have changed the nature of telecommunications work by reducing the levels of skills required and offering greater possibilities for the centralized control of employees. Workers are being required to perform a much wider range of duties than before, as the boundaries between types of work have become increasingly blurred. There are very real fears that there will be considerable redundancies in the near future. So far BT has managed to achieve staff reductions through early retirement and voluntary redundancy schemes, but according to management this will not last for much longer. A new digital exchange is being opened every day of the year and it is only a matter of time before BT will have to have a compulsory redundancy programme.

The process of reorganization has effectively split British Telecom into a range of smaller units, each of which is charged with the requirement to make a contribution to BT revenue and profits quite independently of the others. This was a principle laid down in the licence awarded to BT when it was privatized and was designed to undermine the principle of cross-subsidization upon which the service had been based over the previous fifty years. The new organization has not just sought to meet the requirements of this licence but has been aimed at applying modern managerial principles to this new company with the express intention of replacing the old service and engineering ethos and of making BT a major multi-national telecommunications company designed to exploit the new international markets for information technology.

In short the national telephone company has developed a new structure, has had its market opened up to competition, provides new services, has constructed a new internal culture, competes in the international market, has diversified its operations and fundamentally changed the relationship between management and unions. Privatization has played a part in these developments but is not totally responsible for all of them. It can be argued that in some ways liberalization has had a much more profound direct effect. Competition has forced the company to construct systems that can allocate costs more accurately, leading to the development of profit centres and divisionalization. Indeed both these processes were under way well before privatization. The net effect of this has been a shift away from the provision of domestic services to the concentration on services needed by industry. It was no longer possible for there to be cross-subsidization from the profitable parts of the operation to the maintenance of the public-service aspects.

The particular contribution made by the 1984 Act was to relieve BT of the restrictions of the PSBR, and for this reason it was a policy that received considerable support from senior BT management. The main function of selling shares in the company has been to seek public support for both the package of changes in this central industry and the ideology of the government's approach to restructuring the public sector.

I suggest that it was the opening up of the telecommunications network to competition and the removal of BTs' exclusive privelege that was the foundation stone that supported most of the government's expressed aims. Privatization can be seen as the keystone that was designed to hold the government's economic policy in place by use of a cash relationship to ensure public support and commitment for the policies. The government must have known that selling shares in the company would not directly affect company policy; since shareholding interests would be dominated by the huge institutions, it would be organizationally very difficult for millions of small shareholders to present a coherent single voice; and the government had effectively determined the main elements of BT policy through the clauses contained within the operating licence. The government has used privatization in an attempt to make the restructuring of this industry, and others, irreversible.

References

Batstone, E., Ferner, A., and Terry, M. (1984) *Consent and Efficiency: Labour Relations and Management Strategy in the State Enterprise*, Oxford: Blackwell.

British Telecom (1983) *Area Reorganization*, London: British Telecom.

British Telecom (1985) *British Telecom response to the NCU (Engineering Group) 32 hour claim*, London: British Telecom.

British Telecom (1986) *Report and Accounts*, London: British Telecom.

British Telecom (1987a) 'What the new deal involves', *British Telecom Today*, March 1987.

British Telecom (1987b) 'Wide horizons', *British Telecom Today*, March 1987.

British Telecom (1987c) 'Lessons of the dispute', *British Telecom Today*, April 1987.

British Telecom (1987d) 'Teamwork is the key to the future', *'British Telecom Today'*, May 1987.

British Telecom (1987e) 'BTI forges links with districts', *'British Telecom Today*, May 1987.

British Telecom (1987f) 'Need for a mastery of technology', *'British Telecom Today'*, July 1987.

British Telecom (1987g) '999', *British Telecom Today*, July 1987.

British Telecom (1987h) *Report and Accounts*, London: British Telecom.

BTUC (1983a) *The Great American Disaster*, London: British Telecom Union Council.

BTUC (1983b) *The American Experience*, London: British Telecom Union Council.

BTUC (1983c) *Licence To Neglect*, London: British Telecom Union Council.

BTUC (1984a) 'Who will benefit', evidence to the GLC Public Enquiry into the effects of the privatization of British Telecom.

BTUC (1984b) *British Telecom – How Selling It Off Will Harm Britain*, London: British Telecom Union Council.

BTUC (1987) *A Fault On The Line*, London: British Telecom Union Council.

CIS (1982) *Private Line – The Future of British Telecom*, London: Counter Information Services.

Communications Campaign (1985a) *In The Know*, London: Communications Campaign.

Communications Campaign, (1985b) *Inside the Black Box*, London: Communications Campaign.

Coventry Workshop (1979) *Job Loss in Telecom*, Coventry: Coventry Workshop.

Coventry Workshop (1982) *Joint Trade Union Project On The Impact Of New Technology On Trade Union Organization*, London: Coventry Workshop.

Curwen, P. (1986) *Public Enterprise*, Brighton: Wheatsheaf.

Downing, H. (1987) 'Total Quality Management', internal National Communications Union Research Department document (unpublished).

GLC (1984) *The Future of Telecommunications in London*, London: Economic Policy Group, Greater London Council.

GLC (1985) 'Ten key issues for the future of telecommunications and the future of London, a discussion document, London: Greater London Council.

Hallett, R. (1987) 'Privatization and industrial relations: the re-structuring of British Telecom, unpublished dissertation, Warwick University.

Haywood, P. (1987) 'Trying to put a great past behind us', to be published in *Trade Unions and Britain's Industrial Future*.

Kleinwort Benson (1983) *British Telecom: The Power Behind The Button*, London: Kleinwort Benson Ltd.

Murphy, B. (1983) *The World Wired Up: Unscrambling the New*

Communications Puzzle, London: Comedia.

NCU (1985) *The Back To Front Office*, London: National Communications Union.

NCU (1986a) *BT Privatization: Staff Numbers*, London: National Communications Union.

NCU (1986b) 'Manpower survey', *Letter To Branches 1203*, May 1986.

NCU (1987a) *'BT Privatization – Effects On Staff*, London: National Communications Union.

NCU (1987b) *Main Annual Conference 1987*, London: National Communications Union.

OECD (1983) *Telecommunications – Pressures and Polices for Change*, Paris: Organization for Economic Co-operation and Development.

OFTEL (1986) *Review Of British Telecom's Tariff Changes*, London: Office of Telecommunications.

POEU (1981) *The American Telecommunications System*, London: Post Office Engineering Union.

POEU (1984) *Making The Future Work: The Broad Strategy*, London: Post Office Engineering Union.

Shaiken, H., Herzenberg, S., and Kahn, S. (1986) 'The work process under more flexible production', *Industrial Relations* 25, 2, spring 1986.

Society of Telecom Executives (1987) *The Review*, London: Society of Telecom Executives.

Solomon, J.H. (1986) 'Telecommunications evolution in the UK', *Telecommunications Policy*, September.

Chapter eight

Private power and public relations: the effects of privatization upon industrial relations in British Coal

Jonathan Winterton

Introduction

Privatization has been a key element in Conservative economic strategy to promote efficient allocation of resources, reduce public-sector borrowing, and remove state interference in industry. Privatization of the energy industries has been a priority because of their size and their strategic role in the economy. The government argues that privatization will create competition and that the resultant lower energy costs will benefit industry, while a guaranteed market is attractive to potential investors. At the same time, energy-sector workers are among the most organized and include the symbolic vanguard of the labour movement, the NUM. Oil and gas have already been taken out of public ownership, the privatization of electricity generation is under way, and the government has formally announced its intention to sell off British Coal (the corporate name adopted as a symbol of the new commercial orientation of the enterprise and a break with the traditions of the National Coal Board (NCB)). The order of privatization appears to have been influenced by the industries' profitability, technological infrastructure, and strength of trade-union organization. Coal mining was less ready than the other industries for privatization on each count, but the privatization of electricity generation will hasten the changes that are a prerequisite for removing coal from the public sector. Paradoxically, those changes were initiated to secure the long-term viability of coal mining but have now become subsumed under measures designed to improve short-term profitability.

The first oil shock of October 1973 reversed coal's decline, enhanced the miners' bargaining power, and reinforced the resurgence of militancy that had begun with the 1969 strike over surface workers' hours (Winterton 1981). The 1974 miners' strike and the re-evaluation of coal in the energy economy resulted in a tripartite agreement outlined in *Plan for Coal* to increase coal capacity through investment in new mines and new technology (Burns *et al.* 1983). Trans-national corporations also exploited new coal reserves in Australia, Colombia, and South Africa in anticipation of increased coal demand (Wright and Rutledge 1985). Actual coal demand proved much lower because of economic recession, reduced energy intensity, and conservation measures, and by 1981 world coal capacity was substantially in excess of requirements. In Britain this prompted a coal crisis of acute surplus capacity (Winterton 1985b) which necessitated an acceleration of the restructuring programme already under way (Burns *et al.* 1985). The 1984–5 strike arose out of these profound changes, although the dispute focused more narrowly upon the resultant pit closures rather than their origin (Winterton 1985a).

British Coal (BC) has a virtual monopoly of indigenous coal production but this market power is outweighed by the monopsonistic advantage of the Central Electricity Generating Board (CEGB), which has pursued a policy of fuel supply diversification. Both oil and nuclear power are part of CEGB diversification strategy, but power-station infrastructure changes slowly as the lead time from planning to operation is about ten years and a station may remain in service for fifty years. In place of changes in the fuel mix, the key element of CEGB diversification strategy since 1979 has been the use of imported and opencast coal to provide multiple sourcing and to drive down the price of indigenous deep-mined coal. The allocation of profits between public-sector enterprises is arbitrary but the electricity-supply industry has been treated as though it is already part of the private sector, with its profits maintained at the expense of the coal industry. The mechanism through which CEGB monopsony has operated is in a series of Joint Understandings between the CEGB and the NCB whereby future prices and orders are agreed for tranches of coal. Five such contracts were made between 1979 and 1986, each successive one entailing an increased proportion of the total to be bought at the price available on the international market irrespective of the costs of production (Gladstone and Dewhirst 1988). In the 1980s the spot price of coal has generally been well below the contracted price. The new coal reserves opened up by transnational corporations after the 1973 oil crisis created a surplus when demand was lower than anticipated due to the recession. These modern opencast operations with favourable geological conditions and exploited labour have considerable cost advantages over European deep-mined coal and, in an effort to recoup massive infrastructural investment, the transnationals have maintained production and dumped coal on the international market.

The privatization of electricity supply guarantees that the pressures on BC from internationally traded coal will intensify. Privatizing electricity will remove the remaining constraints on the CEGB and South of Scotland Electricity Board (SSEB) to purchase the bulk of their coal from BC. Advocates of coal privatization have argued that the industry should first be liberalized through relaxing constraints on coal imports and opencast production (Turner 1984; Robinson and Marshall 1985). Electricity privatization will effectively liberalize the coal industry. Once exposed to international competition, BC will be forced to implement international production standards. The second stage of coal privatization could entail measures to expand private mining operations, to encourage more extensive use of subcontracted labour by BC, and to provide miners with an opportunity to run collieries earmarked for closure as co-operatives (Robinson and Sykes 1987). Before it is possible to privatize BC, either as a complete enterprise, by area, or, as is most likely, by the sale of individual production units, management need to establish patterns of industrial relations and working practices commensurate with private-sector coal mining. This paper analyses the managerial offensive which has been apparent since the defeat of the 1984–5 strike and assesses its effect upon pit-level industrial relations in Yorkshire.

Privatizing coal

The coal industry has long been on the Conservatives' privatization agenda, although their priority was to denationalize more lucrative enterprises and those in which labour was less well organized. In December 1983, when Financial Secretary to the Treasury, John Moore announced in the Party pamphlet *Why Privatise?* (Moore 1983) the government's intention of looking at 'further ways of increasing competition and introducing privatization into the energy sector'. The National Union of Mineworkers (NUM) (1983) had already noted in its *Campaign for Coal*:

> disturbing talk of the peripheral coal fields being allowed to go to the wall with private capital invited for stakes in the lucrative central coal field. It is not at all inconceivable that Selby, paid for and developed at tremendous cost to the taxpayer, could be sold off at a knock-down price to private buyers.

During the early part of the 1984 strike the government was careful not to reawaken fears of a return to private ownership, although Norman Tebbit commented in April 1984 that there would have been no strike if the coal industry had been denationalized. Within a month, a Cabinet sub-committee agreed that the NCB should be allowed to seek private capital to develop a new generation of highly profitable pits, with companies like Taylor Woodrow investing in coal for use in privatized power stations.

A *Times* editorial noted that before coal could be privatized:

> the political power of Mr Arthur Scargill and the National Union of Mineworkers should be broken. It is unlikely that private investment

could be attracted if Mr Scargill was able to stop the current programme of pit closures. If he won that battle he could prevent privatization. (*The Times*, 5 May 1984)

In September 1984 the Adam Smith Institute recommended that the NCB should cease to be the licensing authority for independent opencast operators and independent deep mines, arguing that both of these should be allowed to expand (Adam Smith Institute 1984). The report also recommended that the NCB should be divided into at least twelve independent units which would become autonomous corporations. The Monopolies and Mergers Commission (1983) had similarly recommended that NCB areas should 'be operated, as far as possible, as separate business units'. Ian MacGregor declared his intention to decentralize the NCB, believing that the ability 'to tap private capital' was an indication that 'the industry has a future', and claiming that it would be 'wonderful' to sell 'uneconomic' pits to miners.

With the miners' defeat in the 1984–5 strike, the chorus of support for coal denationalization became more vocal. As the strikers returned, *The Times* (5 March 1985) proclaimed 'the year-long dispute has reinforced the lesson of history that a state monopoly is a wholly unsuitable structure for the British coal industry' and suggested how opencast operations and the more profitable areas could soon be privatized. Peter Rost, MP (1985) claimed that 'nationalization had proved itself a disastrous failure', and that the need for privatization had 'been privately acknowledged throughout the NCB and in the Government'. Robinson and Marshall (1985) stressed the importance of decentralization 'to build on Mr Scargill's work in weakening the monolithic power of a politicized NUM, which remains the major concern for potential private investors'. They argued the case for liberalizing the coal industry by privatizing small, competitive units rather than selling off the NCB as an enterprise. Restrictions on imports, opencast and licensed mines could immediately be lifted since these were more profitable and would promote deep-mine efficiency if allowed to compete. As a first step towards privatizing deep-mined coal production they recommended joint ventures involving private capital in the development of super-pits and looked forward to the sale of packages of pits and power stations.

To extract the maximum profit under private ownership, high-cost collieries must be shed: as the *Financial Times* (17 September 1984) noted, 'many parts of the coal industry are profitable . . . even though the NCB with its trail of high-cost pits is running at a loss'. The need to be free from maintaining costly capacity explains why the Conservatives are reducing the size of the coal industry. The Energy Committee Report on the Coal Industry in February 1987 recommended that 'for the immediate future British Coal should remain in the public sector' but argued that further productivity improvements were the best defence against international competition (Energy Committee 1987). Five months later a Centre for Policy Studies pamphlet argued that another 75,000 jobs would need to be shed to make BC internationally competitive and called for its privatization in 1988 together with the CEGB on an area-by-area basis (Robinson and Sykes 1987). The government confirmed its 1987 election manifesto commitment to privatize electricity in February 1988. In October 1988, Energy Secretary Cecil Parkinson made his 'historic pledge' to the Tory Party Conference: if elected again the government will be ready for the 'ultimate privatization': the sale of the mining industry. Privatizing the electricity industry will effectively remove any protection of BC from international competition; Gladstone and Dewhirst (1988) estimate that 51,500 jobs will be lost by 1992 as a result. As the pressures on BC are intensified, so will the offensive which management has already begun in order to reduce labour costs and increase productivity.

A management offensive

When the 1973 oil crisis returned the miners' bargaining power, a hidden agenda of objectives was drawn up within the NCB and pursued in implementing the 'Plan for Coal'. During the 1973 overtime ban, former East Midlands Division Chairman Wilfred Miron had outlined, in a confidential report to NCB Chairman Sir Derek Ezra, strategies to reduce the influence of the NUM membership and to increase management control (Winterton 1987a). The Miron Report predicted that the left would gain control of the NUM Executive and recommended the introduction of area incentive schemes to fragment bargaining and restore the influence of moderate area leaders. To increase management control over the labour process, Miron argued for the development of automated systems which would introduce 'skilled engineers or supervisory staff' in place of NUM members. Miron recommended the establishment of a 'high powered confidential Working Group at Headquarters' to oversee the strategy; shortly afterwards the Central Planning Unit was created to co-ordinate investment projects. A high priority was given to the systems-engineering programme out of which MINOS (Mine Operating System) was developed (Burns *et al.* 1982).

The objectives outlined by Miron remained covert and were not widely publicized even among senior NCB managers since the whole approach was at variance with the corporate industrial-relations philosophy of pluralism laced with benevolent paternalism. The conjuncture of several factors ensured that the Miron objectives would become more prominent in the 1980s. Economic conditions caused coal demand to fall and reduced the miners' strategic importance. The implementation of new technology added to over-capacity and provided the means to alter the balance of power in management's favour. Finally, the political context altered with the election of Conservative governments committed to reducing the public-sector and trade-union influence. These developments led to the appointment of Ian MacGregor as NCB Chairman in September 1983 and confirmed that a major confrontation was both inevitable and imminent (Winterton 1985c; Feickert 1987).

The intention to privatize the coal industry dictated the need for a management offensive to weaken the terms and conditions established by almost forty years of public ownership. Well before the strike, the new-style NCB industrial relations was evident in management provocation during the overtime ban and MacGregor's 'off your butts' productivity drive. The pit conciliation machinery was rigidly enforced by managers refusing to negotiate until men were working normally and the Union was back in procedure. However, it was during the strike, and partly through the opportunities afforded by the strike, that the major changes were instituted. The back-to-work campaign was particularly significant, suggesting that the objective was not only to break the strike, but also the Union (Winterton and Winterton 1989). Geoffrey Kirk, Public Relations Director, and Ned Smith, Industrial Relations Director, strongly objected both to the back-to-work campaign and the involvement of union-busting consultants. MacGregor also used Area Directors Ken Moses and Albert Wheeler to undermine the Union. Both Kirk and Smith questioned MacGregor's policies and the conflict of ideologies ultimately led each to take early retirement. To bring the commercial perspectives of the private sector to the NCB, MacGregor replaced Board members committed to the British coal industry with part-timers representative of international capital (Wilsher *et al.* 1985: 181–2). When Bob Haslam replaced MacGregor as Chairman in September 1986, the management style became more conciliatory but BC objectives were unaffected.

The outcome of the 1984–5 strike demonstrated how the balance of power between the forces of production had altered since 1974. The miners' defeat facilitated the pursuit of managerial objectives which may be traced to the Miron Report but which take on a new significance with the prospect of denationalization. In October 1985 the NCB released details of stringent cost objectives in the 'New Strategy for Coal', which was prepared by Moses without trade-union involvement. The Moses Strategy defined a cost ceiling of £1.50/gigajoule (GJ), on average equivalent to £38/tonne depending upon the calorific value of the coal being produced.

In November 1986 a plan formulated by Wheeler, the former Scottish Area director who took responsibility for the key Nottinghamshire Area, was endorsed by Haslam as BC strategy for the future. The Wheeler

Plan outlined a number of means to attain the £1.50/GJ target which amounted to lengthening the working day, intensifying supervision and reducing safety standards, an approach reminiscent of the coal owners' strategy after the 1926 lockout. The Miron Report had recommended the reintroduction of the 1965 Bevercotes Agreement relating to remotely-operated longwall faces, which allowed seven-day working under continental shift patterns. Under the Wheeler Plan the aim is to increase working time by producing coal six days per week with miners working four continental shifts of up to nine hours per day underground and shafts winding at full capacity for 23 hours per day.

The problem of decreasing returns is endemic to coal mining, and a major cause is the reduction of productive time as coal workings become more remote from the shaft. In the Durham coastal pits travel time has such an effect that BC calculates the optimum shift length (to allow continuous production) to be in excess of 9 hours. Four 9-hour shifts would increase machine available time by 30 per cent. For some time BC has considered asking the government to amend the Coal Mines Regulation Act, 1908 (as amended by the Coal Mines Act, 1932), which limits the underground shift length to 7.5 hours plus one winding time. The Durham Area resisted pressure from BC to allow longer shift times, having recognized that union acceptance of a shift length of 8 hours in that Area would have been used by BC to advocate removing statutory limitations on the length of the working day for all miners. If BC were able to introduce optimum shift lengths, NUM researchers estimated 50,000 miners' and deputies' jobs would be lost nationally, 4,000 of them in South Wales.

The reduction of statutory limitations on hours of work underground would undoubtedly have an adverse effect upon miners' health; evidence on health and safety was used to support the 1908 Act. Other aspects of the Wheeler Plan are also likely to worsen conditions, as new working practices are being introduced from America, including the use of diesel-powered free-steered vehicles and roof bolts in place of conventional supports. There are plans to reduce the number of deputies and officials, partly owing to automation, and to alter their function from safety to supervision. In order to introduce these changes in working practices BC has been pressing the Health and Safety Executive (HSE) to relax statutory standards. Under the Health and Safety at Work, etc., Act 1974, the HSE have drafted general regulations to replace the detailed provisions of the Mines and Quarries Act, 1954. The 1974 Act was enabling legislation designed to promote the more effective application of existing provisions and to replace these progressively with detailed regulations which would 'maintain or improve the standards'. The NUM and the National Association of Colliery Overmen, Deputies and Shotfirers (NACODS) argued that the new general regulations constitute a dilution of standards and in 1986 withdrew from consultative discussions in protest:

The changes to existing regulations do not just flow from the Health and Safety at Work Act, but are inspired by the NCB's new strategy for production. It is clear from Wheeler's proposals that the Board see existing Regulations as a constraint on the technological revolution. It is not merely a question of replacing out-of-date statutes. From the Board's viewpoint it is as much a question of establishing highly flexible working practices, *in all parts of a mine*. (NUM 1986)

Having failed to alter working hours in Durham, in February 1987 BC made the development of a £900m. super-pit at Margam conditional upon union acceptance of six-day working, in breach of the national Five Day Week Agreement. National union opposition was stifled and, after a four-hour meeting on 7 March 1987, two years after the strike ended, South Wales delegates agreed to discuss the concept of six-day working. Area President Des Dutfield claimed the decision was taken because of the responsibility to school leavers and the unemployed in South Wales, while Arthur Scargill accused the Area of violating NUM rules.

In June 1987 BC made a formal Strategy Presentation to the trade unions. The medium of the presentation was as significant as its message since the management team used transparencies and an overhead projector in the style of an American 'teach-in'. The presenters reviewed 'progress' made in the two years since the strike: a reduction of 35 per cent in the number of collieries, 37 per cent in manpower, and 24 per cent in overheads. While the proportion of heavy-duty faces had increased from 16 to 39 per cent, productivity had increased by 73 per cent. The overall objectives for the future were shown to include attaining financial break-even in the year ended March 1989, generating surplus, and earning a sufficient return on capital by concentrating on low-cost production. Minimum UK coal consumption was projected at 105 megatonnes (Mt) by 1995–2000 and management argued that BC's share would depend upon competitiveness with imports. Provided the unions cooperated with the new strategy, management claimed that an output of 90 Mt deep-mined, and 15 Mt opencast could be sustained.

The presentation outlined the logic of cost-parameter rules, and established three current cost parameters:

1 closure of collieries not producing below £1.65/GJ
2 incremental output to cost no more than £1/GJ
3 major project expansion only at collieries operating below £1.50/GJ

Management stressed the need to improve asset utilization using the examples of a hotel and a passenger aeroplane. The key to improved asset utilization was shown to be *flexibility*, which would entail:

1 more shifts per face
2 more days worked per colliery
3 increased machine running time
4 reduced travelling time

For an existing mine with capital costs of £5m. per year and an output of 2 kt per day, the cost per tonne was shown to vary from £10.73 with 233 days' operation over the year to £8.06 with 310 days' operation. For a new mine with capital costs of £15m. per year and an output of 1 kt per shift, the cost per tonne was shown to vary from £30 with 10 machine shifts per week to £15 with 20 machine shifts per week. The examples illustrated two variations on the BC theme of increased working time: six-day working (310 days per annum) and seven-day production (20 machine shifts per week). The point was therefore made that collieries under threat of closure might be saved by agreement to six-day working and that capital investment would only be forthcoming if agreement was secured on seven-day coaling.

Flexible working inevitably dominated the 1987 NUM Conference, and a few days earlier BC reiterated that Margam would not produce coal until six-day working was agreed. The NEC split 10–10 on the issue which was therefore debated by Conference delegates without an NEC recommendation. South Wales Area delegates supported flexible working, while opposition was led by delegates from Durham and the Midlands. After extensive debate, delegates rejected flexibility, including six-day working, by more than 2–1, and agreed to hold an individual membership ballot with a recommendation to support the conference resolution. No such membership ballot was organized and flexibility was overshadowed by ballots on a new BC disciplinary code and the presidential election following Scargill's resignation at the November 1987 Executive meeting. At the November meeting the South Wales Area NUM representatives agreed to abide by union policy but proposed to hold discussions with BC to establish what their proposals were for flexible working at Margam; this was supported by 13 out of 22 on the NUM Executive Committee.

Relations at colliery level

The emergence of the Union of Democratic Mineworkers (UDM) emphasized the weakness of the NUM following the 1984–5 strike. BC used the UDM as a lever on the NUM in establishing industry-wide rates of pay and attempting to introduce flexible working. The UDM breakaway institutionalized a division which had always existed but had become more significant since bargaining was fragmented by the 1977 agreement on area incentives. BC sought to exploit this division further and to establish managerial prerogative in its new conciliation and consultation machinery (Taylor, 1988). In the Yorkshire coalfield, where less than 10 per cent of the workforce had abandoned the 1984–5 strike and there was no support for the UDM, the management offensive nevertheless has had a profound effect upon pit-level industrial relations. The pursuit of the new strategy was underpinned by a variety of tactics aimed at restricting the influence of the NUM.

In the immediate aftermath of the strike management was concerned to prevent the harassment of strike breakers, while the union sought the reinstatement of sacked activists. In an effort to rehabilitate the strike breakers some pit managers negotiated over sacked miners. At Savile, for example, men were reinstated in return for union agreement to accept scabs from Fryston and Wheldale. Management similarly used sacked miners as a lever to gain union agreement over introducing contractors, by accepting the sacked men as part of the contractor's workforce. At the end of January 1986 there were still 143 men sacked in Yorkshire, and by August 1986 the national total of sacked miners had only fallen to 500. MacGregor's replacement by Haslam did not radically affect the pattern of labour relations, although Haslam promised to review 400 cases of sacked miners. Two years after the strike ended, 135 were re-employed (though not reinstated in their former jobs) nationally, but there were still 134 sacked miners in Yorkshire and little prospect of their being re-engaged. Activists were naturally a target for management reprisals. Six months after the strike Rossington colliery came out for two weeks over management's refusal to uphold the Doncaster Deployment Agreement relating to manning levels and the allocation of work by rota; management would not give face work to 'activists of a disruptive nature'. At Barnsley Main management tactics similarly provoked a stoppage in the first year after the strike, when in contravention of custom and practice the undermanager attempted to remove unilaterally a team who had taken a hard line against scabs. Despite the local strike being solid, it was settled by the parties' agreement that the decision on which team to remove should alternately fall to management and the branch.

The balance of power between management and union, however, hinged upon control over the majority of miners who were neither victimized activists nor intimidated strikebreakers. Even before the strike had ended many pit managers made unilateral changes to working arrangements. At Gascoigne Wood, miners who had gone back to work rejoined the strike when management introduced continental shifts. Although only 7 per cent had gone back before the end in Doncaster, Area Director Albert Tuke showed most enthusiasm for initiating the post-strike regime. Several concessions were withdrawn throughout the Doncaster Area, including the practice of paying craftsmen one half-hour's overtime for completing reports required under safety legislation.

Craftsmen's report money was unaffected in Barnsley, where 12 per cent had gone back to work. After several months the union negotiated back a portion of report money in Doncaster. At Woolley, where 30 per cent gave up the strike, management stopped all concessions, including water money. Six months after the strike ended Houghton Main miners walked out over management's refusal to implement the Yorkshire water agreement. At Frickley, where only 1 per cent had broken the strike, management altered shift times unilaterally and dropped rates for outbye workers to 50-per-cent bonus from the 65 per cent formerly agreed locally; shift times were restored within six months but it took over a year for the branch to get outbye workers back on 65-per-cent bonus. At Wheldale, where about 7 per cent had gone back to work, colliery management gradually eroded demarcation, using workers' increased flexibility to reduce manpower. The need to earn bonus money to clear strike debts removed any possibility of concerted restriction of output, but there were still disputes over productivity as management attempted to increase the rate of production.

Although the *extent* of the crack-down depended upon local management attitudes and the strategic importance of the operating unit, rather than upon the incidence of strike-breaking, it was nevertheless the breaking of the strike and the damage inflicted upon union organization which made it possible. The first four months after the strike were regarded by many branch officials as a 'punishment period'. Management put branch officials back on three shifts and allowed only one official to remain on the surface, thereby reducing the union's effectiveness and exposing union officials to complaints about the deterioration of working conditions. Branch officials fulfilled the role of personnel officers smoothing out local difficulties and acting as a brake on the militants. Management were so successful in reducing time off for union business that the NUM head office circulated details of trade-union rights to local officials, and Roy Mason raised the matter in the Commons. Later, managers offered to 'make life easier' for branch officials in return for their co-operation in relaxing restrictions on overtime working.

As well as restricting union officials and discriminating against activists, BC management continued the union-busting tactics begun during the strike using the law and appealing directly to the men without involving the union. These tactics were particularly evident in the Selby complex. In January 1986 miners at Stillingfleet walked out because management stopped pay after men arrived one minute late due to adverse weather. The manager wrote to the branch secretary, Ted Scott, claiming he had 'deliberately caused men to take strike action' and warning that any future action would be regarded as 'a serious breach of the existing machinery'. The branch instituted an overtime ban to pressurize management into repaying the men and agreed to organize a strike ballot if union officials were disciplined for carrying out trade-union duties, but Area officials prevented the ballot as BC was seeking a court injunction. Miners were encouraged to take their problems to management without involving the union and chargehands' meetings were held every month as part of a 'quality circle' approach. Management regularly used the incentive scheme to enforce discipline in the Selby complex. In February 1987 management stopped a week's bonus pay for 'restricting output' after workers had walked out over visits from local Conservative MP Spencer Batiste and Bob Siddall, who had reputedly told miners to 'eat grass' during the 1984–5 strike. In response all 3,000 Selby miners staged a week-long protest strike which was unanimously supported, even by those who had given up the strike before Christmas.

A further challenge to union organization came with management's unilateral introduction of a new disciplinary code in 1987. The new code sanctioned summary dismissal for 'gross industrial misconduct', including acts committed away from the workplace, thereby ignoring the criticisms of hard-line management made by the House of Commons Employment Committee (Employment Committee 1985). The code also gave management control over the representation of offenders; pit managers could refuse to allow union representatives to attend members' disciplinary interviews on the vague grounds that they were 'not acceptable'. Shortly after the 1987 NUM Conference, the use of the new code provoked a stoppage at Frickley colliery, deflecting attention from the flexible-working issue. The stoppage began after five Frickley miners, who had allegedly left work early on the eve of their holiday, refused to attend a disciplinary interview with the colliery manager and were suspended. The colliery's 900 miners walked out and the next day picketed out six other Doncaster pits. A day later pickets spread the strike to the remainder of South Yorkshire, so 16 pits and 14,000 miners were involved. The colliery manager wrote to all Frickley strikers warning that they would be sacked unless they returned to work; copies of the letter were sent to other strikers in South Yorkshire. The NEC agreed to hold a national ballot on the disciplinary code, and the Yorkshire Area Executive instructed the strikers to return to work pending the outcome of the ballot. The Frickley branch secretary was dismayed by the decision; 'for the first time since the strike there is resistance to the management's dictatorship and the Executive are telling fifteen thousand miners to go back to work'. Although other collieries agreed to abide by the executive's instruction, Frickley pickets again stopped nine South Yorkshire pits and two Barnsley pits in the neighbouring village of South Kirkby before voting to return to work. The Frickley dispute presented the union with a classic dilemma; they chose the legitimacy and unity of an official dispute in preference to the gathering momentum of a spontaneous strike movement.

While the Frickley dispute brought the entire South Yorkshire coalfield to a standstill, a simultaneous disciplinary case brought the threat of a strike throughout North Yorkshire. Stillingfleet's branch secretary, Ted Scott, was dismissed for instructing miners not to shear at the weekend. This was potentially a far more dangerous situation for BC than the Frickley dispute, for three reasons. First, the dispute linked the issues of the new disciplinary code with flexible working. Second, the manager was disciplining a branch official for attempting to uphold a national agreement which, for all the rhetoric of Area leaders, was being steadily undermined at a number of Yorkshire collieries. Third, management clearly wished to avoid a stoppage at Selby. The Frickley dispute pre-empted action over Scott's case and fragmented the Yorkshire collieries because in North Yorkshire this was 'bull week' when miners worked exceptionally hard to increase their holiday pay; South Yorkshire collieries had already taken their annual holidays so were more willing to take action. Its timing suggested that the Frickley dispute was deliberately provoked by management to divide North and South Yorkshire. At the height of the Frickley dispute, Area Director Tuke wrote to all North Yorkshire miners warning that, if they struck over Scott's dismissal, their involvement in the action would be recorded in their personal files. A later letter informed miners that Scott had been offered re-employment at Wheldale (which was expected to close within six months) and that any industrial action would guarantee the closure of seven named collieries.

The North Yorkshire Panel discussed the possibility of a 'rolling strike', involving groups of collieries taking action alternately, but activists expected Scott's case to become subordinate to any national programme of action against the code. The ballot on the new code was organized during August and sought authority for the NEC to call 'various forms of industrial action' if BC failed to withdraw the code. Following a three-hour meeting with the NUM and the involvement of the Advisory, Conciliation and Arbitration Service (ACAS), BC agreed to re-examine the code, but not to withdraw it. The membership ballot authorized industrial action by a majority of 77.5 per cent nationally, 80 per cent in Yorkshire, in response to which BC made the minor concessions of agreeing not to veto union representation and to accept the decisions of industrial tribunals. Viewing these concessions as inadequate, the NUM instituted an overtime ban, prompting Haslam to write to all miners warning that the Five Day Week agreement would be suspended to lay off men in the event of a backlog of maintenance work. Yorkshire Area Council postponed its proposed ballot and at the November NEC meeting there was considerable confusion on the issue. Following a national membership ballot in March 1988, the ban was called off.

In January 1988 another strike spread through the Yorkshire coalfield when three development workers were redeployed by the manager at Bentley colliery for allegedly making insufficient progress. Management had suspended the colliery conciliation machinery since the 1984–5 strike and disputes were no longer referred to a pit Umpire. In anticipation of an assertion of managerial prerogative, reinforced by the new disciplinary code, Bentley miners struck and picketed out other Doncaster pits. The colliery manager wrote to all strikers warning that the dispute could only be resolved once the pit was working normally, but the South Yorkshire Panel voted to continue the action involving 12 pits and 10,000 miners. A day later, with 19 Yorkshire pits at a standstill, the South Yorkshire BC Area Industrial Relations Officer sent a copy of the Bentley letter to every miner's home. The spontaneous action and management's immediate direct appeal to the workforce surprised Area NUM officials, who feared BC would seek an injunction to stop secondary picketing. Bentley miners were persuaded to call off the action but struck again a week later when ten miners were threatened with dismissal after management had identified them from video tapes as flying pickets.

Conclusions

Most of the significant developments in British Coal since the miners' strike can be viewed both as consequences of the planned privatization of electricity generation and as prerequisites for privatizing coal. These developments stem from management strategies and tactics adopted in pursuit of substantive and procedural corporate objectives.

The overriding substantive objective has been to achieve profitability and international competitiveness by introducing private-sector mining standards. The cost parameters were outlined in the Moses Strategy in October 1985, since when more high-cost collieries unable to operate below £1.65/GJ have been closed. The Wheeler Plan in November 1986 revealed that the major mechanisms for reducing production costs to £1.50/GJ were flexible working, new technology, and a relaxation of safety standards. The Strategy Presentation to the unions in June 1987 confirmed that the Moses cost parameters derived from the price of imported coal and elaborated upon the Wheeler Plan as a means of attaining these financial targets. Since the 1984–5 strike there has been a substantial increase in productivity and some reduction in production costs; the continued application of new technologies is expected to lead to further improvements over the next five years (Winterton 1988c). One consequence of the increase in productivity will be further job losses through the 1990s (Winterton 1988b).

These substantive objectives are a direct result of energy privatization which, in the case of coal mining at least, is contrary to the public interest. Britain's energy self-sufficiency is being damaged by British

Coal's investment strategy of restructuring coal production to meet short-term financial objectives with little regard for the conservation of indigenous reserves (Winterton 1988a). As peripheral reserves are sterilized and central reserves worked more intensively, Britain's coal could be exhausted in 50 years rather than the potential 300 years (Winterton and Winterton 1986). Sterilization also represents a strong case for protecting indigenous deep-mined capacity from import competition to insure against the cartelization of the international coal market by transnationals (Winterton 1987b).

The procedural corporate objectives may be viewed as supplementary in that they relate to the means adopted to neutralize worker resistance to the substantive issues. After the defeat of the 1984–5 strike, management attempted to restrict local union officials and victimize activists, introduced a new disciplinary procedure, and made unilateral changes to the conciliation machinery. Public-relations consultants have been used to undermine or circumvent the union with quality circles or team briefings, and by making direct appeals to the membership. Moreover, increasing numbers of private contractors are being employed, particularly in sensitive operations, effecting a further reduction in NUM membership, co-operation with flexible working and back-door privatization. Nevertheless, the offensive on union organization has been only a partial success in Yorkshire for three reasons. First, the centrally directed hard-line management introduced in conjunction with a process of decentralization created a paradox: pit managers continued to enjoy the autonomy to decide whether to adopt the new approach. Second, sufficient cohesiveness remained in the core of the coalfield to resist the most flagrant attempts at asserting managerial prerogative. Third, even where the strike had been broken, the strategic importance of key locations still demanded the co-operation of the workforce to achieve development rates and productivity targets.

Organized labour represents the major barrier to the attainment of corporate objectives which have been identified as prerequisites for the privatization of coal mining. Management control over the labour process has steadily increased, but several major stoppages have been provoked by management's contravening local agreements and making unilateral changes in working arrangements. However, the miners' power at the point of production has proved largely irrelevant in opposing pit closures and job losses. It is questionable how long corporate objectives relating to flexibility can be resisted at pit level, given the external pressure of privatized electricity generation. It is, perhaps, significant that the unions' campaign against electricity privatization includes the coal and rail unions but excludes the power workers in the Electrical, Electronic, Telecommunications and Plumbing Union (EETPU), the Engineers and Managers' Association (EMA), and Amalgamated Union of Engineering Workers

(AUEW). During January 1989 market researchers employed by BC were visiting miners' homes in Yorkshire asking their views on the privatization of electricity and coal, whether they would take shares in BC if offered them, and crucially, whether they would take industrial action to oppose the privatization of BC.

References

Adam Smith Institute (1984) *Energy Policy*, London: Adam Smith Institute.
British Coal Corporation (1987) 'Strategy presentation to trades unions', June [mimeo].
Burns, A., Feickert, D., Newby, M., and Winterton, J. (1982) *An Interim Assessment of MINOS*, Report No. 4, Bradford: Working Environment Research Group, University of Bradford.
Burns, A., Feickert, D., Newby, M., and Winterton, J. (1983) 'The miners and new technology', *Industrial Relations Journal*, 14, 4, 7–20.
Burns, A., Newby, M. and Winterton, J. (1984) *Second Report on MINOS*, Report No. 6, Bradford: Working Environment Research Group, University of Bradford.
Burns, A., Newby, M., and Winterton, J. (1985) 'The restructuring of the British coal industry', *Cambridge Journal of Economics*, 9, 1, 93–110.
Employment Committee (1985) Sixth report, session 1984–5 *The Dismissal of National Coal Board Employees*, HC 416, 19 June, London: HMSO.
Energy Committee (1987) First Report, session 1986–7, *The Coal Industry*, HC 165, 24 February, London: HMSO.
Feickert, D. (1987) 'The midwife of mining', *Capital and Class*, 31, 7–15.
Gladstone, B. and Dewhirst, D. (1988) *Electricity, Linked Industries and Privatisation*. Coalfield Communities Campaign Special Report No. 4, Barnsley: Coalfield Communities Campaign.
Monopolies and Mergers Commission (1983) *National Coal Board: A Report on the Efficiency and Costs in the Development, Production and Supply of Coal by the NCB*, Cmnd. 8920, London: HMSO.
Moore, J. (1983) *Why Privatise?*, London: Conservative Political Centre.
National Coal Board (1985) 'New strategy for coal', Joint Policy Advisory Committee, Memorandum, 15 October, London: National Coal Board.
National Coal Board (1987) *Code of Conduct*, London: National Coal Board.
NUM (1983) *Campaign for Coal*, Sheffield: National Union of Mineworkers.
NUM (1986) 'Hours of Work: 1908 Coal Mines Regulation Act', National Union of Mineworkers Research Department, December [mimeo].
Robinson, C. and Marshall, E. (1985) *Can Coal be Saved?*, Hobart Paper 105, London: Institute of Economic Affairs.
Robinson, C. and Sykes, A. (1987) *Privatise Coal*, Policy Study No. 85, London: Centre for Policy Studies.
Rost, P. and Pargeter, M. (1985) 'Pits, privatisation and politics', *Economic Affairs*, 15, 4, July–September.

Taylor, A.J. (1988) 'Consultation, conciliation and politics in the British coal industry', *Industrial Relations Journal*, 19, 3, 222–33.

Turner, L. (1984) *Coal's Contribution to UK Self-Sufficiency*, London: Heinemann.

Wilsher, P., MacIntyre, D., and Jones, M. (1985) *Strike: Thatcher, Scargill and the Miners*, London: Coronet.

Winterton, J. (1981) 'The trend of strikes in British coal mining, 1949–1979', *Industrial Relations Journal*, 12, 6, 10–19.

Winterton, J. (1985a) 'Computerized coal: new technology in the mines', in H. Beynon (ed.) *Digging Deeper: Issues in the Miners' Strike*, London: Verso.

Winterton, J. (1985b) 'The source of the crisis', Coalfield Communities Campaign Working Paper No. 1, Barnsley: Coalfield Communities Campaign.

Winterton, J. (1985c) 'The crisis in British coal mining', *Insurgent Sociologist*, 13, 1–2, 53–62.

Winterton, J. (1987a) 'The politics of new technology in British coal mining', Conference of Socialist Economists, Sheffield, 10–12 July.

Winterton, J. (1987b) 'The role of new technologies in coal policy', European Parliament Committee on Energy, Research and Technology, Public Hearing on European Coal Policy, Brussels, 1–2 December.

Winterton, J. (1988a). 'The investment strategy of British Coal: a question of public interest', Memorandum of evidence to Monopolies and Mergers Commission Inquiry into the efficiency and costs of the capital investment activities of the British Coal Corporation, April.

Winterton, J. (1988b). 'The size and structure of the British coal industry in the 1990s: a projection', International Symposium on Modern Mining Technology, Tai-an People's Republic of China, 11–15 October.

Winterton, J. (1988c) *The Effect of New Technologies on the Productivity and Production Costs of the British Coal Mining Industry*, Report No. 12, Bradford: Working Environment Research Group, University of Bradford.

Winterton, J., and Winterton, R. (1986) 'The coal industry', Memorandum No. 60, House of Commons Select Committee on Energy, *The Coal Industry*, HC 165-I, HMSO, 314–20.

Winterton, J., and Winterton, R. (1989) *Coal, Crisis and Conflict: The 1984–85 Miners' Strike in Yorkshire*, Manchester: Manchester University Press.

Wright, P., and Rutledge, I. (1985) 'Coal worldwide: the international context of the British miners' strike', *Cambridge Journal of Economics* 9, 4, 303–26.

Chapter nine

A testing road for Chinese industry: the Enterprise Responsibility System (ERS)

Li Hong

This paper examines a new practice of Chinese industrial reform – the Enterprise Responsibility System (ERS). As an experiment to invigorate publicly owned enterprises in China, the system appeared only a few years ago. Now it is growing more and more popular and has become, more or less, a dominant approach to Chinese industrial reform. By the end of 1987 the ERS was practised in 82 per cent of the large and medium-sized industrial enterprises owned by the public. Under the circumstances, questions related to the system might be raised, such as 'How did the ERS come into being?', 'What is it about?', and 'What impacts would it have on Chinese industrial reform?' This paper is going to answer these questions respectively.

The paper is organized as follows: part 1 looks at the background of Chinese industrial reform. Part 2 throws light on the nature of the ERS, within which three aspects of the ERS are discussed. After that the effects of the ERS, in part 3, are viewed from different angles. Then part 4 discusses some problems in connection with improving the system. Finally the author comes to conclusion in part 5.

1 Background

As far as the economic system is concerned, China used to have a highly centralized planning economy which came originally from the Soviet Union. The implementation of such a system in China was due to historical reasons. At that time, centralized planning was even believed to be a distinguishing feature and a major advantage of the socialist system. Objectively, the system of mandatory planning once played a positive role but, with economic development and rapid advance of science and technology, its defects became more and more obvious.

Under the centralized planning economy, decision-making is basically concentrated in the central planning authority. The authority is responsible for making the national plan which is supposed to cover production, allocation of resources, and exchange of products. Based on it, subplans for industries and enterprises could be made. As far as China's experience is concerned, to do such a work is very time- and resource-consuming. Nevertheless, the ties between enterprises and markets are arbitrarily cut off, replaced by the mandatory plans from superior administrative bodies. In this situation, enterprises have no access to direct feedback from consumers. All they need to do is just complete the production plan. However, they share no responsibility for marketing the products they have produced. Moreover, because of commonly accepted ideas of egalitarianism, enterprises could lose their motivation to improve performance, becoming reluctant and passive. In other words they look more like annexes of government departments than economic agents.

Therefore, a long-standing problem for Chinese enterprises is what they call lack of incentives. In other words, the problem involves the relationship between the state and enterprises. In fact, during the course of Chinese industrial development, some measures had been taken to tackle the problem, such as decentralizing administrative powers to local governments or ministries, and enterprises paying taxes to the state instead of directly delivering profits, but they seemed either irrelevant or ineffective. Under the circumstances, the ERS seems to be a better option.

Historically China's economic reform started in 1979, and initial reform happened in rural areas. In order to overcome inefficiencies of Chinese agriculture under the commune system, a sort of 'responsibility system' was put into practice in some areas, then officially adopted, since the rapid increases in agricultural output and farmers' income in the following years had supported the system. Later focus of the reform was shifted into urban areas.

In 1980 some limited industrial reforms were adopted. Four years after that, however, only little progress in industrial efficiency had been achieved. Observing the limited changes in the urban industrial sector and stimulated by further success in agriculture, the Twelfth Central Committee of the Chinese Communist Party (CCP) at its Third Plenary Session on 20 October 1984 made a substantial decision to carry out overall economic reform. This decision laid a foundation for the Chinese economic reform later on.

Six key elements of the decision on 20 October 1984 concerning industrial reform include:

1 Giving state enterprises autonomy in decisions regarding production, supply, marketing, pricing, investment, and personnel as independent profit-seeking economic units.
2 Reducing the scope of central planning, except for certain important products, and shifting from mandatory planning to indicative planning.
3 Allowing prices of more products to be determined by supply and

demand in the market rather than by central control.

4 Introducing macroeconomic control mechanisms, mainly through fiscal and monetary policies directed at improving goods and money markets.

5 Establishing various forms of economic responsibility system within enterprises, and encouraging differential wage rates to compensate for different kinds of work and levels of productivity.

6 Fostering the development of private and collective enterprises.

All these reform measures or loosening of policies left room for new ideas and consequently created a favourable environment for reformed system. As a result, various forms of reform measure have been put into practice, and the Enterprise Responsibility System is one of them. Dealing with the relationship between the state and enterprises, the ERS has attracted considerable attention since it emerged. One of the pioneers to try the new system is the Capital Iron and Steel Company, a large complex, occupying a significant position in the production of iron and steel in China. Up to now, the implementation of the ERS in the company has resulted in a ten-year increase of profit at a rate of 20 per cent. Therefore, compared with other systems, the ERS seems to be a feasible way of injecting new vigour into Chinese industrial enterprises, especially large and medium-sized ones owned by the public. Based on such an understanding, more and more enterprises have adopted the ERS in line with their own situations.

Now the ERS has been officially recognized. On 27 February 1988, the State Council issued the Provisional Regulation on Responsibility System for Industrial Enterprises Owned by the Public. The regulation, with 45 articles in seven chapters, formally identifies principles, content, and forms of the ERS. Thus the practice of the ERS in China has reached a new stage of development.[1]

In reviewing the development of the ERS, there are two points worth mentioning: the first is that the system has absorbed some successful experience from the rural reform. The other is that practice comes before theory in the evolution of the ERS.

2 The nature of the ERS

In essence, the ERS refers to a managerial system at enterprise level. Under the system an administrative body would specify tasks or responsibilities for subordinate enterprises through contracts, whilst granting them certain managerial powers. The objective of the ERS is to revitalize enterprises, next, to promote efficiency, and finally to transform enterprises into independent commodity producers. As a managerial system, the ERS consists of a few major points:

New forms of ownership

Taking public ownership for granted

Guaranteed by its dominant public ownership of the means of production, China is a socialist country. This fundamental principle is defined by China's Constitution. The current Chinese industrial reform is going to overcome the drawbacks of the traditional planned economy, rather than to change its social and economic nature substantially. So it does not involve any change in the public ownership in China. The ERS, like other industrial reform measures, is only concerned with the methods of economic operation and management. As far as my understanding is concerned, the patterns or methods of economic operation and management under different economic systems could be applied to each other. This application has no real influence over its social and economic nature. For instance, capitalist countries, especially advanced ones, now lay much stress on government macroeconomic control as well as on regulation and planning, while socialist countries introduce market mechanisms. For Chinese industrial reform, the public ownership is a premise, so the ERS has to take this establishment for granted.

Separating ownership from management

The ERS is based on the principle of separating ownership from management, because under this system, enterprises are given the rights to possess, use, and transfer property owned by the public. By making effective use of the property granted by the state, enterprises are expected to fulfil the financial quotas and property increase as laid down by the state. In this way, the public ownership of the property will be realized. In addition, while ensuring that their property belongs to the state, enterprises could adopt various forms of managerial system, through either contract or leasing methods, in accordance with the regulations of relevant administrative departments. Thus the enterprises could be less dependent on the state and run their own business risks. Now enterprises have got more decision-making, they could establish effective managerial organizations within them, and conduct their own production and marketing. Anyway enterprises have got more chance for self-development.

Separation of ownership from management is a breakthrough in socialist economic theory. Although the practice could be dated back to last century when share ownership emerged in some capitalist countries, it is entirely a new idea in the field of public ownership. The bold practice of the ERS in China, to some extent, means that there is a possibility for separating ownership from management in the situation of the public ownership as well. The practice has enriched socialist economic theory, and its influence will be far beyond China's industry itself.

Recognizing the economic interests of enterprises

Obviously economic interest is a prerequisite condition of motivation in a commodity economy for both enterprise and individuals. The ERS admits that differences will exist between enterprises in terms of economic interests, and this factor will be fully considered when drawing up the contract requirements. First, all enterprises are allowed to select or create a form of contract suited to their own conditions, so that the economic interests and responsibilities of both the state and the enterprises could be clearly specified to the satisfaction of all parties. Second, the ERS stipulates that there should be a correlation between remuneration and an enterprise's efficiency. The linkage is expected to embody the principle of better payment for harder work. Furthermore, enterprises could adopt their own forms of distribution in order to connect payment with performance, in other words, wage increases for employees will be closely linked to growth in the enterprise's profits. Finally, the ERS ensures benefits for enterprises and safeguards them against social reactions of political risks that price and tax reforms may cause. This also implies that all potential benefits to enterprises lie in their economic success.

Strengthening the rights and responsibilities of the enterprise's director

Once the director or manager is decided by bidding of contracts or the other ways, he or she is going to be a legal representative of the enterprise, based on the requirements of the ERS. This represents an important change from the former enterprise leadership system in China. Under the ERS, directors or managers have powers to make decisions concerning production, management, and personnel. This implies that the party organizations in enterprises will no longer exercise 'monist' leadership; on the other hand, the directors are going to shoulder the responsibilities for production and development of socialist ideology. The responsibilities will be reflected in their own incomes. Normally a director's income may vary from one to three times the average income of employees in the enterprise, provided he can make profits from production and fulfil other tasks specified in the contract; otherwise he may lose part of his wage as a penalty if he fails to complete the contract.

Usually an enterprise, represented by its director or manager, signs a contract with the superior administrative authority under the ERS. The contract usually includes:

1 agreed form of the ERS.
2 valid terms.
3 target figures for profits to be delivered or deficits to be made good.
4 mandatory plans of supply and production.
5 product quality and other economic and technological requirements.

6 requirements for upgrading, maintenance, and increment of fixed assets.
7 use of retained profits; repayment of loans and methods for settling outstanding credits and debts.
8 rights and obligations of both parties.
9 responsibilities for disobeying the contract.
10 directors' rewards and penalties.
11 other items.

As far as the period of validity is concerned, there are sometimes different ideas due to different expectations. In order to avoid shortsighted behaviour on the part of enterprises, the terms of a contract usually extend over three to five years, giving both sides enough time to meet their promises.

Another crucial item in the contract is to determine the amount of profits to be delivered. By setting it both parties will compromise on economic interests. For the state, the profit may be seen as a compensation for granting rights to use a certain amount of property. For the enterprises, on the other hand, the profit may be taken as a base above which part of the profits could be retained by them. Generally both parties determine the base collectively, through taking full consideration of all affecting issues. In practice this base mainly depends on three factors: (1) maximum capacity of production; (2) the enterprise's actual level of production in the past years; (3) possible changes in markets for the coming years. Nevertheless, different weights will be put on these factors under various circumstances.

Once the base of profits to be delivered is set up, the enterprise is expected to achieve, or even surpass it. by scientific management, increased production, or decreased cost, and technological innovation. As a result of that the enterprise will be able to retain some profits, while it is making a contribution to the state.

3 The effects of the ERS

The impacts of the ERS are multifold. First of all, the ERS puts more pressure on enterprises. Under this system, the enterprises have to take greater risks in exchange for greater decision-making powers, greater chance of self-development, and greater economic benefits. More or less the ERS has created an environment of equal competition, and it enables the enterprises to be more active than before. In fact, most enterprises are changing their passive and reluctant pattern of behaviour. Now they are more concerned about any market changes. Anyhow, the changes in enterprise behaviour could certainly be reflected in their performance. In 1987, 72 cities in China were chosen by the state to try out comprehensive reform. In these cities a majority of the large public-owned enterprises have implemented various forms of the responsibility system, and about half the small enterprises were contracted or leased to collectives or individuals. As a result of that total industrial-output value in these cities increased by 17.2 per cent. The figure is 14.3 per cent when village-run industries are excluded. Both the figures are higher than the national average. As expected, by stimulating enterprises, the ERS has promoted production and improved efficiency as well.

The second point in the effects of the ERS is that it could reshape enterprises. By implementing the ERS the enterprises would not only improve their performance, but also change gradually their internal organization. Along with strengthened responsibilities of the director, the enterprises could necessarily establish more effective and flexible production, marketing, and personnel systems in order to respond promptly to market changes. In doing so the former production-orientated enterprises are likely to turn into market-orientated ones, and their mechanisms would be extended greatly. In addition, the ERS would help to create entrepreneurs, because competent managers could be selected on the basis of bidding for contract targets, and competitive markets would provide them with more room to show their skills.

Third, from the viewpoint of macroeconomic control, the ERS seems to have influence on the co-ordination of economic development. In the past decades Chinese industry has been maintaining a rather high rate of growth. However, most increases in output were based on the increase of inputs. In other words, although the economy has expanded, ratio of output over input was still low and production was relatively inefficient. Moreover, growth and efficiency could seldom co-exist in the development of China's industry. Whenever pursuing growth, we had to sacrifice efficiency, or vice versa. This dilemma was due to the irrational structure of industries and the internal organization of enterprises under the former system. Fortunately the practice of implementing ERS in recent years has sent out some signals to help sort out the problem, getting the growth and efficiency consistent with each other. According to published statistics of the Chinese economy during 1982-7, calculated on comparative prices, the industrial-output value of 1987 totalled 1,378 billion yuan, more than double the 1982 figure and representing an annual increase of 15.3 per cent.[2] At the same time, the gross national product (GNP) increased from 503.8 billion yuan in 1982 to 1,092 billion yuan in 1987, a 68.9 per cent increase. More importantly, the national income rose from 426.1 billion to 915.3 billion yuan, a 66.2 per cent increase. The figures show that Chinese industry is getting rid of the problem. In short, all these results are good for reforms to other aspects of economic structure and to establishing a socialist market system.

Now let us take the railways in China as an example to see the comprehensive effects of the ERS. Although the ERS has been widely practised in large public-owned enterprises, the railways are pioneering a very large-scale implementation of the system. There are 52,611 km of railways in China, including 11,186 km of double-tracked lines, carrying 71 per cent of China's freight and 56 per cent of its passengers. The Chinese railways, which employ 3.2 million people and have fixed assets worth 100 billion yuan, used to be a state monopoly with centralized management and revenues. In March 1986 it adopted the ERS in the following way: the Ministry of Railways makes a contract with the State Council; the targets set then become the goals of the 12 railway bureaux and 56 sub-bureaux, the railway sections, stations, and workers. Rewards and penalties are built in. The contract covers carriage, locomotive building, extra capacity, capital construction and upgrading, distribution of profits, and safety.[3] In relation to distribution of profits, formerly 85 per cent of profits were handed over to the state and in return all construction funds were allocated by the state. Since the introduction of the ERS, a proportional tax has been levied, and all extra profits retained and used for production, collective welfare projects, wage increases, and bonuses. In 1985, before the implementation of the system, railway departments earned 21.4 billion yuan, of which 8.12 billion yuan were turned over to the state as tax, and the state, in turn, allocated 8.04 billion yuan to the railway departments for railway construction. But in 1986 and 1987, the railway departments earned 50.05 billion yuan, and the state netted 3.1 billion yuan in tax. Eventually both the state and the enterprises benefit from the ERS. This fact is also supported by further study of the Guangzhou Railway Bureau which was the first to implement the system. In 1987 the Guangzhou Railway Bureau, staffed by 150,000 people, had a total income of 1.98 billion yuan; this was 14 per cent more than 1986 and is in excess of its target. The bureau paid tax to the state, accumulated funds for the Ministry of Railways totalling 336 million yuan, and retained 557 million yuan for its own construction projects. The average income of its employees was 8.3 per cent more than the year before, too.

After several years' experiment, people are realizing step by step that the ERS might be one of the most practical choices for Chinese industrial reorganization. Under the circumstances, it is necessary to have specific legislation to support the ERS. On 13 April 1988, the First Session of the Seventh National People's Congress (NPC) passed the Public Owned Industrial Enterprise Law of China.[4] This is a milestone for Chinese industrial reform. Before being issued, the law had been on the drawing board for over nine years. The draft was discussed and revised several times by the NPC Standing Committee. In addition, on 11 January 1988, the draft law was published in the press to solicit other opinions. It was the experience of reforms in practice, including the ERS, that made a contribution towards the enactment of the law. Anyway, the law applies directly to the more than 90,000 state industrial enterprises now operating in China, and accounting for more than 70 per cent of the nation's total industrial-output value. Its implementation will therefore make a massive impact on the development of China's national economy as a whole.

The Public Owned Industrial Enterprise Law of China has 69 articles, set out in eight chapters. Most of its provisions are closely related to the practice of the ERS. The law, in no uncertain terms, confirms the legal status of enterprises, and it clearly restates some important principles embodied in the ERS, such as separating enterprise ownership from management power, combining the rights and duties of the enterprise, and implementing the director responsibility system, etc. As a matter of fact, the law provides safeguards for the implementation of the ERS. Under this law, relations between enterprises and the state are different from former ones. Now enterprises are acting as entities. In line with the principle of 'the state regulating markets and the markets guiding enterprises', the government should serve enterprises and exercise control and supervision over them in accordance with their responsibilities and relevant legal stipulations. So it could be said that the law heralds the freedom of the enterprises from the trammels of direct government control. This law came into effect on 1 August 1988, and similarly other relevant statutes will come into being soon.

4 Relevant issues

As a newborn thing, the ERS needs to be developed and improved. In fact, some practices of the ERS are open to debate. Although a majority of the people argue for the ERS, some still hold opposing views:

a With the distorted system of pricing and taxation current in China, because enterprises now have greater decision-making powers, making bigger profits does not necessarily mean an improvement in economic performance. Nevertheless, within the distorted system of pricing, the misallocation of resources and production would be likely to result in an automatic readjustment of production according to changes of prices. Consequently this would lead to an imbalance between aggregate supply and demand, and make indirect macroeconomic control more difficult. Besides, the ERS could allow some inefficient enterprises to continue to operate at a low standard, thus obstructing the rationalization of the enterprise's structure.

b The contracts between administrative bodies and enterprises could not keep up with the constant change of supply and demand in markets, so it will lead to endless amendments to the contract requirements, over which both parties will haggle. In this sense the elimination of intervention by administrative bodies is impossible; sometimes the intervention may become even more closely linked to the enterprise's operation and, more or less, lead to bureaucracy and corruption. On the other hand, attempts to reduce future uncertainty through the convenience of contracts may tend to make both parties accept old methods of mandatory planning, fixed prices, and fixed interest rates, something that is in contradiction to further development of market mechanisms and indirect regulation by the government.

c Enterprises will still display shortsightedness when their contracts approach expiry. Extending the terms of the contract does not provide a solution to the problem, but simply delays the outcome. Many contracts that had been signed are due to expire in 1990, and there exists considerable pressure to extend the contracts. The implication is that some more substantial reform measures are needed.

d Competent managers are not easily selected through the bidding of the contract targets, since target bidding relies on an uncertain estimate for domestic and world market in the future; it is a problem of expectation, rather than ability. Assessment of a manager can be made only on the basis of his or her performance in competition.

Existence of different views on the efficacy of the ERS does reveal some imperfection of the system or, in other words, some inconsistency in the outer environment. In fact, most of the problems derive from the old economic system. It is a foolish idea to give up the ERS completely at the moment, so what Chinese industrial reform should do is to improve the system, or carry on some supplementary reforms so that the ERS could play a full role. With the present situation in China, three aspects of inconsistency with the ERS should be pointed out, they are:

1 Current pricing system

Two points about the pricing system in China could be made in relation to the ERS. One is that unreasonable prices still exist. The prices of agriculture and associated products, mineral products, fuel and other raw materials remain relatively low. Raising prices of these products and narrowing the differences between them and processed goods are very urgent. Otherwise the situation in these 'bottle-neck' sectors could not be changed. And as mentioned before, the distorted prices would likely misdirect production and allocation of resources, resulting in an imbalance between aggregate demand and supply. These tensions between various elements of the economic system are not good for implementing the ERS. Moreover, the temporary 'double-track system' adopted for goods in short supply, that is, the coexistence of state-set prices and market prices, has opened some loopholes with some negative results. In this sense, pricing reform is inevitable. However, China's recent experience of partial price readjustment has shown that the pricing reform is a complicated project, and it must be carried on cautiously, because at the moment Chinese pricing reform is facing two difficulties: the overheated state of the economy and the tendency for various sectors to vie against each other to raise prices. Second, enterprises play only a limited role in the matter of pricing. Generally speaking, the enterprises should seek inputs of production and set prices for their own products. The freedom to do so is very important to the decision-making rights of enterprises. Anyway, if political considerations require delays or postponements to pricing reform, industrial policies should use taxation to adjust distorted prices.

2 Imperfect money market

Since it started economic reform, China has developed a more market-orientated economy. Currently markets for agriculture and sideline products and consumer goods have basically taken shape, and the market for the means of production is developing, but markets for money, technology, labour, and real estate are just emerging; they are lagging behind the pace of the ERS. Under the circumstances of commodity economy, an enterprise needs not only decision-making rights, but also a favourable environment, which includes a well-developed money market. At present following works should be done in the field:

a strengthening the function of the central bank.
b establishing different kinds of specialized bank and financial institution.
c connecting banks and enterprises more closely.

With a perfected money market, enterprises could possibly expand their scope of business activities in terms of adjusting production and development. On the other hand, the government could influence, guide, and monitor the activities of enterprises through business in the market, such as preferential policy and change of interest rates. Thus the indirect macroeconomic control could be implemented effectively.

3 Lack of competition policy

Introducing market forces into the economy is the intention of Chinese economic reform. However, a competitive market could not be formed automatically. In other words, the government could play a positive role in terms of promoting competition. Now the ERS and the law of enterprise have put enterprises into a world of competition, therefore Chinese industry has got two reasons to call for a policy of competition. First, there are various forms of monopolies and artificial barriers in China which hamper competition among enterprises. Second, after implementing the ERS, problems like merger and bankruptcy will certainly arise with the current situation in China. Competition policy could help to regulate markets on the one hand, and remove blockades to competitions on the other hand. It is apparent that the ERS could not bring about expected results without competition policy.

Because of the limitation of this paper's length, other points about improving the ERS cannot be discussed here. All in all, it could be predicted that the contents of the ERS would be greatly enriched with the widening of economic reform in China.

5 Conclusion

The ERS is a test under the circumstances of the public ownership. The purpose of the system is to promote efficiency of enterprises by granting them more decision-making rights with more responsibilities. The principle of separation of ownership from management is the core of the ERS. Now the ERS has become a dominant form of Chinese industrial reform. Although it is still early to make a definite statement on the ERS, it seems that Chinese industrial reform has embarked on a solid road. In spite of its imperfection, the ERS could be seen as a signal of diversification of managing form for the public-owned enterprises in China.

Notes

1 'The Provisional Regulation on Responsibility System for Industrial Enterprises Owned by the Public', *People's Daily*. 3 March 1988.
2 'Economic growth between 1983–1987', *Beijing Review*, 31, 23, 1988.
3 Li Rongxia (1988) 'The contract system on the rails', *Beijing Review*, 31, 14.
4 'The Public Owned Industrial Enterprise Law of China', *People's Daily*, 16 April 1988.

Reference

Ricketts, M. (1987) *The Economics of Business Enterprise*, Brighton: Wheatsheaf.

Part 3

Profit-sharing, buy-outs, and franchise ownership

Chapter ten

Profit-sharing and company performance: some empirical evidence for the UK

Charles Hanson and Robert Watson

Introduction

Since the late 1970s there has been a steady expansion in the number of UK companies operating all-employee profit-sharing schemes.[1] A succession of Finance Acts which give favourable tax treatment to profit-sharing bonuses paid out by 'approved' schemes appears to have been largely responsible for this recent interest in profit-sharing (Poole 1988; Richardson and Nejad 1986). Thus the vast majority of schemes in operation today are 'approved' schemes which have been expressly designed to take full advantage of these tax concessions.

An important point regarding these tax concessions is that they are available 'across the board' to all companies irrespective of any organizational and industrial relations characteristics. The main justification put forward by the UK government in 1978 for introducing these across-the-board tax concessions was what has recently been termed the 'morale and productivity argument' (Blanchflower and Oswald 1987). In essence it was presumed that profit-sharing 'will help to improve efficiency and productivity and, therefore, the effectiveness of the corporate sector as a whole' (Barnett 1978).

However, nowhere was it suggested that any relationship between profit-sharing and improved performance may be a contingent relationship which is likely to be crucially moderated by other firm-specific factors such as existing industrial-relations practices. Thus the legislation appears to be based upon the assumption that grafting a profit-sharing scheme on to any business entity will necessarily improve performance. Whilst this views business organizations in an unduly simplistic or mechanistic fashion, it has nevertheless continued to be the major justification underpinning all subsequent legislation regarding both profit-sharing and profit-related pay.[2] Moreover, this belief that a more direct linking of remuneration to company profitability makes employees feel more committed to the company and/or work harder was not based upon any substantial empirical evidence. This is because, at the time when

165

the legislation was drawn up, no such empirical evidence did, or could, exist.

The present paper examines a sample of 382 UK listed companies, of which 107 had profit-sharing schemes, to determine whether any systematic differences in performance consistent with the 'morale and productivity' hypothesis exist.[3] The paper adopts a very broad-brush approach. This is largely because the empirical analysis has been based upon publicly available data and, therefore, a great many potentially important variables which may have an affect upon performance and the influence of profit-sharing have had to be ignored.

The paper is structured as follows. The history and existing empirical evidence in respect of profit-sharing and company performance in the UK are briefly examined first. This is followed by a description of the dataset to be used and a section which develops a number of hypotheses regarding the likely effects of profit-sharing upon various performance measures. The main empirical findings are then presented and the paper concludes with a summary of the main findings and a discussion of their implications.

Profit-sharing: history and evidence for the UK

Neither profit-sharing nor the belief that the sharing of profits with workers will lead to better economic performance is a new idea. Over the past one hundred years or so, several eminent economists have strongly endorsed profit-sharing as a means of inducing greater co-operation between capital and labour and/or better economic performance by business firms. For instance in 1870 W.S. Jevons stated that 'the sharing of profits is one of those apparently obvious inventions at the simplicity of which men will wonder in an after-age' (Jevons 1883).

In addition, Alfred Marshall (1920: 256 and 521) wrote approvingly of the arrangment and both D.H. Robertson and J.M. Keynes were members of the committees which produced the famous 'Yellow Book' (*Britain's Industrial Future*, 1928) in which it was emphatically stated that 'the system of profit-sharing should be extended as widely and rapidly as possible'.

Nevertheless, despite such encouragement from economists, until very recently only a relatively small number of firms had actually introduced profit-sharing schemes. Thus, since reasonable comparisons between profit-sharers and non-profit-sharers could not be undertaken, the presumed effects upon firm performance could not actually be measured or tested. That practical difficulty has now largely disappeared and a recent study has estimated that in the UK there are currently over two million employees that participate in some form of profit-sharing in about 700 companies (Bell and Hanson 1987).

The presumed positive consequences of profit-sharing for employee morale and attitudes first attracted the attention of academic researchers. Already there is a growing body of empirical evidence which suggests 'that profit-sharing has small, but significant, effects upon employees' attitudes to work' (Blanchflower and Oswald 1987). In particular, employees' attitudes towards their firm and its objectives become more positive and employees generally become more profit-conscious as a result of participating in profit-sharing schemes (Bell and Hanson 1984).

Evidence regarding the productivity effects of profit-sharing is slightly more mixed, but a distinct majority of empirical studies show that profit-sharing and/or employee shareholding produces higher productivity. A recent review article by Estrin, Grout, and Wadhwani (1987: 45) stated that:

> the work of Cable and Fitzroy (1980) for Germany, Jones and Svejnar (1985) for Italy, and Defourney, Estrin and Jones (1985) for France, all report significant positive associations between total factor productivity and the extent of profit-sharing or employee shareholding.

Estrin, Grout, and Wadhwani conclude (page 50) that 'most of the studies suggest that profit-sharing raises worker productivity'.

As regards the UK, the available evidence also indicates that profit-sharing firms tend to do better than similar non-profit-sharing firms on most generally accepted performance measures (Richardson and Nejad 1986; Bell and Hanson 1987). However, the first of these studies was very limited in scope. It only examined changes in the stock-market price of company shares and the empirical results were based upon 41 companies in the multiple-stores sector, of which 23 had some form of share-ownership scheme in operation by the end of 1984. By contrast, the Bell and Hanson study examined a much greater number of companies, sectors, and performance measures. However, Bell and Hanson presented only univariate analyses and, moreover, did not provide any statistical significance tests of the differences between profit-sharing and non-profit-sharing companies.

The sample and data

The dataset used by the Bell and Hanson (1987) study is also used for this paper. That study compared the performance of 113 profit-sharing companies with that of 301 non-profit-sharing companies. These 414 companies were all UK public companies which were listed in the *Financial Times* in both 1978 and 1985. Thus, companies which had been newly listed, taken over, or merged between 1978 and 1985 were excluded from the sample.

Sectors where almost all companies had profit-sharing schemes, the most obvious of which is banking, were not considered as this would render comparisons between the performance of profit-sharing and non-profit-sharing companies impossible. Only companies in the following ten sectors were, therefore, included:

beers, wines and spirits
building, timber, roads
chemicals, plastics
drapery and stores
electricals
engineering
food and groceries
industrials (miscellaneous)
paper, printing, advertising
textiles

This sample selection procedure resulted in 827 companies fulfilling the necessary criteria. These companies were then sent a simple 'post-card-type' questionnaire asking them:

1 Did they operate an all-employee profit-sharing scheme?
2 If so, when was it introduced?
3 Was it set up within the terms of the 1978 Finance Act?

A total of 470 replies were received, giving a response rate of almost 57 per cent. This compares very favourably with other questionnaire surveys of a similar type and is large enough considerably to reduce any possible non-response 'bias'.

These ten sectors were reduced to seven because three sectors, beers, etc., paper, etc., and textiles had too few cases for reasonable comparisons to be made. These three small sectors were, therefore, merged with 'industrials (miscellaneous)'. The final dataset of 113 profit-sharers and 301 non-profit-sharers was arrived at after excluding companies which returned incomplete replies and, since this would give at least four years of post-introduction performance data, those profit-sharers which introduced schemes after 1981. The final number of profit-sharing and non-profit-sharing companies in each sector are shown in table 10.1.

Thus, for the purposes of this study, a firm was defined as being a profit-sharing company only if it introduced an all-employee profit-sharing scheme prior to 1982. Only companies which had not introduced a profit-sharing scheme by the end of 1985 were considered to be non-profit-sharing companies. Table 10.2 presents the dates at which the 113 profit-sharers first introduced their schemes.

For each of the 414 companies, the annual accounting data necessary

Table 10.1 Distribution of profit-sharing and non-profit-sharing companies by sector

Sector	No. of profit-sharing companies	No. of non-profit-sharing companies	Total
Building, timber, roads	10	40	50
Chemicals, plastics	6	12	18
Drapery and stores	19	25	44
Electricals	6	23	29
Engineering	10	59	69
Food, groceries, etc.	8	21	29
Miscellaneous*	54	121	175
Totals	113	301	414

*Includes beers, wines and spirits; industrials (miscellaneous); paper, printing, advertising; textiles.

Table 10.2 Distribution of profit-sharing companies by year in which profit-sharing introduced

Year/ period	No. of companies	%
Before 1977	34	30.1
1977/78	2	1.8
1978/79	5	4.4
1979/80	24	21.2
1980/81	48	42.5
Total	113	100.0

for the construction of the accounting-based performance measures was collected from the *Hambro Company Guide* for the years 1978 to 1985 inclusive. In addition, annual investor returns (defined as dividends plus capital gains/losses) for each company were calculated from the 'London Share Price Data Tape Returns File'.

The Bell and Hanson (1987) study examined nine performance measures. However, some of these, such as return on equity and return on capital employed, were highly correlated and consequently produced almost identical results. Moreover, some of the performance measures are irrelevant to the hypotheses examined in this paper. Thus, we will be concerned with only the following four performance measures:

return on equity (%)
return on sales (%)
growth in sales (%)
total investor returns (%)

The results presented here are based upon a slightly smaller number of companies than the 414 companies used in the Bell and Hanson text. This is because, for the statistical tests used to compare the performance of profit-sharing and non-profit-sharing companies, full data are required for all eight years, and for a small minority of the Bell and Hanson sample values for some data items were missing for one or more years. The exact number of companies used differs slightly for different performance measures. The number of cases for each measure will, therefore, be reported in the tables along wth the results.

Research design, measures of performance, and profit-sharing

Given the above dataset, derived primarily from publicly available information, we are unable to test directly the validity of either the morale or the productivity hypotheses. Nevertheless, if the 'morale and productivity argument' has a measure of empirical validity, then it is to be expected that this will be reflected in the relative performance of profit-sharing and non-profit-sharing companies. In this paper, therefore, we shall be solely concerned with examining differences in publicly available performance measures between profit-sharing and non-profit-sharing companies. Quite simply, if the observed differences in performance between the two groups are as anticipated, then we can infer that the productivity hypothesis has some empirical validity.

Of course, different performance measures are likely to be affected at different times, in different ways, and to differing extents. An examination of the likely consequences which the introduction of a profit-sharing scheme may have upon each of the four individual performance measures is therefore required. Moreover, in practice, company performance will be a function of many variables. These other variables will have an important effect upon performance independent of the existence of a profit-sharing scheme. Thus, the purpose of this section is to develop specific hypotheses and multivariate models for testing each of the four performance measures.

As the timing and/or degree of 'permanency' which profit-sharing may have upon the individual performance measures is likely to differ, the empirical analysis will be based upon the following comparisons:

1 the 'all-company analysis' where the performance of all profit-sharers is compared with all non-profit-sharers over the full eight-year period.
2 the 'before-and-after analysis' where the performance of all profit-sharers that first introduced schemes in 1980–1 is compared with that of all non-profit-sharers for the two subperiods 1978–81 and 1982–5.

The primary purpose of 2 is to conduct a 'before-and-after' comparison

comparison of performance in order to ascertain whether the performance of the two groups differed significantly prior to the introduction of the profit-sharing scheme, and whether the introduction of the profit-sharing scheme had any appreciable effect upon subsequent performance.

Since both the initial size and the industry within which the company operates will be likely to have an effect upon performance, the general model for each performance measure will be as follows:

$$PM = \alpha + PS + Size + IND_1 + IND_2 + IND_3 + IND_4 + IND_5 + IND_6$$

where PM (the dependent variable), for the 'all-company analysis', is the average level of performance (i.e. return on equity, return on sales, sales growth, and investor returns) over the eight-year period 1978–85; for the 'before and after analysis', PM is the difference in performance between 1978–81 and 1982–5.

α	=	constant term plus Industry 7 (dummy reference category).
PS	=	profit-sharing dummy variable coded 1 if company is a profit-sharer and O otherwise.
Size	=	log of size measure (i.e. balance-sheet equity, turnover and market capitalization) in base year (1978).
IND_1 to IND_6	=	dichotomous (dummy) variables representing industries 1 to 6.

For the investor-returns measure, an additional variable, which is a measure of 'volatility' or 'risk', will be included in the model. According to financial-market theory, investors will require a higher return if the 'market' or 'systematic risk' of a share is high (i.e. the share is more volatile with respect to general market movements). Thus, a large difference in investor returns for the two groups may be due entirely to differences in the relative risk of the two groups.

To examine this possibility, the so-called 'beta' weights (simple regression slope coefficients) for each company were calculated by regressing each company's 60-monthly observations immediately prior to 1 January 1978 upon the monthly FTA-index returns over the same period. These estimated beta weights for each company will be included as an additional explanatory variable in the investor-returns model.[4]

Given the limitations of the current dataset, the above model necessarily excludes a number of potentially important determinants of company performance. In particular, we are unable to control directly for factors such as the degree of unionization, existing market shares, industrial-relations practices, or the 'quality of management'. We now examine the main anticipated effects which profit sharing is likely to have upon each of the four individual performance measures.

Return on equity

If, as a consequence of the introduction of a profit-sharing scheme, workers become more productive, then return on equity for profit-sharing companies should increase. This is because, whilst profits will be greater than otherwise, assuming of course that companies are able to sell the additional production at a profit, there will be no requirement for the amount of equity and/or loan capital needed to produce this level of profit to increase.

Return on sales

If companies tended to set up profit-sharing schemes primarily because of the perceived morale and productivity effects, then profit-sharing schemes would be most likely to be introduced in companies which were currently already highly profitable and where product demand was strong. That is, companies with high profit margins (return on sales) will be most likely to introduce profit-sharing schemes because, in these companies, the expected benefits from increased output would be highest for two main reasons. First, the link between increases in output (extra effort) and increases in profits (additional remuneration) will be most direct, and thereby most motivating. Second, if product demand is strong, then companies will be able to sell the increased output without significantly reducing the profit margin on existing production.

A priori, it is difficult to determine the effect upon the return-on-sales variable that profit-sharing may have subsequent to its introduction. This is because the return-on-sales variable will be largely determined by the profit margins that companies can obtain from the sale of any additional output. Hence, whilst both the numerator (profits) and denominator (sales) seem likely to increase for profit-sharing companies, the relative rate of change of these two variables will depend more upon market-demand factors than upon profit-sharing. Thus, once prior period performance has been incorporated in the model, the estimated coefficient on the profit-sharing dummy may be either positive or statistically insignificant.

Growth in sales

If positive productivity effects occur, then this measure seems likely to be most directly affected by the introduction of profit-sharing: sales growth should increase at a faster rate than otherwise. However, superior sales growth within the profit-sharing companies may not persist indefinitely. A 'once and for all' step change in the two to three years after the introduction of a profit-sharing scheme seems a more plausible consequence since, after an initial increase in output, further increases in productivity by working harder become more difficult to achieve. Thus, even if workers in profit-sharing companies were highly motivated, it seems unlikely that productivity, and hence sales, will continue to rise at faster rates than in non-profit-sharing companies. Any effect of profit-sharing upon sales growth may, therefore, only be apparent in the first year or two after the introduction of the scheme.

Investor returns

The efficient-market hypothesis implies that any 'publicly available' information relevant to the valuation of a company's shares, such as the introduction of a profit-sharing scheme which increases productivity and/or profits, will be rapidly incorporated into the share price. One would not, therefore, expect to see the profit-sharers consistently outperforming the non-profit-sharers once the consequences for the future value of the company had been assessed by the market-makers.

The timing of the market's reaction to the introduction of profit-sharing is, however, difficult to determine a priori. Depending upon market-makers' expectations regarding the future value consequences of profit-sharing, the market could react either at the time that the profit-sharing scheme was first announced, at the time that it was actually introduced or at the time that an improvement in sales growth or profits actually occurred. To test this issue empirically, the before-and-after model for investor returns will consist of two separate models where the dependent variables will be average returns 1978–81 and average returns 1982–5.

Empirical results

The main empirical findings will be presented in two subsections consisting of the all-company analysis and the before-and-after analysis for companies which first introduced profit-sharing in 1980–1.

All companies

Table 10.3 presents the univariate empirical results for the four performance measures based upon all profit-sharing and all non-profit-sharing companies. Section A of table 10.3 presents the number of companies in each group for each performance measure, the group means for each of the individual eight years and, in the extreme right-hand column, the overall results for the period 1978–85.

Table 10.3 Section A: annual mean values for all companies

Performance measure	Number	Type	1978	1979	1980	1981	1982	1983	1984	1985	Average 1978-85
Return on equity (%)	100	PS	33.7	29.9	22.5	19.1	19.0	19.7	23.0	22.7	23.7
	279	NPS	30.5	27.5	19.9	13.1	12.4	14.5	18.6	18.1	19.3
Return on sales (%)	101	PS	9.9	9.6	8.1	7.1	7.2	7.8	8.5	8.4	8.3
	281	NPS	7.7	7.3	5.6	3.9	4.1	4.9	5.8	5.6	5.6
% change in sales	100	PS	17.9	17.3	14.0	8.5	11.9	11.7	18.1	12.8	14.0
	279	NPS	17.6	18.5	14.8	4.3	8.1	9.7	13.1	11.7	12.3
Annual investor returns (%)	107	PS	26.0	7.6	15.8	21.9	40.4	21.3	31.8	27.4	24.0
	269	NPS	23.1	0.9	9.0	16.3	14.9	30.4	24.4	25.4	18.0

PS = Profit-sharing companies
NPS = Non-profit-sharing companies

Section B: statistical tests for all companies

	Profit-sharing companies		Non-profit-sharing companies		Test statistics
	$\bar{M}$	SD	$\bar{M}$	SD	T
Return on equity (%)	23.7	10.8	19.3	11.6	3.3***
Return on sales (%)	8.3	4.9	5.6	4.8	4.9***
% change in sales	14.0	6.3	12.3	10.2	2.0**
Annual investor returns (%)	24.0	11.7	18.0	13.3	4.1***

*   = Sig at 10% ⎫
** = Sig at 5% ⎬ 2-tail test
*** = Sig at 1% ⎭

As can be seen, for both return on equity and return on sales, the profit sharing group outperforms the non-profit sharers in all of the eight years examined. The difference between the two groups over the full period averages 4.4 per cent and 2.7 per cent for return on equity and return on sales respectively. From Section B of table 10.3 it can be seen that this difference between group means is statistically significant at 1 per cent levels of confidence (t = 3.3 and 4.9 for return on equity and return on sales respectively).

Section A indicates that the percentage growth in sales for the two groups differs by an average of 1.7 per cent per year in favour of the profit-sharers. In only two years, 1979 and 1980, do the non-profit-sharers outperform the profit-sharers. The difference between group means for the full eight-year period is statistically significant at 5-percent levels of confidence (t = 2.0).

The profit-sharing group obtained higher annual investor returns in seven out of the eight years. The average annual difference in returns of 6.0 per cent is statistically significant at 1-per-cent levels of confidence (t = 4.1).

The empirical results for the multivariate models for the all-company analyses are presented in table 10.4. As can be seen from the positive and statisitically significant coefficients on the profit-sharing variable (PS), the multivariate results reinforce the univariate findings. With the exception of sales growth, which is significant at 10-per-cent confidence levels, the average differences in performance over the eight-year period between the profit-sharers and the non-profit-sharers are significantly different from one another at 1-per-cent confidence levels.

Before-and-after analysis

The results so far have been based upon all profit-sharing companies irrespective of when they introduced their schemes. From table 10.2, it will be recalled that more than a quarter of the 113 profit-sharers had a scheme in operation prior to 1978 and that 42.5 per cent did not introduce their scheme until 1980 to 1981. The annual and overall univariate means for those companies that introduced profit-sharing schemes in the period 1980 to 1981 are shown in table 10.5, along with the comparable figures for all non-profit-sharing companies.

The overall figures are very similar to those presented earlier in table 10.3 for all profit-sharers except that average return on sales is 1 per cent lower for the 1980–1 profit-sharers than for all profit-sharers. As may be seen from Section B of table 10.5, the statistical significance of the difference between group means for all four performance measures are also very similar to, though generally slightly lower than, the previous analysis.

Table 10.4 All companies: period = 1978–85: estimated regressions

Return on equity

$$29.017 + 3.951PS + 1.822E - 12.422I_1 - 12.216I_2 - 9.997I_3 - 14.667I_4 - 16.078I_5 - 8.395I_6$$
$$(12.65)^{***} \quad (3.08)^{***} \quad (2.38)^{**} \quad (5.56)^{***} \quad (4.74)^{***} \quad (3.06)^{***} \quad (5.44)^{***} \quad (6.55)^{***} \quad (2.84)^{***}$$

$\bar{R}^2 = 13.9\%$ $F = 8.64^{***}$ $N = 379$

Return on sales

$$10.746 + 2.664PS + 0.049S - 4.885I_1 - 5.585I_2 - 3.615I_3 - 6.593I_4 - 6.693I_5 - 7.520I_6$$
$$(10.57)^{***} \quad (5.00)^{***} \quad (0.16) \quad (5.27)^{***} \quad (5.20)^{***} \quad (2.65)^{***} \quad (5.87)^{***} \quad (6.56)^{***} \quad (6.09)^{***}$$

$\bar{R}^2 = 16.8\%$ $F = 10.63^{***}$ $N = 382$

Change in sales

$$18.522 + 1.749PS - 0.156S - 5.440I_1 - 4.642I_2 - 7.687I_3 - 8.515I_4 - 9.924I_5 - 3.601I_6$$
$$(9.07)^{***} \quad (1.66)^{*} \quad (0.25) \quad (2.92)^{***} \quad (2.15)^{**} \quad (2.80)^{***} \quad (3.78)^{***} \quad (4.83)^{***} \quad (1.45)$$

$\bar{R}^2 = 6.5\%$ $F = 4.27^{***}$ $N = 379$

Investor returns

$$29.812 + 5.436PS - 1.937MC_{t-1} - 11.780B - 2.817I_1 - 0.120I_2 - 7.063I_3 - 2.514I_4 + 8.645I_5 + 1.540I_6$$
$$(8.83)^{***} \quad (3.71)^{***} \quad (1.79)^{*} \quad (3.84)^{***} \quad (1.07) \quad (0.6) \quad (1.86)^{*} \quad (0.79) \quad (2.97)^{***} \quad (0.46)$$

$\bar{R}^2 = 11.5\%$ $F = 6.40^{***}$ $N = 376$

* = Sig at 10%
** = Sig at 5% } 2-tail test
*** = Sig at 1%

Table 10.5 Section A: before and after analysis: annual mean values

Performance measure	Number	Type	Year 1978	1979	1980	1981	1982	1983	1984	1985	Average 1978–85
Return on Equity (%)	43	PS	33.2	30.4	21.8	19.2	19.4	19.6	23.1	23.4	23.8
	279	NPS	30.5	27.5	19.9	13.1	12.4	14.5	18.6	18.1	19.3
Return on sales (%)	42	PS	10.7	10.5	9.0	6.3	6.5	6.6	7.4	7.0	7.3
	281	NPS	7.7	7.3	5.6	3.9	4.1	4.9	5.8	5.6	5.6
% change in sales	41	PS	17.2	17.7	11.2	15.4	16.4	13.0	18.1	25.0	14.6
	279	NPS	17.6	18.5	14.8	4.3	8.1	9.7	13.1	11.7	12.3
Annual investor returns (%)	46	PS	27.0	14.6	15.2	24.9	45.1	17.5	34.4	24.9	25.5
	269	NPS	23.1	0.9	9.0	16.3	14.9	30.4	24.4	25.4	18.6

Section B: before and after: statistical tests

Performance measure		PS companies M̄	SD	NPS companies M̄	SD	Test statistics T
Return on equity (%)	Before	26.1	9.8	22.8	13.4	2.0**
	After	21.4	11.8	15.9	12.9	2.6***
	Full Period	23.8	10.0	19.3	11.6	2.4**
Return on sales (%)	Before	7.8	4.9	6.1	4.8	2.1**
	After	6.8	4.4	5.1	5.5	2.3**
	Full Period	7.3	4.4	5.6	4.8	2.2**
% change in sales	Before	13.7	6.9	13.8	12.2	0.1
	After	15.4	9.7	10.7	13.3	2.7***
	Full Period	14.6	6.5	12.3	10.2	1.9*
Annual investor returns (%)	Before	20.4	18.6	12.3	20.7	2.5***
	After	30.5	17.4	23.8	19.9	2.1**
	Full Period	25.5	12.1	18.0	13.3	3.5***

* = Sig at 10%
** = Sig at 5%   } 2-tail test
*** = Sig at 1%

PS = Companies which introduced profit-sharing 1980–1
NPS = Non-profit-sharing companies

These overall comparisons seem, however, to mask some important trends over the period, particularly with respect to growth in sales. Section B of table 10.5 also presents details of the performance of the two groups over the two subperiods 1978 to 1981 and 1982 to 1985. The earlier 1978–81 period includes the three to four years immediately prior to the introduction of profit-sharing and the period covering its introduction. The later subperiod covers the four years immediately after the introduction of profit-sharing.

For both return on equity and return on sales measures, the mean differences between profit-sharers and non-profit sharers in the four-year period prior to the introduction of the profit-sharing schemes are significant at 5 per cent confidence levels (t = 2.0 and 2.1 for equity and sales respectively). Thus, it appears that the profit-sharing companies were generally performing significantly better than the non-profit-sharing companies prior to the introduction of the profit-sharing schemes.

For both of these measures the statistical differences between the two groups in the four-year period after the introduction of profit-sharing are slightly greater than for the previous four-year period. Thus, on a univariate basis, on average the profit-sharers appear to have improved their position relative to the non-profit-sharing group in the four years after the introduction of the schemes.

The growth in sales figures show that for the four-year period prior to the commencement of the profit-sharing schemes, differences between the groups were minimal and not significant (t = 0.1). In the subsequent four-year period, however, the performance of the profit-sharers was markedly better than that of the non-profit-sharers. The profit-sharers achieved an additional 4.7-per-cent per-annum growth in sales above that of the non-profit-sharers. The t-statistic of 2.7 indicates that this difference in means is significant at 1-per-cent confidence levels. This tends to imply that, as anticipated, the introduction of profit-sharing and subsequent sales growth were very closely associated.

The total investor-returns figures for both subperiods indicate that the differences between the profit-sharers and non-profit-sharers are statistically significant at 1-per-cent and 5-per-cent levels of confidence for the earlier and later periods respectively.

The empirical estimation of the multivariate models for the before-and-after analysis are presented in table 10.6. These results are broadly consistent with the productivity hypothesis detailed earlier. Turning to the sales-growth measure first, since this variable will be most directly affected by any morale and productivity improvements, the results show that the coefficient on the profit-sharing dummy variable is positively and just statistically significant at 5-per-cent confidence levels (t = 1.97). This indicates that the profit-sharers had significantly higher sales growth relative to the non-profit-sharers over the four-year period following the

Table 10.6 Before and after multivariate analysis

DEPENDENT VARIABLE

Change in return on equity

$$15.614 + 5.666PS + 2.603E - 16.412I_1 - 15.888I_2 - 16.761I_3 - 19.117I_4 - 20.882I_5 - 10.958I_6$$
$$(5.52)^{***}\ (2.76)^{***}\ (2.72)^{***}\ (5.96)^{***}\ (5.05)^{***}\ (4.22)^{***}\ (5.71)^{***}\ (6.98)^{***}\ (3.10)^{***}$$

$\bar{R}^2 = 17.3\%$ $F = 9.39^{***}$ $N = 322$

Change in return on sales

$$8.331 + 1.798PS + 0.413S - 7.411I_1 - 7.931I_2 - 8.538I_3 - 9.789I_4 - 9.507I_5 - 7.280I_6$$
$$(6.54)^{***}\ (2.05)^{**}\ (1.03)\ (6.41)^{***}\ (5.98)^{***}\ (5.07)^{***}\ (6.93)^{***}\ (7.55)^{***}\ (4.87)^{***}$$

$\bar{R}^2 = 16.3$ $F = 8.85^{***}$ $N = 323$

Change in sales growth

$$8.024 + 4.949PS - 3.522S - 6.195I_1 - 3.970I_2 - 1.329I_3 - 7.577I_4 - 6.242I_5 - 2.360I_6$$
$$(2.23)^{**}\ (1.97)^{**}\ (3.11)^{***}\ (1.90)^{*}\ (1.06)\ (0.28)\ (1.90)^{*}\ (1.75)^{*}\ (0.56)$$

$\bar{R}^2 = 3.6\%$ $F = 2.47^{***}$ $N = 320$

INVESTOR RETURNS

Before

$$41.816 + 8.043PS + 4.471MC_{t-1} - 20.419B - 16.285I_1 - 8.861I_2 - 21.286I_3 - 17.680I_4 - 23.176I_5 - 8.154I_6$$
$$(7.34)^{***}\ (2.54)^{**}\ (2.42)^{**}\ (4.0)^{***}\ (3.63)^{***}\ (1.68)^{*}\ (3.32)^{***}\ (3.22)^{***}\ (4.73)^{***}\ (1.48)$$

$\bar{R}^2 = 12.9\%$ $F = 6.17^{***}$ $N = 315$

After

$$19.917 + 4.630PS - 0.533MC_{t-1} - 1.511B + 5.504I_1 + 5.546I_2 + 3.864I_3 + 18.693I_4 + 3.792I_5 + 6.524I_6$$
$$(3.48)^{***}\ (1.45)\ (0.29)\ (0.29)\ (1.22)\ (1.04)\ (0.6)\ (3.38)^{***}\ (0.77)\ (1.18)$$

$\bar{R}^2 = 3.8\%$ $F = 2.38^{***}$ $N = 315$

* = Sig at 10%
** = Sig at 5%   } 2-tail test
*** = Sig at 1%

introduction of their schemes. The results for the return-on-equity measure also tend to support the productivity hypothesis since the coefficient on the profit-sharing dummy variable is likewise positive and is statistically significant at 1-per-cent confidence levels.

The results for the return-on-sales measure indicate that the profit-sharing companies had managed on average to increase their profit margins by 1.8 per cent above that of the non-profit-sharers. This slight increase in return on sales is statistically significant at 5-per-cent confidence levels.

The results for the before-and-after investor-return models also suggest that the market may have anticipated a positive productivity effect. The market performance of the profit-sharing companies, as indicated by the positive coefficient on the dummy variable, was significantly better at 5-per-cent confidence levels than that of the non-profit sharers over the 1978–81 period. The lack of significant differences in the latter four-year period after the introduction of profit-sharing is also consistent with this efficient-markets view. If the subsequent superior performance of the profit-sharers regarding the other performance measures had been anticipated by the market, then these expectations would have been rapidly 'impounded' in share prices. Thus, no significant differences between the two groups would be expected once the likely consequences of the schemes had been absorbed by the market.

Concluding remarks

The results presented here demonstrate that companies with all-employee profit-sharing schemes outperform similar non-profit-sharing companies to a statistically significant extent. The before-and-after analysis provides some evidence of an improvement of performance, particularly in respect of growth in sales, soon after the introduction of the schemes. The results also indicate that the stock market appeared to recognize this improvement.

Of course, this apparent correlation between profit-sharing and superior performance may be entirely due to any one of several omitted factors. In particular, we believe that the observed improvement in performance may be a reflection of generally good corporate management and industrial-relations practices. That is, profit-sharing may be merely one element of an integrated business strategy which leads to improved performance, rather than profit-sharing possessing any causal influence on its own. This interpretation seems plausible since the results show that only relatively successful companies tend to introduce such schemes.[5] Thus, the empirical findings do not unambiguously demonstrate that profit-sharing schemes on their own are a major cause of this better performance. It may be that, as Bell and

Hanson (1987) and Poole (1988) have recently argued, the existence of all-employee profit-sharing in a company indicates a certain management style which is conducive to high relative levels of performance. The results presented here are certainly consistent with such a view.

Notes

1   Throughout this paper the term 'profit-sharing' is used in its traditional sense of a bonus, related to profits, over and above established wages or salaries. For an expansion of this definition and a discussion of the importance of distinguishing between profit-sharing and 'profit-related pay', see chapter 1 of Bell and Hanson (1987).
2   For instance, a recent consultative document on the benefits of profit-related pay stated that it 'should lead to a closer identification of employees with the companies in which they work. . . . The most important consequence . . . is likely to be . . . enhanced competitiveness and better business performance' (HMSO 1986: 3).
3   Other justifications for encouraging profit-sharing, such as the 'wage flexibility argument' (see Blanchflower and Oswald 1987) and Weitzman's (1984, 1985, and 1987) macroeconomic arguments, are not considered in this paper.
4   On a univariate basis, the 107 profit-sharing companies appeared to have slightly higher betas than the 269 non-profit-sharers. However, the difference between the two groups was marginal, betas of 0.96 and 1.01 respectively for profit-sharers and non-profit sharers, and not significant at 10 per cent ($t = 1.4$).
5   This ties in with the conclusions of Cable and Wilson (1989) who found that profit-sharing firms in the UK engineering industry were more productive than non-profit-sharers. They argued that 'the effect (of profit-sharing) is entwined with the firm's choice of technology, internal organisation and labour force characteristics'.

References

Barnett, J. (1978) 'Second reading of the 1978 Finance Bill', *Hansard*, 27 April: 1657.
Bell, D.W. and Hanson, C.G. (1984) '*Profit-sharing and employee shareholding attitude survey*', London, Industrial Participation Association, November.
Bell, D.W. and Hanson, C.G. (1987) *Profit sharing and profitability*, London: Kogan Page.
Blanchflower, D.G. and Oswald, A.J. (1986) 'Profit sharing: can it work?', *Oxford Economic Papers*.
'*Britain's Industrial Future*' (1928) 'The Yellow Book', London: Benn.
Cable, J. and Fitzroy, F. (1980) 'Co-operation and productivity: some evidence from West German experience', *Economic Analysis and Worker's Management*: 163–80.

Cable, J. and Wilson, N. (1989) 'Profit-sharing and productivity: an analysis of UK engineering firms', *Economic Journal*, 99: 366–75.

Defourney, J.S., Estrin, S., and Jones, D.C. (1985) 'The effects of worker participation on enterprise performance', *International Journal of Industrial Organization*: 197–217.

Estrin, S., Grout, P., and Wadhwani, S. (1987) 'Profit sharing and employee share ownership', *Economic Policy*, April: 14–62.

HMSO (1986) '*Profit-related pay: a consultative document*, July, Command paper 9835.

Jevons, W.S. (1883) *Methods of Social Reform*, London: Macmillan.

Jones, D.C. and Svejnar, J. (1985) 'Participation, profit sharing, worker ownership and efficiency in Italian producer co-operatives', *Economica*: 449–65.

Marshall, A. (1920) *Principles of Economics*, eighth edition 1920, London: Macmillan.

Poole, M. (1988) 'Factors affecting the development of employee financial participation in contemporary Britain: evidence from a national survey', *British Journal of Industrial Relations*, March: 21–36.

Richardson, R. and Nejad, A. (1986) 'Employee share ownership schemes in the UK – an evaluation', *British Journal of Industrial Relations*, July: 233–50.

Weitzman, M.L. (1984) *The Share Economy*, Cambridge, MA: Harvard University Press.

Weitzman, M.L. (1985) 'The simple macroeconomics of profit sharing', *American Economic Review*, 75: 937–53.

Weitzman, M.L. (1987) 'Steady state unemployment under profit sharing', *The Economic Journal*, 97: 86–105.

Chapter eleven

Options for workers: owner or employee?[1]

Harvie Ramsay, Jeff Hyman, Lesley Baddon, Laurie Hunter, and John Leopold

Introduction

A number of related effects concerning employee behaviour and attitudes have been predicted for employee share ownership at both micro and macro levels. At the level of the enterprise, the basis for this prediction derives from the significance attributed to property possession and from an assumption that share ownership is associated with employee involvement and with participation by employees as shareholders in the overall supervision and management of their companies.

In other words, employee share schemes are thought to possess valuable transformative properties and, unlike other participative approaches, the key to this transformation rests in ownership and its presumed effects upon employee orientations and attitudes, in turn leading to increased productive efficiency and work performance. Recent studies demonstrate the weight attributed by managers to this transformative potential when introducing schemes. Research by Smith (1986), Bell and Hanson (1987), and Baddon *et al.* (1987) clearly shows that steering general employee attitudes toward closer identification with company objectives and profitability and emphasizing a common frame of reference have formed a major part of management expectations. Consequently share schemes are being introduced as part of the move by companies to adopt 'human resource' management styles which emphasize the relationship of the individual employee to the enterprise.

With these putative benefits firmly in mind, the government has set about extending the base to share ownership as a vital part of its campaign to broaden the distribution of wealth among the employed population and thereby to reinforce the principle of a democracy in which individual freedom is directly linked with access to property ownership. This campaign has found expression in numerous exhortative statements, supported by regular legislative moves designed to encourage companies to offer shares to their employees.

Major questions faced by researchers concern whether share-ownership

183

patterns are changing as a consequence of employee share programmes and, second, the nature of any impact that schemes are exerting on employees and their relations to work in terms of behaviour and attitudes. With regard to the first question, a rise in the number of companies offering some form of share provision has been noted (Baddon *et al.* 1989). Millward and Stevens (1986) estimated that the proportion of companies offering share schemes had risen from 13 per cent in 1980 to 23 per cent by 1984. By January 1989, some 788 Approved Deferred Share Trust (ADST) schemes granting shares to all eligible employees had received Inland Revenue approval. Since 1980, employees have also been offered the opportunity to purchase shares in their companies on favourable terms through SAYE all-employee option schemes. The number of such schemes has shown steady (if unspectacular) growth. By the end of January 1989 some 795 all-employee schemes offering options to purchase shares were in operation.

This figure is dwarfed, however, by the 3,689 discretionary share schemes granted approval since their endorsement by legislation in 1984. These schemes offer options only to selected, usually high-ranking, employees. Despite the overall growth in the number of share programmes, Millward and Stevens estimate that employee share participation only rose from 5 per cent in 1980 to 7 per cent in 1984. Employee share ownership continues, therefore, to be a minority habit. This can be accounted for largely by the continuing majority of companies without schemes open to all employees and by the relatively small numbers of those eligible who avail themselves of the opportunity to participate in all-employee option schemes, a hitherto unexplored area which will be given more exposure in this paper.

Both government and share-scheme ideologues see unitarism as the principal channel by which 'attitude changes which can result from the introduction of employee share schemes put management and employees rather more on the same side' (Copeman *et al.* 1984). An equally positive unitarist claim has been made by Cable and Fitzroy (1980) who contend that: 'Participatory firms – with or without profit-sharing – will produce better outcomes than traditional firms if the negative collusion to maximize one party's share . . . can be replaced by positive collusion to maximize joint wealth'. The extent to which share schemes are able to persuade employees in these directions has, however, yet to be established, and in this respect, evidence rather than ideology has become a major priority.

For researchers, employee share schemes pose two very major questions. The first concerns the nature and extent of attitudinal effects which can be positively traced to share schemes. The second question asks how these 'effects' are to be identified and measured.

Thus far, research findings have been mixed but are far from unanimous in their support for attitudinal changes based upon emergent unitarist sympathies. While the work of Bell and Hanson has tended to demonstrate positive attitudinal effects in their recent research projects, a number of other findings on employee responses have been more circumspect, summarized by Klein and Rosen (1986) as 'mixed and inconclusive'. In his review of West German studies, Estrin, too, comments that 'few of the attitudinal effects suggested by the theory show in the West German sample' (Estrin and Wadhwani 1986). Other recent findings also point toward a possibly more limited impact (Poole and Jenkins 1988).

The inconclusive nature of many of these findings can, of course, be traced to the difficulties inherent in evaluating employee responses and relating these accurately to the effects of a share scheme. Perhaps for this reason, support for the effects of the application of share schemes is tinged with a good measure of caution (e.g. Richardson and Nejad 1986). Advocates such as Bell and Hanson are also inclined to exercise restraint by adding imprecise qualifications when discussing their purportedly unremittingly positive research findings: '*Most* managers we have met in profit-sharing companies have said that, at least to a *modest* extent, profit-sharing, as *part* of their total employee participation arrangements, has had *some* effect . . .' (1987: 6) (emphasis added).

The obstacles faced in trying to decipher employee responses and attitudes to share arrangements specifically are formidable; what is being measured? How persistent are 'attitudes' over time? This latter point is particularly important as most studies have tended to rely upon surveys offering little more than a snapshot of employee views at a particular time and as revealed by means of a written questionnaire. A further potential shortcoming concerns the difficulty in accurately identifying the agents responsible for influencing employee dispositions, a point well illustrated by the above reference to profit-sharing exerting an effect within a broader participative framework and confirmed by the number of studies showing that financial participation is more likely than not introduced in companies which cater for other forms of participation (Baddon *et al.* 1987).

These limitations to the accurate measurement of attitudes are well recognized by researchers who have recently explored ways of securing more reliable measures. In particular, there have been moves to supplement survey material with appropriate case-studies. For example, Dewe and his colleagues (Dewe *et al.* 1988) have attempted to obtain reliable data through conducting an initial assessment of employee opinion and attitudes in a case-study company prior to the introduction of a scheme, to be followed by subsequent follow-up studies within the same company after introduction.

The 'Glasgow' study

Our approach also adopts a multi-dimensional approach using a range of surveys supported by case studies. The study comprised three main stages: namely a wide-ranging postal survey of 1,000 companies conducted during summer 1985, and which elicited 356 responses. Over two-thirds of these reported at least one type of scheme, and many more than one. In total, details of 396 schemes were supplied. The survey was followed by extended, tape-recorded interviews with management representatives in each of 35 companies with profit-sharing arrangements. These interviews were designed to reveal the motives and management philosophies which underlie the introduction of schemes. Finally, six case studies in five separate companies were conducted in late 1986 and early 1987.

The case-study companies ranged in size from 70 employees to 30,000

Table 11.1 Characteristics of case-study companies

Company	Owner ship	Sector	Union-ized	Type of PS/ESO scheme(s)	Approxi-mate employ-ment size	HQ location	Case-study location
Fairbrush	Private limited company	Manu-facturing (tools)	Yes	Cash based: employee trust	340	Midlands	Midlands
Norbrew	plc	Manu-facturing (food/drink)	Yes	ADST: SAYE	6,000 (group)	North England	North England
Goodbake (i) Breadline	plc	Manu-facturing (retail)	Yes	SAYE: (discre-tionary (profit sharing)	30,000 (group)	South-east	Scotland
(ii) Scotcake		Manu-facturing* (food/drink)					
Bossguide	Private limited	Manage-ment services	No	Discre-tionary profit-bonus; share option	70	Midlands	Midlands
Thistle	plc	Manu-facturing	Yes	SAYE	20,000	North-west	Scotland

* In this case there is also a productivity bonus scheme.
ADST Approved Deferred Share Trust
ESO Employee share ownership
PS Profit-sharing
SAYE Save-as-you-earn

and covered both service and manufacturing concerns. Further details of these companies are shown in table 11.1. From the table it can be seen that three of the companies, covering four case-studies, operated SAYE share-option schemes. The case studies involved taped interviews with representatives from both management and employees, chosen because of their influence, involvement, or interest in establishing and maintaining the share schemes. Appropriate documentation (e.g. minutes of consultative meetings) was also examined. Finally, a work-place survey was conducted resulting in replies from just over 500 employees and including 413 in those companies with SAYE schemes. In addition to seeking details of employee views and orientations, the questionnaire was designed to gather valuable information about patterns of share acquisition and disposition as well as background information of SAYE participants and non-participants.

In this paper we have decided to focus our analysis on an assessment of the impact of one type of share programme, namely SAYE all-employee share-option schemes, through an evaluation of the responses, both material and attitudinal, of participants and non-participants to their schemes. The reasons for this derive from our earlier discussion. First, analysis of employee responses would be expected to yield valuable information regarding the characteristics of participants as against non-participants in the SAYE schemes across a number of companies. An opportunity is thereby provided to explore differences and similarities exhibited by the groups towards share participation and to examine linkages with other aspects of their work lives or general attitudes. By choosing SAYE it is possible to differentiate between the two groups in an environment where other participative arrangements are common to all employees. This would then help to isolate those particular influences which help to determine the extent and level of SAYE participation.

Second, these schemes operate according to principles of choice in that employees actively decide whether to take part in the five-year (minimum) savings period by diverting an element of their personal wealth into the share plan. They choose again at the end of this period whether to take accumulated cash, continue saving for a further two years, or to convert their savings into company shares, purchased at a price (often discounted) set when the employee joined the scheme five years earlier. The opportunity provided to analyse employee responses in terms of their rates and extent of participation would also add significantly to the findings for the groups across a number of companies. The general directions of the questionnaire analysis can be illuminated and enhanced by individual case-study material. Third, an option scheme requires approval according to specific criteria from the Inland Revenue prior to introduction, thus ensuring an element of commonality between schemes operating in otherwise diverse circumstances.

Scheme participation

In the four establishments operating an approved SAYE scheme, overall participation rates were not high; about 20 per cent at Norbrew (encouraged by opening the scheme in 1986 to part-time employees), 10 per cent overall for the two establishments at Goodbake, and 20 per cent for employees at Thistle. These figures are consistent with findings reported elsewhere (Baddon *et al.* 1987). The original survey figures indicate progressively higher participation rates by occupational group, ranging from 8 per cent for manual employees, through 13 per cent in non-manual to 26 per cent for managers (ibid.)

The questionnaires distributed to employees in the four case studies positively indicate more interest in completing the questionnaire among SAYE participants than the majority non-participant employees (see Fogarty 1987 for similar responses) leading to significantly more data from the former than the latter. The overall impression provided by the case-study survey was that participants are more likely to be male than female, though not proportionately so. Union membership is proportionately less common among participants and these are more likely to be engaged in white-collar rather than manual work. As table 11.2 shows, participation is also likely to be associated with levels of pay.

Table 11.2 Percentage of respondents participating in the SAYE scheme, by pay band

Weekly pay	Under £100	£100–129	£130–159	£160–199	£200–299	£300+
Participants (%)	40.2	56.5	54.3	70.5	75.5	83.3

Owning shares: a new window on the world?

We begin by considering how far the attitudes of employees on labour–management relations in general are influenced by (or at least covariant with) participation in SAYE schemes or offer support for any hypothesis of an ideological shift to a unitarist view of the world arising from share purchase. We are able to consider these through the prism of responses to questions on the nature of management/employee relations in Britain, on the issue of union power, and to the results of a series of statements inviting agreement or disagreement on general industrial-relations issues. Though the survey approach of necessity offers a snapshot of currently expressed attitudes and opinion and is unable to separate cause and effect, this potential methodological weakness is of little significance in our study which found little effect attributable to share ownership.

Overall just under one-third of answers saw labour–management relations in Britain generally in terms of opposite sides, three-fifths saw them as embodying a combination of shared and conflicting interests, and one in twelve felt interests were predominantly shared. There was some minor variation in the proportional distribution between firms operating SAYE schemes, but they all conformed to the same broad pattern, as indeed did Fairbrush with its cash-based scheme; Bossguide (which had both profit bonus and share options) saw a markedly greater concentration in the middle category.

Table 11.3 View of management–employee relationships in Britain generally and in own company compared

Statement	Britain Generally			Own Company		
	All%	P%	NP%	All%	P%	NP%
Management and employees basically have common aims and objectives	8	5	12	23	26	21
Management and unions have some shared interests, but also some areas of conflict	59	60	56	63	64	62
Management and employees are basically on opposite sides	33	34	32	14	11	17
(N)	(319)	(182)	(133)	(328)	(187)	(136)

P = SAYE share-option-scheme participants
NP = Non-participants

Reference to table 11.3, which covers only the three firms with SAYE schemes, allows a comparison of views between participants and non-participants in the share purchase offer for this question. There are differences between the two groups, but they are extremely small. Moreover, they are not in the direction which would be predicted by any claim that participants should have a more unitarist view of the firm: only 5 per cent of participants selected the description according with such a view, as compared with 12 per cent of non-participants.

As we turn to the question of trade-union power, it should be recalled that it has been a long-established feature of public-opinion surveys that a very large proportion see unions in general as having too much power. Among the employees of our five case studies, in total two-fifths took this view, a few less thought the level of power about right, and one-fifth thought it too low. Again the proportions varied somewhat, with just over half of both Bossguide and Norbrew employees adopting the 'too much power' view, compared with only a third in Fairbrush and Thistle, and two-fifths in Goodbake.

Table 11.4 Views on trade-union power in Britain generally and in own company compared

| | All SAYE Schemes | | | | | |
| | Britain generally | | | Own company | | |
	All%	P%	NP%	All%	P%	NP%
Too much power	39	48	30	7	9	4
About right	35	32	39	64	68	57
Too little power	21	18	25	27	21	33
Don't know	4	3	5	3	1	6
(N)	(401)	(222)	(173)	(389)	(221)	(162)

P = SAYE share-option-scheme participants
NP = Non-participants

Table 11.4 allows comparison of participants and non-participants in the companies with SAYE schemes. This time participants display somewhat different views as a group to non-participants, and in a direction which would be predicted by those who would argue participation in a share scheme weakens support for trade unionism. Thus participants are markedly more likely to see unions as having too much power, and correspondingly less likely than non-participants to feel they have the right amount or too little power.

If we turn to consider the responses to general statements about management, we are again struck by the absence of strong evidence that those who purchase shares do so because they hold a more middle-class or managerial view of the world. Across the entire sample of employees in all our case studies, a clear majority, repeated in all the case-study firms, disagreed that management know what is best and should be left to make decisions (66 per cent overall), and that workers should never strike for reasons of loyalty to the company (71 per cent overall). There was strong agreement in each study that a good management should consult (90 per cent overall). The other statements brought less uniform reactions, with 50 per cent overall disagreeing that management have the welfare of their employees at heart, 49 per cent agreeing that management treat employees as numbers, and 58 per cent disagreeing that people like themselves had no chance to use their abilities.

The statements are set out in full in table 11.5 which separates out once more respondents from the case-study firms with SAYE schemes and compares participant and non-participant responses therein. The unitarization hypothesis would predict greater support among participants for the first, second, and fifth statements, more frequent rejection of the fourth and sixth, and possibly (if the inclination to trust management is taken as contrary to the perceived desirability of consultation) of the third. Each of these expectations is fulfilled, but in most cases by a margin so small that, even if one were to attribute the differences to participation itself, it would be necessary to conclude that only a very small proportion of participants were being influenced thereby. Indeed, for every question the similarities of response between the two groups are far more notable than the differences.

Table 11.5 Views of SAYE share-option-scheme participants and non-participants towards various general statements of management–employee relations compared

Statement	All SAYE schemes					
	Agree		Disagree		No opinion	
	P%	NP%	P%	NP%	P%	NP%
In the end management knows best and employees should let them make the decisions	32	21	64	71	7	8
Workers should never strike for reasons of loyalty to the company and management	19	14	72	76	9	10
A good management always consults its workforce	89	91	9	7	1	2
Management tend to treat people like me as numbers	48	59	48	35	4	6
Most managers have their employees welfare at heart	39	35	47	56	14	9
People like me have no opportunity to use their real abilities at work	32	33	60	53	8	14

P = SAYE share-option-scheme participant maximum N = 226
NP = Non-participant maximum N = 177

Such differences as we have discovered in this comparison of SAYE participants and non-participants have been small and fail to confirm any marked and sustained tendency to view labour-management relations in general differently. This is all the more striking a finding, given that even the discovery of such a relationship might readily have been accounted for in the different profiles of the two groups and their self-selection for share purchase. As such, it implies that the decision to participate in the SAYE schemes was mainly associated with factors other than prior ideological stance; it certainly allows little space for claims that share ownership is instrumental in changing ideology.

It may be, however, that the claims for ownership could migrate to focus on attitudes to employee relations and views of management in the employing concern itself. In fact, it would be possible to draw some implications from the views on management and enterprise control which we have just examined, but it is easier and more effective to attend directly to the hypothetical argument that employees who purchase shares will have a more favourable and unitarist view of their employer.

Share purchase and perceptions of the employer

For this aspect of the analysis we can turn first to the second parts of two questions reported on in the previous section. Respondents were asked to consider union power and the nature of labour–management relations in their own company. On the latter, previous research had suggested that employees are more liable to see conflict as prevalent in their own workplace than in enterprises generally (Brown *et al.* 1972; Ramsay 1982).

In all five of our case studies, however, respondents were more likely to see management and employees as on opposite sides in Britain generally than in their own company. Overall, only 13 per cent felt that interests were divided in their own company (compared to 31 per cent for Britain generally), and 29 per cent saw interests as shared (8 per cent). None the less a clear majority perceived a combination of shared and conflicting interests (58 as against 61 per cent for Britain generally). Whether this result marks a change of atmosphere in the 1980s, the overall management style of these companies, or something about financial participation schemes in particular, is largely a matter for conjecture: we can only examine the last possibility here. As table 11.3 above shows, participants are more likely to endorse the unitary view of interests in their own company, and less so to support the oppositional one. The differences are once again extremely marginal, however.

If we turn to the evaluation of trade-union power, it is intriguing that on this subject respondents do confirm earlier research (see e.g. Cannon 1967; Parkin 1971; Hill 1976; Ramsay 1982) which suggested that the acceptance of media images of over-mighty unions elsewhere would not be borne out by local experience. In every firm where unions existed (i.e. all of the case studies but Bossguide), employees were far less likely to see that union (or those unions) as having too much power in the company than in Britain generally. Overall the figures were 6 per cent 'too much power' (40 per cent Britain generally), 61 per cent 'about right' (37 per cent), and 30 per cent 'too little' (19 per cent). As table 11.4 shows, once again SAYE participants differed from non-participants in the predicted direction, but only marginally, so that only 9 per cent even of participants thought unions had too much power in their organizations.

In neither of these instances does the pattern of views for participants diverge from that of non-participants on judgements involving their own company to a greater extent than for Britain generally, so the possibility from which this section took its departure has thus far found no support. A more rigorous test involves direct questions concerning particular features of the employment relationship, however. For this purpose, respondents were asked to evaluate their employer overall and on a number of dimensions.

In general it was noticeable that evaluations were markedly more favourable concerning the company overall as an employer than on particular matters, with only job security (in three of the five case-study companies) showing comparable levels of 'above average' ratings. This pattern is also apparent in table 11.6 which covers only the three firms with SAYE schemes. Apart from job security, only pay receives a sizeable 'above average' rating (and then primarily at the 'little above average' level rather than 'well above'). The comparison between participants and non-participants repeats the now familiar configuration of a marginally more favourable evaluation of the company by the former. Such differences are submerged by the scale of the differences in the attitudes of all employees to specific employment characteristics.

Table 11.6 SAYE participants and non-participants: views of company (percentages)

View of company	Very good/ well above average		Moderately good/ a little above average		Average		Rather poor/ a little below average		Very poor/ well below average	
	P	NP	P	NP	P	NP	P	NP	P	NP
Overall as employer	39	31	38	38	21	22	2	6	0	2
on pay	3	1	35	29	41	41	17	20	4	9
on management openness	3	4	16	13	45	35	23	32	13	16
on management skill	6	8	17	15	57	45	14	19	5	13
on chances to get on	4	2	18	17	38	41	26	27	13	13
on job security	27	34	42	34	26	26	3	2	2	5
on employee participation decisions	3	3	14	7	36	39	18	24	29	27

P = Participants
NP = Non-participants

A consideration of the three cases from which these results are derived reveals that in Norbrew and Thistle the above pattern is confirmed; in Thistle, participants in the SAYE scheme actually seemed more critical than non-participants at times. In Goodbake, the marginal nature of differences between the two groups holds for the Scotcake side, but in the Breadline subsidiary participants are markedly more favourable in their opinions of the firm. This last divergence followed almost exactly the differences emerging from a comparison of management and manual respondents, however.

It is further worth remarking that the results of this question demonstrate that, even where financial participation is operated, companies are far from automatically regarded as open or participative on other dimensions. In the total sample, only 18 per cent rated their employers above average on participation in decisions, and only 23 per cent similarly on management openness. If there is a management style of employee relations favouring the adoption of financial participation then, its impact on employees seems nugatory.

Employees and share-ownership schemes

In order to illuminate the apparent lack of impact of financial participation schemes on employee attitudes, it seems logical to examine their views of the schemes themselves, and their reasons for participation or non-participation. We can usefully begin by considering views on ownership and control in general. Across the sample, 31 per cent agreed employees rather than shareholders should receive profits, and 26 per cent that employees with shares should elect management, leaving clear majorities against these radical, non-managerial views. Meanwhile, 39 per cent took the more managerial line that employees should share losses as well as profits, and only 26 per cent supported the more ambiguously liberal statement that employees should own the companies they work for. The patterns of response were fairly similar in the three companies with SAYE schemes, though there were some greater divergences with the other two cases.

Table 11.7 Views of SAYE share-option-scheme participants and non-participants towards ownership and control issues compared

Statement	All SAYE schemes					
	Agree		Disagree		No opinion	
	P%	NP%	P%	NP%	P%	NP%
Profits should belong to employees not shareholders	27	39	62	46	11	16
Employees with shares should elect managers	21	28	70	59	9	14
Employees should own the companies they work for	24	25	59	57	17	18
Employees should share losses as well as profits	41	33	49	56	10	11

P   = (N = 219) SAYE share-option-scheme participant
NP = (N) = 174 Non-participant

Table 11.7 once more separates out the views of participants and non-participants in the SAYE scheme companies. A majority of both groups disagreed with all four statements. Non-participants were somewhat more likely to support the first two, more radical proposals; views were very similar on the more ambivalent third statement; and participants gave stronger backing to the more managerial fourth view. On this last result, it is noteworthy that as many as two-fifths of participants accept the logic of loss-sharing (though one could equally emphasize the 49 per cent who do not) – and that this applies also to one-third of non-participants who seem therefore to accept that their fellows who take profits in the good times should also properly bear risk. Lastly, it hardly needs to be said that once more differences between the two groups are relatively small.

The results so far are not readily consistent with participants having ideological or other strong attitudinal reasons for participating. An examination of reasons given by respondents for their decision to enter the SAYE scheme or not lends credence to this supposition. Figure 11.1 shows the reasons endorsed by participants for their involvement. The question is not as discriminatory as one would like, since nearly all the supplied reasons are checked as at least 'quite important' by a large majority, but an examination of the 'very important' category does provide contrasts. From this it will be seen that the two most important reasons given are low risk and financial rewards. Some way behind these come facility of saving and of buying shares. Least significance is attached to having a stake in the company, or a part in the company's future. Thus the highest ratings go to essentially financial or instrumental motivations, while the lowest go to the attitudinal, involvement-oriented options.

An examination of reasons for non-participation shows the reverse side of the same coin. The most prominent reason, given by 44 per cent, was an inability to afford involvement, while a further 20 per cent indicated lack of sufficient knowledge. Positive objections on specific grounds, including risk as well as an aversion to shareholding, accounted for only 11 per cent of responses. This finding is consistent with the income profile of participation in SAYE reported earlier. The central role of this factor was confirmed individually in each of our case studies with SAYE schemes and was reinforced by our interviews in each company to explore our findings in greater depth. It was also apparent in the share-option scheme in Bossguide, where the attractions from a high accrual rate in the notional share value were powerful. In that case, however, an additional factor seems to have been that an offer of options was seen as indicative of a positive top-management assessment of a member of staff, and acceptance was seen as a mark of personal commitment to the firm for consultants, which in turn might be reflected in their internal career prospects.

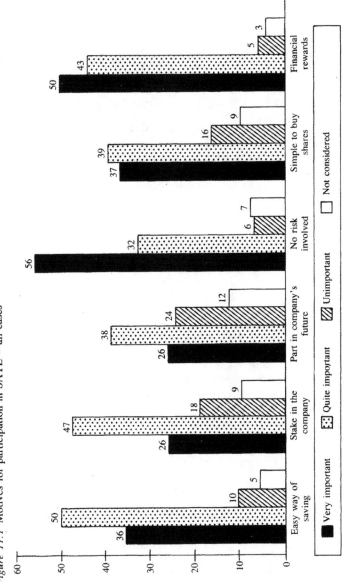

Figure 11.1 Motives for participation in SAYE – all cases

It is worth recording that share ownership was not confined to their companies for some of our sample. In all (across all five case studies) 27 per cent reported owning shares outside the company, and of these almost half (47 per cent) said they had bought shares before their company's scheme commenced.

Employee assessment of financial participation

The take-up and retention of shares obtained through an option scheme provide one measure of the attraction of a scheme. As yet, for many schemes started in recent years, not even the first echelons of employees opting into Inland Revenue schemes are yet able to make any decisions about what to do with their options. Among our case studies, in Norbrew retentions among the first group to reach the end of the five-year savings period had been high in the short time before our study at least. Almost all had exercised the option to take shares (unsurprisingly as the value of the shares had risen almost threefold since the original offer), and many groups had retained all the shares. Only manual workers (where 44 per cent had made significant disposals) and, interestingly, management (where one-third had done likewise) broke from this pattern at all. In Thistle, too few had been able to exercise options to bear analysis. In Goodbake, 75 per cent had opted for shares, and capital gains made were typically very high, with the earliest contributors almost five times to the good on their original commitment.

Despite these figures, the auguries for the achievement of the most prominent objectives expressed by management for financial participation, namely a change of attitudes entailing greater loyalty, commitment, and awareness of the need for management policies, have not been good in the runes cast by the above findings. The portents are generally confirmed by the results of our question-seeking reactions to a series of statements encapsulating different possible outcomes of schemes. Table 11.8 sets out the findings for participants and non-participants. Given the importance of these assessments in the context of the wider claims concerning financial participation which we recalled in our introduction, we will also pass comment on the overall judgements. The discussion below is thematized roughly according to the broad categories of management objectives for schemes which we identified in our research.[2]

The *incentive* effect can be assessed through responses to statements (1) to (5). The idea that hard work would be linked to rewards was accepted by 51 per cent of the respondents across all the case studies, including those with schemes other than SAYE, and rejected by 34 per cent. Table 11.8 shows that participants were rather more likely to accept this view than non-participants. Meantime the risk of lost earnings is discounted (44 per cent disagreeing and 37 per cent agreeing overall),

197

and by both groups in the companies with SAYE schemes. The participants in the latter disagreed on a 5:1 ratio, whereas non-participants split only 2:1. Since the risks of losses from SAYE are very small (until the decision actually to purchase shares is taken), this is a reasonable assessment, but carries few necessary implications for other types of scheme.

Figure 11.8 Views of SAYE share-option-scheme participants and non-participants towards various statements about experience of profit-sharing compared

| Statement | | All SAYE schemes | | | | | |
| | | Agree | | Disagree | | No opinion | |
		P%	*NP%*	*P%*	*NP%*	*P%*	*NP%*
(1)	If I work hard I know I can share in the results	53	40	37	32	10	28
(2)	There are better ways of improving benefits	43	44	23	18	34	38
(3)	Just another kind of bonus	47	43	44	27	9	31
(4)	Employees risk losing part of their earnings	14	23	71	41	15	35
(5)	As you cannot predict the bonus you cannot plan spending	46	46	36	22	18	33
(6)	It has made me less likely to move to another job	44	30	46	36	11	33
(7)	I am more likely to notice if my colleagues are not pulling their weight	28	32	58	38	14	31
(8)	Made me more aware of the problems which management faces	33	27	47	34	20	30
(9)	Enabled me to participate more in the way the company works	27	21	60	42	13	38
(10)	Employees should have more say in fixing the profit share	29	45	50	24	21	30

P = SAYE share-option-scheme participant (maximum N = 215)
NP = Non-participant (maximum N = 136)

The other responses relating to financial incentives were less positive concerning the effects of schemes. A strong majority of those expressing an opinion across the entire sample (45 to 21 per cent) agreed that there are better ways of improving benefits, and in the companies with SAYE this was accepted by both participants and non-participants. Overall, a majority agreed that their scheme amounted to just another kind of bonus (47 to 37 per cent), and a clearer majority accepted that unpredictable bonuses undermined planning of expenditure (51 to 28 per cent). If we return to the participants in SAYE schemes, they prove to be fairly evenly split on the dismissal of the arrangement as another type of bonus, indicating a large proportion who accept this; non-participants were more likely to agree. A majority of both groups agreed on the problems of bonus unpredictability, though one-third of participants did not accept this.

Other motivational issues are covered by items (6) and (7). Overall, a majority (44 to 37 per cent) of those expressing opinions disagreed that their company's scheme(s) had made them less likely to change jobs. In the SAYE companies, both groups were evenly divided on this – hence for every participant who feels less likely to move, another feels unaffected.

Overall, 49 per cent disagreed and only 31 per cent agreed that financial participation schemes had made them more likely to notice whether colleagues were pulling their weight. In the SAYE cases, contrary to expectations from most management theories favouring financial participation, participants were *more* likely to disagree, with almost three-fifths rejecting the notion. This brings us to the *attitudinal* aspects of schemes, covered here by item (8). Our research on management objectives (Baddon *et al.* 1989) indicates that this is the area of greatest management aspiration and optimism. Many of the findings above already suggest that attitudes are much less influenced in a unitarist direction than these expectations would allow, and the finding overall on awareness reinforces this impression: 43 per cent disagreed and only 30 per cent agreed.[3] In the SAYE cases, this pattern is reaffirmed, but once again participants are actually more inclined to disagree than non-participants, rather than the reverse.

Finally, we can consider the question of control. Overall opinions were fairly divided on whether employees should have more say in fixing any share in profits (38 per cent thought so, 39 per cent not). In the SAYE schemes, participants clearly rejected this view, while non-participants equally clearly supported it, providing perhaps the clearest division of opinion between the two groups that we encountered. This does imply a preparedness to accept management decisions by participants which provides, perhaps, some mild comfort for managerial perceptions of financial participation.

The idea that there is a link from financial participation in practice to wider involvement in company decisions is strongly rejected overall (52 to 26 per cent),[4] a rejection echoed by both groups in companies with SAYE, and more strongly by participants than by non-participants. This is a conclusion which all aspects of our case-study research tended to confirm, and it was reinforced by the almost total exclusion of trade unions from negotiation or other involvement in the design or operation of schemes.

Throughout our research we found little opposition to and many positive evaluations of the idea of financial participation among employees, in SAYE and other forms. In the case studies with cash-based profit-sharing, for example, 66 per cent approved of the schemes unconditionally, and a further 27 per cent did so with some reservations (these often concerning the system of distribution), while only 1 per cent were opposed. Yet the tendency to equate the approval of a concept, or even of schemes in practice, with the achievement of the popularized effects claimed for such arrangements is hasty to say the least (Ramsay and Haworth, 1984). The chain of effects runs from idea to scheme, to employee opinion thereof, to nature and degree of effect of this on outlook to effects on actual employee behaviour, to the effect of any change in behaviour on company performance. This chain is long and fragile at many points. Evaluation thus requires a more balanced, cautious and considered analysis.

Concluding comments

To recap, high hopes have been expressed for financial participation as a management instrument to generate and reinforce employee loyalty and commitment to the workplace through its predicted unitarist impact. Prominent among these is the anticipated transformation in values for employees who also become shareholders. The means by which this potential is assumed to translate into improved work performance have been outlined by Estrin (1986). The most pervasively predicted effect, and one which constitutes the central plank that links shareholder employees with productive efficiency and performance, concerns attitude; employee shareholders assume attitudes and opinions thought congruent with and directly related to their share ownership, which in turn generates beneficial effects for the employing organization, these ultimately rewarding the shareholder/employee in a virtuous circuit of mutual gain.

Our paper has attempted to examine the extent to which employee shareholding can be associated with those attitudinal stances predicted to mark out shareholder employees from non-shareholders. SAYE schemes provide an excellent opportunity for this observation owing to the requirement for employees to allocate a portion of personal wealth to the company scheme over a sustained period (which in itself also presupposes an element of pre-existing loyalty toward the company).

Certainly our research on management aims in our interviews and case-study programme confirms that diffuse expressions of loyalty and commitment provide the chief motivation behind the instigation of schemes which was almost always on the initiative of senior management. These general ambitions mean that very few companies monitor the performance of their share schemes in any meaningful way. In our case-study companies, for example, little attempt was made to analyse progress in terms of share acquisitions and disposals or through examination of labour statistics.

As we have shown, attitudinal differences between participants and non-participants across a range of criteria have been marginal, and in some instances barely discernible, notwithstanding the different profiles presented by the two groups. Participants tend to be male, white-collar, non-union employees, often with medium to long periods of service with their companies. Pay seems to be a crucial factor, influencing not just participation/non-participation, but also directly related to savings levels and, as far as can be judged from the small number of participants who have passed the five-year savings mark, to retentions or disposals of shares. In a similar vein, the most frequently expressed reason for non-participation was given as inability to pay.

It appears, therefore, that in contradistinction to management objectives, employee participation in SAYE schemes tended to be based more on financial opportunism than on company identification. Participants evaluate schemes in terms of material benefits and freedom from risk, rather than as an ideological expression of company attachment. In these terms, at least, it is doubtful whether share schemes make other than a marginal contribution to the development of unitarist values within the organisation. Our doubts grow when we examine the limited numbers as well as characteristics of employees who choose to participate in SAYE.

To what extent, if any, are we able to generalize our findings to other forms of share-ownership scheme? It could be argued that option schemes may trigger different employee responses than, for example, all-employee ADST schemes whose specific intent is to provide a blanket scheme which includes the great majority of employees within a company as an expression of corporate identification and of reward for shared endeavour. Yet our findings for all-employee programmes do not signal any great impact in terms of employee attitude, nor one markedly distinct from that charted for SAYE schemes. Nor did we find any great evidence of management discrimination in choosing schemes for their differential potential impact; it was the SAYE scheme at Goodbake, for example, which was introduced with the professed intent of 'trying to create the concept of a commonwealth'.

Conversely, one might expect that, if we were to find evidence of employee conversion to unitarism, or a strengthening of existing ideology, then SAYE participants would be the exemplars. These employees would anticipate staying with the company long enough to benefit from their additional contributions, would be expected to exhibit sufficient commitment as to divert personal wealth into company shares, and interest in the company, coupled with desire for it to do well would be expected to be high. Most employee participants, however, tend to regard their scheme as 'just another kind of bonus', and display attitudes little different than their non-participating colleagues.

Implications for the management of companies can also be traced out. It is very unlikely that the combination of low participation rates, small individual shareholdings, and variable retention rates are going to pose any challenge to management in terms of shareholder influence. Further, the schemes themselves offer little scope for active participation in company affairs. We were unable to detect any noticeable move to 'employee participation' or diminution of management authority as a consequence of financial involvement. Most schemes, indeed, go to considerable lengths to insulate their financial participation arrangements from routine aspects of employee management.

Often financial participation schemes are initiated by senior management and co-ordinated within the finance function or by the company secretariat. Personnel departments tended to be charged merely with routine administration of schemes. The schemes are given little further publicity following the 'hype' which accompanies their introduction and subsequently are not given a high profile by management. The case studies demonstrate that financial participation rarely enters mainstream employee-relations activities, either through negotiation or by consultation. Forming no part of contractual terms and conditions of employment, the schemes are regarded by employee representatives as a management gratuity, appearing to offer no overt challenge to established bargaining procedures or to relations with their members. Consequently, scheme introduction is rarely marked by demonstrative or principled opposition by union representatives.

Finally, we can ask why the attitudinal effects of SAYE appear to be limited. First, if there is an 'ownership' effect (as has been suggested by American studies; see for example, Klein and Rosen 1986), the low contribution levels and small consequent bonuses which are typical appear insufficient to trigger it. Hence, there is little influence on orientations and opinion. Second, the workplace surveys indicate that the complexity of attitudes is such that one small 'bonus' is unlikely to make any great impact. Also seemingly contradictory attitudes can and do co-exist. It was not unusual to find apparent overall satisfaction with the company disaggregating into a number of dissatisfied components, but with one or two major factors (e.g. security) helping to determine the assessment of overall satisfaction. Participant views gave no indication that SAYE should be regarded as one such major influence. One aspect of this ambiguity is that option schemes may also promote instrumental orientations, especially in an environment of profitable enterprise and in a materialistic culture. Ideology then may work towards reinforcing monetary values, with satisfaction contingent upon continuing company success.

Third, SAYE is detached from other features of organizational experience, chiefly as a consequence of management practice. Employees are not likely to associate the scheme with other organizational values, or therefore to judge the organization in a way substantially influenced by their involvement, in the absence of other and major changes in the way management not only purports to manage but is actually experienced as managing.

Notes

1 This paper arises from the findings of a larger research study funded by the Leverhulme Trust, to whom we express our appreciation.
2 It should be noted that where companies operated more than one scheme, this question did not ask respondents to distinguish the effects of the different schemes; thus the responses cannot be attributed to the effects of SAYE alone.
3 This is confirmed for other attitudinal responses; see, for example, Poole and Jenkins 1988.
4 The absence of such links has also been reported recently in a study conducted by Pryce and Nicholson 1988.

References

Baddon, L., Hunter, L.C., Hyman, J., Leopold, J., and Ramsay, H. (1987) *Developments in Profit-sharing and Employee Share Ownership*, Centre for Research in Industrial Democracy, Glasgow: University of Glasgow.

Baddon, L., Hunter, L.C., Hyman, J., Leopold, J., and Ramsay, H. (1989) *People's Capitalism? A Critical Analysis of Profit-sharing and Employee Share Ownership*, London: Routledge.

Bell, D.W. and Hanson, C.G. (1987) *Profit-sharing and Profitability*, London: Kogan Page.

Brown, R.K., Brannen, P., Cousins, J.M., and Samphier, M.L. (1972) 'The contours of solidarity: social stratification and industrial relations in shipbuilding', *British Journal of Industrial Relations*, X(1), March.

Cable, J., and Fitzroy, F. (1980) 'Co-operation and productivity: some evidence from West German experience', *Economic Analysis and Workers' Management*, vol. XIV.

Cannon, I.C. (1967) 'Ideology and occupational community: a study of compositors', *Sociology*, 1(2).

Copeman, G., Moore, P., and Arrowsmith, C. (1984) *Shared Ownership*, London: Gower.

Dewe, P., Dunn, S., and Richardson, R. (1988) 'Employee share option schemes: why workers are attracted to them', *British Journal of Industrial Relations*, XXVI(1).

Estrin, S., and Wadhwani, S. (1986) *Will Profit-sharing Work?*, London: Employment Institute, London School of Economics.

Fogarty, M.P. (1987) 'Share-ownership plans: employees' views', *Policy Studies*, 7, 3, January: 30–49.

Hill, S. (1976) *The Dockers: Class and Tradition in London*, London: Heinemann.

Klein, K., and Rosen, C. (1986) 'Employee stock ownership in the United States' in *International Yearbook of Organizational Democracy*, vol. III, New York: Wiley.

Millward, N., and Stevens, N. (1986) *British Workplace Industrial Relations 1980–1984*, Aldershot: Gower.

Parkin, F. (1971) *The Social Analysis of Political Order*, London: Paladin.

Poole, M. and Jenkins, G. (1988) 'How employees respond to profit sharing'. *Personnel Management*, July.

Pryce, V. and Nicholson, C. (1988) 'The problems and performance of employee ownership firms', *Employment Gazette*, June.

Ramsay, H.E. (1982) 'Participation for whom? A critical analysis of worker participation in theory and practice', PhD thesis, University of Durham.

Ramsay, H.E and Haworth, N. (1984) 'Worker capitalists? Profit-sharing, capital-sharing and juridical forms of socialism', *Economic and Industrial Democracy*, 5(3), August.

Richardson, R. and Nejad, A. (1986) 'Employee share ownerships in the UK – an evaluation', *British Journal of Industrial Relations*, XXIV(2), July.

Smith, G.R. (1986) 'Profit sharing and employee share ownership in Britain', *Employment Gazette*, September.

Chapter twelve

The impact of profit-sharing, worker participation, and share ownership on absenteeism and quits: some UK evidence

Nick Wilson[1] and Mike Peel

Introduction

High levels of labour turnover, represented in terms of (voluntary) quit rates, can impose considerable costs on firms and organizations. These include recruitment costs (e.g. the opportunity costs of those employees participating in the recruitment process), loss of output until replacements are found, formal and informal training costs, and, more indirectly, the negative effects on worker morale and productivity (see e.g. Freeman and Medoff 1984).

Labour absenteeism (voluntary or involuntary), like turnover, is costly for organizations for much the same reasons. Hence the costs associated with absenteeism include the direct or explicit costs in terms of lost output, expenditure on labour which is not supplied, and extra expenditure on cover workers; and the indirect or implicit costs associated with low employee morale and the increased costs emanating from management's attempts to implement controls (see e.g. Dilts, Deitsch, and Paul 1985).

In this paper we analyse variations in the average quit and absenteeism rates experienced by a random sample of 52 firms operating within a narrow product range of the UK engineering industry. Hence, we control for industry-specific characteristics, whilst attempting to isolate the determinants (or predictors) of quits and absenteeism in terms of firm-specific characteristics, at the same time controlling for labour-market conditions. We then focus on the impact of remuneration schemes (including fringe benefits and profit-sharing), the extent of employee involvement in decision-making, and the impact of union and other 'voice' mechanisms on temporary or permanent labour withdrawal. The richness of our data set enables us to control for a wide range of (previously neglected) variables which might affect quit and absenteeism rates (as suggested by the extant empirical/theoretical literature).

The remainder of this paper is organized as follows: In the second section we discuss the theory and evidence pertaining to temporary and permanent labour withdrawal. The third section (page 218) outlines our data and model specification, whilst the fourth (page 219) presents the empirical results on the determinants of quits and absenteeism. In the fifth (page 224), we investigate whether the processes resulting in temporary (absenteeism) and permanent (quits) withdrawal are related; more particularly, employing 'seemingly unrelated regression' techniques, we examine whether there is evidence of common factors (omitted variables) which appear to be correlated with both absenteeism and quits (i.e. which may be responsible for both temporary and permanent withdrawal). The final section (page 226) concludes with the salient points to emerge from the empirical analysis, together with an an outline of suggested areas for further research.

Theory and evidence on quits and absenteeism

In this section we discuss the key variables which have been shown to be related to turnover and absenteeism by previous research. But more specifically, we examine some of the implications relating to the impact of profit-sharing, share ownership (which we discuss in the context of the total remuneration package), and employee participation on employee retention. In particular, we investigate the hypothesis of the 'exit-voice trade-off' in the labour market, introduced by Hirschman (1970), and applied by Freeman and Medoff (1984). We do this by taking into account the effects of unions and the extent of employee participation in decision-making (see Spencer 1986). After developing our theoretical framework, we highlight the possible determinants of turnover and absenteeism, as suggested by previous work, which we include as control variables in our empirical analysis.

A full list of the explanatory variables used in this study (together with their definitions) is given in the appendix. Due to space constraints, we are only able to list the control variables and their expected influence on quits and absenteeism in this section (For a full discussion of the extant theoretical/empirical evidence pertaining to each variable, see Wilson and Peel 1989).

Unionization, employee involvement, and 'voice'

During recent years, the concept of the 'exit–voice trade-off' (Hirschman 1970) has been applied to the study of internal labour markets. In their pioneering paper, Freeman and Medoff (1984) extended Hirschman's thesis to suggest that unions may act to improve the productivity/performance of firms and thus the welfare of the economy as a whole. The exit-voice hypothesis states that a disgruntled worker has the option of temporarily or permanently quitting the firm (exit option) or, alternatively, articulating his grievance (voice option) if dissatisfied with his working conditions. Freeman and Medoff (1984) have argued that unions serve as an important vehicle for workers to express their wishes and to highlight workplace problems. If the exit–voice trade-off applies, then unionization should, *cet. par.*, reduce quits and absenteeism by making the voice option available.

The impact on quits

In their empirical investigations of the influence of unionization on quit rates, Freeman and Medoff (1984) find a strong negative correlation between unionization and quits, suporting their voice-option hypothesis. For US manufacturing data, both Pencavel (1977) and Freeman and Medoff (1984) report a significant negative relationship between the proportion of employees covered by collective bargaining in an industry and the industry quit rate. This is a relationship which holds even after controlling for wage rates (suggesting that unions do not simply lower quits by raising wages). For the UK, Stewart (1987) demonstrates that voluntary separations are lower among union members than non-union members. However, it could be argued that the effect of unionization (in the US) on quits may to a certain degree emanate from unions pursuing non-wage bargaining outcomes (e.g. improving fringe benefits or seniority based personnel policies). The costs associated with quitting are then higher for both employer and employee. However, as Metcalfe (1988:23) noted: 'It is possible, but unlikely, that the impact of these factors on turnover could be offset if unions lower search costs by providing information on jobs or because union membership gives access to a larger pool of jobs.'

A number of recent papers (Spencer 1986; Cotton 1980; and Florkowski 1987) have also suggested that employee participation, through organizational mechanism other than unions, may influence the rate of employee exits. Hence we incorporate a number of alternative channels of 'voice' and levels of employee participation into the model determining turnover. The hypothesis underlying this approach is that it is not solely the degree of representation of workers' interests by an intermediary institution *per se* that determines work satisfaction and the inclination to quit, but rather their perceived influence and the individual rights of workers at the workplace. Hence the exit-voice hypothesis can be extended to consider organizational settings where workers have the opportunity to participate in decisions concerning their immediate workplace and participate financially in the firms' profits. The propensity to quit, we argue, will be reduced in such a climate (irrespective of union representation).

The impact on absenteeism

Many of the arguments applied to the determinants of quits also have

207

relevance for the determinants of absenteeism. For instance, Hirschman (1970) suggested, in his exit-voice loyalty model (EVL), that workers could 'exit' permanently (quits) or temporarily (absenteeism) from an organization.

In relation to temporary exit via absenteeism, Allen (1984), after controlling for a number of othr factors, tested the EVL model empirically by assessing the impact of trade-union membership on absenteeism. He noted, however, that the a priori effect of union membership was ambiguous; since, irrespective of voice, union members may exhibit a higher propensity to be absent because – through union 'protection' – they may face smaller penalties from management and/or because managers in union plants may have less flexibility to tailor work schedules to satisfy individual worker preferences. Allen's empirical evidence certainly suggested this latter effect dominated his estimated model.

As noted earlier, Florkowski (1987: 629) has argued that, although as the mode of participation becomes more formal and widespread in a firm, employees should feel they exert greater influence in decision-making, it is actually: 'the quality of participation in decision-making which is expected to affect employees' perceived influence on decision-making'. Hence a measure of perceived (*de facto*) involvement in participation is emphasized as being relevant (see below), in addition to *de jure* formal participation modes (e.g. quality circles, works councils, union-management committees).

Hence our analysis incorporates measures of union presence and information on formal and informal mechanisms of employee involvement and communication channels within, and outside, union settings. In addition, we construct, from employee interview responses, a measure of perceived employee involvement in decision-making which categorizes firms along a scale from low to high participation. In line with the above rationale, we expect to observe a negative relationship between this participation scale and quit and absenteeism rates.

Financial incentives, profit-sharing, and share ownership

In this section we examine the implications of all-employee profit-sharing and share-option schemes on quit and absenteeism rates. We do this within the context of the total employee-remuneration package (i.e. wages, bonuses, and welfare benefits).

Most recent studies of labour turnover give cognizance to the employer's utility function, manifested by competitive wages and training programmes, as being important determinants of quits.

We therefore assumed that workers plan quits on the basis of a weighted combination of both the monetary and non-monetary rewards attached to their current employment – compared to those offered by alternative (available) employment. We also note that wages include the returns from specific human-capital investment. The higher this is, the higher is the expected wage rate, since human-capital theory predicts a sharing of the costs and returns of specific investment (Oi 1964). Clearly specific skills are worthless to an organization if a worker leaves his employment; hence high investment in specific human capital should act to increase the wage rate and decrease the probability of voluntary quits.

Another important dimension of workers' remuneration package is the level or proportion of fringe benefits (including pensions and other welfare schemes, bonuses, and share options). Freeman and Medoff (1984) noted that most existing datasets do not fully control for union-monopoly effects (a point we return to later). The implication is, the higher are the fixed costs of employment, the lower is the expected quit rate; since it is in the interests of both employers and employees for workers to continue in their present employment (see Hart 1987).

From various perspectives, a widespread interest in profit-sharing and employee share ownership has been rekindled in recent years (see e.g. Blanchflower and Oswald 1987). This is at least partly attributable to possible productivity and efficiency enhancing characteristics of both employee involvement and the reconciliation of ownership with control (as exemplified by the success of co-operative labour-management relations).

Moreover, in a series of well publicized articles and a book, Weitz-man (1983, 1984, 1985a and b, 1986) has claimed that in profit-sharing he has found a remedy for the world economic problems. Hence it is largely macro-economic (employment) issues that have stimulated policy interventions, such as recent UK government schemes to encourage profit-related pay (HMSO 1986). However, micro-economic aspects, concerning the effects of profit-sharing on worker attitudes, loyalty, commitment, and ultimately (via reduced turnover) productivity have received less attention and have often been regarded as separate issues.

One would expect, however, that employees who take up share options are more likely to remain with the organization – but the argumentation may be fraught with complexities. As Dewe *et al.* (1988: 13) suggested:

> The option scheme gives preferential access to an asset, and the demand for it would therefore depend largely on the worker's assessment of its expected financial return, with due allowance for risk and the availability of finance. A necessary condition for joining the scheme would be that the workers expect to stay with the firm for at least five years, because otherwise they would not be able to exercise the option when it fell due.

In our sample, we can distinguish between firms with or without an all-employee share-option scheme, but we have no information relating to the extent to which employees take up these options, nor the frequency and timing of individual take-up levels.

Estrin and Wilson (1988), analysing the present sample, found a significant difference in the means of labour turnover and absenteeism between sub-samples of profit-sharing and non-profit-sharing firms.

However, this result is somewhat at odds with Cable's (1986) earlier study of German firms, where he found that labour turnover was actually higher in profit-sharing firms. It is possible that this inconsistency is explained by differences in the type of firm which introduced profit-sharing. In the German sample, profit-sharing occurred in much larger firms which relied more heavily on mass-production techniques. Indeed, profit-sharing appeared to complement, rather than act as a substitute for, individualized incentives to motivate workers in these relatively less attractive workplaces.

In relation to absenteeism, several previous studies have found an inverse relationship between satisfaction with pay and absenteeism (Mowday *et al.* 1982). Smith (1977), for example, found absenteeism was negatively correlated with wages. However, in relation to pay rates, Allen (1984: 334) has noted 'the effects of wages on absence rates cannot be unambiguously predicted. It will depend on whether the substitution effect of higher wages (lowering absences) dominates the income effect (raising absences).'

For example, through the substitution effect, the availability of overtime has been found to exert a positive influence on absenteeism (Martin 1971). Where, however, pay rewards are explicitly tied to attendance, absenteeism has (not surprisingly) been found to be significantly lower (Lawler 1971). Furthermore, two studies (Taylor 1967; Taylor, Pocock, and Sergeant 1972) found that shift workers exhibited significantly lower rates of absenteeism than day workers.

A number of theoretical commentators have argued that both profit-related pay and share-ownership schemes may act to reduce absenteeism through their impact on employee commitment (Florkowski 1987); employment involvement/satisfaction (Long 1980); and through employees' psychological and financial motivation (Hammer *et al.* 1981; Mowday *et al.* 1982).

Some indirect support for these hypothesized relationships has been found in recent survey evidence. For example, Bell and Hanson (1984: 26), who interviewed 2,703 employees in twelve UK companies, concluded: 'profit-sharing does significantly improve attitudes and employee views of the company.' Furthermore, Poole and Jenkins (1988: 38) discovered, from a survey of 2,000 employees in twelve firms, that in relation to other schemes employee share-option schemes had a 'marginally greater effect on overall satisfaction at work and communication between management and workforce'.

Direct empirical support is found in two studies of individual firms, both of which found absenteeism declined following the introduction of worker share ownership (Rhodes and Steers 1980; Hammer *et al.* 1981). In the latter study, the authors reported (p. 68) that it was 'ownership *per se*, rather than the amount owned (by employees), that affects perceptions and attitudes'.

Control variables

As noted earlier, pressure of space permits us to list only the expected influence of the control variables (defined in the appendix) on quits and absenteeism (table 12.1). A full treatment is given in Wilson and Peel (1989), and full references are given in this paper.

Variables denoted (+) (−) indicate that the weight of evidence suggests the variables will exert a positive/negative impact. A variable denoted (?) indicates that existing evidence suggests that the variable is an important determinant of quits/absenteeism; but that the influence of the variable is not clear cut.

Table 12.1 Expected influence of control variables

Control variables	Expected influence	
	Quits	Absenteeism
Regional unemployment (UNEM)	−	−
Based in South of England (SOUTH)	?	−
Firm size (TOT)	?	+
No. of plants (PLANT)	?	−
Flow production (FLOW)	?	?
Intermediate technology (IT)	?	?
Proportion male (MALE)	?	?
Proportion blue collar (RATIO)	+	+
Proportion of apprentices (APPO)	−	?
Proportion of unskilled workers (UNSKILL)	+	+
Proportion overtime worked (OVER)	+	+
Proportion working shifts (SHIFT)	?	−
Proportion wage in piece rate (PIE)	?	−
Average wage rate (WAGE)	−	−
Training expenditure (TRT)	−	−
Level (and proportion) of fringe benefits (FRINGE)	−	−
Workers per supervisor (SPAN)	?	?

Data and model specifications

Estimating framework

The estimating framework developed in the previous section was implemented for our random sample of 52 UK engineering firms. Data for each firm was available for 5 years (1978–82) which provides us with 260 observations when pooled. For the absenteeism equations, three firms were omitted from the sample. These firms experienced a strike in at least one of the five years, and we were unable to separate out the working days lost due to absenteeism/sickness for these years. This leaves 245 observations for estimating the absenteeism equations.

Our analysis of inter-firm quit/absenteeism rate differentials centres around the following linear regression models:

QUITS = f(L, EARN, SIZE, TECH, UNION, PART, ECON)
ABSENTEEISM = f(L, EARN, SIZE, TECH, UNION, PART, ECON)

Where L is a vector of labour-input variables representing labour force composition and quality; EARN consists of variables measuring earnings, incentive payments, profit-sharing, employee share ownership, and fringe benefits; UNION includes various measures of unionization and union presence in the firm; TECH and SIZE are vectors of independent variables which control for the predominant type of technology, production methods, and firm size; PART attempts to control for perceived and actual employee participation in enterprise decision-making; and ECON for the economic climate in which the firm operates.

Our dependent variable (QUIT) is specified as the ratio of the number of employees giving notice to total employees in a given year (see Mobley 1987).

For the absenteeism equation, the dependent variable (ABSENT) is the average annual number of working days lost per employee – excluding days lost through industrial stoppages. A few previous researchers (see e.g. Hammer *et al.* 1981) have been able to report the determinants of both voluntary and involuntary absenteeism rates. This proved impossible in the current study, since only a small minority of firms had this disaggregated information readily available. In any event, except in cases of obvious (usually lengthy) illness, short absences – which are recorded as illness (involuntary) – may be *de facto* voluntary in nature (see e.g. Dilts *et al.* 1985). Furthermore, we would argue that the incidences of 'genuine' illness should not differ significantly between firms in the same industrial sector.

We argued earlier that it is the level of quasi-fixed costs of employment per employee that should be negatively related to quit rates. The data problems inherent in accurately distinguishing between fixed and variable labour costs may account for the variables' poor performance in the various reported regression equations.

PS, PVA and SHARES are the three dummy variables representing the existence of a profit/value added sharing scheme (PVA); the

212

existence of a share-ownership scheme covering all employees (SHARES); and a composite variable (PS), representing the existence of an all-employee share-ownership scheme and/or profit-sharing scheme.

Firm size could be measured in a number of ways, asset values, total numbers of employees, sales or output (value added). These were all used as proxies for size, with little difference to the reported results. In the event it was decided that size as measured by employees (TOT) was the most relevant measure for the purpose of our analysis.

Technology has been regarded as an important factor in explaining turnover and other measures of employee dissatisfaction such as absenteeism (Wilson and Peel 1989). To incorporate differences in the production base of firms in our sample, a dummy variable for predominantly flow production (FLOW) was constructed – the zero category being predominantly batch. A second dummy variable representing intermediate technology (IT) was constructed from survey information on the type and mix of machine tools operated in each plant (see Wilson 1985).

The industrial sector under consideration is highly unionized and is characterized by multi-unionism. Our sample firms, for instance, exhibit an average union density of 78 per cent – with more than one shop-floor and staff union typically present.

So far as union presence is concerned, our survey data contains a number of alternative variables to capture union effects. These include the number of unions and shop stewards at plant level and the extent of formal committees and channels of union-management communication. In this analysis we proxy union presence by the percentage of employees belonging to a trade union (PERUN), the number of shop-floor and staff unions (NOUNH, NOUNS) and the existence or otherwise of union–management committees (UMC). In the course of our estimation we experimented with a number of other union variables (e.g. the number of shop stewards per worker and the existence of a closed shop, UNION). In addition to entering several individual indicators of union presence into the equation, we also include an alternative composite index of union presence (INDEX) as described below.

In this analysis we use the variables WC (works council), JOBEVAL (the existence of a joint job-evaluation scheme), and SPAN (the number of workers per supervisor) amongst our variables representing employee involvement. In addition, a 'participation' dummy variable (PART) was included in the models (below).

In experimental regression runs we encountered multicollinearity problems, particularly with the EARN vector of variables. From simple correlations it was evident that WAGE, PERUN, INDEX, FRINGE, and FRINGE1 were all negatively related to quits (as expected from our earlier argumentation). WAGE was highly (positively) correlated with our measure of the level of employee fringe benefits; and unionization in turn was positively correlated with fringe benefits, wages, and profit-sharing. To attempt to minimize this multicollinearity, fringe benefits (which consistently failed to find significance in our regression runs) were omitted from final specifications.

Indices of union presence and participation

As noted earlier, we proxy union presence by the percentage of employees belonging to a trade union (PERUN), the number of shop-floor and staff unions (NOUNH, NOUNS), and the existence or otherwise of union-management committees (UMC). In addition to entering these separate indicators of unionization into the equations, we constructed an alternative index of union presence (which is a linear combination of the various components). This index (INDEX) is defined as:

$$I = \sum_{i=1}^{n} \varphi \, V_i$$

where V_i is the component, φ is the weight attached to V_i and there are n components. The index is constructed as a linear combination of the V_i using the weights implied by the first principal components of the variance–covariance matrix of the various constituents of the index. Four components are used to form the index: PERUN, UNION, NOUNH, NOUNS. The first principal component accounted for some 47 per cent of the variation in the four variables. The strongest measure of union presence occurs for a firm with 100-per-cent union membership, a closed shop, and multiple staff and shop-floor unions.

Hence, INDEX is included as an alternative to entering the several union indicators simultaneously. As noted earlier, if unions are an effective channel of 'voice' then we would expect high levels of unionization (INDEX) to be associated with lower turnover.

So far we have outlined the direct and indirect channels of consultation and communication between management and shop floor. The last section of our questionnaire attempted to discover the effects of these internal systems in practice by measuring the degree of perceived employee involvement in decision-making. Separate interviews were conducted with a senior manager, a representative from the production supervisory level and shop-floor representatives. We specified five decision-making issues and asked for respondents' perceptions of how each issue was dealt with on the last occasion it arose. This enabled us to gauge which issues were dealt with solely by management (with or without prior information or opinion from the workforce); which issues required further consultation; and which issues were

214

subject to a joint decision-making process (see Wilson 1985).

Finally, respondents were asked whether they felt that within the firm, employee involvement (generally) had increased, decreased, or not noticeably changed within the last five years.

Following Cable (1985) we used Guttman scale analysis to derive an overall scale of employee involvement from these survey responses. The resulting variable G3 is an ordinal scale (ranging from score 0 to 5) which is used to partition the sample into high- and low-participation categories. This was done on the basis of G3 > 2 being the high participation category; in effect a participation dummy variable (PART) was formed for inclusion in the estimated models.

Model determining quits

The model determining turnover was specified as a linear regression equation with the dependent variable the proportion of total employees giving notice per annum (annual quits). The stochastic specification takes the form:

$$\begin{aligned}
QUIT = a &+ b_1MALE + b_2UNSKILL + b_3APPO + b_4RATIO \\
&+ b_5OVER + b_6WAGE + b_7PIE + b_8PS \text{ (PVA or} \\
&\text{SHARES)} + b_9TOT + b_{10}PLANT + b_{11}FLOW \\
&+ b_{12}INDEX + b_{13}PART + b_{14}WC + b_{15}JOBEVAL \\
&+ b_{16}SPAN + b_{17}UNEM + b_{18}SOUTH + b_{19} \, ERROR
\end{aligned}$$

Our theoretical expectations suggest that firms with a relatively high proportion of unskilled employees should experience higher voluntary quits; and variables proxying investment in human capital (APPO, TRT) should be negatively correlated with voluntary turnover. In the event TRT (training expenditure per employee) was never found to be a significant predictor in any of the estimated models and is omitted from the reported results.

Our earlier analysis suggested that training expenditure is clearly endogenous. It may, for instance, be higher than average in firms experiencing a high turnover rate (retraining) but, on the other hand, firms with lower turnover may be more willing to invest in workers who are expected to provide returns over a longer time horizon. In this respect, table 12.2 shows that TRT is positively correlated with quits but at a level which is not significantly different from zero.

We also incorporate into the empirical specification a variable reflecting the percentage of overtime hours worked (OVER). We argue that overtime is associated with capital-intensive, highly automated plants in our sample and, in consequence, is expected to be positively associated with quit rates. In addition, the availability of overtime may reduce quit costs for firms, since it extends the period over which specific investments are discounted. On the other hand, firms with overtime availability presumably provide higher-total-earnings opportunities for employees and this may serve to reduce turnover. Hence,the association between overtime and quits may be considered ambiguous.

The vector of variables under EARN include our profit-sharing/share-ownership dummies (PVA, SHARES, PS) and remuneration measures (WAGE, PIE). From our earlier survey, we expect these variables to be negatively associated with quits (other than PIE, whose sign is ambiguous).

Fringe benefits (FRINGE, FRINGE1) never entered the regressions significantly and had only a negligible effect on the coefficients of the other explanatory variables. This may be explained by our inability to measure the fixed costs of employment (as discussed earlier), or may be due to multicollinearity problems with the variables under EARN.

From simple correlations (table 12.2) we note that WAGE, FRINGE, FRINGE1, and INDEX are all negatively related to turnover (WAGE was positively correlated with fringe benefits, and union presence was positively associated with fringe benefits, wages, and profit-sharing).

A South of England dummy (SOUTH) and regional unemployment rates (UNEM) are included in the model to capture time and regional variations in economic conditions. Unemployment is expected to reduce the propensity to quit – as McCormick (1988: 92) has noted:

> We have found evidence that the share of new jobs secured by those already employed is virtually unaffected by a rise in the proportion of the labour force that is unemployed. However, a rise in unemployment does discourage quits into unemployment.

Turning to employee 'voice' and participation, we include the union presence indicator (INDEX) and the individual union density variables in separate specifications. If unions are an effective channel of 'voice', then we would expect high levels of unionization to be associated with lower turnover. Further, following Spencer (1986) we would expect a significant relationship between the total number of voice mechanisms that an organization has and its voluntary turnover rate.

Hence, work's councils (WC), job evaluation schemes (JOBEVAL), and the level of worker supervision (SPAN) are all expected to be negatively associated with quits (the latter on the grounds that, *cet. par.*, the lower is job autonomy, the greater is the propensity to quit).

The binary worker-participation composite variable (PART) was included in alternative specifications of the turnover model; since as Price (1977) has noted, in his extensive review of the literature, successive 'amounts' of participation result in successively lower 'amounts' of turnover (i.e. a cumulative effect).

Model determining absenteeism

The linear regression equation for absenteeism, with the dependent variable the number of annual working days lost (voluntary and involuntary) per employee, is given by:

$$
\begin{aligned}
\text{ABSENT} = c &+ d_1\text{MALE} + d_2\text{APPO} + d_3\text{UNSKILL} + d_4\text{SHIFT} + d_5\text{TRT} \\
&+ d_6\text{WAGE} + d_7\text{PIE} + d_8\text{PS (PVA/SHARES)} \\
&+ d_9\text{TOT} + d_{10}\text{FLOW} + d_{11}\text{PLANT} \\
&+ d_{12}\text{INDEX} + d_{13}\text{PART} + d_{14}\text{JOBEVAL} + d_{15}\text{WC} \\
&+ d_{16}\text{SOUTH} \\
&+ \text{error}
\end{aligned}
$$

In line with our previous analysis, we would expect TRT and MALE to be negatively related to absenteeism, whilst UNSKILL is expected to have a positive sign.

Furthermore, there is existing evidence (Taylor 1967; Taylor *et al.* 1972) that shift workers have significantly lower rates of absenteeism than their fellow day workers. In consequence, we expect SHIFT to be negatively associated with absenteeism.

The effects of earnings on absenteeism is not so clear cut and appears to depend on workers' income–leisure trade-off. For instance, although we would a priori expect a negative sign on WAGE, it is possible that workers with higher earnings may pursue leisure opportunities by being absent more frequently.

For the (common) rationale explained in respect of quits, we anticipate that the financial and non-financial participation variables (SHARES, PVA, PS, PART, WC, JOBEVAL) will all be negatively associated with absenteeism. As noted earlier, voice mechanisms are expected to lower absenteeism, though the expected impact of union presence is ambiguous (Allen 1984).

Univariate analysis

Table 12.2 reports simple correlation coefficients between the explanatory variables and quits/absenteeism. Most of the significant correlations are consistent with a priori expectations. For example, wage rates and fringe benefits (FRINGE1) are negatively correlated with quits; whereas joint job-evaluation schemes, flow production, and high overtime and apprenticeship ratios, are positively correlated – as is firm size, perhaps reflecting greater internal job-mobility opportunities.

Table 12.2 Descriptive statistics

Variable	Mean	Standard deviation	Correlation coefficient (quits)	Correlation coefficient (absenteeism)
QUIT	6.312	6.931		− 0.043
ABSENT	11.850	23.270	− 0.043	
MALE	80.000	17.110	− 0.008	0.146 *
UNSKILL	44.089	23.780	0.039	0.192 **
APPO	0.033	0.031	0.385 **	− 0.029
RATIO	2.674	2.105	0.010	− 0.019
TRT	0.189	0.695	0.073	− 0.059
SHIFT	6.937	11.752	− 0.127	− 0.041
OVER	5.279	4.719	0.191 **	0.011
PIE	20.46	22.370	− 0.142 *	0.001
WAGE	0.00254	0.00079	− 0.278 **	0.024
FRINGE	0.174	0.039	− 0.179 *	− 0.058
FRINGE1	0.891	0.310	− 0.251 **	− 0.005
PS	0.519	0.500	− 0.041	− 0.140 *
PVA	0.404	0.492	− 0.124	− 0.107
SHARES	0.269	0.444	− 0.068	− 0.059
INDEX	0.507	0.323	− 0.305 **	0.266 **
WC	0.269	0.444	0.122	− 0.126
UMC	0.462	0.449	0.007	0.165 *
JOBEVAL	0.346	0.477	− 0.233 **	0.154 *
SPAN	13.491	6.741	− 0.121	0.041
PART	0.519	0.500	− 0.079	0.144 *
FLOW	0.038	0.193	− 0.154 *	− 0.061
IT	0.365	0.482	0.049	− 0.113
TOT	1153.10	1800.00	− 0.251 **	0.305 **
UNEM	8.067	3.548	− 0.101	0.035
SOUTH	0.674	0.469	0.062	− 0.255 **
PLANT	1.461	0.919	− 0.091	− 0.068

**,* Significant at 1 per cent, 5 per cent levels

In addition, and consistent with expectations, we note that profit-sharing/share ownership schemes (PVA, SHARES, PS) and union presence (INDEX) are negatively related to quits – though only significantly so in the latter case.

Turning to those variables significantly correlated with absenteeism, we note that in the industry under consideration male workers appear to exhibit a higher propensity for temporary withdrawal (perhaps reflecting the fact that fewer women work on the shop floor). Larger firm size and higher proportions of unskilled workers are (not surprisingly) positively correlated with absenteeism. Also consistent with previous evidence, firms in the south of England appear to experience significantly lower absenteeism rates.

Although all the binary profit-sharing/share ownership variables are negatively associated with absenteeism, only the composite variable (PS) is significantly correlated. In addition, high perceived employee participation in decision-making (PART) and the existence of job-evaluation schemes (JOBEVAL) are positively correlated with temporary withdrawal. Further, the composite measure of union presence (INDEX), and the presence of union–management committees (UMC), are also positively associated with absenteeism. Hence on a univariate basis, the 'protection' effects of union presence appear to dominate 'voice' effects – a result consistent with previous empirical evidence (Allen 1984).

Finally we would note that, although a number of explanatory variables exhibit signs which suggest a common directional impact on temporary and permanent withdrawal, a significant proportion is inversely related (e.g. SIZE, WC, PART). Indeed absenteeism and quits are not significantly correlated in our data set (r = − 0.04). Further consideration of these complex issues is postponed to page 224.

Estimation and results

In this section, we present the results of the estimation of the basic equation structures discussed in the previous sections. The following section explores the relationship between voluntary turnover and absenteeism using 'seemingly unrelated regression' techniques.

The equations are estimated by ordinary least squares (OLS) with diagnostic tests for autocorrelation and heteroscedasticity in the residual term. Although there was no evidence of serial dependence, it was apparent that heteroscedasticity could be a problem with the absenteeism equation – and the presence of both could not be excluded for the quit equation. In consequence we report OLS results for the absenteeism equation using a 'heteroscedasticity-consistent' covariance matrix for calculation of the standard errors.

The quits equation is estimated by generalized least squares/instrumental variable techniques (GLS/IV), which is based on Kmenta's (1971) procedure for autocorrelated and heteroscedastic error structures.

In addition, some mention should be given to possible simultaneity problems in the determinants of the turnover equations. Our initial endogeneity assumptions (which apply to both equations) were that a firm's capital stock, technology, internal organization structure and workforce composition, are predetermined in this way (and thus are not treated as endogenous).

Hoel and Vale (1986) in an efficiency-wage-theory context, argue that quit rates and wages are simultaneously determined. The firm is treated as a wage setter and its optimizing behaviour includes reacting to potential increases in quit threats, and/or the costs of quits, by upwardly adjusting the wage rate.

Table 12.3 Determinants of voluntary turnover: GLS/IV estimates

Independent	Coefficient	Coefficient	Coefficient	Coefficient	Coefficient	Coefficient
MALE	− 0.006	− 0.004	− 0.033 *	− 0.0052	− 0.0024	− 0.0047
UNSKILL	0.013	0.017	0.001	0.0199 *	0.0179	0.0145
APPO	86.64 **	77.04 **	86.27 **	95.920 **	86.530 **	103.76 **
RATIO	− 0.087	− 0.015	− 0.248 *	− 0.1090	− 0.0890	− 0.1350
OVER	0.094 *	0.076 *	0.076 *	0.0760 *	0.0640	0.0560
PIE	− 0.009	− 0.006	− 0.025 *	− 0.0090	− 0.0030	− 0.0270 *
WAGE	129.56	113.20	28.95	− 49.320 *	− 19.927	− 110.05
FLOW	− 1.579	− 1.082	− 2.276 *	− 1.1350	− 0.7960	− 3.0110 *
UNEM	− 0.206 **	− 0.157 **	− 0.184 **	− 0.1400 **	− 0.1630 **	− 0.1210 **
SOUTH	0.362	0.441	− 0.065	0.1270	0.2310	− 0.4070
TOT	− 0.0001	− 0.0001	− 0.0001	− 0.0001	− 0.0001	− 0.0001
PLANT	0.131	0.057	0.640 *	0.2226	0.2340	0.5970 *
WC	4.644 **	4.733 **	4.771 **	2.2920 **	2.3860 **	1.5540 *
JOBEVAL	− 1.036 *	− 0.333	− 2.851 **	− 0.4770	0.8890	− 0.1770
SPAN	− 0.011	− 0.029	0.005	− 0.0490	− 0.0330	− 0.0570
PART	− 0.603 **	− 0.925 **	− 0.216 *	− 0.2620	− 0.0080	− 0.9150
UMC	3.147 **	2.479 **	4.362 **			
PERUN	0.007	0.005	0.003			
NOUNH	− 0.341 *	− 0.452 **	− 0.337 *			
INDEX	− 2.678 **			− 3.4900 **	− 3.785 **	− 3.972 **
PS		− 1.876 **		− 1.6700 **	− 1.759 **	
PVA						
SHARES			− 4.531 **			3.156 **
CONSTANT	3.151 *	2.579	5.581 **	4.7250 **	4.836 **	5.786 **
R-squared	0.63	0.61	0.68	0.689	0.687	0.688

**, * Significant at 1 per cent, 5 per cent levels

To incorporate this possible effect the variable WAGE was instrumented prior to being incorporated into the final estimating equations.

Table 12.3 reports GLS/IV estimates of six quit equations, with the profit-sharing/share option variables entering jointly and separately. The key results appear quite robust. The equations explain approximately 70 per cent of the variation in the dependent variable (as indicated by the Buse R^2). We find that collective 'voice' (INDEX) acts to produce a significant negative impact on average quit rates in all specifications.

When the union-presence indicators are entered separately, we note that the proportion of the workforce unionized (PERUN) does not produce a significant coefficient, but that the number of shop-floor unions (NOUNH) has a significant negative impact.

The participation dummy variable (PART) does not enter significantly in all equations – but there is some evidence of a negative impact of the perceived degree of participation on permanent withdrawal, giving support to the idea that 'voice', however achieved, reduces workers' propensity to quit.

The existence of a works' council (WC) provides an anomaly, since this has a very small (but positive) impact on quit rates. We notice, however, that there is some evidence that joint job-evaluation schemes act to reduce quits; this is perhaps consistent with Price's view (1977) that 'successively higher amounts of formal communication will probably produce successively lower amounts of turnover. What is critical in reducing turnover . . . is job related information', the rationale being that it is the most immediate and relevant forms of participation which produce the desired effect on quits.

Profit-sharing and share-option schemes, it appears, have a significant (and consistently) negative impact on quits in all specifications, confirming our prior expectations. The impact of these schemes could thus be one of the routes to higher firm productivity (see Bell and Hanson 1984; Estrin and Wilson 1988).

Hence, our measures of profit-sharing (PVA), share ownership (SHARES), and the composite variable (PS), all have a significant negative impact on voluntary turnover, a result which is very robust across alternative specifications. Interestingly, it appears that the existence of share-option schemes has the strongest impact in reducing quits (about 4 per cent lower in firms who have adopted these schemes), with profit-sharing appearing to reduce quits by approaching 2 per cent.

UNEM has the correct anticipated sign, whereas relative wages do not feature; and there is no evidence to suggest that quits are higher in the healthier southern economy.

Company size and technology did not enter the quit equation significantly, although firms with flow production appear to have lower than average quit rates. This is perhaps explained by the fact that these firms tend to devote more effort to researching and reducing turnover and take steps to compensate workers for their relatively less attractive work environment. An alternative explanation is that the introduction of modern flow-line production techniques, in this particular industry, actually improves the work environment and hence job satisfaction.

In respect of labour-force composition, it appears that firms with higher ratios of blue-collar workers experience higher voluntary turnover – possibly in consequence of white-collar workers being more tied to firms by fringe benefits.

Firms that invest in general training, as proxied by the number of apprentices, tend to lose through quits – perhaps because skilled apprentices are more mobile or (alternatively), it may be that certain firms use apprentices as a form of 'cheap labour'.

Table 12.4 reports the regression results for six alternative specifications of the multivariate determinants of absenteeism. All equations are reasonably well determined with R^2s varying between 0.46 and 0.51 (which is somewhat lower than the quit equations, a finding consistent with previous research).

We are particularly interested in the behaviour of the variables representing profit-sharing/share ownership, worker participation, and 'voice'. As with the quit equations, we note that the binary profit-sharing/share ownership variables (PVA, SHARES) are highly significant predictors in all specifications and exert a strong negative influence on absenteeism; with firms adopting one or other of these schemes (PS) experiencing an average rate of absenteeism some 13 per cent lower than firms who had not (with share-option schemes again exhibiting the strongest effect).

Perhaps more surprisingly, however, firms where employees had expressed the view that worker participation in decision-making was relatively high (PART) appeared to (perversely) experience higher average-absenteeism rates. This result is hard to explain, other than in terms of a more 'relaxed' approach to absenteeism being adopted in firms with these apparent attributes.

Most of the union presence and 'voice' variables, however, do conform with prior expectations. Hence the index of union presence, the number of blue-collar unions, and the existence of works councils all appear to exert a negative influence on absenteeism; whereas the proportion of the workforce unionized has an insignificant impact.

Overall, and in contrast to the univariate results, union 'voice' effects appear to dominate 'protectionism' effects in our multivariate models. Contrary to prior expectations, however, union–management committees and joint job-evaluation schemes appear to be associated with higher absenteeism. One possible explanation is that firms who are

Table 12.4 Determinants of absenteeism OLS-HETCOV

Independent	Coefficient	Coefficient	Coefficient	Coefficient	Coefficient	Coefficient
MALE	0.439 **	0.452 **	0.354 **	0.404 **	0.415 **	0.332 **
UNSKILL	0.216 **	0.214 **	0.179 **	0.234 **	0.234 **	0.209 **
APPO	− 226.11 **	− 310.48 **	− 199.13 **	− 179.98 **	− 264.27 **	− 168.57 **
TRT	− 1.495	− 1.459 *	− 0.169	− 1.515 *	− 1.379	− 0.132
SHIFT	− 0.316 **	− 0.371 **	− 0.352 **	− 0.191 *	− 0.249 **	− 0.224 *
PIE	− 0.108 **	− 0.078 *	− 0.095 *	− 0.161 **	− 0.131 **	− 0.144 **
WAGE	− 5498.90 **	− 6534.4 **	− 5687.2 **	− 6019.9 **	− 7134.9 **	− 6662.6 **
TOT	0.006 **	0.007 **	0.007 **	0.006 **	0.006 **	0.006 **
PLANT	− 7.263 **	− 8.845 **	− 6.894 **	− 5.449 **	− 7.111 **	− 5.427 **
FLOW	− 62.15 **	− 60.21 **	− 62.294 **	− 58.52 **	− 56.65 **	− 57.36 **
WC	− 4.214	− 3.497	− 5.146 *	− 12.65 **	− 11.78 **	− 14.74 **
JOBEVAL	6.665 *	7.603 *	4.219 *	7.935 *	9.097 *	6.621 *
SOUTH	− 21.594 **	− 21.792 **	− 24.041 **	− 19.56 **	− 20.01 **	− 21.91 **
PART	− 0.455	− 2.979	1.344	3.239 *	0.995	5.293 *
PERUN	0.009	− 0.011	− 0.013			
NOUNH	− 2.223 *	− 2.594 *	− 2.695 **			
UMC	11.77 **	11.58 **	14.50 **			
INDEX	− 13.33 **			− 3.781	− 6.923 *	− 7.565 *
PS		− 8.252 **		− 12.79 **		
PVA					− 7.755 **	
SHARES		15.07	− 15.07			− 11.60 **
CONSTANT	20.55 **	26.94 **	27.08 **	23.12 **	25.16 **	26.21 **
Time dummies	Yes	Yes	Yes	Yes	Yes	Yes
R-squared	0.51	0.49	0.50	0.484	0.462	0.466

**,* Significant at 1 per cent, 5 per cent levels

experiencing deteriorating absenteeism rates introduce these mechanisms as a last-resort measure. (This hypothesis is currently being further researched.)

If we turn to the control variables, consistent with prior expectations, relatively large firms appear to experience higher absenteeism; but this effect appears to be mitigated when companies have instituted a number of separate plants.

Companies with a high proportion of unskilled workers suffer higher absenteeism rates, whereas a high proportion of apprenticeship workers is associated with lower absenteeism rates (perhaps in consequence of apprentices having a relatively higher motivation to attend than unskilled/trained workers).

In common with the quit equations, flow production appears to exert a significant negative impact on temporary withdrawal, perhaps for reasons similar to those discussed in relation to quits.

Finally, we note that the signs on, and significance levels of, WAGE and PIE are consistent with prior expectations and suggest that higher wage rates and higher proportions of workers paid on piece rates are negatively associated with temporary withdrawal.

The determinants of temporary and permanent withdrawal: seemingly unrelated?

Turnover and absenteeism are often considered to be part of the same withdrawal process (see e.g. Mowday *et al.* 1982, for a review). However, as Mowday (1980:13) has noted, although some forms of absenteeism may be a diagnostic of, or precursors to, turnover: 'where an individual wishes to quit an undesirable job but is constrained (e.g. by a lack of alternative jobs), alternative forms of withdrawal may be expected in the form of apathy, absenteeism etc'.

Hence, the expected causal relationship (if any) between quits and absenteeism is ambiguous (as is existing empirical research, which has produced inconclusive results). For example, empirical evidence based on simple correlations is contradictory – with few studies supporting the (positive) 'sequential withdrawal' process, and even fewer the (negative) 'alternative withdrawal' process (see Mobley 1987). Where correlations have been found, they mostly suggest weak associations only.

Hence, although empirical studies have identified some variables which appear to be common determinants of temporary and permanent withdrawal, evidence of a direct causal link is weak. As Porter and Steers (1973: 131) have noted: 'Too often in the past, absenteeism has been considered simply an analogue of turnover, and it has been assumed without sufficient evidence that the two shared identical roots.'

In this section we novelly provide some new evidence on the 'common roots' debate by estimating 'seemingly unrelated regressions' (Zellner 1962) for the quit and absenteeism equations.

We noted earlier, that there is an insignificant negative correlation ($r = -0.047$) between quits and absenteeism in our dataset. On page 219 we also drew attention to a number of independent variables which did not appear to share a common influence on temporary and permanent withdrawal.

An appropriate estimator in these circumstances is Zellner's (1962) 'seemingly unrelated least squares' (SUR). As Pindyck and Rubinfield (1976: 325) have noted: 'The seemingly unrelated model is a special type of recursive model . . . which consists of a series of endogenous variables which are considered as a group because they bear a close conceptual relationship to each other'.

The rationale behind the technique is that disturbances in the error terms in the individual quit and absenteeism equations may be correlated. Hence in this application we are testing the hypothesis that quits and absenteeism may be affected by some common omitted variables which might be evidenced by linked error terms across the equations.

Table 12.5 Seemingly unrelated regressions: turnover and absenteeism: GLS systems estimates

Independent	Equation 1 – Quits		Independent	Equation 2 – Absenteeism	
	Coefficient	T-ratio		Coefficient	T-ratio
MALE	0.028	1.22	MALE	0.365	4.76 **
UNSKILL	− 0.049	− 2.97 **	UNSKILL	0.234	4.49 **
APPO	135.55	9.02 **	APPO	− 179.38	− 3.71 **
RATIO	0.144	0.74	TRT	− 1.136	− 0.66
OVER	0.198	2.54 *	SHIFT	− 0.184	− 1.68
PIE	− 0.041	− 2.51 *	PIE	− 0.167	− 3.09 **
WAGE	− 2500.6	− 4.15 **	WAGE	− 5669.6	− 2.68 *
FLOW	− 2.42	− 0.99	TOT	0.006	6.94 **
UNEM	0.09	0.76	PLANT	− 5.768	− 3.98 **
SOUTH	1.71	2.01 *	FLOW	− 58.61	− 7.51 **
TOT	− 0.00003	− 0.13	WC	− 12.92	− 4.29 **
PLANT	0.431	1.10	JOBEVAL	7.28	2.48 *
WC	1.893	1.87	SOUTH	− 19.76	− 7.08 **
JOBEVAL	− 2.511	− 3.05 **	PART	3.22	1.37
SPAN	− 0.051	− 0.98	INDEX	− 3.60	− 0.79
PART	0.288	0.39	PS	− 12.36	− 4.31 **
INDEX	− 0.992	− 2.68 *	CONSTANT	25.90	2.94 **
PS	− 2.052	− 2.39 *			
CONSTANT	8.336	2.92 **			
SYSTEM R-SQUARED	0.73				

**,* Significant at the 1 per cent, 5 per cent levels

Zellner (1962) suggested that gains in estimator efficiency are produced if the system of SUR equations is treated as a single (large) equation, which is then estimated using generalized least squares.

Table 12.5 reports the results of the Zellner estimates. We note that the error terms of the quit and absenteeism equations are significantly correlated ($r = 0.14$). This may be partly indicative of common (omitted) variables and hence that temporary and permanent labour withdrawal do share some common roots.

We also note that the explanatory variables which are included in the system's estimates, explain a high proportion (73 per cent) of the variation in temporary and permanent withdrawal.

Consistent with the individual equation estimates reported in tables 12.3 and 4, table 12.5 shows that the composite profit-sharing/share-ownership binary variable (PS) exhibits a highly significant negative influence on both quits and absenteeism.

The signs on and significance levels of the other explanatory variables are broadly consistent with our previous estimates. However, some noticeable differences are apparent. For example, in the quit equation, WAGE is highly significant and negative; whereas INDEX is still significant, but the size of the coefficient indicates a much smaller impact.

The absenteeism equation, however, remains remarkably stable, and in accord with the specification reported in table 12.4, indicating the same overall pattern of variable effects.

Conclusions

This paper has focused on the impact of profit-sharing/share ownership schemes, voice mechanisms, and worker participation on temporary and permanent labour withdrawal in a random sample of 52 UK engineering firms. Evidence was also presented relating to the common-roots hypothesis of the process underpinning quits and absenteeism.

A larger number of firm-specific and macro-control variables were included in the multivariate models to allow for important factors suggested by the extant literature.

The key empirical findings were as follows:

1 Firms which had adopted profit-sharing and/or share ownership schemes exhibited significantly lower absenteeism and quits rates – a finding which was consistent and robust under numerous alternative specifications (and in the presence of a large number of control variables).

Hence, in our sample, at any rate, the effects attributed to sharing arrangements are not simply proxies for other relevant variables.

2 Consistent with this, the multivariate models estimated for the quit

equations indicated that 'voice' mechanisms exerted a negative impact on voluntary turnover. Similarly, a relatively high degree of perceived employee participation in decision-making was also associated with lower quit rates.

3 The evidence pertaining to the effects of participation and 'voice' on temporary labour withdrawal were more mixed. Some forms of participation (e.g. works councils) did appear to lower absenteeism – others, however, had the opposite impact (e.g. job evaluation, union–management committees).

Indeed, in specifications where the employee participation index was significant, the sign on the variable suggested that firms with a high perceived degree of participation experienced higher absenteeism rates.

These seemingly inconsistent and conflicting results are certainly deserving of further research – particularly in respect of simultaneity and interaction effects.

4 New evidence was presented relating to the common determinants of voluntary and permanent labour withdrawal. Employing 'seemingly unrelated regression' techniques, our system equations offered some evidence to the effect that there might be common omitted variables responsible for a significant proportion of the variation in both quit and absenteeism rates in our sample. To the extent that error correlation was due to omitted variables, this evidence is supportive of the common-roots hypothesis. A topic for further research is to discover what these omitted variables are.

Although we must be cautious in ascribing 'causal effects' to what may be simply 'associations', the key finding that employee profit-sharing and share-option schemes exert a negative influence on absenteeism and quits, in the presence of a large number of control variables, does appear to support the perceived rationale for their introduction – a finding not without a practical, as well as purely academic, import.

Appendix

Variable	*Definition*
ABSENT	Annual working days lost per employee (exc. industrial disputes)
QUIT	Proportion of employees giving notice (quits/total employees)
MALE	Percentage male employees
UNSKILL	Percentage unskilled operatives
APPO	Ratio of apprentices to operatives
RATIO	Ratio of blue- to white-collar workers

OVER	Percentage overtime hours worked
SHIFT	Percentage of employees working shifts
PIE	Percentage of wage as piece-rate bonus
WAGE	Average hourly wage payment (£000s)
TRT	Training expenditure per employee
PVA	Existence of profit-sharing schemes (dummy)
SHARES	Existence of share-option scheme (dummy)
PS	Existence of profit-sharing/share-option scheme (dummy)
PERUN	Percentage of employees unionized
UNION	Existence of a closed shop (dummy)
UMC	Existence of union–management committee (dummy)
NOUNH	Number of blue-collar unions
NOUNS	Number of white-collar unions
INDEX	Index of union presence
FLOW	Predominantly flow-line production (dummy)
IT	Intermediate technology (dummy)
UNEM	Regional rate of unemployment (per cent)
SOUTH	South of England (dummy)
TOT	Number of Employees (SIZE)
PLANT	Number of plants in company
G3	Employee-participation scale
PART	High/low-participation (dummy)
WC	Existence of works council (dummy)
JOBEVAL	Existence of job-evaluation scheme (dummy)
SPAN	Workers per supervisor
FRINGE	Ratio of non-wage costs to wages
FRINGE1	Non-wage costs per employee (£000s)
KL	Capital labour ratio

See Wilson (1985) for a detailed discussion of survey methods and variable definitions.

Note

1 We gratefully acknowledge Economic and Social Research Council support under grant no. F00232021.

References

Allen, S.G. (1984) 'Trade unions, absenteeism and exit-voice', *Industrial and Labour Relations Review*, 37,3, 331–45.

Baddon, L., Hunter, L., Hyman, J., Leopold, J., and Ramsay, H. (1987) 'Developments in profit sharing and employee share ownership', Centre for Research in Industrial Democracy, Glasgow: University of Glasgow.

Barmby, T. and Treble, J. (1987) 'Absenteeism in a medium-sized manufacturing plant', Labour Economics Unit No. 88/1, Hull: University of Hull.

Bell, D.W. and Hanson, C. (1984) 'Profit-sharing and employee shareholding attitude survey', London: Industrial Participation Association.

Blanchflower, D.G. and Oswald, A. (1987) 'Profit-related pay: prose rediscovered', London: London School of Economics, mimeo.

Brown, C. and Medoff, J.L. (1978) 'Trade unions in the production process', *Journal of Political Economy*, 86, 2, 145–62.

Cable, J.R. (1985) 'Some tests of employee participaton indices', *Warwick Economic Research Papers* no. 258, Warwick: University of Warwick.

Cable, J.R. (1986) 'Production, efficiency, incentives and employee participation: some preliminary results for West Germany', *Kyklos*, 33, 100–21.

Copeman, G.H. and Paterson, P. (1985) *Report*, Wider Share Ownership Council.

Cotton, J.L. (1980) 'Employee participation: diverse forms and different outcomes', *Academy of Management Review*, 13, 1, 8–22.

Crowther, B.J. (1957) 'Absence and turnover in decisions of one company', *Occupational Psychology*, 31, 256–70.

Dewe, P., Dunn, S., and Richardson, R. (1988) 'Employee share option schemes: why are workers attracted to them?', *British Journal of Industrial Relations*, 26, 1, 1–20.

Dilts, D.A., Deitsch, C.R., and Paul, R.J. (1985) 'Getting workers back on the job: an analytical approach', New York: Quorum Books.

Duncan, G.J. and Stafford, F.P. (1980) 'Do union members receive compensating wage differentials', *American Economic Review*, 70, 355–71.

Estrin, S. and Wilson, N. (1988) *The Micro-economic Effects of Profit-Sharing: The British Experience*, London: Centre for Labour Economics, London School of Economics.

Florkowski, G.W. (1987) 'The organizational impact of profit-sharing', *Academy of Management Review*, 12, 622–31.

Freeman, R.B. (1980a) 'The exit-voice trade-off in the labour market', *Quarterly Journal of Economics*, 94, 643–73.

Freeman, R.B. (1980b) 'The effects of unionism on worker attachment to firms', *Journal of Labour Research*, 1, 29–61.

Freeman, R.B. and Medoff, J.L (1984) 'What do unions do?', New York: Basic Books.

Goldfarb, R.S. and Hosek, J.R. (1976) 'Explaining male–female wage differentials for the same job', *Journal of Human Resources*, 11, 1, 98–108.

Hammer, T.N., Landau, J.L., and Stern, R.N. (1981) 'Absenteeism when workers have a voice: the case of employee ownership', *Journal of Applied Psychology*, 62, 319–27.

Hart, R.A. (1987) *The Economics of Non-Wage Labour Costs*, Allen & Unwin.

Hirschman, A.O. (1970) *Exit, Voice and Loyalty*, Cambridge, Mass.: Harvard University Press.

HMSO (1986) 'Profit-related pay: a consultative document', Cmnd 9835, London: HMSO.

Hoel, M. and Vale, B. (1986) 'Effects on unemployment of reduced working time in an economy where firms set wages', *European Economic Review*, 30, 1097–104.

Income Data Services (1986) 'Profit-sharing and share ownership', Report No. 357, London: Income Data Services.

Kmenta, J. (1971) *Elements of Econometrics*, London: Macmillan.

Lawler, E.E. (1971) *Pay and Organizational Effectiveness*, New York: McGraw-Hill.

Long, R.A. (1978a) 'Relative effects of share ownership vs control on job attitudes in an employee owned company', *Human Relations*, 31, 753–63.

Long, R.A. (1978b) 'The effects of employee ownership on organizational identification, employee job attitudes, and organizational performance', *Human Relations*, 31, 29–48.

Long, R.A. (1980) 'Job attitudes and organizational performance under employee ownership', *Academy of Management Journal*, 23, 726–37.

McCormick, B.J. (1988) 'Quit rates over time in a job-rationed labour market', *Economica*, 55, 81–94.

March, J.G. and Simon, H.A. (1958) *Organizations*, New York: J. Wiley and Sons.

Martin, J. (1971) 'Some aspects of absence in a light engineering factory', *Occupational Psychology*, 45, 77–91.

Mathewman, J. (1983) *Controlling Absenteeism: Industrial Relations in Practice*, London: Junction Books.

Metcalfe, D. (1988) 'Unions and productivity', London: London School of Economics, mimeo.

Mobley, W.H. (1987) *Employee Turnover: Causes, Consequences and Control*, London: Adison-Wesley Publishing Company.

Mowday, R.T. (1980) 'Unmet expectations about unmet expectations: employee reactions to disconfirmed expectations during the early employment period', paper presented at the 40th annual meeting of the Academy of Management, Detroit, August.

Mowday, R.T., Porter, L.W., and Steers, R.M. (1982) *Employee–Organization Linkages: The Psychology of Commitment, Absenteeism and Turnover*, London: Academic Press.

Nicholson, N. (1977) 'Absence behaviour and attendance motivation: a conceptual synthesis', *Journal of Management Studies*, 14, 231–52.

Nicholson, N. and Payne, R. (1987) 'Absence from work: explanations and attributes', *Journal of Applied Psychology*, 36, 121–32.

Nicholson, N., Brown, C.A., and Chadwick-Jones, J.K. (1977) 'Absence from work and personal characteristics', *Journal of Applied Psychology*, 62, 319–27.

Oi, W. (1964) 'Labour as a quasi-fixed factor', *Journal of Political Economy*, 532–55.

Parsons, D.W. (1972) 'Specific human capital: an application to the quit rate and layoffs', *Journal of Political Economy*, 80, 1120–43.

Parsons, D.W. (1977) 'Models of labour turnover', *Research in Labour Economics*, 1, 185–223, Greenwich: JAI Press.

Pencavel, J. (1977) 'The distributional and efficiency effects of trade unions in Britain', *British Journal of Industrial Relations*, 15, 137–56.

Pindyck, R. and Rubinfield, D. (1976) *Econometric Models and Economic Forecasts*, New York: McGraw-Hill.

Poole, M. (1988) 'Who are the profit-sharers?', *Personnel Management*, January: 34–6.

Poole, M. and Jenkins, G. (1988) 'How employees respond to profit sharing', *Personnel Management*, July: 30–4.

Porter, L.W. and Steers, R.M. (1973) 'Organizational, work and personal factors in employee turnover and absenteeism', *Psychological Bulletin*, 80, 151–76.

Price, J.L. (1977) *The Study of Labour Turnover*, London: Iowa State University Press.

Rhodes, S.R. and Steers, R.M. (1980) 'Conventional versus worker-owned organizations', *Human Relations*, 34, 1031–5.

Roots, P. (1988) 'Financial incentives for employees', London: BSP Professional Books.

Smith, F.J. (1977) 'Work attitudes as predictors of specific day attendance', *Journal of Applied Psychology*, 62, 16–19.

Smith, G.R. (1986) 'Profit sharing and employee share ownership in Britain', *Employment Gazette*, September: 380–5.

Spencer, D.G. (1986) 'Employee voice and employee retention', *Academy of Management Journal*, 29, (3), 488–502.

Steers, R.M. and Mowday, R.T. (1981) 'Employee turnover and post-decision accommodation processes', *Research into Organizational Behaviour* (3), Greenwich: JAI Press.

Steers, R.M. and Rhodes, S.R. (1978) 'Major influences on employee attendance: a process model', *Journal of Applied Psychology*, 63, 391–407.

Stewart M. (1987) 'Collective bargaining arrangements, closed shop and relative pay', *Economic Journal*, 97, 140–56.

Taylor, P.J. (1967) 'Shift and day work', *British Journal of Industrial Medicine*, 24, 93–102.

Taylor, P.J., Pocock, S.J., and Sergean, R. (1972) 'Shift and dayworkers' absence: relationship with some terms and conditions of service', *British Journal of Industrial Medicine*, 29, 338–40.

Weitzman, M.L. (1983) 'Some macroeconomic implications of alternative compensation systems', *Economic Journal*, 93, 762–83.

Weitzman, M.L. (1984) *The Share Economy*, Cambridge, Mass.: Harvard University Press.

Weitzman, M.L. (1985a) 'The simple macroeconomics of profit-sharing', *American Economic Review*, 76, 937–53.

Weitzman, M.L. (1985b) 'Insiders versus outsiders: macroeconomic externality and the NAIRU under profit-sharing', Massachusetts Institute of Technology, mimeo.

Weitzman, M.L. (1986) *The Case for Profit-Sharing*, London: Employment Institute.

Wilson, N. and Peel, M.J. (1989) 'Quit rates, absenteeism and the impact of participation and profit-sharing: empirical evidence from the UK engineering industry', Bradford: University of Bradford Management Centre, Occasional Paper.

Wilson, N. (1987) 'Unionization, wages and productivity: some British evidence', Bradford: University of Bradford Management Centre, Occasional Paper.

Wilson, N. (1985) 'Work organization, incentives and economic performance in British Industry', Economic and Social Research Council End of Award Report.

Zellner, A. (1962) 'An efficient method of estimating seemingly unrelated regressions and tests of aggregation bias', *Journal of American Statistical Society*, 57, 348–68.

Chapter thirteen

Incentives for senior managers: share options and buy-outs

Alistair Bruce, Trevor Buck, John Coyne, and Mike Wright

Introduction

Oliver Williamson has always emphasized the wide spectrum of governance structures that are present within and between economic systems. This chapter is concerned with the problems experienced in market-based economies surrounding the incentivization of key employees inside the vertical hierarchies of large corporations. While the rest of this compilation is concerned with broader issues of employee ownership, the focus here is on incentives for senior managers, although we also touch upon the position of more junior employees.

The chapter combines for the first time the preliminary results of two research projects that the authors continue to undertake at the University of Nottingham; although quite separate, the executive share-option project and the management buy-out (CMBOR) survey are concerned in part with similar issues and have many parallels.

The first section presents a short review of incentivization problems for senior managers in large companies and then discusses two potential solutions to these problems – executive share options (ESOs) and management buy-outs (MBOs), in each case pointing out unresolved conflicts. Our conclusions are presented on page 246 and details of the surveys are given in the appendices.

Incentives for senior managers

In the UK, ESOs apply to senior managers in virtually every large company (Coopers and Lybrand 1987:9) and about three-quarters of management buy-outs (MBOs) occur as divestments from large companies or large groups (Chiplin *et al.* 1988; Wright and Coyne 1985).

The motivational problems within these large firms can be understood best within the framework of *agency theory*. Inside firms, shareholders are considered as principals to managerial agents, who in turn become principals to other employees. We concentrate here on

233

shareholders and senior managers, with only passing reference to the rest of the workforce which is the subject of the remainder of this book.

In a conventional firm, shareholders arguably bear most of the uncertainty. Employees risk some income in the form of bonus and over-time payments and face the possibilities of dismissal and redundancy. However, they receive a weekly or monthly income which in the short term is paid irrespective of ultimate profitability. The balance of these 'downside' and minor 'upside' risks leads to the usual assertion that risk-averse employees are more conservative and defensive than shareholders, favouring projects with lower variances, since they gain little from above-average expected outcomes. On the other hand, shareholders' income is determined by variations in profits and losses, i.e. shareholders are residual claimants. As residual claimants and principals, shareholders can issue instructions to managers and other employees and can introduce a system of vertical monitoring in an attempt to ensure that employee agents do as they are told.

Unfortunately for shareholders, over-monitoring is possible, and monitoring can be obstructed where the measurement of employees' out-puts (productivity) and inputs (effort) involves high transactions costs. This will tend to be the case where production has a strong 'team' element, and especially where the tasks delegated to employees require delicate *judgements* in an uncertain environment. It is unlikely that employee agents on (almost) fixed salaries will voluntarily make judgements that are considered efficient by shareholders concerned only with profitability and its variability. Of course, the proportions of routine to judgemental tasks will vary by industry, company, and occupation, and Knight (1921: 294) insisted long ago that 'even the coarsest and most mechanical labour involves in some sense meeting uncertainty, dealing with contingencies which cannot be *exactly* foreseen.'

Once employeès realize that their shareholder principals cannot monitor their judgements closely, all the usual problems of asymmetrical information arise, i.e. adverse selection, moral hazard and hold-ups (Barney and Ouchi 1986: 440). These problems may be particularly severe where shareholders try to monitor employees who are hired to make specialized judgements in the cost centres of a unitary firm (U-form) organization. Indeed monitoring problems provide one explana-tion why shareholders resort to a wide variety of decentralizing reforms which may economize on transaction costs. These can range from a holding company (H-form) structure, through the divisionalized com-pany to the looser arrangements of franchises, co-partnerships, and joint ventures. In particular, the multidivisional (M-form) company is extremely popular as a governance structure in large companies, where the shareholders arrange for the concentration of strategy, objective setting, and monitoring functions at head office, while profit-centre divisions are responsible for day-to-day operations within this broad framework. Head office can now leave operational judgements to the divisions and reward them through internal labour and capital markets according to divisional profit, without detailed monitoring. In this compromise between markets and hierarchies, the M form tries to encourage in divisional managers behaviour consistent with a status of residual claimant.

The M form has a number of potential weaknesses as well as strengths, however, and ESOs and MBOs may be seen as attempts to solve them. In the divisions, employees may perceive the M-form's incentive structure as an encouragement for 'short-termism' in relation to divisional profit. In any case, they may feel powerless to influence divisional profit on their own and be tempted to 'free ride' on the efforts of others. If shareholders wish to compare the financial out-turns of comparable divisions, this implies that functions must be 'wastefully' duplicated in the divisions, although competition (real or simulated) always depends upon such static duplication, if any dynamic gains from competition are to be realized.

At the same time, the M form may produce weaknesses at head office. The M form can reduce divisional opportunism, but there is no guarantee that senior managers may not behave opportunistically at head office, although this opportunism ought to be more 'transparent' to shareholders. The concentration of strategy at head office may, however, produce a lack of diversity in strategic thinking, and the quasi-competition between M-form divisions remains bureaucratic and lacks the impersonal discipline of markets. This will be particularly true where head-office managers have divisional allegiances, subsidizing pet projects out of 'cash cow' divisional profits.

It is between the divisions and head office, however, that the main M-form weaknesses may show themselves. Some specialist functions must be retained at head office depending on circumstances, and this can lead to all the standard opportunistic behaviour attributed to U forms, where functions compete for 'free' central services. Strategic thinking may also become distanced from the operational shop-floor and, in any case, strategy and operations can never be totally separated. The quality of strategic decisions will influence divisional profits differentially and operational performance will reflect upon attempts to evaluate strategic decisions. In these circumstances, head office and divisions may feel a *joint* responsibility for divisional performance, and the situation is ripe for the cover-ups and blame-shifting that the M form was designed to avoid.

For these reasons, the M form and other forms of partial decentralization within large companies may leave shareholder principals and employee agents dissatisfied. Shareholders may continue to feel that employees have dissonant objectives, and employees may in turn feel frustrated that the quality of their performance goes unrecognized and unrewarded.

In these circumstances shareholders may consider giving residual claims to employees to reduce dissonance and encourage employees to make profitable decisions that pay proper attention to risk. Residual claims can take the form of profit-related pay (PRP), but this may lead to free-riding by employees who feel that their share of residual income is insignificantly small, and PRP can do nothing towards bridging the alleged time-horizon differences between shareholders and employees.

Employee share ownership can solve any time-horizon problems, but the benefits for employees from shares are longer term and therefore less tangible than the fairly instant case of PRP. In addition, employee shares can run into risk-bearing difficulties where employees with their livelihoods and equity holdings at stake in the same company may feel that their human and financial asset portfolios are too undiversified. It follows that risk-averse employees may be particularly unwilling to hold shares where their company operates in a turbulent environment, e.g. where product sales are made to an undiversified set of buyers. Indeed, Fama and Jensen (1983: 315) explain the survival of residual-sharing partnerships in accountancy, law, and architecture in terms of their diversity of clients and the need for partners to use their judgement to cultivate a profitable clientele. High risks and risk-averse attitudes on the part of employees may threaten the effectiveness of PRP and employee shares in general. A short-term attitude is evident in a tendency for employees to hold shares for relatively modest periods when there is a ready market in the shares (e.g. at Vickers). The rational risk-averse employee would in any event sell shares to diversify his portfolio.

These difficulties will all be recognized in the surveys reported below on experiences with ESOs and MBOs.

Executive share options

ESOs represent an attempt by hierarchical corporations to motivate senior managers, reduce their frustrations, and restrict levels of opportunistic behaviour to proportions acceptable to shareholders. In contrast with MBOs, ESOs are an attempted solution *within* the existing boundaries of the firm.

As opposed to PRP and employee shares, the share option has two characteristics that may commend it to employee motivation, in addition to any favourable tax treatment.

First, the funding of share options is quite different to PRP and employee shares. The beauty of share options is that they apparently involve no financial cost to shareholders who simply give employees written promises that they can buy (call) in the future stated quantities of shares at a price set at the time of granting (often the prevailing market price, or close to it). If share prices do not rise, then, of course, opportunity costs are low, limited to opportunities foregone as a consequence of the potential 'lock in' effect of options. Shareholders' costs do occur if prices exceed the exercise level and the equity of existing shareholders may be diluted by the discounted sale of shares to employees. However, shareholders would only consent to options where the net benefit after dilution when options are exercised is positive. If the options granted are on shares bought in at the time they are granted, not through the creation of new shares, then there is no dilution.

Second, besides being apparently cheap to fund, share options have the additional property of being worth more, the riskier the underlying share. The risks on options are apparently asymmetrical, since a call option is simply worthless if share prices fall below the exercise price, and any subsequent price falls incur no extra penalty. If shareholders perceive employees as otherwise having relatively conservative attitudes to risk and profit, however, this may be no bad thing. Indeed, share options may be regarded as correcting the asymmetry in a typical employee's contract, which implies some penalties but few rewards for profitable behaviour. On the other hand, once share-option holders have built up 'paper gains', the possibility of future 'paper losses' arises and the risks associated with options becomes symmetrical again. During October 1987, many call-option holders were made only too aware of the two-sidedness of their risks.

The act of targeting ESOs on senior managers offers a number of advantages in addition to the general advantages of employee share options, explained above. Of course, the restriction of options (and subsequently shares) to a small group of senior employees makes the costs for shareholders even smaller than for more general awards, and any dilution of equity is similarly limited. In the UK, ESO schemes approved by investment-protection committees in 1988 cannot give executives more than 5 per cent of total equity, and this limit is well below holdings produced by most MBO schemes. Furthermore, restricting options (and thus shares) to small groups of employees, reduces the possibility of free-riding.

Finally, it could be argued that ESOs restrict profit-related rewards to those key senior managers who must make a high proportion of decisions that are judgemental, and therefore difficult to monitor, and strategic, having a substantial impact on the profitability of the whole company. At one stroke, ESOs may be claimed to encourage senior managers to pay attention to the profitability and riskiness of their decisions, to eliminate any truncated time horizons and generally to remove any conflict with shareholders, simply by turning senior managers into shareholders. Unlike the gift or subsidized sale of shares to executives, shareholders can be sure with ESOs that executives cannot gain unless other shareholders gain too.

On top of these advantages, the UK government has offered significant tax incentives for ESO schemes, although these were substantially withdrawn in the 1988 Finance Act. As a result of the underlying strengths of ESOs and these tax advantages, most large firms in the US and UK now use ESOs. By March 1988, the UK Inland Revenue had approved 2,949 schemes, and approvals were increasing by about 90 a month. Our survey, conducted in February 1988 by the Confederation of British Industries (CBI) and described in Appendix 1, showed that 33 per cent of all UK manufacturing firms had approved ESOs. In any one year, the highest initial value was between 1.5 and 2.2 times other emoluments, see Appendix 1.

Table 13.1 What were the main objectives of your ESO?

	Main objectives %	Average ranking	% rank 1	% rank 2	Objective achieved
To provide tax-efficient remuneration for executives	21	1.9	8	9	10
To sharpen the relation between effort and reward	29	1.4	23	1	11
To enhance the firm's competitive position in the labour market	14	2.5	4	2	5
To tie executives to the firm	12	2.4	2	3	6
To forestall a management 'buy-out'	1	5.7	0	0	0
Other	3	1.0	2	0	2

See Appendix 1 for details of survey

For tax and efficiency reasons, shareholders may find that ESOs are an effective means of raising profits and reducing risks, and table 13.1 shows that the main objectives cited by companies for ESOs relate to the improved performance of managerial agents, with the highest average ranking (1.4) given to 'sharpening the relationship between effort and reward'. At the same time, however, a number of difficulties have been encountered with ESOs concerning the extent to which executives feel responsible for profits and difficulties associated with the divided loyalties of executives as shareholders. ESOs may actually encourage moral hazard in executives, even though shareholders intend that they prevent it.

The objectives that shareholders set for ESO schemes (see table 13.1) may be jeopardized if executives have *too much control* or paradoxically, *too little control* over profit out-turns. Shareholders' fears about opportunism and too much executive control apply to accounting profits, share values in the short term, and the possibility that executives may influence the design and operation of ESO schemes to suit their own pockets. The whole issue therefore cannot be divorced from the organizational framework within which decisions are made. Moral hazard in the design of schemes depends crucially on whether the main board, the executive board, or specialist board committees design an ESO scheme. It is common for remuneration committees to have a majority of non-executive directors. Nevertheless, it is possible that 'creative' accounting, for example, involving companies that are controlled but not subsidiary, may influence book profits. Table 13.2 reveals considerable anxieties on the part of shareholders, and 18 per cent of companies did not contemplate an ESO for fear of executives' diluting their equity. For companies with an ESO scheme, it is significant that the only important barrier to larger ESO allocations has been the organization of

Table 13.2 CBI survey on ESOs, 1988: examination of ESO characteristics

	Yes	No %	N/I
Was a larger ESO ever considered in terms of executives covered and/or the number of options to be awarded?	8	24	66
For those who answered 'Yes' to the previous question, was a larger ESO not implemented because of:			
Constraints imposed by the 1984 Finance Act?	1		
Constraints imposed by an investment protection committee?	6		
Shareholders' anxieties about the dilution of equity?	1		
Executives' uncertainty regarding ESO benefits?	0		
Jealousy on the part of the employees not covered?	0		
Other constraints?	0		
Are you currently considering an extension of ESO in terms of coverage or size?	8	26	65
If you are not currently operating an ESO			
(i) Is your company currently contemplating an ESO?	5	55	38
(ii) Is your company awaiting Inland Revenue approval for an ESO?	3	52	43
For those who answered 'No' to both parts of the previous question:			
What was the most important reason for not considering ESO?			
Constraints imposed by the 1984 Finance Act?	1		
Constraints imposed by an investment protection committee?	0		
Shareholders' anxieties about the dilution of equity?	18		
Executives' uncertainty regarding ESO benefits?	4		
Jealousy on the part of the employees not covered?	0		
Other constraints	32		

Source: Survey of CBI Companies, 1988. Percentages have been rounded down to the nearest whole figure

shareholder interests into investment-protection committees (IPCs). These committees impose stricter constraints on ESO schemes than the Inland Revenue in the UK, but there are still good reasons to fear excessive executive control. Although most IPCs insist that only one set of options is granted every ten years, table 13.3 reveals that in our 1988 survey 5 per cent of companies openly admitted that they had reissued ESOs with lower option prices after falls in the company's share price had made earlier ESOs worthless. Such behaviour seems to confirm the worst fears of the former chief executive and chairman of ITT, Harold Geneen, who observed that (Incomes Data Services, 1985:4) 'when the stock market goes up, everybody cashes in – when it goes down the board issues new options at lower prices'. One way of safeguarding the interests of shareholders is to make ESO awards conditional upon the fulfilment of target rates of share-price performance or on local performance indicators for managers, but table 13.3 shows that only 4 per cent of companies relate ESOs to performance. In addition, table 13.2 shows that an important objective of ESOs before 1988 was simply to help executives minimize their tax liabilities. There is a danger that executives may wield such power that ESOs become a standard feature of any executive remuneration package and lose any value as a performance incentive.

Table 13.3 CBI survey on ESOs, 1988: reissue and performance triggers

	Yes %	No %	N/I %
Options only have a money value to executives if share prices rise. Have Executive Share Options ever been reissued with lower initial share values during period of decline in the company's share price?	5	27	66
Is the award of Executive Share Options related to performance triggers?	4	29	65

See Appendix 1 for survey details

Although ESOs may fail to prevent opportunistic executive behaviour in some circumstances because of too much executive control over accounting results, over the release of information to which share prices are sensitive, and over the design of ESO schemes themselves, it seems likely that elsewhere ESOs will fail as an incentive because executives feel that they have *too little control* over profits and hence share values. Executives may feel powerless, for example, in the face of inflation or exchange-rate uncertainties, or their efforts may be swamped by the performance of employees without ESOs. Such feelings of powerlessness were widely voiced after the general fall in share prices of October 1987 had reduced the value of ESOs held, and Lewellen *et al.* (1987) show that stock-based remuneration for executives is relatively unpopular in firms with a high BETA value, i.e. share prices that are highly sensitive to systematic, market-wide movements. Shareholders with faith in ESOs would insist, however, that ESOs do give executives an incentive to provide contingency plans for uncertainties like mail strikes, natural disasters, political changes, and so on.

Besides difficulties concerning the degree of executive responsibility for share prices and the success of ESOs as incentives for senior managers, there are also problems concerning loyalties. On the face of it, the last question reported in table 13.2 reveals that at least *companies* remain unconcerned about any resentments felt by managers and other employees excluded from ESO schemes. This does not mean that such resentments do not exist, however, even within the group of executives with ESOs. In a large British company recently, the chief executive sold shares obtained through an ESO scheme, the market interpreted the sale of shares as a pessimistic act, the company's share price fell, and other executive shareholders could sell only at the new lower price.

The foregoing example illustrates the potential for ESOs to create more general conflicts where executives are managerial agents of the shareholders and also managers of their own personal assets. If the frequency of ESO awards is rationed, perhaps by an IPC, then the exercise of an ESO by an executive may be taken as a signal that the company's share price is not expected to continue to rise. Furthermore, once shares under option have been purchased by executives, other shareholders and the capital market may draw conclusions about the company's prospects if the executive chooses to sell them or even buys 'put' options in the company's shares. The market may tend to disregard explanations of the transactions in terms of an executive's attempts to broaden an undiversified personal-asset portfolio and the importance of this point is emphasized by the existence of specialist research services which provide investors with analyses of (perfectly legal) 'insider' share dealings, see, for example, *Investors' Chronicle* (5 February 1988:12–13).

Finally, it is relevant to note that attempts have been made to predict and test the prevalence of stock-based remuneration (including ESOs), see Lewellen *et al.* (1987). Although they are able to demonstrate that such schemes are influenced by efficiency considerations like effort levels, risk, and time-horizons, and not tax, they are only able to explain 22 per cent of inter-firm variations. Remaining variations could depend to some extent on the degree of executive control over remuneration packages. Either ESOs may provide shareholders and managers with exactly the incentive scheme that they seek, or managers may behave opportunistically and design ESOs to suit their own pockets, or managers may find ESOs insignificant, leaving them still frustrated in the sense that their efforts, decisions, and judgements are felt to go inadequately rewarded. In the latter two cases a more drastic solution, like the MBO, may be added to the agenda. It must be recognized, however, that it is still early days in the UK and few schemes are sufficiently mature to make reliable judgements concerning the overall impact.

Management buy-outs

In contrast to the internal solution proposed by ESOs, the MBO constitutes a possible solution to the problem of inadequate incentives for senior managerial agents that breaks open the existing hierarchy. Although table 13.2 showed that ESOs rarely have the explicit objective of forestalling a buy-out, they could obviously be considered long before the possibility of an MBO has arisen, to deal with the motivation and frustrations of management.

The meaning of MBO is explained in Appendix 2. The managerial-incentive problems explained earlier are an important peripheral element in MBOs which are traditionally associated with resolving difficulties faced by companies that have over-diversified, perhaps through the acquisition of a 'string-bag' of activities, some of which fit uncomfortably into a company's portfolio. There are two broad issues on which evidence from management buy-outs may illuminate the debate on managerial incentives. First, there is the motivation to do an MBO, and for an organization to permit it, a recognition that separation is the best option for both parties. Second, the subsequent structure of ownership and control and its associated incentives may demonstrate the effects of residual claimant status. In the discussion here it is implicitly assumed that incentive problems, as well as strategic-fit considerations have prompted the MBO, and we can then question post-buy-out effects.

Table 13.4 Percentage of shareholdings held by management in buy-outs

Range	Number	%
5–24.9%	17	9.4
25.0–49.9%	24	13.3
50–74.9%	71	39.2
75–99.9%	40	22.1
100%	29	16.0
	181	100.0

Average size of management team = 5.5; SD = 19.4; median = 4.0

Note: One respondent did not disclose management equity stake out of the total sample of 182.
Source: Centre for Management Buy-out Research Survey of 1984 and 1985 buy-outs. All buy-outs identified in this period were sent a mailed questionnaire, with one reminder also being administered.

How may MBOs affect the motivation of senior managers who previously felt that rewards were insensitive to their performance or that their division or subsidiary had a low priority at head-office? First, and most importantly, table 13.4 shows that managers in MBOs become very substantial equity-owners as well as peak-tier decision-takers. In 16 per cent of MBOs, managers are the only shareholders and, overall, the CMBOR survey reported in table 13.4 showed that MBO managers on average owned two-thirds of total equity. It can be seen therefore that MBO managers are much more substantial residual claimants than ESO-holding managers within large firms and therefore have a greater incentive, as principals rather than agents, to make more profitable judgemental decisions that pay proper attention to risk.

However, it must be appreciated that many MBO deals are highly geared, and owner-managers are committed in most cases to servicing very heavy borrowing, often secured by mortgages on their homes and other assets. This situation may be expected to concentrate the minds of managers fully on their company's financial results and the 'downside' risks are much greater than the holders of ESOs experience. Although massive downside risks may reintroduce conservative attitudes to risk, such borrowings effectively *bond* managers to their company. It is difficult, however, to be certain whether it is the expectation of 'upside gain', also experienced by ESO participants, or the fear of 'downside' loss which is the key factor.

Table 13.5 Existence of an employee share-option-scheme in MBOs

	No.	%
Yes, at time of survey	19	10.4
Intention to introduce	49	26.9
Existed prior to buy-out	11	6.0

Base for percentages = 182

Source: Centre for Management Buy-out Research Survey of 1984 and 1985 buy-outs. All buy-outs identified in this period were sent a mailed questionnaire, with one reminder also being administered.

As an antidote to conservatism, to spread the pattern of incentives, and to create an amenable attitude to risk, MBOs have often extended the constituency-holding equity or options in the new company. This may be done at the time of buy-out or subsequently and may include the second tier of management or a deeper penetration. The choice may be a matter of fairness or a recognition of where true influence over company performance rests. In 10.4 per cent of buy-outs surveyed (see table 13.5) an employee share-option scheme was in place at the time of the survey, with a further 26.9 per cent intending to introduce one. Given the conservative attitude which may be created by leverage, and the apparently symmetrical effect of restricted share options which favour high-risk projects, then MBOs with ESOs may be synergistic.

The imposition on managers of performance-contingent equity rewards (or 'ratchets') by MBO-financing institutions may further stiffen the regime of rewards and penalties. Table 13.6 shows that although such ratchets existed in only about a quarter of the MBOs surveyed, they were more common in the larger transfers of ownership. More generally, funding institutions tend to impose a whole battery of monitoring devices that are designed to reduce managerial opportunism further. These devices can include board representation, monthly performance reports, and generally more detailed information than firms would normally provide to outside lenders (see Wright *et al.* 1989). Care must be taken in the balance between debt bonding and the re-creation of alienating principal–agent pressures experienced earlier.

Table 13.6 Ratchets in management equity stakes in MBOs

Presence of a ratchet		44 (24.2%)
Maximum attainable	– Average	50.2% of equity
	– SD	22.6%
	– Range	7–100%
Minimum attainable	– Average	32.0% of equity
	– SD	22.3%
	– Range	0–80%

Source: Centre for Management Buy-out Research Survey of 1984 and 1985 buy-outs. All buy-outs identified in this period were sent a mailed questionnaire, with one reminder also being administered.

Vertical monitoring by lenders can work both ways, and the MBO may *weaken* managerial incentives in a number of ways.

In the first place, intrusive lenders may effectively put managers back into the sort of vertical-hierarchy they were anxious to escape from: in this case the hierarchy of the lending institution. The institutions may force managers to concentrate on static cost economies within the new firm at the expense of any flexibility of managers to respond to unforeseen opportunities and problems, see Scherer (1984) and Jensen (1986).

The other potential problems introduced by MBOs also featured in the ESO survey. With much higher equity stakes under MBOs compared with ESOs, managers will consider their asset portfolios to be insufficiently diversified. A Stock Exchange flotation may provide managers with an opportunity to realize capital gains and to diversify, but, of course, such diversification must weaken the incentive package, albeit with a more symmetrical risk profile. Alternatively the sale of the

MBO company to a third party may permit portfolio diversification of individual portfolios, but at the same time will reintroduce a vertical hierarchy. If no such portfolio widening occurs, MBO firms may be effectively protected from the disciplines of the external capital market and the market for corporate control and may therefore experience performance decline (see Chiplin and Wright 1987).

The other problem that MBOs share with ESO schemes concerns the effect of peak-tier shareholdings on excluded managers and other employees. Table 13.7 shows that the majority (85.7 per cent) of 'other employees' contributed nothing to the MBO and, from the remaining 13.6 per cent who gave a survey response, only an average of 5 per cent of total funding was contributed by other employees at the time of buy-out. These results make it possible that MBOs will develop incentivization problems below the level of the MBO team, especially among managers *just* below the team who now see their career path blocked. They may feel they can move neither upwards nor diagonally to another subsidiary or division.

Table 13.7 Proportions of other employees providing funds and amounts invested in management buy-outs

Percentage of shareholdings/funding	Number of employees		Amount of funding	
	No. of respondents	*%*	*No. of respondents*	*%*
0	156	85.7	156	85.7
1–4	4	2.2	7	3.8
5–24.9	12	6.6	13	7.1
25–49.9	3	1.6	3	1.6
50–74.9	3	1.6	2	1.1
75–99.9	3	1.6	—	—
100	1	0.7	—	—
Not stated	—	—	1	0.7
Total	182	100.0	182	100.0
Average	27.2%		14.6%	

Source: Centre for Management Buy-out Research Survey of 1984 and 1985 buy-outs. All buy-outs identified in this period were sent a mailed questionnaire, with one reminder also being administered.

It would appear therefore that the MBO can be no general panacea for incentivization problems in vertical hierarchies. It offers many potential costs as well as benefits and the net outcome can only be determined empirically in particular circumstances. So far, there have been few published studies on the net performance effects of MBOs, although those that are available do suggest that performance improves as a result of better incentives for senior managers and the opportunities for greater flexibility produced by the changeover to an MBO (see Thompson and Wright 1987; Hanney 1986; Scherer 1984; Jones 1988).

Conclusions

The presence and prevalence of ESOs and MBOs demonstrates that problems exists in motivating senior managers in large corporate hier-archies. If shareholders experienced no agency problems with managers, there would be simply no need for ESOs and less pressure for MBOs.

Our surveys would emphasize the need to keep an open mind on the best way to motivate managers, which must depend on a firm's circumstances. Where managers make a majority of decisions that are non-routine and judgemental, shareholders will find it very costly to monitor them, and managers will inevitably feel frustrated in the sense that they consider that their judgemental efforts go unacknowledged and unrewarded.

In these circumstances, a degree of profit-related rewards seems appropriate and, if decisions are predominantly long-term ones, stock-based remuneration has a significant advantage. ESOs and MBOs both involve an element of stock-based rewards, much larger in the case of the MBO. Indeed, it has been shown that ESOs and MBOs may be complementary in that ESOs apparently involve no 'downside' risks and MBOs may lead to conservative attitudes to risk, where manager-owners must service large borrowings.

Of the two approaches, ESOs involve more organizational inflexi-bility. In fact, the tying of senior executives to the firm is one of their explicit objectives, while MBOs are a potential solution to monitor-ing problems but by definition can be accomplished only by separating from the organization. The new owners are subsequently bonded to the MBO.

It seems important to tailor solutions to the particular circumstances of a company. In more turbulent environments, where managerial deci-sions comprise exclusively non-routine judgements, the MBO may be a very strong candidate. In less turbulent circumstances, ESOs may provide the degree of stock-based rewards that reduces the dissonance between shareholders and managers. Most of the other chapters in this compilation also emphasize that where *all* employees make non-routine judgements, the restriction of ESOs and MBOs to a small elite group may bring fresh hierarchical problems.

Appendices

1 The CBI Survey

In February 1988, a questionnaire on ESOs was completed and returned by 862 manufacturing companies in a special survey sent out as a supplement to the regular industrial-trends survey of the Confederation of British Industry (CBI). An industrial disaggregation of the survey responses could not be provided by the CBI since it is anxious to conceal the identity of its survey respondents. The results were therefore provided as percentage responses weighted according to the system employed in the *CBI Industrial Trends* survey. This system is designed to reflect the importance both of individual respondents relative to their industry group and of industry group relative to aggregate manufacturing (in terms of value added).

Because the CBI's survey was restricted to manufacturing industry, the size and prevalence of ESOs reported was much lower than in other surveys which embraced the services sector. For example, Income Data Services (IDS) (1985:5) showed ESOs in 41 per cent of the 'Times Top 1000' companies and in 63 per cent of the 'Top 100'. This report also showed (page 6) that chief executives tended to receive ESOs to the value of four times salary, the maximum for Inland-Revenue-approved schemes. Survey details are shown in table 13.8 and it can be seen that salary multiples are lower than in the IDS survey.

2 The Centre for Management Buy-out Research Survey

In the autumn of 1986 a mailed questionnaire was administered to all the management buy-outs taking place from 1983, second quarter, to the end of 1985 as identified by CMBOR. Some 182 complete replies were received, after the sending of one reminder, representing a response rate of 36 per cent.

The questionnaire sought a great deal of information on many aspects of management buy-outs including quite detailed financial information. The questions on equity stakes, ESOs, and incentives should be seen in this context. The response rate was regarded as exceptionally good in these circumstances.

Management buy-out refers to the transfer of ownership of a firm whereby the incumbent senior management, taking the initiative, acquire a majority equity stake, having previously held none, or very little. However, there are a number of other transactions which share many characteristics of the pure buy-out, varying in only minor details. Variations relating to 'incumbent management' and size of 'equity stake' are given in table 13.9, with the terms generally associated with them.

247

Table 13.8 CBI special survey – executive share-option-schemes (ESOs) – February 1988; percentage responses except where indicated; number of respondents: 862. Responses of firms were weighted according to their sector's share of the overall CBI sample

		Yes	No	N/I
Does your company operate a scheme or schemes for	(a) executive share options?	34	65	0
	(b) share ownership for all employees?	29	68	2
Do you operate an Executive Share Option Scheme which is	(a) approved by the Inland Revenue under the 1984 Finance Act?	33	1	65
	(b) unapproved by the Inland Revenue?	5	8	85
Please indicate which of the following are eligible to participate in your ESO	(a) chief executive	32	1	65
	(b) other directors	33	0	65
	(c) other senior directors	29	4	66

The initial value of shares over which options are granted may be calculated as a multiple of an executive's current emoluments. For each category, please enter the highest multiple awarded in any one year of the initial value of shares covered by options to other emoluments.

Chief executive	2.2 times emoluments
Other directors (highest year's average for all in category)	1.9 times emoluments
Other senior executives (highest year's average for all in category)	1.5 times emoluments

Please indicate:

	£ (× 1000)
the total initial value of shares covered by ESOSs	3,548.2
the total value of shares acquired by executives upon the exercise of their options	1,334.2

Table 13.9 The definition of management buy-out

Key factor	Variation	Categorization
Incumbent management	Senior managers/directors	MBO
	Wider management team (2nd tier?)	MBO
	All employees have opportunity	EBO/ESOP
	External management team	MBI
	External management but with existing internal	MBO/MBI
	All employees must have shares	EBO/ESOP
	Managers take on contracts not the business	MCO
Equity stake	Controlling stake	MBO/EBO
	Largest single stake	MBO/EBO
	'Significant' stakes in terms of incentive and personal wealth	MBO/EBO
	Insignificant minority participation	LBO
	Existing management, but vendor retains significant (often majority) equity stake	Spin-out/ spin-off

MBO	Management buy-out
EBO	Employee buy-out
LBO	Leveraged buy-out
MBI	Management buy-in
ESOP	Employee share ownership plan
MCO	Management contract-out

References

Barney, J.B., and Ouchi, W.G. (1986) *Organizational Economics*, London: Jossey-Bass Publishers.

Chiplin, B., and Wright, M. (1987) 'The logic of mergers – the competitive market in corporate control in theory and practice', *IEA Hobart Paper 107*.

Chiplin, B., Wright, M., and Robbie, K. (1988) *Annual Review from CMBOR*, Nottingham: Centre for Management Buy-out Research.

Coopers and Lybrand (1987) *Employee Share Schemes in Practice*, Saffron Walden: Monks Publications.

Coyne, J., Wright, M., Robbie, K., and Lloyd, S. (1987) *Trends in UK Management Buy-outs 1986*, London: Venture Economics.

Fama, E.F., and Jensen, M.C. (1983) 'Separation of ownership and control', *Journal of Law and Economics*, 23(3), 301–25.

Garvin, A. (1983) 'Spin-offs and the new firm formation process', *California Management Review*, 25(2), 3–19.

Hanney, J. (1986) 'The management buy-out: an offer you can't refuse', *Omega*, 14(2), 119–34.

Incomes Data Services (1985) *Executive Share Options*, London: IDS Top Pay Unit.

Jensen, M.C. (1986) 'Agency costs of free cash flow, corporate finance and takeovers', *Papers and Proceedings of the American Economic Association*, 76(2), 323–9.

Jones, C.S. (1988) 'Management buy-outs and accounting control systems', mimeo, presented at BAA Annual Conference, Nottingham, April.

Knight, F.H. (1921) *Risk, Uncertainty and Profit*, Boston and New York: Houghton Mifflin.

Lewellen, W., Loderer, C., and Martin, K. (1987) 'Executive compensation and executive incentive problems', *Journal of Accounting and Economics*, 9(3), 287–310.

Mills, A. (1987) 'The neglected spin-out', *Acquisitions Monthly*, November, 36–8.

Scherer, F.M. (1984) 'Mergers, sell-offs and managerial behaviour', mimeo, presented to the 11th EARIE Conference, Fontainebleau, August.

Thompson, R.S., and Wright, M. (1987) 'Markets to hierarchies and back again: the implications of management buy-outs for factor supply', *Journal of Economic Studies*, 14(2), 1–22.

Wright, M. and Coyne, J. (1985) *Management buy-outs in British Industry*, London: Croom-Helm.

Wright, M., Robbie, K., and Thompson, R.S. (1989) 'On the financial and accounting implications of management buy-outs', *British Accounting Review*, forthcoming.

Chapter fourteen

A chance to be your own boss: the myth or reality of franchise ownership?

Alan Felstead[1]

Introduction

One of the central themes of Conservative policy since 1979 has been the reversal of the decline in direct share ownership that continued throughout the 1960s and 1970s. The policy consists of two strands. The first is the promotion of wider share ownership in its most general form, i.e. the encouragement to individuals to own shares directly in companies in which they have no direct involvement. This has been prompted most notably through the sale of nationalized industries, often at give-away prices (Vickers and Yarrow 1988: chapter 7). Personal Equity Plans have been introduced with a similar aim in mind although with less significance. Second, certain tax advantages have been offered to encourage individuals to own shares in the company in which they work. Instruments here include the promotion of employee share ownership and share-option plans (Grout 1987a). The combined aim of wider share and employee ownership is an attempt to create an 'enterprise culture' in which workers' incentives and attitudes towards the creation of wealth are fundamentally changed (Richardson and Nejan 1986; Grout 1987b; for a wide-ranging review, see *International Journal of Industrial Organization*, May 1988).

Independent of government, the 1980s have also seen the growth of a new wave of co-operatives, the expansion of self-employment, and the rising importance of management buy-outs (Oakeshott 1988; Meager 1987; Coyne and Wright 1988). By giving many more people a common goal with management, these growing forms of ownership, have allegedly improved worker incentives and company performance. Franchising forms another way in which businesses might harness these improvements.

In the light of the small-enterprise sector becoming the renewed focus of government and academic attention, franchised businesses are also notable for their relatively small size. Except for one-person van operations, most franchises take on staff to help them run their units. On average, each unit has in addition to the franchisee 5.5 full-time and 3.1 part-time staff; full-timers being split more or less evenly between men and women but part-timers being made up of predominantly women workers (Power Research Associates 1987:10).[2]

Franchising remains poorly understood, even though it is predicted to be one of the few areas of economic activity in which substantial growth can be expected. In the United States, for example, it is estimated that 34 per cent of retail sales in 1988 will occur through franchise-company outlets, and that total franchise-company sales of goods and services will reach $553 billion by the end of the year (US Department of Commerce 1988:15). Caution should none the less accompany these figures, since over three-quarters of these sales are made up of new motor vehicles and of petrol where franchising as a method of distribution has a long pedigree. In addition, they include sales for company-owned and franchised units. Unfortunately in the UK there is no comparable official database from which to draw. Instead one has to rely on an annual survey conducted independently on behalf of the British Franchise Association. The latest puts British franchising at around 2 per cent of retail sales. However, a comparison of these raw data figures is meaningless since the British estimate excludes categories included by the Americans (Power Research Associates 1987). A more accurate comparison can be made by excluding from the US figures the 75 per cent or so franchised sellers of cars and petrol. The exercise reveals US and UK franchise penetration to be far narrower than a straight comparison of statistics might first imply – 7.7 per cent of retail sales in the US compared to 2 per cent in the UK.

Nevertheless the upward direction and rapid pace of the franchise boom in the UK is largely undisputed. Over the last two years franchising has doubled both in terms of sales and employment. Today the sector's turnover stands at around £3.1 billion with employment levels running at about 169,000.[3] Turnover is expected to reach £7.7 billion by 1992, at current prices, while the number directly employed is forecast to top 420,000.[4]

It is the intention of this chapter to assess the 'industry's' claim that the franchise route offers franchisees 'a chance to be their own boss'. In so doing, the aim is to clarify the status of the franchised business for those attempting to aid the small-business sector. The chapter begins by defining a franchise. The key issue which, at least in some minds, separates the franchised business from the conventional small business – that of independence – is then examined from a formal and operational level (Stanworth *et al.* 1986).

The chapter argues that, while providing a useful starting point, such an approach provides an incomplete set of tools with which to assess the claim that franchisees are 'their own boss'. Two limitations in particular are noted. First, the assessment has previously been made in a static framework, with no attempt to assess changes that might occur over time. Second, the exclusive focus on the formal and operational dimensions to independence sidesteps an analysis of the franchisor-franchisee relation as exercised through royalty payments and/or a mark-up on supplies which in turn is legitimated and sustained by the franchisor's 'know how'.

The chapter concludes that a comprehensive analysis of the relations of production under which franchisees operate is required before clarification of franchisee status can be made. The following need to be considered: the ownership of the means of production; the control over the productive process; and distribution of the surplus generated. On each of these strategic variables, franchisees exhibit an ambiguous position. They are often owners of the physical but not mental means of production, required to operate within procedures laid down and subject to change, and contributors to the process of capital accumulation outside their own limited sphere of autonomy. Franchisees must therefore occupy an intermediate position between waged workers and the truly self-employed (and *independent* small employers) who own their own means of production and reap the full rewards of their own (and others') labour (Wright 1978). Any unequivocal answer to the question posed at the top of this chapter must therefore conceal a far greater level of analytical complexity than 'industry' advocates are willing to acknowledge. The chapter begins with the issue of definition.

Definition of a franchise

Although franchising began to grow rapidly in the UK during the late 1970s and early 1980s, it has a much longer commercial heritage. Indeed the first franchises in the modern commercial sense were established in the eighteenth and nineteenth centuries. The term itself, though, has an even longer ancestry. Originally it was used to refer to the granting of various rights and obligations from the sovereign which would otherwise be reserved for the Crown. Today its original meaning remains in widespread usage – governments still confer upon individuals or corporations the right to exercise some special privileges or engage in some particular enterprise, such as broadcasting on independent television (see Domberger and Middleton 1985), operating cable television systems and services (Home Office 1983; Veljanovski 1987) and often allows its citizens the right of self-determination through the ballot box.

More recently, a number of writers have suggested that this form of franchising might be extended to the sale of publicly owned 'natural' monopolies, such as electricity transmission (cf. Sharpe 1983; Domberger 1986). Advocates of such a strategy are in agreement with one of the major criticisms levelled at the current privatization programme, namely that transferring ownership from the public to the private sector will do little to promote competition, which ostensibly at least, is the overriding policy objective (Kay and Silberston 1984: 16). In contrast, franchising is said to combine the desirable elements of competition – through franchise bidding – with a regulatory framework which may be essential for the prevention of monopolistic and other 'inefficiencies'. The issues this debate raises are beyond the scope of this chapter; nevertheless given the currency of the debate, it is essential to be aware of the distinction between the franchises the state has within its power to grant and those granted by capital. It is with the latter issue that we are concerned.

Franchising as a form of business organization is frequently seen as a very recent phenomenon imported from the US. However, it has been widely used in some industries for several decades, and in others for centuries. In petrol retailing, for example, the operation of independently owned petrol stations in association with one or other of the major oil companies has been common for several decades. Today it is estimated that around 15,000 outlets operate on this basis (Euromonitor 1986: 24). Similarly, new car dealers who distribute a manufacturer's vehicles through their own retail outlets under the manufacturer's name and trade mark can be described as operating under a franchise arrangement, and one that has been practised for several decades.

In the brewing industry the franchising concept has been prevalent since stricter licensing laws introduced towards the end of the eighteenth century prompted the 'tied' public house. The tightening of the licensing laws had the effect of greatly raising the value of the remaining premises, often beyond the resources of the publican. The magistrates' insistence on raised standards in licensed premises was an added problem for the licensee who turned to the brewers for financial, and sometimes supervisory, help. Brewing companies, anxious to secure outlets for their products, and fearing competition, bought some premises outright, and gave credit to publicans (often in return for a mortgage), on condition that the publican would sell no beer other than that produced by the brewer (Housden 1976; *Financial Times*, 23 and 30 July 1986). Most of today's brewers sell their beer through the same system of 'tied' public houses, of which 33,600 are tenanted and almost 13,000 brewery-owned and managed (Brewers' Society figures).

Other types of franchise arrangement can also be identified. Franchising can refer to the arrangement where a second party is licensed to undertake a manufacturing or processing operation and to sell the product to a retailer under the franchisor's trade name and/or mark. On becoming a Coca-Cola or Pepsi-Cola franchisee, for instance, the independent bottler receives the exclusive rights to bottle and distribute soft drinks for that company in an exclusive geographical territory.

There are also franchise links between wholesalers and retailers. This method of wholesale distribution is best known for its usage by American drugstores, vehicle part outlets, and the food and hardware chains. British voluntary chains such as VG and Mace, as well as European chains such as Spar, operate a similar system.

The final type, and the one around which much of the more recent growth has centred, is known as the business-format franchise. Under this system, the franchisee not only sells the franchisor's product and/or service, but does so in accordance with a set of precisely laid-down procedures or 'format'. The franchisee provides the capital for the business and usually pays both a one-off initial licence fee and some form of continuing royalty payment, either as a percentage of turnover or a mark-up on products supplied by the franchisor. In return, the franchisor provides the franchisee with assistance in carrying on the business. This includes training in the operation and methods of the business prior to opening, in addition to continued advice and assistance in the areas of staff training, managemment, marketing, research and development and so on. Clearly, some of these elements are to be found in many of the franchise arrangements discussed above. However, the business-format franchise involves the use of, not merely goods and services identified by a trade mark or invention, but a package/'blueprint' containing all the elements necessary to establish the business and run it profitably on a predetermined basis. The package/'blueprint' is carefully prepared from the company's wholly owned and/or pilot operations, thereby minimizing the risks involved in setting up a conventional small business.

Many businesses are currently operating and offering franchises on a business format basis (see tables 14.1 and 14.2). They cover a number of market sectors and scales of operation. Overall, though, the 'industry' is still dominated by food and drink, followed by home maintenance and business services (this is mainly composed of high-street print shops). Despite having more units, greater turnover, and being the heaviest users of labour, the food and drink sector (this refers mainly to fast-food restaurants) have fewer franchisees than both home maintenance and business services (see table 14.3). This would seem to suggest a higher proportion of multiple unit/outlet franchisees than elsewhere.

Variations are also evident across market sectors in terms of set-up costs, licence fees, and levels of royalty payments. Take set-up costs, for example. These range from just over £140,000 for a fast-food outlet to nearer £10,000 for a domestic-service franchise. Likewise with royalty payments; from an average of 2 per cent of turnover in franchised confectioners to around 18 per cent in domestic services (see table 14.4).

This chapter focuses attention on those franchise opportunities currently available in the UK and often billed as a 'chance to be your

Table 14.1 Franchise opportunities in the UK

Automotive/car hire
Autopro
Autosheen Car Valeting
Avis
Better Brakes
British Damproofing
British School of Motoring
Budget-Rent-A-Car
Car Market
Clean Machine
Computa-Tune
Fittapart
Highway Windscreens
Hometune
Hot Wheels
Identicar
Jet Clean
Kenprest and Kentred
Kleenacar Valeting
Masterserve
Midas
Mobiletuning
Mr Autobrill
Mr Clutch
Novus Windscreen Repair
Panarama Sunroofs
Practical Used Car Rental
PRB Self Drive Hire
Professional Appearance Service
Revolution
Silver Shield
Town and Country Car Rentals
Tune Up
UK School of Motoring
Wash 'N' Wax
Ziebart Rustproofing

Building maintenance
A1 Damproofing
AMK Damproofing
Bath Transformations
Brick-Tie Services
British Damproofing
CICO Chimney Linings
Complete Weed Control
Countrywide Garden Maintenance
Cover Rite
Creteprint Paving
Dampco
Dampcure-Woodcure/30
Damptechnik
Drainmasters

Dyno-Electrics
Dyno-Plumbing
Dyno-Rod
Enviraflo
Fersina
Guardia Shutters
Gun-Point
Hire Technicians Group
Isodan
Jet-Rod
Master Thatcher
Metro-Rod
Microelec
Mixamate
Pass and Co
Potholes
Power-Rod
Quattro Seal
Trace Heat Pumps
Ventrolla

Beauty/fashion
Alan Paul
Barry 'M' Shop (The)
Body and Face Place (The)
Body Reform
Body Shop (The)
Caroll Fashions
Command Performance
Copy Cats
Direct Salon Services
House of Colour
Keith Hall
Lady K Salon Services
Natural Life Products
Nature's Way
Nectar Cosmetics
Soap Shop
Weightguard Slimming Centres
Yves Rocher Beauty Centres

Cafes/pubs/restaurants
Chantegrill
Berni Restaurants
Fatso's Pasta
Morley's
Pancake Place
Pizza Express
Ponderosa
Poppins Restaurants
Strikes
Tippy's Taco House

Table 14.1 continued

Computers/business services	**Fast food baking/confectionery**
Accounting Centre (The)	Baskin-Robbins Ice Cream
ACT Computerworld	Bellina Belgian Chocolates
AIDS Computer Services	Big Orange (The)
Amicro Systems	Burger King
Britannia Business Sales	Chicken George
Business Transfer Consultants	Confetti
Computerland	Cookie Coach Company
Future Training and Recruitment	Dial-A-Dino's
Micropulse	Dixy Fried Chicken
Personal Computers	Domino's Pizza
Prodata	Don Millers
Programs Unlimited	Donutland Yog-Ice
RBS Accountancy and Book-Keeping	Kansas Fried Chicken
Recognition Express	Kentucky Fried Chicken
Regional Business Services	Lyons Maid
VDU Services	McDonald's
Wetherby Training Services	Merryweathers
Wordplex Wordprocessing	Mister Softee
	Mr Big
Delivery service/distribution	Mr Cod
Alpine Soft Drinks	Olivers
Amtrak Express Parcels	Perfect Pizza
Anaco	Pizza Galley
ANC Parcel Service	Pizza Hut
Bread Roll Company (The)	PJ's Drive-In
Brewer and Turnbull	Snappy Tomato Pizza
Business Post	Southern Fried Chicken
Captain Cargo	Spud-U-Like
City Link	Subway
Coffeeman	Thorntons
Crispflow	Wendy
Fidelity	Wimpy International
Freezavan	Yankeeburger
Hornets	
Inter-Teddy Worldwide	**Glass engraving**
Interlink	The Compleat Engraver
Lazeron Batteries	
Northern Dairies	**Health/leisure**
Retail Milk Rounds	Barry 'M' Shop
Stroud Creamery	Bodysense
TNT Parcel Office	Castle Fairs
Unigate	Great Adventure Game (The)
	Herbal World
Estate agents	Poppy's Body Centre
Balmforth and Partners	Skirmish
Cornerstone	Slim Gym
Country Properties	Splatoon
Everett Masson and Furby	Team
New Moves	Tumble Tots
Seekers	Video Events

257

Table 14.1 continued

Weider Health and Fitness
West Coast Video

Interiors/DIY/security
Bath Doctor
Bath Doctor (The)
Bath Wizard
Betterware
Carpet Master
Colour Counsellors
Curtain Dream
Decorating Den
Fersina
Fuel Boss
Guardia Shutters
House of Colour
Intoto Kitchens
Knightguard
Kwik Silver
Kwik-Strip
Mr Boilerserviceman
National Security
Newlook Bath Services
Original Kitchen Company (The)
Pandel Tiles
Renubath
Scotchcare Services
Stained Glass Overlay
Stop-A-Thief!
Uticolour
Vinyl Master
Wallspan Bedrooms

Laundry/dry cleaning/cleaners
Chem-Dry
Dial-A-Char
Euroclean
Global/The Maids
Magna Dry
Molly Maid
Mr Slade Dry Cleaning
National Vacuum Cleaners
Poppies
Rainbow International
Safeclean
ServiceMaster
Sketchley

Personalization services
BadgeMan
Banaman

Geoffrey E. Macpherson
Meistergram
Signtalk
System-Text

Printing/photography
AlphaGraphics Printshops
Concord One Hour Photo Labs
Foto Inn
Fotofast
Kall-Kwik Printing
Langwood's One Hour Photo
Microfilm Express
PDC Copyright
Photomaid
PIP Printing
Prontaprint
Snappy Snaps

Recruitment and training
Alfred Marks Bureaux
Ashfield Personnel
Future Training & Recruitment
Priority Management

Retail outlets
Apollo Window Blinds
Athena
Ballon
Bally
Benetton
Bike
Bob's Tiles
Bundles
Caroll
Chapter and Verse
Circle 'C' Convenience Stores
City Bag Store
Clarks Shoes
Compleat Cookshop
Crown Eyeglass
Curtain Dream
Dash
Descamps
English Rose
Eye Shop
Fastframe
Fikipsi
Fires and Things
Frame Factory (The)
Garden Building Centres

Table 14.1 continued

H-Plan Bedroom Furniture	Strachan Studio
House of Something Different	Swinton Insurance
Intoto Kitchens	Tandy
Kimberley's	Tie Rack (The)
Knobs and Knockers	Youngs Formal Wear for Men
Late Late Supershop (The)	
Leatherland	*Tool hire and sales*
Lenniz Kitchens	Agricultural Plant Hire
Lifestyle	Banson Tool Hire
Mainly Marines	Fixit
Millers Cookies	Hire Technicians Group
Oasis	Mr Lift
Oilily	Snap-On-Tools
On the Wall	
Openshop	
Original Art Shop	*Travel/holiday*
Pandel Tiles	Exchange Travel
Phildar	Holiday Inn
Phone-In	Hyde-Barker Travel
Pier Cargo	Intacab
Pineapple	Yellow Cab
Portico Canopies	
Prima	*Vending*
Pronuptia de Paris Bridalwear	Carebridge
Rodier Paris	Infopoint
Rymans	
Singer	*Workshop consumables*
Snappy Snaps	Motabiz
Spar Discount	Snap-On-Tools
Stefnal	Trust Parts

Note: This list is by no means exhaustive, but it should give some idea of the breadth of franchise opportunities available in the UK. It should also be pointed out that the companies listed have various degrees of involvement and historical commitments to franchising as a business arrangment (for all firms in that franchise in the US, the US Department of Commerce (1988:2) estimates that 82 per cent of the units are franchised and 18 per cent centrally owned).

Sources: Compiled from *Franchise World, The Franchise Magazine,* Barrow and Golzen (1987), Baillieu (1988), franchise 'fairs' as well as from information supplied by the companies themselves.

Table 14.2 Company ranking by number of UK outlets, 1986[1]

Company	Number of business format franchised outlets/units in UK
TNT Despatch[2]	435
Wimpy	364
Snap-On-Tools	312
Prontaprint	286
Kentucky Fried Chicken	280
Benetton	270
Home Tune	230
ServiceMaster	175
British School of Motoring	150
Kall-Kwik Printing	120
Budget Rent A Car	114
Identicar	100[3]
Apollo Window Blinds	100
Auto-Smart Distributorship	90[3]
The Body Shop	77
Dyno-Rod	75
Pronuptia de Paris Bridalwear	70
Safeclean	65
Youngs Formal Wear for Men	60
Isodan	60
Retail Milk Rounds	60
Tie Rack	56
The Cookie Coach Company	54
Mobiletuning	54
PIP Instant Printing	53

Notes: 1 The figures given here are those supplied by the companies concerned and are correct as of September 1986.
2 This type of franchise is known as a fractional franchise, that is one in which the franchise forms part of an existing business operated by the franchisee. TNT Despatch Post franchised reception points are often found in various locations such as petrol stations, High-street shops, and so on.
3 These figures are the most up-to-date available and they apply to 1984. They have been taken from Golzen, Barrow, and Severn 1984: 238.
Source: Company information (correct at time of inquiry)

Table 14.3 Distribution of business format franchising by market sector

Market sector	% of all active franchisees	% of all units	% of total turnover	% of all employees
Food and drink	16	42	56	59
Home maintenance	28	23	18	12
Business services	19	12	8	8
Vehicle maintenance	8	14	8	10
Transport	4	5	10	5
Leisure	8	1	2	—
Health and beauty	6	2	1	1
Clothing and fashion	3	2	1	1
Other	3	1	2	1
Personal durables	3	—	—	—
Instruction	1	1	—	—
Communications	1	—	—	—

Note: Column totals may not add up to 100 because of rounding.
Source: Power Research Associates 1985: 7

Table 14.4 Business format franchising: set-up costs, licence fees, and royalties
by market sector

Market sector	Average licence fee	Average initial investment	Royalties (as % of turnover)
	£	£	
Fast food	7,125	142,170	7.8
Computer retailers	8,488	79,350	5.8
High-street print	11,063	58,776	10.0
Consumer services	6,227	48,613	10.1
Food specialists	4,750	47,750	5.9
Clothiers	5,417	40,500	5.7
Other retailers	3,700	38,050	4.2
Commercial services	4,442	18,521	9.1
Automotive	8,419	17,850	11.2
Confectioners	1,150	14,700	2.0
Domestic services	4,214	10,325	17.7

Note: Ranked by level of initial investment. According to Power Research Associates (1987: 24)
the initial outlay across franchising as a whole averages £43,270. To this total must then
be added the ongoing costs – averaging 7.8 per cent of turnover for royalties or management charges, 2.6 per cent contribution to advertising (where this is itemized separately),
and a 25.7 per cent mark-up on supplies which becomes 8.6 per cent if these are taken to
account for one-third of turnover.
Source: Company information (correct at time of inquiry)

own boss' for the aim of the chapter is to guide policy-makers, bankers,
and academics to clarify the position of franchised businesses. Most of
these opportunities can be defined as business-format franchise systems.

Formal limits to and operational scope for independence

Independence from external control is often taken as one of the defining
characteristics that separates small firms from the small units of a larger
enterprise (and the self-employed from the directly employed, see page
265). In the words of the Bolton Committee: 'the owner-manager should
be free from outside control in taking their practical decisions' (Bolton
1971: 1. However, as the Committee itself pointed out, the independence
of even the conventional small business is always less than total and often
difficult to assess accurately in practice. Many are reliant on much larger
firms for their custom. For example, widely dispersed networks of small
clothing manufacturers often produce for one large retailer who in turn
lay down the exact specifications for an acceptable item – the number
of stitches to an inch, the number of inches to a hem, dates for delivery
and the price for the completed item. In return for acceptance of these
disciplines, suppliers are rewarded with long production runs (Rainnie
1984; Stanworth 1988). These constitute severe limitations on the

independence of the small entrepreneur in practice, without in any way compromising the nominal or legal independence they are deemed to enjoy. The *Bolton Report* estimated that 35 per cent of small firms were dependent on one customer for 25 per cent or more of their business (Bolton 1971: 32).

The problems of assessing the independence of the franchised small business are even more difficult to resolve than those connected with the conventional small business. Additional problems mainly arise because of the close and explicit links between franchisor and franchisee. To overcome these problems Stanworth *et al.* (1986) suggest that franchisee independence needs to be examined from a formal *and* operational level. In this section we critically outline this approach and the conclusions its originators reach.

By the formal level Stanworth and his colleagues refer to the legal contract binding franchisor and franchisee. Close analysis at this level reveals a very comprehensive specification of the business relationship between franchisee and franchisor. In addition to setting out the exact nature of the services to be provided, payment levels, royalty charges, and the basis of their calculation, the contract also includes other more restrictive clauses. One contract the Stanworth team examined, for example, stipulated that the franchisee:

> Will conduct his [sic] franchised . . . business in all respects as shall be laid down by the Company from time to time in the Manual or otherwise. The franchisee will keep a copy of the Manual in his [sic] possession up to date with all variations thereto which the Company may make.
>
> (Quoted in Stanworth 1984: 83.)

This type of contract commits the franchisee to an open-ended agreement whereby 'franchisees find themselves in the tenuous positon of being bound to a contract that can be modified *unilaterally* by the franchisor' (Hunt 1972: 37, emphasis in original). In a wider review of franchise contracts in the US simlar clauses were found (Hunt 1972).

Franchise contracts also lay down the conditions on which a franchisee is allowed to dispose of the franchised business, particularly the standards by which the franchisor may approve or reject any prospective assignee or purchaser should the franchisor not exercise the right of first refusal to purchase often contained in the contract. As part of its obligation of confidentiality the franchisee is normally prohibited from setting up a business in competition with that of the franchisor for a fixed period, even after the termination of the franchise agreement. And finally, since the franchisor runs the risk of becoming liable for the acts of the franchisee, the franchise agreement often states that the franchisee is an independent contractor responsible for all acts and defaults made by him/herself and any others he/she may employ. This indemnifies the franchisor.

At the formal level the restrictions on franchisee independence appear severe. However, Stanworth (1984) and his colleagues (Stranworth *et al.* 1986) suggest that such a conclusion is misleading. Although central in a formal sense to franchisor–franchisee relations, the franchise contract is not permitted a similarly explicit position in their day-to-day relations. Franchisor–franchisee relations as exercised operationally are not revealed by detailed examination of the franchise contract.

By shifting the analysis to the *operational* level and an examination of the everyday relationship that exists between franchisor and franchisee, the Stanworth team suggest that an altogether different picture emerges.

When franchisors and franchisees were questioned on the division of responsibilities on key aspects of decision-making at the outlet, broad agreement emerged. Franchisors claimed responsibility for control over the product mix and pricing, while franchisees claimed control over hours of opening, employment of personnel, bookkeeping, and quality standards. However, there were sizeable minorities holding contrary views on these aspects and particularly on quality control and product mix changes (Stanworth *et al.* 1986: 241).

The research also measured the extent of the franchisee's operational freedom by using the yardstick of the frequency of contact. Almost 35 per cent of franchisees reported contact with their franchisor as occurring at least once a week, most of which were franchisee-initiated rather than franchisors exercising a more explicit supervisory role. Similarly with franchisor visits to the outlet: less than 10 per cent were visited more frequently than once a fortnight, with most franchisors visiting on a monthly or bi-monthly basis. These figures hardly betoken close supervision.

On this basis the originators of the formal/operational approach have reached the conclusion that, although a portion of a franchisees' independence has been 'traded' for an element of security and support, those seeking to promote the small enterprise in our society can legitimately include the franchised outlet among the alternatives to be realistically considered' (Stanworth 1986: 54).

However, in reaching this conclusion no account has been taken of the changes that might occur over time within a franchise chain, although different levels of independence that a franchisee might exercise across systems has been noted by one of the Stanworth team (Hough 1986). Three possible sources of dynamic variation can be singled out.

First, when franchising is adopted by a company from its inception (see Felstead 1988), the franchisor will usually lack impressive head office facilities, have few existing outlets to show potential franchisees, may have uncertain sales levels due to a lack of pilot outlets, and be relatively unknown. These factors severely limit the ability to recruit franchisees. However, as the franchise system matures, these limitations become more relaxed, thereby allowing the franchisor to offer franchises to preferred candidates on a take-it-or-leave-it basis. It has been recently suggested that one in seven of those who enquire after a business-format franchise are interviewed, while only 4 per cent are actually appointed (Power Research Associates 1987: 36). Thus 'the greater the over supply of labour [would-be franchisees], the more selective employers [franchisors] can be, and the more important recruitment becomes as a means of control' (Maguire 1986: 73). As franchise systems mature, this means of control is enhanced.

Against the background of lengthening waiting lists some franchisors have developed more sophisticated and more thorough 'vetting' procedures. In the US, for example, McDonald's franchise candidates are required to work for a *minimum* of 500 hours in a local store. As part of the training programme franchise candidates receive no pay. Instead they are assessed on their capabilities to run a successful store.

A second way in which operational independence may be tightened up over time is through the easing of the capital constraint which often provides the incentive for franchising in the first place. Initially franchisors may be short of funds and hence driven to rely on those provided by franchisees. This scarcity becomes less of a constraint over time, especially for successful franchisors, as they become self-financing. The availability of a ready supply of managerial talent and labour to train the less experienced franchisee also increases the franchisor's hold on the franchisee as well as ultimately creating a pool of labour to substitute for their existing franchised labour force.

The third factor relates to the promotion and protection of the trade mark. This is central to the franchise relationship because consumers possess information about the price and quality of goods or sevices sold by establishments under a given trade mark. Consumers have this information precisely because the franchisor polices the system and maintains quality according to a predetermined set of standards (Caves and Murphy II 1976).

In the 1950s many US fast-food franchisors, including McDonald's, lacked the disciplining force of uniformity. For example, some of McDonald's earliest franchisees were buying only the blueprints to the red and white tile building, the right to use the arches, a fiffteen-page operating manual describing the Speedy Service System, and the McDonald's name. Each franchisee also received one week's training in the company-owned store. After that they were free to operate as they wished, and most did. They sold hamburgers at different prices, some added new items to the menu, others added more serving windows, and one licencee decided to bring the golden arches to a point and rename his drive-in, 'Peaks'.

By granting large franchising territories to franchisees who could then sublicense to others, some of McDonald's contemporary fast-food operators found it even more difficult to exert central control over the development of the chain. Large territorial franchisees, with considerable amounts of money invested in their local operations, developed their territories as they saw fit. Thus, Dairy Queen (a chain of ice-cream stores), for example, operated differently in different parts of the country. Some had food; others did not. They even offered different sizes of cones and types of sundaes. With little centralized supervision, the quality of local operations varied all over the United States. While some operators provided a quality product and service, others would 'cheat' by adding water to their dairy mix and their toppings.

Real problems also lay in the duplication of a poor franchisee which territorial franchising implied. If a franchisor has a poor franchisee in one store, he/she has one type of problem. But if the same operator has a contractual right to put up as many stores as he/she wishes, the franchisor's problem can be duplicated many times over. As a result the franchising of large territories has become relatively rare.

Instead most of today's franchisors grant franchises on store-by-store basis, equipping each franchise with a detailed operations manual. The current McDonald's operating manual runs to 600 pages and covers cooking methods and procedures, standard food portions, daily cleaning requirements, quality control, as well as specifying the organization of production and the division of labour. Although all franchisors do not have such detailed manuals, the trend is towards greater uniformity as franchise chains expand and mature. The consequences for franchisees are particularly severe when the franchisee is committed to an open-ended agreement of the sort discussed above.

However, even the identification of factors which suggest that a tightening up of franchisee independence might take place as franchise systems expand and mature provides an incomplete set of tools with which to assess the claim that franchisees are 'their own boss'. Its exclusive focus on the relative, albeit shifting, autonomy of the franchisee in the production process sidesteps an analysis of ownership and distributional relations. It is to the provision of a more complete analysis that we now turn.

Small employers, self-employed or a disguised wage-labour force?

The class position of the self-employed, and small employers more generally, has been the source of much debate (see Mackenzie 1982 for a review). This has been fuelled by widespread indications of a revival in their fortunes. A recent estimate suggests that there are 2.6 million self-employed people in Britain – a sharp increase over previously recorded levels (Creig *et al.* 1986: 13). Despite evidence to the contrary (Storey and Johnson 1987), the small firm sector is increasingly seen by the government as a source of new jobs and as playing an important role in economic change and innovation. The government has therefore sought to promote the small enterprise using the strong ideological appeal of 'being your own boss'.

Seemingly persuaded by the claim that the controls placed upon the franchisee by the formal contract are not translated into operational practice, and in the absence of wage payments, the government has begun to treat franchisees as part of the *independent* small business sector. Indeed in October 1986 the rules governing the Enterprise Allowance Scheme were relaxed to allow unemployed people to take up a franchise and qualify for the £40 weekly allowance, provided they had the £1,000 to qualify, not to mention some £10,000–£15,000 to buy even the cheapest franchise (cf. table 14.4). A number of other training and employment programmes have also been modified. The Loan Guarantee Scheme, for example, provides a government guarantee against default by borrowers, enabling banks to make loans to franchisees who might otherwise have been regarded as too great a risk. Through the Business Expansion Scheme investors in franchises can benefit from tax relief at top rates on their investment, and there is currently pressure to allow franchisors to participate in the Scheme as well. Other government programmes such as the Technical and Vocational Education Initiative (TVEI), Youth Training Scheme, Community Programme, and Voluntary Projects have also been modified to give young people an understanding of franchising (*Employment Gazette*, December 1987).

At a superficial level, franchisees appear to operate under conditions not as rigid as suggested by the franchise contract (see page 262), own the physical means of production, and receive compensation levels directly tied to the profits of the outlet. If the defining feature of wage labour is the payment of a wage, then franchisees clearly fall outside the category of waged labour. If, however, wage labour is defined as the contribution labour makes to the process of capital accumulation, then franchisees may, in part, constitute a form of wage labour since payments are made to the parent company (usually proportional to turnover), thereby contributing to a process of capital accumulation *outside* their own limited sphere of autonomy.

As research in other areas has suggested, the absence of direct supervision and/or conventional wage payments need not mean that those who work under these conditions are no longer part of the wage-earning class (cf. Birkbeck 1978; Gerry and Birkbeck 1981; Allen and Wolkowitz 1986). The status of franchisees must therefore rest on an analysis of their location in the wider process of capital accumulation, and not upon legal definitions (see Dale 1986) nor the appearance of 'own-account' working.

By granting certain workers property rights in the business, franchising, like other forms of financial participation (cf. Poole 1988), attempts to enlist support for the extraction of labour from labour power. For example, the nominal status of the franchisee as self-employed (with or without employees) may bring the franchisor considerable benefits in terms of increased levels of motivation and commitment without costly supervision. Franchisees, are, for instance, likely to work longer hours. Of a sample of self-employed, Gallup found that 45 per cent regularly worked more than 60 hours a week, with an average of just over 55 (Legal and General Assurance Company 1985). In addition, unpaid contributions were also in evidence. Gallup found that 60 per cent of self-employed men and 48 per cent of self-employed women had the help of their spouse, 41 per cent of whom received no remuneration at all. Eleven per cent of those surveyed also had their children working for them, one-third of whom went entirely unpaid. Many franchisors specify the need for complete family 'commitment' in their screening of potential franchisees, thereby allowing such reserves of unpaid labour to be tapped (Edens *et al.* 1976). The outcome is to raise labour's input (that of both the franchisee and his/her staff) without the costly monitoring across a widely dispersed network of outlets/units that might otherwise attend company ownership.[5]

Since franchisees do not experience direct work discipline as exercised through the wage relationship, it may appear, and they may also feel, independent. However, their relative autonomy should not be confused with independence from the generation of surplus value and its distribution; although franchisees may appropriate some of the surplus value created by others, they also contribute to the production process of their parent franchisor.

The main source of returns for the franchisor is the royalty (and/or mark-up on goods supplied). Using this method for obtaining returns, the franchisor benefits from an income stream that gives it a share in the enlarged sales of its franchised outlets. Furthermore, the franchised establishment need not make a profit for the franchisor to do so. Instead some franchises may be terminated for poor performance, i.e. low sales. Higher sales volume, less expensive supervisory mechanisms, and greater net profits for the franchisor make franchising the preferred business strategy, particularly for marginal and outlying outlets.

Franchising also ensures that franchisors bear a smaller than 'normal' share of the costs associated with capitalist production. Associated payroll costs and employment rights are no longer the responsibility of the franchise company. Instead National Insurance contributions, paid holidays, sick leave, and other fringe benefits are borne by franchisees. For those who employ others, franchising effectively transfers these labour costs to franchisees. As a result it may serve to forestall collective organization by fragmenting the labour force across the franchise through heterogeneous terms and conditions of employment. The effect is, however, more likely to be a consequence of franchising than a major incentive for organizations to franchise all or parts of their business.

In addition, franchising off loads many of the risks associated with expansion. In order for production to take place, both the physical means of production (raw materials, plant, equipment), labour power, and the mental means of production (know-how and methods of operation) are required. Before production can be set into motion, money capital must be advanced for the purchase of the physical means of production for each outlet established, whilst the mental means of production acquired for one outlet are simply applied with little variation to others in the chain. A company-owned and -managed chain is therefore reliant for its expansion upon either internal generation of capital or borrowing from financiers. As a result an expanded network of outlets is either slow or else costly to establish and is a problematic source of profit. By raising capital from outside the firm, however, franchising reduces the level of capital injection required of franchisors, thereby diminishing any potential loss and quickening the pace at which the network is able to expand.

The implication might be drawn that the franchisor's knowledge and know-how is scarce and thus a factor that a competitive market will properly reward (on the issue of knowledge and power see Marglin 1984; Berg 1984). Under conditions of Pareto-optimality goods and services will command a price so long as they are scarce and possess the property of 'private' goods, that is more for one person will mean less for another. However, the peculiar nature of the services provided by franchisors violates the latter condition. More specifically, the supply of the business format and the knowledge and 'know-how' associated with it to more than one franchisee does not diminish the supply available to others. As a result each franchisor has an incentive to share his/her know-how with an expanded circle of clients without reducing either the supply to existing recipients or the reward per client. Other franchisors offering 'turnkey' operations in the sector can be expected to retaliate in two ways: one is to cut the prices of their services to their existing franchises, the other is to undercut the price of services provided by competitor franchisors, thereby invading the markets of others. The competitive outcome will be zero pricing, hence no 'reward' nor role for franchisors (Marglin 1984).

In fact, many of the early business-format franchisors, such as McDonald's, were often so generous in providing visitors to their stores with information about their production procedures, their equipment, and their suppliers, that no one really needed a franchise to learn the McDonald's secret. However, the returns for franchisors rest heavily upon strategies that make it difficult, if not impossible, for a franchisee to operate without their assistance. By restricting the transference of relevant know-how and accumulated business experience to its franchisees alone, a franchisor is able to engender a dependent relationship from which a return is then drawn. This is often embodied within the franchise contract itself. Clauses relating to the disclosure and resale of know-how and restrictions on ex-franchisees from operating similar types of businesses are aimed at tying a franchisee to a franchisor, thereby legitimating and sustaining the income of the latter. Issues of this kind were most recently raised in a High Court action by Prontaprint against one of its former franchisees. Given the importance of the case to franchising generally, it is worth examining the case in more detail.[6]

The case concerned a Prontaprint franchisee who declined to renew his contract but continued to trade at the same premises in the same type of business, yet under a new name. The terms of the original agreement entered into, however, contained specific clauses restraining ex-franchisees from engaging in similar types of businesses – either directly or indirectly. The restrictions were to operate for a period of three years following termination/expiry, with the geographical extent of the limitation confined to within half a mile of the original premises and three miles from existing Prontaprint outlets (most franchise contracts contain similar restrictions).

The company claimed that by entering into an agreement of this kind, the franchisee was supported in the setting up and successful operation of a business about which they really knew little about until Prontaprint's know-how was made available to them. They also benefited from the goodwill attached to the Prontaprint name.

Counsel for the ex-franchisee did not dispute that Prontaprint was a name which in fact acquired considerable goodwill. Rather the franchisee's position was that the restrictions on ex-franchisees was unreasonable. Prontaprint had already received an initial payment – the franchise fee – for the use of the trademark, know-how, and for the help and support given in setting up the business. In so far as additional assistance and know-how were given thereafter, a percentage charge on turnover was levied. The ex-franchisee submitted that the business was one mainly built by the franchisee with Prontaprint having been paid for such contribution as they made during the life of the agreement. On expiry, Prontaprint no longer had an interest in the business and, as such, it would be unreasonable for the franchisor to restrict the activities of an independent business.

The judgement found in favour of the franchisor's upholding the duration of the restraint and its geographical coverage. Two main grounds for doing so were offered. The first was that, if the former franchisee were entitled to operate from the same premises, albeit with a different name (Laserprint), they would still draw advantage from the Prontaprint name. In all local directories, including the 'Yellow Pages', anybody seeking printing services would, for some time, find under the name of Prontaprint the address and telephone number of Laserprint.[7] Furthermore, existing customers returning to where they would naturally expect to find a Prontaprint service, would find a competing service yet with the same faces greeting them. They might well assume that it was, in substance and effectively, the same business and they would not bother to go elsewhere. Indeed by displaying a notice on the window bearing the words 'Same Team, New Name' shortly after the franchise agreement came to an end, the ex-franchisee actively encouraged old and new customers to make just such an assumption.

The second reason for ruling in favour of the franchisor, lay in Prontaprint's know-how. Without this having been made available to the franchisee, it was argued that the business would not have been set up, let alone become a success. On these grounds the court upheld the restrictions placed upon former franchisees.

In giving his judgement, Mr Justice Whitford, recognized the importance of the case to franchising more generally:

> if a convenant of this kind [restrictions on the activities of ex-franchisees] is unenforceable, as soon as they [franchisees] have managed to get going on the expertise, advice and assistance given to them by the plaintiffs [Prontaprint and other franchisors], other franchisees are going to either withdraw or not renew their agreements and franchising will, effectively, become inoperable.
>
> (quoted from *Franchise World*, March/May 1987: 15.)

In upholding the terms of the franchise agreement the court therefore reinforced the franchisor's hold over the franchisee by declaring it lawful for restrictions to be placed on the activities of the latter on termination or expiry of the agreement.[8] As a result the franchise relationship and the contract in particular make it difficult, if not impossible, for the franchisee to do without the franchisor. Know-how, like capital itself, becomes a social relation of production and, as such, a source of power from which income can be drawn. The outcome of the specific case itself was that the former Prontaprint franchisee rejoined the chain, and as a result royalties continued to be paid.[9]

Other more mature franchisors have further strengthened the tie between themselves and franchisees through the ownership of the property and land on which outlets are built. Again McDonald's provides the classic example of this sort of tie. Indeed the control which this gave the company over its franchisees was not lost on the chain's founder, Ray Kroc:

It [the franchisee's sublease] says that if at any time McDonald's System Inc., notifies Franchise Realty Corporation that the operation does not conform in every way to the McDonald's standards of quality and service, this lease will be cancelled on thirty-day notice. Now we have a club over them, and by God, there will be no more pampering or fiddling with them. We will do the ordering instead of going around and begging them to co-operate.

(quoted in Love 1987: 157.)

However, the available evidence suggests that, in general, UK franchisees are more often tenants of landlords rather than their franchisors (only 17 per cent of the Power sample reported themselves to be tenants of their franchisor, Power Research Associates 1987: 29).

Conclusion

Concentration on the outward manifestations of independence provides a somewhat simplistic basis on which to assess the 'industry's' claim that franchisees are 'their own boss'. In addition, consideration must be given to the ownership of the means of production – physical and mental – and the distribution of the surplus generated. In this way a more complex picture emerges.

The conclusion reached in this chapter has wider implications than those simply relating to franchising. It also has implications for the study of small businesses more generally. Given that 'independence' is a relative notion, previous research (Stanworth 1984) has often compared the experiences of franchisees with owners of conventional small businesses. This is justified on two grounds. First, both are small units and, second, entry through one is often a substitute for entry through the other.

However, as already noted, the independence of conventional small businesses is often limited by a heavy reliance on a few large firms. Moreover, the label of self-employed or small employer says nothing about the economic and social reality that might lay behind (Rainbird 1988). In other words, the contribution small firms might make to the process of capital accumulation outside their own limited sphere of automony is not assessed. As a consequence, while the law makes the selection of employment status critical, 'it has failed singularly to provide clear guidance as to how this should be done' (Leighton 1983: 197). The class position of many small-business owners is therefore confused.

This confusion is most acute in the case of the franchise relationship. Here the franchisee owns the physical means of production, conducts his/her operations within procedures laid down by the parent organization, and is a recipient of most, but not all, of the surplus generated. The franchisor, on the other hand, retains the intellectual

271

property rights in the business, is able to change procedures almost at will, and receives a share of franchisee turnover.

But like the employment relationship the franchise relationship typically involves an imbalance of consequences. According to the *Donovan Report* there was, in practice, 'no comparison between the consequences for an employer if an employee terminates his [sic] contract of employment and those which will ensue for an employee if he [sic] is dismissed' (Donovan 1968). A similar imbalance is reinforced in the franchise relationship by the fact that the franchisee often has his/her life savings invested in and/or a second mortgage on the franchised business. A franchisee can lose much more than just a job if the franchise contract is not rewritten or else is terminated (Stanworth *et al.* 1983).

Franchisees therefore occupy an intermediate position between waged workers and the truly self-employed (and *independent* small employers) who own their own means of production and reap the full rewards of their own (and others') labour. Any unequivocal answer to the question posed at the top of this chapter conceals a far greater level of analytical complexity than 'industry' advocates are willing to acknowledge. While the slogan 'be your own boss in franchising' provides an appealing catch-phrase, it is prone to conceal much more than it reveals – it is of this that researchers, policy-makers, bankers, and would-be franchisees should be well aware.

Notes

1 I would like to thank all those who have commented on earlier drafts of this chapter and for the financial support given to the Franchising Project by the Edward Heath Charitable Trust. I am particularly grateful to Bill Westerman, Peter Hunt, the Franchising Project Steering Committee, Peter Nolan, Al Rainnie, and Andrew Scott for their remarks. However, I alone remain responsible for any errors.

2 To date, no satisfactory or agreed definition of 'smallness' has emerged: 'Asking anyone to define just what constitutes a small business is rather like asking the length of a piece of string and there are probably around the world as many definitions of a small firm as there are small firms' (Woodcock, 1982). Even so the number of workers typically employed by franchised units falls well short of the *Bolton Report*'s upper limit of 200 or less (Bolton 1971:3). On average, Kentucky Fried Chicken stores employ 15 full- and part-time workers, the typical Wimpy table-service restaurant between 15 and 20, while its counter-service restaurants have a staff of around 50 (company information). Even Coca-Cola's US bottlers in the mid-1970s, were predominantly small plants, with 85 per cent having less than 100 employees, although considerable concentration has since taken place (US Federal Trade Commission 1975: 24).

3 In this paper the words 'sector' and 'industry' refer to those

companies and firms using franchising as well as those operating under a franchise arrangement.

4 These statistics must, however, be treated with some caution since the response rate to the survey was a poor one on which to make such large claims. Only 23 per cent (87) of franchisors mailed and 16 per cent (84) of franchisees responded to the survey (Power Research Associates 1987: Appendix B). Needless to say, however, they are better than no statistics at all (*Hansard*, 29 April 1976: 183).

5 According to a survey of American fast-food franchisees, each franchisee works on average 60 hours a week. For a married franchisee with two children living at home, it would not be unusual for the family to work over 120 hours per week in the franchised business – 60 by the franchisee, 35 by the spouse, 25.5 by the children (Ozanne and Hunt 1971: 147).

6 The High Court also ruled in favour of Kentucky Fried Chicken in its refusal to renew the contracts of certain franchisees on expiry of their agreements (an automatic option to renew was not included). At least two rival chains – Favorite Fried Chicken and Dixie Fried Chicken – have been set up by ex-franchisees as a result (here Kentucky Fried Chicken conceded in allowing former franchisees to continue trading as chicken take-aways and restaurants) (*Franchise World*, March/May 1987; *Franchise Magazine*, spring 1987).

7 In the very next issue of the 'Yellow Pages' (published on a yearly basis) the Prontaprint advertisement suggested that customers contact the company's corporate headquarters in Darlington for their nearest Prontaprint branch.

8 Similar restrictions are also placed on the holders of master licences. The managing director of the company holding the Sir Speedy licence for Western Europe, for example, is restricted for a period of one year after termination of his employment, neither to compete with the company, nor enter the employ of, nor render any consulting services to, any other company engaged in a similar type of business (Sir Speedy ceased trading in the UK in September 1988).

9 Another former Prontaprint shop began trading under a new name, Reliance Print, in May 1987. But following the High Court ruling against Laserprint (see text), Reliance Print quickly rejoined the Prontaprint chain (*Franchise World*, May–July 1987).

References

Allen, S. and Wolkowitz, C. (1986) 'The control of women's labour: the case of homeworking', *Feminist Review*, 22, spring.

Baillieu, D. (1988) *Streetwise Franchising*, London: Hutchinson Business.

Barrow, C. and Golzen, G. (1987) *Taking Up a Franchise*, London: Kogan Page.

Berg, M. (1984) 'The power of knowledge: comments on Marglin's "Knowledge and Power"', in Stephen, F.H. (ed.) *Firms, Organization and Labour: Approaches to the Economics of Work Organization*, London: Macmillan.

Birkbeck, C. (1978) 'Self-employed proletarians in an informal factory: the case of Cali's garbage dump', *World Development*, 6, 9/10.

Bolton, J.E. (1971) *Report of the Committee of Enquiry on Small Firms* (referred to as the *Bolton Report*), Cmnd 4811, London: HMSO.

Caves, R.E. and Murphy II, W.F. (1976) 'Franchising: firms, markets and intangible assets', *Southern Economic Journal*, 2, 4, April.

Coyne, J. and Wright, M. (1988) 'Buy-outs and British industry', *Lloyds Bank Annual Review*, 1.

Creig, S., Roberts, C., Gorman, A., and Sawyer, P. (1986) 'Self-employment in Britain', *Employment Gazette*, June.

Dale, A. (1986) 'Social class and the self-employed', *Sociology*, 20, 3, August.

Domberger, S. (1986) 'Economic regulation through franchising', in

Kay, J., Meyer, C., and Thompson, D. (eds.) *Privatisation and Regulation: The UK Experience*, Oxford: Clarendon Press.

Domberger, S. and Middleton, J. (1985) 'Franchising in practice: the case of Independent Television in the UK', *Fiscal Studies*, 6, 1, February.

Donovan, Lord (1968) *Royal Commission on Trade Unions and Employers' Associations, 1965-1968*, London: HMSO.

Edens, F.N., Self, D.R., and Douglas, T.G. 1976) 'Franchisors describe the ideal franchisee', *Journal of Small Business Management*, 14, 3, July.

Euromonitor (1986) *Service Stations in the UK*, London: Euromonitor Publications.

Felstead, A. (1988) 'Franchising: a case of large firm decentralization?', The Franchising Project Research Paper No. 3, June 1988, Nuffield College, Oxford.

Gerry, C. and Birkbeck, C. (1981) 'The petty commodity producer in Third World cities: petit bourgeois or "disguised" proletarian?' in Bechhofer, F. and Elliot, B. (eds.) *The Petite Bourgeoisie: Comparative Studies of the Uneasy Stratum*, London: Macmillan.

Golzen, G., Barrow, C., and Severn, J. (1984) *Taking up a Franchise*, London: Kogan Page.

Grout, P. (1987a) 'The wider share ownership programme', *Fiscal Studies*, 8, 3, August.

Grout, P. (1987b) 'Wider share ownership and economic performance', *Oxford Review of Economic Policy*, 3, 4, winter.

Home Office (1983) *The Development of Cable Systems and Services*, Cmnd 8666 London: HMSO.

Hough, J. (1986) 'Power and authority and their consequences: a study of the relationship between franchisors and franchisees', unpublished PhD thesis, Polytechnic of Central London.

Housden, J. (1976) 'Brewers and tenants: a changing relationship', *Hotel Catering and Institutional Management Association Review*, autumn.

Hunt, S.D. (1972) 'The socioeconomic consequences of the franchise system of distribution', *Journal of Marketing*, 36, July.

Kay, J. and Silberston, Z.A. (184) 'The new industrial policy – privatisation and competition', *Midland Bank Review*, spring.

Legal and General Assurance Society (1985) *The Self-Employed Report*, London: Legal and General Assurance Society.

Leighton, P. (1983) 'Employment and self-employment: some problems of law and practice', *Employment Gazette*, May.

Love, J.F. (1987) *McDonald's: Behind the Arches*, London: Bantam Press.

Mackenzie, G. (1982) 'Class boundaries and the labour process', in Giddens, A. and Mackenzie, G.(eds.) *Social Class and the Division of Labour: Essays in Honour of Ilya Neustadt*, Cambridge: Cambridge University Press.

Maguire, M. (1986) 'Recruitment as a means of control', in Purcell, K., Wood, S., Waton, A., and Allen, S. (eds.) *The Changing Experience of Employment: Restructuring and Recession*, London: Macmillan.

Marglin, S. (1984) 'Power and knowledge', in Stephen, F.H. (ed.) *Firms, Organization and Labour: Approaches to the Economics of Work Organization*, London and Basingstoke: Macmillan.

Meager, N. (1987) 'Self-employment: serious trend or statistical hiccup?', *Manpower Policy and Practice*, 4, 2, summer.

Oakeshott, R. (1988) 'The beginnings of an employee-owned sector', *Lloyds Bank Annual Review*, 1.

Ozanne, U.B. and Hunt, S.D. (1971) *The Economic Effects of Franchising*, Washington D.C.: US Government Printing Department.

Poole, M. (1988) 'Factors affecting the development of employee financial participation in contemporary Britain: evidence from a National Survey', *British Journal of Industrial Relations*, 26, 1, March.

Power Research Associates (1985) *Franchising – The Industry and the Market*, London: Power Research Associates.

Power Research Associates (1987) *Business Format Franchising in the UK*, London: Power Research Associates.

Rainbird, H. (1988) 'Self-employment: a form of disguised wage labour?', paper presented to the 'Questions of Restructuring Work and Employment', Industrial Relations Research Unit, University of Warwick, 12–13 June.

Rainnie, A. (1984) 'Combined and uneven development in the clothing industry: the effects of competition and accumulation', *Capital and Class*, 22, spring.

Richardson, R. and Nejad, A. (1986) 'Employee share ownership schemes in the UK – an evaluation', *British Journal of Industrial Relations*, 24, 2, July.

Sharpe, T. (1983) 'The control of natural monopoly by franchising' in Gretton, J. and Harrison, A. (eds.) *Franchising in the Public Sector* (Papers given to the *Public Money* seminar).

Stanworth, J. (1984) *The Franchise Relationship*, London: Franchise World Publications.

Stanworth, J. (1986) 'Your own boss, or a supervised employee?' in *Directory of Franchising and Franchise Yearbook*, London: Franchise World Publications.

Stanworth, J. (1988) 'Socio-economic factors in franchising', unpublished paper presented to the World Wide Situations and Franchising Development Conference, Universata Degli Studi di Pisa, 11–13 May.

Stanworth, J., Curran, J., and Hough, J. (1983) 'How franchising brings a new perspective to "us and them"', *Personnel Management*, September.

Stanworth, J., Curran, J., and Hough, J.-(1986) 'The franchised small enterprise: formal and operational dimensions of independence', in Curran, J., Stanworth, J., and Watkins, D. (eds.) *The Survival of the Small Firm*, Aldershot: Gower Publishing.

Storey, D., and Johnson, S. (1987) *Job Generation and Labour Market Change*, London: Macmillan.

US Department of Commerce (1988) *Franchising in the Economy* 1986–88. Washington DC: Department of Commerce, International Trade Administration.

US Federal Trade Commission (1975) 'Territories case, administrative law judge, initial decision'.

Veljanovski, C. (1987) 'British cable and satellite television policies', *National Westminster Bank Quarterly Review*, November.

Vickers, J. and Yarrow, G. (1988) *Privatization: An Economic Analysis*, Cambridge: MIT Press.

Woodcock, C. (1982) 'What is a small business?', *The Guardian*, 25 June.

Wright, E.O. (1978) 'Class boundaries and the labour process', *New Left Review*, 98, July–August.

Trade Press

Franchise World
The Franchise Magazine

Part 4

Co-operatives: organization and control

Chapter fifteen

Share-ownership co-operatives – some observations

Laurence Clarke

Introduction

Capital has long been seen as a constraint to the growth of worker co-operatives. Recently more and more interest has been paid to the idea of co-ops limited by shares rather than the conventional structures of Industrial and Provident Societies Act rules or companies limited by guarantee. It is believed that these share-ownership co-ops (SOCs) may attract Business Expansion Scheme (BES) money or ethical investors, whilst retaining the basic co-operative principle of a company owned and controlled by those working in it with a one-person, one-vote philosophy. The more familiar structure of a company limited by shares affords confidence to professional advisors and encourages preference-share investments. As one accountant put it, after sighing with relief when a co-op changed its structure from limited by guarantee to limited by shares: 'Now we don't have to check the relevant Act of Parliament each time we do something just to make sure companies limited by guarantee are treated in the same way as share holding companies.'

SOC's issue each member with one ordinary voting share. This share must be sold back to the company at par when the member leaves. Employees normally become members after a probationary period. No one outside the co-op may hold a voting share.

Although several support organizations have attempted to produce model rules for these companies, only the Scottish Co-operatives Development Committee (SCDC) rules have been used. The National Co-operative Development Agency (CDA) Employee Participation Company rules allow an element of the share-holding aspects but are not concerned with employee share holding and hence are not reviewed here. The SCDC rules lay down that every employee must be accepted as a member after up to one year's probationary employment or cease employment. This reduces the chance of a two-tier structure of members and employees that some co-ops evolve through professional or skill chauvinism or the founders' reluctance to 'give away' control from their group.

279

Most SOCs capitalize the business through investments in non-voting preference shares by the members. Since these investments go on the capital side of the balance sheet and not on long-term liabilities (as loans do in conventional co-ops), they give banks and institutions more confidence when lending to co-ops.

Although there are a few one-off share-ownership co-ops such as Bardrec in Scotland and Manchester Cold Rollers (both have now unfortunately ceased trading), the SCDC rules have been used to set up five companies in the North-east and four in Scotland. It seems likely that these rules will be used much more widely now that the Department of Trade and Industry has approved them for BES investments. Alex Smith, Director of SCDC, argues, however, that as these investments must be in ordinary shares and, in order to retain the co-operative nature of the company, non-voting, this puts co-operatives at a disadvantage over conventional companies as far as BES money is concerned. At present there are no moves at the Department to change the BES regulations to regularize the position of co-ops by allowing co-op preference shares to be included in the scheme.

The recent interest in SOCs has been as a result of these apparent advantages which are summarized as follows:

Members' investment is in capital rather than long-term liabilities and hence this increases the capital base of the company.
Professional advisors easily understand the structure.
Outside investments in capital may be possible (through non-voting shares).

Before the co-op movement clasps this new structure to its bosom and hails it as the long-lost answer to existing co-op structure and capital problems, it is important to take stock of what has been the experience so far and attempt to assess the possible pitfalls of this approach. What follows is a result of my personal experience as a co-operative development officer, a member for a number of years of a co-op limited by guarantee and a SOC, and interviews with several of the SCDC-rules SOCs in the UK.

Issues

Does owning shares change the perception of members?

If we divide co-ops into those set up by a group of philosophically motivated people and those set up by people whose primary aim is employment, and to whom the co-operative structure is perhaps interesting but more of a convenience, we find that there is a greater difference in perceptions between those two groups than between SOCs and conventionally structured co-ops.

Within the philosophically based co-ops much emphasis is put on the fact that what money you have invested is irrelevant. As Hugh Clark of Hadrian Glass Fibre Ltd, a share-ownership co-op, puts it when considering bringing new people into their co-op: 'It wouldn't be critical for the person to put money in.' Indeed he and his fellow members are really only concerned to find someone as committed as they are to their business and their views on co-operation. He points out that many potential people fail their criteria because they can't grasp the concept of shared ownership and control.

However, within the non-philosphically based co-ops, whether you have your 'money in' or not is often a burning question. A knitwear co-operative (limited by guarantee) won't countenance any of the workforce becoming members of the co-op unless they put their money in or take a substantial cut in wages (admittedly to the level of the existing members). In another co-op (limited by shares) it was commented 'Why should they have any say when they aren't willing to put their money in.' It is interesting that of the share-ownership co-ops investigated, those that had an equality of share ownership amongst members seemed to be less concerned about the 'money in' syndrome. It is also worth noting that the shareholdings in most cases were relatively small (up to a maximum of £2,000 per member).

Thus any difference between SOCs and conventionally structured co-ops as far as 'money in' is concerned is difficult to detect, given the small numbers involved and the large difference between philosophically and non-philosophically based co-ops. However, there are some indications in TMS Advertising that their switch to share ownership (they were limited by guarantee previously) has resulted in some members' equating size of share holding with control. Indeed, there was at one time a feeling amongst some members with very few shares that they had little or no status in the company because of this. Their voice was unimportant, they felt. This was probably exacerbated when the company hired a member who was able to put in £10,000 worth of shares, thus helping the co-op through a difficult cash crisis, but creating a vast imbalance in share holdings. It is worth noting that this member felt he owned a significant part of the company and did tend to equate that to control.

One perception detected amongst members of the non-philosophical share co-ops is a belief that they will eventually be 'rich'. Clearly there is a feeling that, if you own shares in your company, you will be able to sell these in the future and make a lot of money. This, of course, could only be true if someone were to buy the shares. The company cannot be sold for personal gain without the unanimous agreement of all the members. This point is tackled later but it should be noted that none of the members talked to had the remotest knowledge of how, or whether, the company could be sold. This ignorance is disturbing and is touched on later.

As the number of SOCs increase, much more work is needed in this area regarding the perceptions of members concerning share holdings, to ensure the structure does not destroy the co-operative principles.

What happens when a person leaves?

When members leave a SOC, most co-ops agree to give them back their money. However, as this is recorded in the minutes of the company and not the rules, practices vary. Hadrian Glass Fibre have minuted that they would pay it back if the company were in a position so to do. North Eastern Technical Services may possibly give some form of compensation in a number of years' time but never more than the original investment. TMS Advertising would buy back shares if they could but, due to acquiring the debt of a previous company, they have no reserves to do this with.

The problem is, that under present legislation, a company may only buy back shares by using reserves. If it does so, it thus reduces the capital of the company. So, not only does the company suffer cash-flow strain, it also weakens its position with its backers, particularly the bank who may react badly to a reducing capital base. Of course, if no reserves exist, no shares can be bought back. Hence in the example of TMS when the member with £10,000 worth of shares, resigned, his shares were bought by all the other members in proportion to salary in order to give him his money back. A deduction was made from each person's salary to pay up his or her share holding as soon as possible. However there is a limit to what the other members can take on, so that departing members now hold more preference shares than are held by employees in TMS. This has resulted in one particular ex-member believing that she has rights because of her shareholding, which she has not, and this can cause distress on both sides.

Clearly provision has to be made at the outset for what happens if a person leaves.

As a corollary, if the members, as in TMS's case are paying up for shares already issued, then, should the company collapse, they would be liable to pay to the liquidator the remainder of the shareholding they had taken on.

In Numac Engineering Ltd, a phoenix co-op (one formed from the ashes of a previous co-op), many of the members felt they had more or less written off their investment, hence getting it back after they left would be a bonus. Interestingly, Bob Richardson, former chair of Craigton Bakery (an Industrial and Provident Societies registered co-op) said after it failed, that he and the rest of the members agreed that the £300 they each had invested (in loans) in the business had bought them five years of employment and that this was a very good buy in an area of high unemployment.

In addition all the SOCs interviewed did not understand the mechanics for giving preference shareholders back their money and the implications to the company's balance sheet.

In co-operatives where members had left, either they had gone before the shares had been issued or the money had simply not been paid back. All ex-members seem to be philosophical about their leaving having virtually written off the money anyway. However, in TMS where the problem is of longer standing and greater, some ex-members are now distinctly unhappy.

With a loan members have some rights on leaving. They can ultimately sue for repayment of the loan. Not so with shares. They are locked into the company unless a buyer can be found. There is a real danger that, at some point in the future, there will be a group of disenfranchised ex-members holding shares in co-ops, believing that they are entitled to their money back, but with no mechanism to achieve some compensation. This would look, and be, extremely bad for the co-op movement.

As years pass and more members leave the SOCs, this issue will not go away.

Value of shares and distribution of profits

In the SCDC rules, profits are distributed (after Corporation Tax) first to pay interest on preference shareholdings and second in such a way as the members decide. But, as we have seen, some reserves are required to fund the repayment of shares of those who have left. If a loss has been made in the past, then there is also a requirement to retain profits in order to wipe out the deficit in the reserves account before any repayment of shares can take place.

Since buying back shares effectively reduces the capital base of the firm, it makes commercial sense to keep the reserves account at or just below zero, thus obviating any requirement to buy back shares.

Thus it would make sense to write into the memorandum and articles of association of the company that a certain percentage of the profits must be retained as reserves (say 40 per cent).

But who owns these reserves?

If it is the ordinary shareholders, then there is a contradiction since they must sell this share back to the company at par when they leave. Clearly the SCDC rules take it that these reserves are held in common ownership as the rules insist, that, on dissolution, any proceeds are distributed to other co-operative enterprises with similar objects and not to the members. This can only be overturned by an unanimous vote of the members. But if they did so vote, what about the previous members. They have apparently no ownership of this money, despite having helped create it.

One way round this is to distribute all profits to the members but mostly in terms of further preference shares. But what happens when there are losses or when a person leaves. Losses could be carried forward and, along with buying back the shares, would have to await future profits. Thus the efforts of future members would pay for the success and failure of previous members. This might be regarded as equitable but could be very demotivating to present members as they see their profits melt away to previous members and losses.

None of the share-ownership co-ops that were contacted had considered this problem (although TMS has it unsolved at present). Indeed it was difficult to be clear that the local CDA development workers had looked that far in advance. Development officers in general tend to be dedicated to getting the company started and have no time to consider the long-term implications of what they are doing. Thus it is essential that a longer-term view is taken now so that this head-down approach does not result in the problems outlined.

Fife Wineries have raised a new problem in share values. They have people keen to invest in the company and take advantage of the Business Expansion Scheme. However, not only are they looking for dividend, they are also looking for capital growth. In order to give value to these non-voting ordinary shares, somebody has to be willing to buy them. This would normally be achieved when the company was sold or floated on the Unlisted Securities Market. If the co-operative is to remain a co-operative, this seems fanciful. Thus the only real buyer would be the company itself. But what should it pay? (Assuming that the co-operative is happy with this foray into capitalism.) Some valuation of the company or agreed formula needs to be worked out at the start.

It would appear that the best way to solve all these problems is to have an element of common ownership built up from a set percentage of the profits (say 40 per cent) being held back to reserves. This would allow SOCs to cover any losses and buy back the shares of former members.

This common ownership fund belongs equally to all ordinary voting-share holders past and present and this is written into the rules so that if a unanimous vote of the present members is taken to change the provision for distribution of proceeds, at least all members past and present would benefit. This would discourage present members taking a short-term, personal-gain view. .

To tackle the appreciation in value of non-voting ordinary shares held by outsiders, a further percentage could be retained in reserves against these shares. The same percentage of losses would be distributed to this reserve. Thus the value of the non-voting ordinary shares would be the size of this reserves fund at any one time.

In co-ops limited by guarantee or only using loan capital from members, losses can be distributed to members' loan accounts in the same way as profits. Also, on leaving, there is a loan to be repaid and hence the relationship is clear. We need to have the same clarity in SOCs. We need to state, on formation, preferably in the rules:

1 How profits (and losses) are distributed and in what percentages, or the mechanism to determine the percentages.
2 How and when members' shares will be bought back when they leave.

Bringing in new people

As we have seen, Hadrian Glass Fibre has had a lot of problems finding the right people to join their firm. TMS found potential members taken aback when they discovered they were expected to invest money in the business and have a percentage of their wage deducted. This did not necessarily dissuade people, but it did mean that they sought other jobs at a higher net wage. This, of course, is not a problem unique to share-ownership co-ops. However, as the member of TMS who left and then misunderstood her standing as a preference-share holder, demonstrates, share-ownership co-ops need to spell out exactly what is happening as far as the share-ownership aspect is concerned.

The existing share ownership co-ops fail to issue share certificates quickly. This is to fail to grasp the motivation and personal identification with the co-op that a share certificate brings. The one-pound voting share is like a membership ticket and should be treated as such. If there is a probationary period, then this should be spelt out at the start and an occasion made of the event of the employee's becoming a member and receiving the share certificate.

In our drive for production we lose sight as co-op members and development officers, of the people aspect of these co-ops and how important it is to make much of membership.

During a time of tight cash flow in TMS, the co-op was asked by its bank to give personal guarantees. It was agreed that, as a co-op, this would have to be all the members or none of them. The bank agreed to all. At the subsequent co-op meeting where the proposal was put to the members, there was a deathly hush as no one wanted to make the commitment. It was left to a 17-year-old girl, just newly made a member, after joining under the Youth Training Scheme, to start the ball rolling by intimating that 'It's our company and we need to support it. I will guarantee the overdraft.' The rest followed suit. If you can make new people feel involved, as co-ops are supposed to do, then the results can be extraordinary.

Development officer – head-down approach

Development officers with local co-operative development agencies are vested with one primary mission and that is to set up co-ops. It is easy to get so embroiled in that process that you lose sight of the longer-term effects of what you are doing. Sometimes you set up co-ops that, at best, need a longer gestation period. Sometimes, there simply is not enough time to ensure that all the founder members understand co-operative principles and what they are letting themselves in for. Rarely is a process set up for the induction of new members to include information on the structure and philosophy of the co-op they are joining.

Often you use tools without completely understanding their long-term effects. The important thing is to set up the co-operative and your time horizon has a clever knack of reducing to the next two or three weeks or months. 'We'll worry about that later.' In share-ownership co-ops (SOC's) we have let this happen and, as we have seen, there are many potential problems down the road which worryingly none of the share-ownership co-ops investigated had considered.

If SOCs are to be the answer to capitalization and professional adviser problems for co-ops, then we must solve these problems now before we create unsolvable ones as happened to the plywood (mule) co-ops in America. (In these 'mule' co-operatives no creation of new worker share-owners is possible because of the extremely high value of existing shareholders' shares.)

The way ahead

In trying to find solutions to the problems outlined, I have taken the stance that whatever we do must be:

simple and understandable to all co-op members
easily carried out by the SOC
workable in terms of profits and losses
equitable

Thus, some of the solutions may not be tax efficient.

Initial equality of preference shareholding is a must. It prevents tensions on democracy and on personal benefits from capital involvement. This throws up a problem when profits are distributed since, if these are in preference shares, this changes the equality.

It would appear sensible to distribute non-cash profits as loans which earn a fixed rate of interest compared to average base rate each year.

This allows much easier repayments when the person leaves as it does not affect the net asset position of the company. It is merely the repayment of a loan and does not reach into the complex area of share buy-back. It also gives the member leaving some rights to repayment of this loan. The timescale of repayment would be negotiated. Some arrangements can be made to allow members to withdraw some of their loan account before leaving or retiring, but this should be kept to a minimum.

The initial preference-share stake should be seen as a long-term investment repayable only when the company is in a position so to do. This repayment should be regarded as a bonus, not a right. However, the shareholding still accrues the same dividend/interest rate as current members' holdings, until bought back.

The profits are distributed in the following order:

1 interest on Loans.
2 Corporation Tax.
3 interest on preference-share holdings.
4 dividend to ordinary, non-voting share holders (if BES investors used).
5 a set percentage (say 40 per cent) to reserves.
6 distribution to all employees, whether members or not, either equally or according to job ranking (this depends on the philosophical nature of the co-op) and in cash or additions to loan accounts.
7 A set percentage to charitable social or co-operative purposes.

Losses are distributed by a set percentage to reserves and the remainder distributed either equally or according to job ranking to existing members' loan accounts. (NB This distribution of losses is only up to the total in any individual's loan account. Any additional losses are credited to the reserves account.

The voting share is always returned to the company on leaving at par when it is exchanged for a non-voting ordinary share of a special ex-members' class. Only if a unanimous decision of the existing members changes the provisions of distribution of proceeds on dissolution of the company, does this share come into effect. Then all proceeds are divided equally amongst members past and present.

BES investment, as the government regulations stand at present, has to be in non-voting ordinary shares. These can have a dividend attraction and a buy-back option based on an agreed percentage of the increase in reserves over the period possibly up to an agreed upper limit on value.

This percentage must be set at the start of the relationship. Alternatively, for ethical investors who want to take advantage of the BES tax advantages, these shares could earn dividend only and have no capital appreciation, merely a par buy-back agreement.

New members and founding members require a short explanation as to the structure, philosophy, and financial implications of their involvement in the SOC. This should be akin to the company rule book for contracts of employment. The Co-operative Development Agency (or SCDC as the developers of the generally accepted standard rules) should produce an outline version of these documents that has blanks for the particular situation of the co-op in question.

More generally, however, the worker co-operative movement needs to assess the implications of present moves and development officers need to be encouraged and trained to assess the long-term needs of their clients and plan accordingly.

Share ownership co-ops are here to stay. It is important that they are set up with as much foresight as possible and monitored to ensure that the decisions that are made today do not have long-term deleterious effects.

Chapter sixteen

So how many co-operatives are there? – a critical note on co-operative statistics

Phil Hobbs and Keith Jefferis

Introduction

> The [worker co-operative] movement has grown beyond all expectations since 1976. We have witnessed a 26-fold increase which has brought 1,400 co-operatives and 12,000 worker-owners into being, the greatest increase in Europe, (superseding even the much-praised co-operatives of northern Spain).
>
> (Whyatt 1987: 5)

Given the confidence that pervades such statements and the optimism for the future that is evident in comments such as those by Sawtell in the preface to the Co-operative Development Agency's 1984 directory (CDA (1984)) it would seem that we are indeed witnessing a renaissance of the producer co-operative:

> They [worker co-operatives] have grown so fast during the last few years that, if the growth continues at the same rate, there will be over 250,000 co-operative businesses by the end of the century. How will the Registrar of Friendly Societies cope with over 1000 registrations every week . . . ?
>
> CDA (1984: v)

Our objective in this paper is to present basic statistics on the number, size, and industrial and geographic distribution of the UK worker co-operative movement and, where possible, compare it to information on the small-firms sector. In presenting this data we show that much of the officially published information on the co-operative sector is misleading as to its true size. The central error in this work appears to be the overzealous inclusion of organizations that are not strictly 'co-operative' (using the definition employed by the International Co-operative Alliance and Common Ownership Principles (see appendix 1)). Furthermore, there is evidence to suggest that the methodology used in compiling such data has an inbuilt bias towards overestimating the size of the co-operative sector.

In the first section of the paper we discuss some of the issues that need to be confronted when collecting data on business organizations. The second considers the published data on the extent of the co-operative sector in the UK and in the third section we present our own data, based on a more rigorous methodology, which is contrasted where possible with information on private firms.[1]

Issues in data collection

The statistical description of the co-operative sector confronts many of the problems that are familiar to the small firms researcher.[2] These issues may, for convenience, be summarized simplistically as 'what, when, and why?'

First, what is it that we are trying to measure or observe? In essence what is the boundary that delimits small firms from larger firms, or co-operative from hierarchy. In the case of the small firm various definitions have been employed, ranging from the detailed, if rather impractical, multi-dimensional definition used by the Bolton Committee (Bolton 1971) to that, say, of VAT registration (Ganguly 1985). However, it should be noted that definitions have tended to vary to suit the data at hand. Thus Colin Mason comments that it is 'essential to ensure that similar definitions have been used when any attempt is made to compare results' (Mason 1983: 40).

Our definition in this paper of a worker co-operative is based on the legal constitution or 'Model Rules' that each co-operative adopts at registration. These model rules define the various rights and structures within the co-operative (Hamwee 1979; ICOM 1977). In particular, we are concerned that a co-operative should have full worker control and conform to the definition of a co-operative provided by the International Co-operative Alliance (ICA 1971) and the Industrial Common Ownership Movement (ICOM) (see appendix 1).

Second, when does the data refer to? The volatility of the small-firms sector is such that data can only ever be the briefest of snapshots. A preliminary analysis of current survey work being undertaken by the Co-operatives Research Unit (CRU) shows that the information provided on employment levels on 1 April specifically is significantly different to that information which referred to the survey date (about two months later). Furthermore, there are problems in obtaining data relating to the same date for all co-operatives – information is gathered over a lengthy period. Therefore it is clear that to refer to data as representing, say, 1986 may in itself be misleading. Our survey data refers to the position in October 1986.

Third, we need to know what is the purpose of collecting the data – the why. Obviously the accuracy and detail required if data is to be used to calculate, say, survival rates needs to be greater than if it is to be used to give a broad view of an industrial sector. Unfortunately it would appear that much of the published data on the extent of the co-operative sector has not adequately addressed these issues. Data that has been collected for promotional purposes has been used to draw important comparative conclusions. This is a view that has some support within the co-operative movement. Thus Jenny Thornley comments 'How many times have the same uncritical speeches been trotted out, boasting of the staggering growth of co-operatives . . . The reality is much less satisfying.' (Thornley 1987).

In collecting and analysing the data used in this paper our objective has been to provide a dataset that allows comparison between privately owned firms and worker co-operatives. This, as is described below, has been achieved through the adoption of a number of rules and criteria which needed to be satisfied to ensure that co-operatives included in the total are bona fide businesses.

Existing national data

Since 1980 the national Co-operative Development Agency (CDA) has conducted surveys of the UK co-operative sector which have been published as 'Worker Co-operative Directories'. The purpose of these directories has tended to be promotional in nature. From discussions with the CDA it appears that their primary use has been to show the extent and development of the co-operative sector to third parties and provide an information resource (a co-operative 'Yellow Pages') rather than a rigorously compiled dataset. This is a view that has been confirmed by local CDAs. For example: 'it [the Directory] has always been of great value in our promotional and training work to be able to brandish an impressive summary of the co-operative movement "at a glance" ' (private communication).

The figures reproduced in table 16.1 suggest a rapid and dramatic growth, with an average annualized growth rate in the stock of worker co-operatives of 30 per cent over the period 1980–6. This is particularly so if one juxtaposes this data with that of the historical decline of the producer-co-operative movement in the period up to 1970 shown in table 16.2. Even so, by comparison with the small-firms sector, worker co-operatives remain a marginal contribution. For example, the co-operative sector employs, using the CDA data, around 8,000 workers compared to the more than 14 million employees in small private firms.[3]

If, as Sawtell (CDA 1986) has suggested, we extrapolate this growth rate, which is indeed more impressive than that of small firms, can the co-operative sector become the third sector promoted variously by Rigge and Young (1983) and Clayre (1980)? The answer we think is likely to be negative. First, comparative growth rates are exaggerated because

Table 16.1 Co-operative Development Agency data on the size of the UK co-operatives sector

Year	1980	1982	1984	1986
No. of co-operatives identified	305	498	911	1,476
Annualized growth rate (%)	—	27	35	27

Source: CDA (1986)

of the very low initial number of co-operatives. Second, simple extrapolations ignore the reasons behind such growth. Given a static social and economic framework, it may well be possible for the recent growth rate to be sustained. However, it would appear to be no coincidence that the growth of the co-operative sector (and similarly that of the small-firms sector) has been during a period of historically high unemployment and unprecedented industrial restructuring aimed at restoring firms' profitability. This intuitive connection has been confirmed in research undertaken in the CRU which looked at the origin of new worker co-operatives. This work found that, of co-operatives replying to a 1986 questionnaire, 14 per cent were formed out of failing capitalist firms. Furthermore, many of the 'new start' co-operatives are taking advantage of the same economic opportunities, created by the restructuring processes of the early 1980s, as capitalist small firms. The growth of co-operatives must be analysed in relation to a set of historically specific economic, social, and political factors which will not necessarily be maintained. For instance, co-operatives derived strong support from the activities of 'municipal socialist' Labour local authorities in the early 1980s which funded co-operative development agencies and other local economic initiatives; the largest of these authorities – the Greater London Council and metropolitan councils – have, of course, since been abolished, and this is likely to have an adverse effect on the formation of new co-operatives.

Table 16.2 The historical decline of the UK co-operative movement: membership of the Co-operative Productive Federation (CPF) for various years 1925–70

Year	No. of co-operatives	Employees
1925	42	5,578
1930	43	6,970
1935	42	7,908
1940	40	7,366
1945	44	5,055
1950	37	5,971
1955	32	4,313
1970	8	706

Source: Jones (1975)

We believe that the totals given in the CDA directories are overly optimistic for a number of reasons. They include co-operatives on the basis of registration rather than positive evidence that they are in fact trading. The inclusion of organizations that are not worker controlled inflates the total number of co-operatives and also dilutes the ideological basis of the sector as a radical alternative to capitalist production and employment. The absence of any minimum employment requirement means that many of the co-operatives included are unable to support one full-time worker[4] (or equivalent) and therefore should not be considered as viable economic units.

With these remarks in mind, research undertaken in the CRU has adopted the following criteria to determine whether a co-operative is included or excluded in the total.

A co-operative must be substantially worker controlled

Thus 'community', 'neighbourhood' and 'instant muscle'[5] co-operatives have been excluded on the grounds that they do not embody this key co-operative principle. Whilst we accept the importance of social responsibility to the wider community, we do not believe that those organizations where membership is open to the local community, or consumers, can correctly be referred to as worker controlled. In the case of 'instant muscle' co-operatives, the absence of capital and the fact that they are frequently, if not exclusively, 'sole traders', again implies that the principle of worker control cannot be realised. The importance of this commitment to worker control is recognised by Bibby in his consideration of community co-operatives:

> The new wave of workers' co-operatives has been concerned to stress the importance of autonomy: Ensuring that workers' co-operatives are self-managing, are not beholden to outside investors, and indeed are controlled by the workforce *and the workforce alone.* This is an important perspective, and is especially important given some of the structures which in the past (and not just in the past) have been allowed to pass as 'co-operative'.
>
> (Bibby 1987: 22 (our emphasis))

It is also emphasized by MacFarlane (1986) that, whilst both worker and community co-operatives are likely to have economic, social, and political objectives, the internal dynamic by which these are pursued is different in each case.

We have also excluded actors' agencies, marketing, property management, and other secondary co-operatives. The membership of these organizations generally consists of other businesses, on whose behalf services are being provided.

293

There must be positive evidence that a co-operative is actively trading

The CDA survey has employed a criteria that excludes a registered co-operative only where there is evidence that it has ceased trading. This rule has a natural bias towards overestimating the size of the co-operative movement, not least because there are many co-operatives that register but never actually trade. Similarly, there are many co-operatives that cease trading but are not excluded from the total, because it is difficult consistently to gather information on such 'failed' co-operatives. This is particularly the case in areas of the country where no local CDA exists to provide independent information on the size of the co-operative sector.

We have, therefore, excluded a co-operative unless we have evidence either from a survey reply, information from a local CDA, or personal/third-party knowledge that it is trading.

Co-operatives are included on the basis that they are able to provide employment for at least one full-time worker

The objective of this rule is to exclude co-operatives which are not the predominant or main source of income for the workers. Furthermore, it also acts to exclude co-operatives that may have returned a survey questionnaire but which are to all intents and purposes dormant. The use of this rule also compares with a similar criteria used by Ganguly, whose work we draw on heavily in our comparative analysis. He notes that 'Within the eligible trades, the VAT statistics will pick up the majority of businesses when they reach *the point at which they become potential employers.*' (Ganguly 1985: xii (our emphasis))

The rules described above are not necessarily exhaustive and admittedly may be interpreted as involving a degree of subjectivity. They have, however, been used, either in full or in part, by other researchers, notably Munroe (1987) in her study of co-operative financing. In this study the criteria described above to determine whether a co-operative was trading were augmented by telephoning each identified co-operative, using a cut-off point of three unsuccessful calls. This work suggested that of the 300 co-operatives identified as trading in London, only 200 could actually be contacted by telephone. Consequently we believe that our method may still produce an overestimate of the number of actively trading worker co-operatives in the UK.

The number, size, and distribution of UK worker co-operatives

The data for worker co-operatives used in this section has been taken from the Worker Co-operative Database operated by the London Industrial Common Ownership Movement with the assistance of the

CRU. Where tables indicate that the source is 'WCDB amended' it means that the raw data taken from the database has been revised using the criteria discussed above; see appendix 2 for full details of sources of data.

The number of worker co-operatives

Our key findings are illustrated in table 16.3. From this the overestimate of the total size of the co-operative sector by the CDA is evident. Our annual stock figures show that the co-operative sector is around two-thirds the size that the CDA finds. Thus, in 1986 (the latest date available), the total number of co-operatives in the UK was 894 compared to a figure of 1,476 claimed by the CDA. The average growth rate for the period 1980–6 from the revised data is 28 per cent which compares favourably with that given by the CDA. However, it should be noted that this average hides the noticeable decline that our data indicates for 1985 and 1986. Evidence that the decline in registrations has continued is borne out by ICOM, who handle around 75 per cent of registrations. Articles appearing in the winter 1987 edition of the journal *The New Co-operator* pointed to a fall in registrations from an expected 250 for 1987 to 206.

Table 16.3 The number of UK worker co-operatives – revised calculations

Year	Co-operatives formed	Co-operative stock	Annual growth (%)
1975	44	32	—
1976	19	48	50
1977	32	75	56
1978	67	134	79
1979	46	165	23
1980	70	217	32
1981	73	267	23
1982	128	366	37
1983	181	506	38
1984	229	651	28
1985	232	765	18
1986	223	894	17

Source: Worker Co-operative Database amended

Size distribution

Contrasting the size distribution of the co-operative sector with that of private firms, we find that the average size of worker co-operatives is much smaller, 86 per cent of co-operatives have less than ten workers compared to a figure of around 76 per cent for private firms[6] – tables 16.4 and 16.5. This finding is perhaps not unexpected. First, the co-operative sector is much younger, on average, than the private sector. Therefore one would expect the immaturity of the co-operative sector to show up as a smaller average size. Additionally researchers have pointed out the structural and organizational problems incurred in co-operatives as they expand are likely to be more intense than those found in private small firms (Paton 1978). Furthermore, the legal structure of co-operatives makes acquisition and takeover activity more complex (Cowe 1988). Perhaps the most noticeable point is not the predominance of small co-operatives but the almost total lack of large co-operatives (over 200 workers).

Table 16.4 Distribution of co-operatives by number of workers, 1986

No. of workers	No. of co-ops	Percent of co-ops	No. of workers	Percent of workers
1-4	527	59	1,344	24
5-9	243	27	1,368	24
10-19	89	10	992	18
20-49	28	3	704	13
50-100	3	1	165	3
100+	4	—	1,018	18
Total	894	100	5,591	100

Source: Worker Co-operative Database amended

Table 16.5 Size distribution of firms (census units) by employment

No. of employees	Percentage of firms
1-10	76
11-24	14
25-49	6
50-100	3
100+	1

Source: Department of Employment Gazette (1978: 39)

Industrial distribution

Historically worker co-operatives have concentrated in particular industrial sectors – printing, bootmaking, metal-working, and building (Cole 1944). In part this is a reflection of the artisan trades of the original co-operators and the desire to protect traditional skills in the face of industrialization.

Within the broad industrial headings given in table 16.6[7] co-operatives appear to be underrepresented in agriculture, building, wholesale distribution, transport, and motor trade. However, those sectors in which co-operatives show a higher representation conceal the fact that co-operatives tend to be concentrated in smaller sub-sectors. Thus, in production, co-operatives operate largely in printing, publishing, light engineering, and clothing manufacture; service co-operatives are predominantly located in media, arts and entertainment, computing and consultancy, and the wholesale and retail of foods (in particular wholefoods, where co-operatives established and, until recently, controlled a substantial proportion of the market). There are a number of factors which contribute to the growth of co-operatives in an industry, including low capitalization, labour and/or skill intensity, and recent industrial decline. For example, within the clothing sector, co-operatives are predominantly based in cut, make, and trim (CMT) operations (Jefferis and Thomas 1988), an industrial sector that conforms closely to the pattern we describe.

Table 16.6 Distribution of co-operatives and small firms by industrial sector

Sector	Co-operatives trading	Percentage of stock	Employment	Percentage of employment	VAT-registered firms (%)
Agriculture	17	2	50	1	12
Building	66	8	300	5	15
Catering	46	5	192	3	9
Finance and professional	56	6	312	6	7
Motor	12	1	30	1	5
Production	243	28	2,250	41	10
Retail	147	18	730	13	18
Services	249	28	1,266	23	12
Transport	19	2	179	3	4
Wholesale	25	2	96	4	8
Total	880	100	5,505	100	100

Source: Worker Co-operative Database amended and Ganguly (1985)
NB. Total may differ from those given in other tables as co-operatives not allocated to a sector have been omitted.

Not all co-operatives are in declining industries, however; the printing industry was one of those least affected by the recent recession, and wholefoods has been expanding rapidly, as have computing and business services. A fuller explanation of why co-operatives should exhibit such sectorial concentration is beyond the scope of this paper. We confine ourselves, therefore, to a brief observation.

The area of large-scale mechanized production, with its detailed and hierarchical division of labour, may be seen as antagonistic to co-operative principles. Therefore it is not surprising that co-operatives should locate in areas where small-scale or 'human-scale' production is possible. Furthermore the inability to raise suitable loan finance may force co-operatives into labour-intensive sectors. Equally important is the political and social dimension. The expansion in the co-operative movement has been characterized by a commitment to production for need, be that need social (nurseries), environmental (wholefoods), or political (radical printing and publishing), which in itself is likely to lead to industrial stratification.

Geographic distribution

Given current concern that the effect of economic change has not been felt equally over the different regions of the UK, we are interested to note that co-operatives exhibit a remarkably similar regional distribution to that observed for private firms. Table 16.7 shows a very high proportion of co-operatives in London and the South-east (35 per cent, cf. 34 per cent for private firms). However, as with the industrial distribution discussed above, on a sub-regional level the co-operative sector appears to be highly skewed. For example, within London some 64 per cent of co-operatives are concentrated in 6 of the 32 boroughs. A similar picture is found in most regions with co-operatives apparently differentially located in the urban and inner city areas. The possible explanation of this distribution is likely to have many features. The more compelling of these are as follows: the recent growth in the co-operative sector is, we have argued, a reflection of the rise in unemployment. Therefore it is likely, given that co-operatives tend to be locally based, that they will locate in areas of high unemployment which are typically in the urban and inner-city areas. Thus, for example, in London there are more co-operatives in inner London (Brent, Hackney, Lambeth) than in the more prosperous outer London boroughs (Merton, Sutton).

Table 16.7 Geographic distribution of co-operatives

Region	Co-operative stock	Percentage of stock	Employment	Percentage of employment	VAT-registered firms (%)
Scotland	74	8	1,443	8	8
North	65	7	285	5	4
Yorkshire and Humberside	91	10	545	10	8
North West	85	10	430	8	10
Wales	62	7	337	6	6
West Midlands	62	7	269	5	9
East Midlands	81	9	953	17	7
East Anglia	23	3	116	2	4
South West	35	4	252	5	10
London	273	31	1,528	27	34
South East	36	4	398	7	
Total	887	100	5,556	100	100

Source: Worker Co-operative Database amended and Ganguly (1985)

An equally compelling explanation would seem to be the influence of local CDAs acting to promote the formation of co-operatives and to provide business advice to those formed. The growth in local co-operative-support organizations has its roots in the rise of municipal socialism in the early 1980s amongst Labour-controlled local authorities. This manifested itself in a commitment (amongst other things) to interventionist support for job-creating locally based initiatives. The existence of, by 1986, some 85 co-operative-support organizations in spatially disjoint areas would seem to be a powerful explanation of the sub-regional bias in the concentration of co-operatives. Co-operative formation rates have also been relatively low (compared to the distribution of small firms) in areas such as East Anglia and the South-west where there are few CDAs. This intuitive view is confirmed in the work of Cornforth and Lewis (1986) who found that co-operative-support organizations generally had a positive effect upon co-operative formation rates.

Despite these variations, it is noticeable that the geographic distribution of co-operatives does not differ markedly from that of small firms in general. This contrasts with distribution by industry, where co-operatives are highly concentrated in certain production processes relative to small firms. This suggests that industrial factors or characteristics are a more significant influence in co-operative formations than geographical characteristics.

Conclusion

The picture that we paint of the co-operative sector is, in many respects, less optimistic than that which the National Co-operative Development Agency suggests.

We have found that the total population of worker co-operatives is roughly two-thirds that which has been claimed in various 'Co-operative Directories', giving a total of 894, compared to that of 1,476 claimed by the CDA, for 1986.

The industrial distribution of co-operatives suggests a concentration in particular industries and services that are characterized by low capitalization, recent decline, and high labour intensity. Whilst in part this distribution might be explained by factors specific to the ideological, political, and social make-up of the co-operative sector, it does suggest that the growth in existing co-operatives may not be as dramatic as that found for formation rates.

In a similar vein to the comments above we find that co-operatives exhibit a locational bias at the sub-regional level, with co-operatives' locating predominantly in urban and inner-city regions. These areas may not offer the greatest opportunity, due to low demand, for expansion and growth.

Appendix 1

The principles of co-operation

The following definition of principles results from the International Co-operative Alliance's commission convened in 1971 and subsequently reporting on the 'Present Application of the "Rochdale Principles"'. It now represents the fundamental principles binding co-operative societies.

1   Membership of a co-operative society should be voluntary and available without artificial restriction or any social, political, racial, or religious discrimination, to all persons who can make use of its services and are willing to accept the responsibilities of membership.
2   Co-operative societies are democratic organizations. Their affairs should be administered by persons elected or appointed in a manner agreed by the members and accountable to them. Members of primary societies should enjoy equal rights of voting (one member, one vote) and participation in decisions affecting their societies. In other than primary societies the administration should be conducted on a democratic basis in a suitable form.
3   Share chapital should only receive a strictly limited rate of interest, if any.
4   The economic results arising out of the operations of a society belong to the members of that society and should be distributed in such a manner as would avoid one member gaining at the expense of others. This may be done by decision of the members as follows:
    (a) By provision for development of the business of the Co-operative;
    (b) By provision of common services; or,
    (c) By distribution among the members in proportion to their transactions with the Society.
5   All co-operative Societies should make provision for the education of their members, officers and employees and of the general public, in the principles and techniques of co-operation, both economic and democratic.
6   All co-operative organizations, in order to best serve the interests of their members and their communities should actively co-operate in every practical way with other co-operatives at local, national and international levels.

The ICA principles are silent on whether co-operatives should be organized on an individualistic or collectivist basis. In Britain these are typically supplemented by principles ensuring common ownership:
    (a) Only people employed in the co-operative can become members.

(b) All those working in the co-operative have the right to become members.

(c) Capital employed is in the form of loan stock or reinvested profits and carries no element of control (it is collectively owned).

(d) In the event of dissolution, the members cannot benefit from the distribution of residual assets.

Appendix 2

Sources of data

Sources of data on co-operatives were:
(a) Worker Co-operative Database (WCDB).
(b) Local CDAs.
(c) Direct contact with co-operatives.
(d) Registry of Friendly Societies.
(e) Personal/third-party knowledge and sectoral research.

Notes

1   Throughout this paper we refer, for convenience, to capitalist firms, based on hierarchy and individual ownership, as 'private firms'. This should not confuse the fact that co-operatives are also privately owned. The key difference is that co-operatives are a form of 'social ownership' in that the means of production are not owned by capitalists.

2   Much of the literature relating to the debate over small firms concerns methodological and measurement issues as much as substantive differences in conclusions.

3   Less than 20 employees.

4   In this paper employment data is given as 'full-time equivalents' (FTEs), valuing a part-time worker as half a full-time worker.

5   Community and neighbourhood co-operatives are owned by members of the community within which the business operates, rather than by workers; they are analogous to 'community businesses'. 'Instant muscle' co-operatives are effectively a form of 'labour-only' subcontracting.

6   Note that for this comparison we are using data for 1976 from the Annual Census of Employment which is the latest date for which data is broken down for all industries on a firm-size basis.

7   The VAT data used in these tables refers to 1985.

References

Bibby, A. (1987) *Co-operative Working and Community Projects*, Leeds: ICOM.

Bolton, J.E. (1971) *Report of the Committee of Enquiry on Small Firms* (referred to as Bolton Report), Cmnd 4811, London: HMSO.

CDA (1984) *The New Co-operatives – A Directory and Resource Guide*, London: Co-operative Development Agency.

CDA (1986) *The National Directory of New Co-operatives and Community Businesses*, London: Co-operative Development Agency.

Clayre, A. (1980) *The Political Economy of Co-operation and Participation*, Oxford: Oxford University Press.

Cole, G.D.H. (1944) *A History of Co-operation*, Manchester: Co-operative Union.

Cornforth, C. and Lewis, J. (1986) *The Role and Impact of Co-operative Support Organizations*, Milton Keynes: Co-operatives Research Unit Open University.

Cowe, R. (1988) 'Where anti-capitalist workers are happy exploiting the system', *Guardian*, 4 August.

Department of Employment Gazette (1978) *How Big is British Business?* January, 37–40.

Ganguly, P. (1985) *UK Small Business Statistics and International Comparisons*, London: Harper & Row.

Hamwee, J. (1979) 'Worker co-operatives', *The Industrial Law Journal*, March, 19–31.

ICA (1971) *Report of the ICA Commission on Co-operative Principles*, London: International Co-operative Alliance.

ICOM (1977) *Industrial Co-operatives: A Guide to ICOM Model Rules*. London: Industrial Common Ownership Movement.

Jefferis, K. and Thomas, A. (1988) 'Measuring the performance of worker co-operatives' in Hopper, T. and Cooper, D. *Critical Accounts*, London: Macmillan.

Jones, D.C. (1975) 'Producer co-operatives and the views of the Webbs on participation and ability to survive', *Annals of Public and Co-operative Economics*, 46,1, 23–44.

MacFarlane, R. (1986) *Councils Support Co-operatives*, CLES Report No. 2, Manchester: Centre for Local Economic Strategies.

Mason, C.M. (1983) 'Some definitional difficulties in small firms research', *Area*, 15, 53–60.

Munroe, C. (1987) *The Financing of Worker Co-operatives: A Comparison with Conventional Small Business and Evaluation of Proposed Mechanisms for Investment*, paper presented to the Tenth National Small Firms Policy and Research Conference, November, Milton Keynes.

Paton, R. (1978) *Some Problems of Co-operative Organization*, monograph, Milton Keynes: Co-operatives Research Unit Open University.

Rigge, M. and Young, M. (1983) *Revolution From Within: Co-operatives and Co-operation in British Industry*, London: Weidenfeld & Nicolson.

Thornley, J. (1987) 'Oiling the movement', *New Socialist* (supplement).

Whyatt, A. (1987) 'Time for change', *New Socialist* (supplement).

Chapter seventeen

The organization and behaviour of UK – worker co-operatives: an empirical investigation

Richard Welford

Introduction

The purpose of this paper is to examine aspects of the organization and behaviour of firms in which labour is the residual claimant and controls the firm. The term labour-managed firm can and will be used in its general sense to describe this sort of organization, although in the UK the term worker co-operative is in more common usage.

The aim of this investigation is to analyse survey data which is able to mirror the state of worker co-operation in the UK economy. This seems to be a worthwhile area of study, given that the number of worker co-operatives in the UK has grown twentyfold in the last ten years. A distribution showing the establishment dates of the co-operatives used in this research is given in figure 17.1, reflecting this growth.

This paper concentrates on discussing just a subset of the larger survey, specifically those parts which lead us to question commonly held notions about the co-operative sector and the behaviour of it in the UK (for full details and results of the survey see Welford 1988a).

The structure of the paper is as follows. First, there is a brief examination of previous questionnaire-based surveys and a description of the size and nature of the survey discussed here. Following this, there is an analysis of the objectives of the co-operatives in the survey. Third, growth aspirations are considered and, fourth, organizational form is discussed. The degree of managerialism with the co-operative firm is then analysed. The final section discusses the results of the previous sections and notes the implications of them.

Previous empirical investigation

The degree to which any theory can be supported or refuted relies on the empirical evidence available. Other than anecdotal evidence, in the case of worker co-operatives, this is in short supply. One of the problems is that the co-operative sector has always been relatively small in the

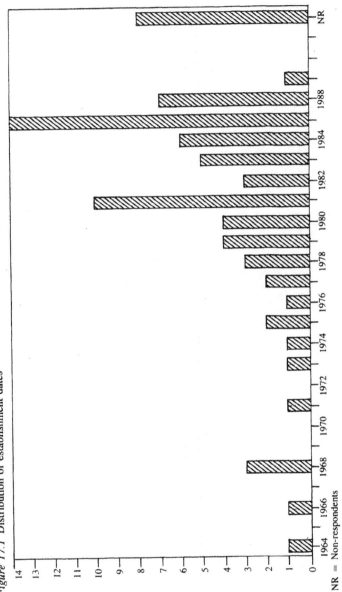

Figure 17.1 Distribution of establishment dates

NR = Non-respondents

UK and has also comprised small firms. In an attempt to add to the empirical evidence it was the intention of this research to mount a survey of a representative sample of co-operatives which are operating in the manufacturing sector of the economy. Two previous attempts at doing this have provided interesting information in areas other than those specified above, but naturally sample sizes were small.

A survey of 57 co-operatives who were members of the Industrial Common Ownership Movement has been carried out by Chaplin and Cowe (1977). The questionnaire was designed to elicit information about how co-operatives started and how they operated, together with the kind of problems met both in starting up and in subsequent operations. The survey indicated that the problems involved in setting up a co-operative were no different to those encountered in establishing a conventional small business. Co-operatives which had been established close to the time of the survey tended to receive a significant amount of help from government finance and loans from the Industrial Common Ownership Fund (ICOF) and other co-operatives. The average size of the co-operatives investigated was nine members.

One aspect of the study which is particularly relevant to the research reported in this paper concerned the organization of the co-operative. It revealed that many co-operatives appeared, to the purist, to fail as co-operatives in one or more of the crucial areas of control, job allocation, and wage payments. Over a quarter of the co-operatives did not indulge in communal decision-making and in three cases those responsible for taking the decisions were not elected by the workforce. One-third of the established co-operatives had no restrictions at all on differentials. Thus commonly elites developed within the workforce against the ideals of longer-term co-operation. Chaplin and Cowe (1977: 50) also note that those co-operatives 'representative of alternative movements seem less concerned about ownership and indeed with financial success'.

In a postal survey of economic aspects of worker co-operatives in Britain (Wilson 1983), 113 co-operatives were analysed. In addition to the questionnaire responses, data was supplemented by information from Companies House and the Registry of Friendly Societies. An unexpected outcome was that many co-operatives proved to be multi-functional. For example, one surveyed co-operative described its activities as 'a nucleus of people looking for friendly, non-sexist socially responsible, flexible work' and listed its trades along the range from building to dressmaking. This was typical of co-operatives who had been set up as alternatives to a more traditional firm, seeking to escape more conventional work relationships, primarily promoting broader causes. This perhaps suggests a correlation between strength of ideological input and diversification into a range of activities.

Generally, the co-operatives surveyed were seen as having broader objectives than their capitalist counterparts. Of the firms surveyed, some were mainly concerned with achieving a desired 'quality of working life' and many placed emphasis on political or religious ideology. Fifty-eight per cent of the survey saw stability of employment and job security as a prime objective.

The questionnaire

The questionnaire used in this research represents an attempt both to answer some of the points raised in the theoretical literature from an empirical stance and to provide a snapshot of the contemporary co-operative sector. The survey was sent to the 216 manufacturing co-operatives listed in the National Directory of New Co-operatives and Community Businesses (CDA 1986); 78 questionnaires were returned completed and a further 37 were returned marked 'gone away' and 8 returned not completed. This represents a return rate of 57 per cent and a response rate of 36 per cent.

The objectives of the co-operative

In the analysis of the traditional capitalist firm the dominant assumption has been the maximization of profits. In the case of the worker co-operative two common characteristics may lead us to challenge the assumption.

First, many co-operatives are established for political and ideological reasons, often as a rebuttal to capitalist values. For example, the exclusive aim of profit maximization may be seen as undesirable. Second, Estrin (1985) notes that the modal size of a UK co-operative is about four members and we are left with the question as to whether small firms, however organized, do or are able to maximize profits.

The results of this research indicates that the modal size is five with a mean of about fifteen, but, if the largest two co-operatives in the survey are ignored, with memberships of 160 and 400, then this mean falls to about nine (a distribution of co-operatives responding to the question-naire by number of members is presented in figure 17.2). Three-quarters of the co-operatives contained members who had prior experience in the area in which they were operating, although only a quarter of the co-operatives contained members who had all had experience.

The questionnaire attempted to elucidate the objectives of the co-operative. Co-operatives were asked about how important a number of factors were in the establishment of the co-operative. Table 17.1 summarizes the responses. What can be seen clearly is the importance of the atmosphere at work, wanting to work for oneself, the provision of a particular product, and a desire for equality with fellow workers.

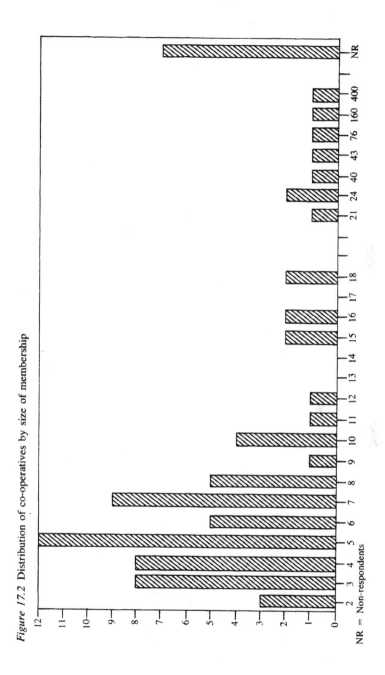

Figure 17.2 Distribution of co-operatives by size of membership

NR = Non-respondents

Table 17.1 The importance of factors in the establishment of the co-operative

	Number of co-operatives reporting the factor to be:				Numbers reporting this to be the most important factor
	Very important	Important	Not important	NR	
Religious reasons	5	4	66	3	5
Political reasons	16	17	39	6	6
A redundancy situation/ factor closure	19	15	38	11	9
A job-creation programme	18	11	40	9	9
The provision of a particular product	31	19	21	7	5
The availability of grants	16	19	38	6	3
The desire for a pleasant atmosphere at work	35	27	12	4	7
Wanting to work for oneself	38	21	12	7	5
Support of a CDA	9	21	39	8	3
A desire for equality with fellow workers	28	30	14	5	23
Others	5	0	0	61	1*

NR = No response
* = Objective stated was the provision of shared childcare support

Whilst the establishment of the co-operative as a direct result of redundancy or as a means of job creation was relatively unimportant amongst the majority of co-operatives, clearly for a significant minority it was the most important aspect of the co-operative's establishment.

Correlations between the reasons for the establishment of the co-operative provide some interesting results:

1 Of the 16 co-operatives who listed political reasons as being very important, half or more also reported the provision of a particular product, the atmosphere at work, working for oneself, and equality with fellow workers as being very important.
2 Of those recording 'working for oneself' as being very important, two-thirds thought that atmosphere was very important, and a half stated that equality was very important.
3 Two-thirds of those stating that atmosphere was very important also saw working for oneself and the issue of equality as being very important.
4 Over half of those who thought that the provision of a particular product was very important also recorded atmosphere and working for oneself as being very important.

Thus there seems to be a number of co-operatives whose objectives revolve around matters of politics, equality, working for oneself, atmosphere, and the provision of a particular product. We find that 39 co-operatives (exactly half) saw two or more of these factors as being very important. In some respect therefore we are able to split the sample in half according to objective. On the one hand there seem to be those co-operatives interested foremostly in non-financial objectives and objectives not aimed primarily at the provision of employment. On the other hand there are those who see employment for members and financial viability as the dominant objectives.

Another question attempted to reveal something of the aims of the co-operative at the time of the survey. This was intentionally left to the respondents to word but nevertheless there are common areas of response. These are reported in table 17.2. Certainly there appears to be considerable overlap with objectives stated above, as one would expect, and comparison of original objectives with present aims shows them to be largely consistent. There is, however, a much larger emphasis put on employment; particularly on security of employment. Thus, whilst for many the original intention of the co-operative was not to create jobs, certainly the maintenance of those jobs once created is important. Again featuring as an important objective is the production of particular (socially worthwhile) goods. In an attempt to group products into similar areas of production, figure 17.3 shows the distribution of co-operatives by product type.

Table 17.2 Aims of the co-operative

Common Areas of Response	
General aim reported	*Number of co-operatives reporting this aim*
The provision of employment/security of employment	26
The production and promotion of socially worthwhile goods	24
Promoting the co-operative sector	13
Profitability and good rates of pay	12
Training and skills development	12
Viability of the co-operative/production to 'make a living'	10
Equal status for women and minority groups	9
Growth	8
High quality of workmanship/creativity	8
Working with and responsibility towards the community	8
Provision of good working conditions	7
Non-exploitation	6
No response	20

Some authors have also argued that the effort expended by members is likely to be higher, and therefore productivity greater, than that expended by workers under capitalism (Tyson 1979; Ireland 1981). Of the respondents to the questionnaire nearly half thought that there definitely were productivity advantages. This may be due to reduced alienation (see for example Reich and Devine 1981) or a sense of loyalty or perhaps a result of the knowledge that the enterprise surplus will return to the members. Sixty-five co-operatives reported that they had made a surplus recently and the distribution of this is reported in table 17.3.

Table 17.3 Distribution of surplus (where applicable)

Destination of surplus	*Number of co-operatives distributing at least some of the surplus to this area*	*Average distributed to this area by co-operatives making a surplus (%)*
Members	54	25
Re-investment	65	61
Charity	20	5
Other co-operatives	7	1

Respondents = 72
Non-respondents = 6

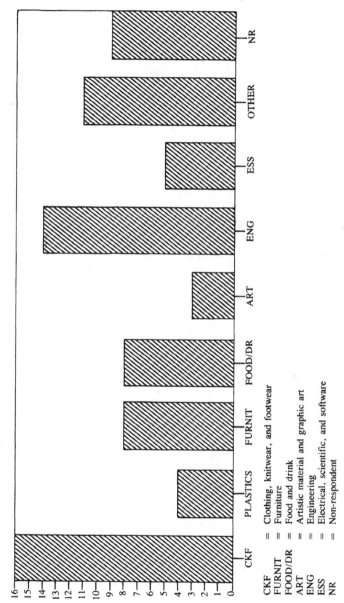

Figure 17.3 Distribution of co-operatives by main product

CKF   = Clothing, knitwear, and footwear
FURNIT   = Furniture
FOOD/DR = Food and drink
ART   = Artistic material and graphic art
ENG   = Engineering
ESS   = Electrical, scientific, and software
NR   = Non-respondent

Much of the literature surrounding alternative maximands in the labour-managed firm assumes that each member behaves in the way which maximizes his/her own utility and may be unaffected by the impact of the behaviour of others. This may seem a naïve assumption when examining any organizational form, but in the case of the co-operative it may be particularly inappropriate. In the case of an income-sharing co-operative one member may be affected by the behaviour of another since one member's effort will in part determine another's income. At issue therefore is the consideration of whether co-operatives demonstrate a degree of altruism, i.e. their members attach some weight to the impact of their behaviour on others' welfare. A definitive answer to this question is impossible on the basis of this questionnaire, but nevertheless amongst the objectives of co-operatives cited one can find mention of worksharing, equal status, democracy, harmony, and one co-operative listed its objectives as:

> The provision of goods and services required by our customers, to look after our members in every respect, to fly the common ownership flag and to be a caring, sharing community.

Growth and the co-operative firm

It is often claimed that the labour managed firm will tend to grow at a slower rate than its capitalist counterpart. The work of authors such as Atkinson (1973) and Bonin (1983) represents a theoretical demonstration that the labour-managed firm chooses a lower rate of growth than the profit-maximizing firm in certain circumstances.

On a level more related to the decision-making machinations of the worker co-operative, one may expect that growth which results in an expansion of the labour force and a consequent diluting of the authority of the original members, may be resisted. Moreover the expansion of the workforce needs to result in a proportional expansion of the surplus if members are not to be made worse off by following a growth strategy.

The results of the survey certainly do not reflect the view that co-operatives will not want to grow. No respondents expected a decline in terms of turnover, employment, or incomes of members. The distribution between those anticipating no growth, a growth rate of less than 10 per cent, and a growth rate of more than 10 per cent, over the next twelve months and three years, is shown in figure 17.4. In every case, over each time period, the majority of respondents expected growth by more than 10 per cent. A relatively large proportion of respondents did expect employment not to change, even though some of them expected turnover to increase by more than 10 per cent, even in the short term. This may lend support to the view that some co-operatives do not wish

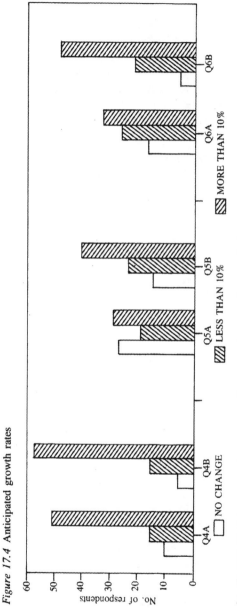

Figure 17.4 Anticipated growth rates

Q4 To what extent do you expect your co-operative to grow in terms of turnover in the next
   A 12 months?
   B 3 years?

Q5 To what extent do you expect employment in the co-operative to expand in the next
   A 12 months?
   B 3 years?

Q6 To what extent do you expect incomes of the members of the co-operative to increase in the next
   A 12 months?
   B 3 years?

to expand employment. In the past the reason for this has been seen in terms of selfish reasons (i.e. not wanting to dilute the shared surplus), but other rational reasons might include not wanting to risk losing a good atmosphere or the relationships between members.

One strategy for overcoming problems associated with employment and reductions in the shared surplus has been examined in terms of the establishment of two or more categories of membership. Termed by Meade (1972) and Zafiris (1983) 'the inegalitarian co-operative', its existence brings into question the most basic principles of common ownership. Another possibility is that the co-operative may actually hire labour. This is common amongst the plywood co-operatives of North America for example, but again it can be easily criticized for its non-adherence to co-operative ideals. Two-thirds of the co-operatives sampled did pay members according to the same rate. Of those that did not, the largest differential reported was between £7000 and £30,000 per annum. Interestingly under half of the co-operatives actually varied wages with the surplus of the co-operative. But this reflects the fact that many co-operatives were not making a surplus and many newer ones were reinvesting all the surplus. Results are summarized in table 17.4.

Table 17.4 Wage payments

Co-operatives paying members regular wages	62
Co-operatives not paying regular wages	12
Non-respondents	4
Wages paid in the co-operative compared with the non-co-operative sector:	
Lower	27
About the same	25
Higher	15
Don't know	9
Non-respondents	2
Co-operatives paying members according to the same rate of pay	53
Co-operatives paying members differing rates	22
Non-respondents	3

Of the twenty-two co-operatives adopting differentials 15 did so because of differences in skills. One co-operative operated a differential with a member who was a YTS trainee, one co-operative paid members with dependents more than those without, one paid wages according to the amount of freelance work members attracted, and the other three had differentials between members who were part-time workers and those who were full-time. In addition, four co-operatives reported that there were non-members in the organization who got paid less.

Organizational form

Of interest here is the extent to which an organizational form specific to the co-operative firm leads to efficiency gains. Drawing on and developing the work of Stewart (1986) and Williamson (1980), it is possible to hypothesize that labour-managed and profit-maximizing production might have different cost functions. There are a variety of suggestions as to possible sources for this differential which can be categorized into four parts.

First, the two organizational forms may have different incentive and monitoring properties. In other words, workers might be motivated and monitored in different ways. Most of the debate centres around the supply of effort but note should also be taken of other aspects of performance such as quality. The questionnaire asked whether respondents considered there to be productivity advantages associated with co-operative organizations which do not exist for conventional firms. Nearly half (37) of the respondents thought that there definitely were advantages. Common reasons for these are summarized in table 17.5, but high on the list are issues such as motivation, flexibility, and commitment. Commitment being the most commonly cited factor and being due in no small part presumably to the fact that, in 56 out of the 78 co-operatives surveyed, at least some of the capital provided came from members. The fact that tasks were self-monitored and that there was no shirking perceived also resulted in some co-operatives considering themselves to have productivity advantages.

Second, there is a need to examine the role of assignment. The extent to which workers are optimally allocated to the various tasks in the organization might be investigated, the ability of labour to assign itself to the most appropriate tasks in the labour-managed firm being a key issue. The fact that members were expected to do any job which needed doing in the organization was commonly recorded and five co-operatives clearly stated that the fact that there was no demarcation or unionization aided productivity. In the majority of co-operatives work is divided, at least in part, on specific skill lines. As can be seen from table 17.6, work is only occasionally allocated by a manager or management team.

Third, as Williamson notes, organizations might differ in terms of atmosphere. It may be argued, for example, that profit-maximizing production alienates workers and that the democratic nature of a labour-managed firm may lead to a greater feeling of self-determination. Certainly commonly cited areas for productivity advantages associated with co-operatives included a happy atmosphere and a feeling that members would receive the full benefits of their effort (see table 17.5).

Fourth, the assertion that, because transactions are not conducted under conditions of perfect competition, bargaining costs may differ

Table 17.5 Responses to question 17: Do you consider there are productivity advantages to be gained from co-operative organizations which do not exist in conventional firms?

Areas commonly cited by those believing there to be productivity advantages:	Number of co-operatives citing this area
Motivation	6
Flexibility	11
Commitment	19
No demarcation/no unionization	5
Self-monitoring/no shirking	8
Members receive the benefits of their labour	5
Happy atmosphere	10

Areas commonly cited by those believing there to be productivity disadvantages:	Number of co-operatives citing this area
Slow decision-making process	5
Work effort is not expected to be so intense	3
Inability to raise money for expansion	4
Humanist aims are not compatible with high productivity	3

Summary of responses	*Yes*	*No*	*Don't know*	*Non-respondents*
	37	13	3	24

Table 17.6 Allocation of work amongst members of the co-operative

Allocation device	*Number of co-operatives citing this as a method of job allocation*
Work is divided on specific skill lines	47
Certain jobs have always been done by the same people	15
Work is rotated	9
There is not specific division of labour	21
Allocation is done by a manager or management team	10
Other	0
Non-respondents	4

between the two organizational forms needs to be considered. For example, where wage bargaining is concerned, the profit-maximizing firm is likely to face significant transactions costs which do not arise for the labour-managed firm. In the case of 54 co-operatives wages did vary with the surplus of the co-operative and therefore productivity/ efficiency bonuses were built-in rather than having to be negotiated. Moreover the non-existence (in most cases) of a separate management structure results in wages being self-determined.

Managerialism

The egalitarian co-operative we may assume will be democratically run with decision-making being done by all the members. In some instances day-to-day running and decision-making may be the responsibility of a member taking on a managerial role or of a management group. Account has to be taken of the interplay between the various individuals and groups who make up the firm. The question which then arises is whether managers will display the same sort of managerial tendencies which we observe in capitalist firms, whether other types of managerial discretion exists, or whether managerialism is absent.

Table 17.7 Decision-making in the co-operative enterprise

Co-operatives reported the following strategies for decision-making			Number of co-operatives
On a day-to-day basis			
A single manager makes the decisions			22
A management team makes the decisions			20
All members decide democratically on decisions			29
Other (not specified)			1
Non-respondents			6
When deciding on longer-term policy			
A single manager makes the decisions			0
A management team makes the decisions			9
All members decide democratically on decisions			61
Other (not specified)			2
Non-respondents			6
Where applicable were managers democratically elected?	*Yes*	*No*	*Not clear/No response*
	27	7	8

Figure 17.5 and table 17.7 summarize the extent of decision-making done by a manager or management team. As far as day-to-day decisions are concerned, it is indeed most common for these to be taken by managers. In all but nine cases though, policy decisions were taken by

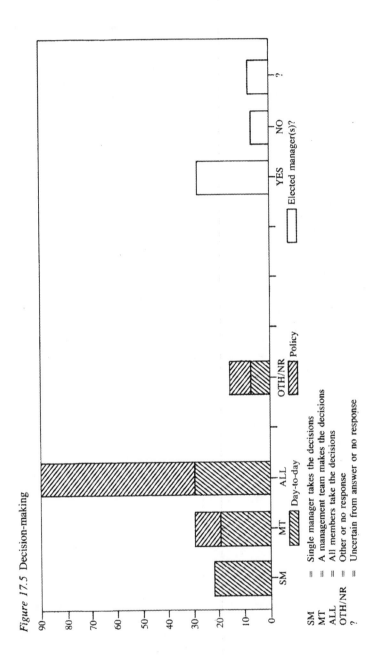

Figure 17.5 Decision-making

SM = Single manager takes the decisions
MT = A management team makes the decisions
ALL = All members take the decisions
OTH/NR = Other or no response
? = Uncertain from answer or no response

all the members. In addition to these nine cases another thirty-three co-operatives used managers. Seven co-operatives from the sample did not elect their managers and in two of these cases the managers decided on policy matters.

Discussion

The evidence presented here highlights some important issues facing the co-operative sector in the UK. Certainly it provides further evidence (see also Welford 1988b) that much of the neo-classical Illyrian theory of the firm, particularly with regard to supply-side effects, appears to be refuted. For the purist, however, the results of the survey may be disappointing. They tend to suggest that there are two distinct categories of co-operative, represented in this survey almost equally. Whilst one type does tend to adhere to the principles and practices of common ownership and has a political nature to its existence, the other does not. There seems to be no real difference between the behaviour and objectives of these latter co-operatives and their capitalist counterparts.

According to Daudi and Sotto (1985), Western capitalism is forcing a metamorphosis on co-operative organizations such that traditional aims and objectives of the co-operative movement are being eliminated or absorbed by both internal and external forces. The implication of their analysis is that in the long run there may be little difference between the co-operative and the small capitalist firm. This may be a pessimistic view but certainly the bidimensional nature of this survey needs explaining.

One of the reasons for differences in the structure and the operation of the co-operative has to be the perception by members of the benefits and costs of operating a structure where democracy and participation are important. In particular, respondents to the questionnaire were split over whether the co-operative organization would have inherent productivity advantages. About one-quarter of respondents clearly felt that there was a trade-off between the 'political' ideals of the co-operative and efficiency, stemming from a slow decision-making process, a lower expectation of work effort, and an inability to raise money for expansion. Although we should remember that the production 'norm' by which co-operatives would have been measuring themselves is set by the prevailing form of capitalism.

It should be remembered that the co-operative is merely an amalgam of a number of individuals. In the traditional co-operative these individuals are likely to be motivated by the existence of self-management, self-determination, and equality. But many organizations were not established first and foremost for these reasons. Reasonably common, for example, was the establishment of the co-operative as a means of job creation. Given this establishment of co-operatives in a labour market under pressure, we may assume that in many cases co-operative ideology is not important. Thus the goals of the co-operative may be more associated with the small capitalist firm. But then why did the individuals establishing an organization decide on the co-operative format? This question can be partly answered by reference to the significant number of positive responses received when asking if the co-operative received support from the Co-operative Development Agency or whether it received financial support because it was a co-operative. CDA and local-authority support may thus sometimes be promoting a co-operative sector in name only.

There are clearly differences in how members of the co-operative organization treat their fellow members. At one extreme a member may view his/her associates as a means to his/her economic ends. On the other hand Pfeiffer (1982) argues that co-operative members are inclined to regard economic ends as a means to the service of his/her fellow social actors. Thus the relationships and interrelationships within the co-operative are important. If members see their own income as a particularly important factor, then co-operative ideals and behaviour may be compromised. The member or members which have the most influence or power may be able to influence the behaviour of the co-operative. Certainly evidence of a degree of managerial control exists in the survey.

Authors such as Cyert and March (1963) and Vernon (1971) have long considered organizations not as homogeneous entities but rather as complex sets of interactions between different competing interest groups. Karpik (1978) views the organization as a loosely coupled political system in which individuals are motivated by a mixture of private, political, and ideological interests. In the co-operative there may be conflict between those with private interests and those with others. If we view the co-operative as having traditional ideals, then this will be because a dominant coalition within the organization has had the power to attain its own ends. Thus the opposite must be true in a co-operative which acts as a capitalist firm. The implication is that any further analysis of the co-operative organization requries an analysis of the members which make up that organization.

The diverse nature of the co-operative sector in the UK reflects the diverse number of objectives of coalitions within the organization. But the survey does suggest that a co-operative sector not wholly based on traditional co-operative ideals is emerging. The new co-operative firm is as likely to be interested in the pursuit of profit as it is in the pursuit of more 'social' goals. Indeed Daudi and Sotto (1985: 38) accuse the co-operative movement of 'going towards the very regions that it used to condemn, or, rather were condemned by its ancestor'. They further claim that a co-operative interested in common ownership and equality no longer exists. I am pleased to be able to report that they are nevertheless wrong on the second count. The future behaviour of the co-operative sector is more questionable however.

References

Atkinson, A.B. (1973) 'Worker management and the modern industrial enterprise', *Quarterly Journal of Economics*, 47, 75–92.

Bonin, J.P. (1983) 'Innovation in a labour-managed firm: a membership perspective', *Journal of Industrial Economics*, 31, 3313–29.

CDA (1986) *The National Directory of New Co-operatives and Community Businesses*, London: Co-operative Development Agency.

Chaplin, P. and Cowe, R. (1977) 'A survey of contemporary British worker co-operatives', Manchester Business School Discussion Paper, University of Manchester.

Cyert, R. and March, J. (1963) *A Behavioural Theory of the Firm*, Englewood Cliffs, New Jersey: Prentice-Hall.

Daudi, P. and Sotto, R. (1985) 'The Sword of Damocles – on the metamorphosis of homo co-operatives', discussion paper, Department of Business Administration, University of Lund, Sweden.

Estrin, S. (1985) 'The role of producer co-operatives in employment creation', paper presented to the Fourth International Conference on the Economics of Self-Management, Liège.

Ireland, N.J. (1981) 'The behaviour of the labour-managed firm and disutility from supplying factor services', *Economic Analysis and Workers' Management*, 15, 21–43.

Karpik, L. (1978) *'Organization and Environment: Managing Differentiation and Integration*, Boston: Harvard University Press.

Meade, J.E. (1972) 'The general theory of labour-managed firms and of profit-sharing', *Economic Journal*, 82 Supp., 402–28.

Pfeiffer, L. (1982) *'Les Conditions de Développement d'un Secteur d'Economie Sociale'*, Aubenas: Leinhart & cie.

Reich, M. and Devine, J. (1981) 'The microeconomics of conflict and hierarchy in capitalist production', *Review of Radical Political Economy*, 12, 27–45.

Stewart, G. (1986) PhD thesis, University of Warwick.

Tyson, L.D.A. (1979) 'Incentives, income-sharing and institutional innovation in the Yugoslav self-managed firm', *Journal of Comparative Economics*, 3, 285–301.

Vernon, R. (1971) *Sovereignty at Bay*, New York: Basic Books.

Welford, R.J. (1988a) 'Aspects of the behaviour of UK Worker Co-operatives: results of a survey', Discussion Paper No. 11, School of Economics, Portsmouth Polytechnic.

Welford, R.J. (1988b) 'Objectives and growth aspirations of UK Worker Co-operatives', *Annals of Public and Co-operative Economy*, 59, 215–28.

Williamson, O.E. (1980) 'The organization of work: a comparative institutional assessment', *Journal of Economic Behaviour and Organization*, 1.

Wilson, N. (1983) 'Economic aspects of worker co-operatives in Britain' in *The Economics of Worker Co-operatives*, Oxford: Plunkett Foundation.

Zafiris, N. (1983) 'The form of maximand of the inegalitarian workers' co-operative', *British Review of Economic Issues*, 5, 13, 39–61.

Chapter eighteen

Changing ownership: meaning, culture, and control in the construction of a co-operative organization

Neil Carter

Introduction

Worker co-operatives provide work for less than 10,000 workers, despite their rapid growth in Britain during the 1980s and the recent political and academic interest in this alternative organizational form. Co-operatives won support earlier in the decade because of the widespread, but over optimistic, hope that the expansion of a 'Third Sector' would substantially reduce unemployment. It is clearer today that co-operatives will remain of marginal economic importance for the foreseeable future, although they continue to be promoted in local economic initiatives seeking to alleviate structural unemployment among specific disadvantaged groups of workers. But there remains a strong *moral* case for promoting co-operative development as a desirable, and possibly more efficient, democratic alternative to the dominant hierarchical, capitalist organizational form. This chapter examines the problems arising from an attempt to convert a small conventional company into a co-operative.

The concept of workers' co-operatives poses a fundamental question about the tension faced by a democratic organization competing in a capitalist market system where most firms pursue profit-maximization and adopt a hierarchical division of labour. The problems generated by this conflict led the Webbs (1914) to conclude that co-operatives tend to degenerate into small businesses run on capitalist lines, although this thesis has been contested by several recent observers, notably Jones (1975), Batstone (1983), and Cornforth (1986). Either way, there is a consensus on one point. Recent British experience suggests that co-operatives must prove commercially viable if members are to obtain long-term satisfaction from their experience of work. Over the last fifteen years many 'defensive' co-operatives, formed after a factory closure, have endured a constant and frequently unsuccessful struggle for commercial survival: Pakenham, Meriden, KME Kirkby, the Scottish *Daily News*, and Unicorn Shirts form a long and familiar litany for students of the co-operative movement (see Wajcman 1983; Coates 1976).

Alternatively, when co-operatives do survive, as have many of the small start-up co-operatives formed during the 1980s, they are concentrated in the secondary sector of the economy. This means that co-operatives are often dependent on sub-contract work from large companies and many workers operate in 'sweated labour' conditions where they endure long hours, low wages, poor conditions, and high insecurity. Both examples offer little scope for the development of democratic structures and processes, or for any permanent impact on worker attitudes and behaviour.

One solution to this problem may involve a profitable conventional company's transferring to a co-operative form of ownership. This would have the advantage that the members avoid having to adapt simultaneously to a new organizational structure whilst coping with the problems of starting a new business or rescuing a declining company. If the considerable legal problems raised by such a transfer were eased, then this might prove an attractive option. One approach is to convert businesses along the lines of the Employee Share Ownership Plans (ESOP) that are common in the USA (Russell 1985) and currently attracting the attention of the British labour movement. Several trade unions have sponsored the Unity Trust Bank to promote ESOPs. There are also a few long-established conversion co-operatives, notably Scott Bader, Landsmans, and Michael Jones, where, in each case, a Christian entrepreneur has imposed ownership on the workforce (Oakeshott 1978). Whilst these co-operatives have continued to prosper as businesses, there is little evidence that they differ markedly from conventional companies in organizational, attitudinal, or behavioural terms.

This chapter examines the case of 'Topline Typewriters',[1] a supplier of office equipment in the London area. The existing owners of the company were approaching retirement and attempted to transfer ownership to the employees rather than sell to outsiders. However, the experiment proved unsuccessful. Within three years, two managers had staged a successful takeover of power and had established themselves as directors of the company; ironically, the attempt to convert to a co-operative resulted in the ascendancy of a new managerial elite. It is argued that this failure can be explained by focusing on the way in which the staff were unable socially to construct an alternative organizational form. Three key aspects of this process are analysed, all of which have been inadequately treated in the majority of the co-operative literature.

First, an examination of the *meanings* that the workforce attributed to the co-operative reveals the existence of a variety of definitions of the new situation. Second, the emphasis is on the issue of control rather than ownership. The co-operative literature has concentrated on formal processes of control resulting in a partial understanding of control (Webbs 1914; Jones 1975; Oakeshott 1978; Batstone 1983). Instead, it is fruitful to adopt a broader perspective on control (Carter 1988). In particular, it is vital to uncover the informal processes of control that influence the relative power of individuals or groups within a co-operative – leadership (Cosyns and Loveridge 1981), information flow (Abell 1979), expertise (Rothschild-Whitt 1979) – and to discover who exercises control over the organization of work (Clarke 1984). Third, in co-operatives, as in any other organization, any change initiative is mediated and shaped by the extant organizational culture (Gherardi and Masiero 1987; Oliver and Thomas 1990).

The use of this approach helps to explain why the transfer of ownership *per se* neither produces a radical change in the distribution of organizational power, nor alters the way that people experience work. Before exploring this problem, it is necessary to outline the key events in the Topline story.

A short-lived experiment

Topline Typewriters was founded by George Dixon in the early 1950s, with the object of selling and leasing typewriters to companies, backed up by quality service and maintenance of equipment. The company grew steadily so that by the 1980s there were some fifty employees.

Dixon described himself as a 'socialist' who now votes SDP due to his disillusionment with 'two-party politics' and the 'power of the trade unions'. He was influenced by 'Human Relations' writers such as Eliot Jaques and Elton Mayo, and the practical achievements of companies like Marks and Spencer and the John Lewis Partnership. Dixon had long cherished the idea that workers should take control of their own destinies in co-operatives and co-ownerships (he used the words interchangeably) and hoped that these organizational forms would encourage workers to be more committed, flexible and responsible. He managed to convey these hopes and beliefs to the workforce, as one area manager reflected: 'I've been here twenty-eight years. Right from the start we knew we were working together for something; we weren't sure what, but there was an idea that kept us together.' This idea lacked clarity until the four company directors began planning for retirement during the 1980s. Dixon saw an opportunity to realize his broader ambitions by transferring ownership of the company to the employees, so he persuaded the other directors to consider the interests of the staff by not imposing outside owners on them.

Dixon drew up a two-stage conversion plan. First, Dixon and one other director would retire, followed five years later by the remaining two directors. The workforce was told that all the shares would be placed in a trust controlled by six trustees who would, initially, be the four directors and two elected employee representatives, but after five years all trustees would be elected by the members. The new sovereign legislative body was the General Assembly where members – employees with a tenure of three years – would make policy decisions at regular monthly meetings. The assembly would elect a four-person management committee with day-to-day control over company affairs.

Dixon made some attempt to prepare the workforce for self-management: for several years an elected committee had worked on specific projects such as reforming the wage structure, the managers were shown a video about the Mondragon co-operatives in Spain, and he arranged regular seminars to explain the business. The managers were asked if they wanted a co-operative in a questionnaire that recorded 80 per cent support for the idea, although many later admitted that they had supported it just to keep Dixon happy, never believing that his scheme would ever materialize. The rest of the workforce were not consulted about the plan.

Immediately after the conversion was initiated, the new committee faced two major problems. First, the application of a wage freeze caused an internal dispute. Two managers registered a grievance at not being regraded. This grievance was rejected after a personal hearing from both the committee and a full meeting of the assembly. The committee's indecisive handling of the issue, against a background of discontent over the wage freeze, lost it credibility. Second, two managers were found to have formed their own company and were poaching customers while still working for Topline. Both men were sacked, but the incident caused further disruption and instability. Convinced that the committee was inadequate and that a more dynamic approach was required, Dixon intervened by winning the support of the other trustees for placing the committee into abeyance. The 'democratic' interregnum had lasted just three months.

Dixon appointed two managers to run the company. He stressed that the co-operative was not abandoned but that the trustees (i.e. the directors) felt that the company was not yet ready for a committee. The assembly was retained as a consultative and information-giving forum, but not as a decision-making body. However, this change also proved unsuccessful with the new senior managers winning little credibility from the staff, partly due to jealousy of their rapid promotion. Conflict among the managers became incessant and staff grew increasingly concerned about the state of the business. Within a year, Dixon again intervened to form a five-person management committee. Initially, this committee made several organizational changes that enabled the company to compete more effectively in the changing market. Furthermore, Dixon was, at last, persuaded to withdraw from the company in order to enhance the credibility of the new management team. But then the committee divided: two ambitious members persuaded Dixon to appoint them as trustees and they subsequently used this body to oust the other committee members. The management committee was disbanded and the two 'young pretenders' were appointed directors. The experiment was over. These two managers now run the company, the assembly rarely meets, many staff have departed, and outsiders have been brought in. The word 'co-operative' is an historical relic.

The meaning of co-operation

Several contrasting definitions of co-operation were prevalent among the workforce during the attempted conversion,[2] each generating different expectations and behaviour from the various organizational factions described in figure 18.1.

Figure 18.1 Organizational structure of Topline Typewriters at conversion (the figure in brackets refers to the number of staff at each level)

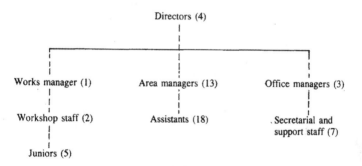

```
                        Directors (4)
                             |
                             |
      ┌──────────────────────┼──────────────────────┐
      |                      |                       |
Works manager (1)      Area managers (13)      Office managers (3)
      |                      |                       |
Workshop staff (2)      Assistants (18)         Secretarial and
      |                                         support staff (7)
  Juniors (5)
```

Dixon intended the co-operative to safeguard the business, employ the same workforce, and retain the standards and principles he had implemented. He hoped that co-operative ownership would provide the stimulus for the workers to assume the responsibility necessary to run the company but, recognizing that such a change in attitudes and behaviour would be gradual, he designed a constitution containing safeguards against rapid, radical changes. However, despite trying enthusiastically to convince staff of the merits of his scheme, Dixon's hectoring style made him a poor teacher. Instead of creating a learning environment he spoke in a way that made people afraid to voice opinions or to ask questions for fear of criticism. By concentrating his efforts on the managers, he also revealed the limits to his planned change, for he anticipated no alteration to the managerial hierarchy.

The managers discussed the co-operative plan most frequently because their seniority and status made them more involved in the company. The managers can be roughly divided into two groups: the 'old guard' and the 'young upstarts', to employ expressions used both humorously and disparagingly by each group about the other.

The 'old guard' all boasted more than twenty years service at Topline. They claimed to enjoy working at Topline and affirmed their commitment to the company. However, their loyalty depended on Topline's relatively favourable wages and conditions, and the limited transferability of their own skills. This instrumentalism made them very conscious of status and embroiled them in continual conflicts over wages and fringe benefits, notably car allowances and bonuses.

The 'old guard' viewed the co-operative plan with trepidation because they saw it as a threat to their status: 'I asked "What have I got for twenty-nine years' service?" A younger member stood up and said "Nothing, we are starting afresh." I suppose he is correct, but is that right? Shouldn't I get some reward for long service?' They had hoped that Dixon would hand the company over to the senior managers as a reward for their loyalty and were unhappy that the co-operative seemed to reward everyone equally. Ironically, when the younger managers prospered after Dixon's intervention, the 'old guard' criticized the disbanding of the committee as 'undemocratic', although their anger was motivated by their own exclusion from the new management team rather than at the loss of the co-operative structure.

The 'young upstarts' were in their early thirties and were united around the need to develop the business by adapting to changes in the product market. They recognized that new, more reliable, electronic technology was making their traditional mechanical skills redundant and shifting the emphasis of the business on to sales and marketing. They eagerly grabbed training opportunities, shared ideas, and were rewarded by Dixon as his own thinking moved in a similar direction. When he advocated the co-operative idea, they supported him, but with a varying commitment to his idealism. Some shared his belief that 'everyone should work together, on an equal footing, more for that way of working than for money'. But most hoped that the co-operative might generate responsibility and commitment through greater consultation and participation for the workforce. When the committee took over, they believed it created conflict and indecision: 'you can't have everyone making decisions all the time, can you?' Consequently, they all supported Dixon's intervention as a way of reintroducing greater managerial control: 'A co-op is about working together for the common good: it's a team game. But I don't think it can work. I'm not against democracy, it's just that people make bloody stupid decisions. You need hard men in charge, making decisions with an iron hand.'

The younger managers were content for control to reside with management, particularly as they now dominated. They began to talk about the old guard as 'wasters', even suggesting that the deadwood be discarded. Like Dixon, they increasingly talked about 'co-ownership', meaning they accepted some limited worker participation but with control retained by management.

The Staff knew less about the co-operative because they were rarely consulted on company policy-making. The young trainees were simply ignorant of the scheme. One youngster asked: 'What's this co-operative lark anway? My mum shops at Tesco's.' Coming several months after the conversion, this comment shows that the co-operative message was not reaching the parts of the organization that other co-operatives reach.

Among the longer-serving assistants and administrative staff, most of whom had worked in Topline for several years, two general attitudes were discernible: one largely dismissive, the other supportive, but in neither case was there a demand for a greater say in company affairs. The majority were unimpressed by the co-operative plan: 'The idea of a co-op doesn't mean a thing to me; it doesn't affect me and things don't seem different.' Some professed to hold only instrumental values: 'I couldn't care less about the co-op. I only work for the money. As long as I've still got my job, I don't care whether it's a co-op or not.' Most felt as powerless as before the conversion: 'The co-op doesn't really mean much to me. I've only been here four years and I'm not very senior, so I don't know what's going on. I still take orders; people tell me what to do and I do it.'

These comments reveal the ignorance and the feelings of distance that remained after the conversion: the workforce simply did not see the co-operative as affecting them.

A smaller group held more positive attitudes towards the co-operative. Some simply associated it with job security: 'I think the co-op is OK. If they had sold the company then anyone could have bought it. What it means to me is that I can carry on doing the job I've been doing for seven years.' Others saw it in terms of the need for greater personal effort and responsibility: 'In a co-operative you work together for each other. Before, I worked for a boss and he told me what to do. Now you work for each other and share the profits'.

These were examples of the success of Topline's socialization, reinforced by Dixon's co-operative vision which supported the unitarist promise that individual effort would be rewarded through worker ownership. Clearly the co-operative did not alter the taken-for-granted assumption that managers would continue to run the company; consequently it was no surprise to anyone when Dixon intervened, for it confirmed the popular belief that nothing had really changed.

Thus there were several sets of meanings regarding the co-operative, including support and opposition, interest and apathy. But no one articulated a definition of co-operation built around democratic or egalitarian principles. Perhaps most important, aside from Dixon, there was no strong desire for a co-operative.

How people define a situation will profoundly influence the way in which they react towards it. This was apparent in the way that very few people initially changed their workplace behaviour, largely because they could not see that this co-operative was any different from what preceded it. Later on, when the new managerial elite assumed power and introduced sweeping organizational changes, there was a noticable growth in discontent and opposition. By this time, members were also upset by the endemic conflict that now pervaded the company. In other words, once people can see that things are different and it affects them in their daily work, then they may respond. One important area affecting all workers is the amount of control that they can exercise over decisions and the degree of autonomy that they enjoy in their job; it is to the issue of control that we turn to next.

The limits on democratic control

The ownership and control structure of the co-operative set considerable formal limits on the extent of control available to the members. However, in addition to these constraints, it is important to analyse the informal processes of control that prevented the workforce's utilizing those few formal controls that did exist.

Informal controls

The co-operative constitution gave the assembly the power to make all key policy decisions, but there was a strict requirement that 80 per cent of members had to attend the assembly and that 80 per cent support from those attending was necessary for a proposal to become company policy. These stipulations denuded the assembly of practical power. However, the ineffectiveness of the democratic mechanisms owes more to other factors than to the existence of these formal constraints.

First, the monthly meeting of the workforce had been introduced ten years earlier, primarily to disseminate information from the directors down to employees. Despite the conversion, nothing happened to make the workforce believe that the committee now possessed any more power: the directors continued to dominate meetings and non-managerial staff remained silent, in deference to their bosses. Consequently, there was a strong undercurrent of rumour, gossip, and moaning, widely acknowledged to be 'unpleasant' and 'destructive', but existing because members, including managers, felt unable to express their feelings in meetings.

Second, the assembly was weakened by low attendance; for although most area managers were present, often only about half the members turned up. This apathy was not surprising, for the agenda at meetings was geared to the needs of area managers with little effort to include assistants and office staff. And, of course, non-members had no vote. The meetings were appallingly handled, usually starting half an hour late, badly chaired, and lasting until after nine o'clock in the evening.

Third, the committee was regarded with disdain by most members. It was formed to prepare members for self-management, yet Dixon had consistently ignored its views. One manager reflected:

> He would never give up his authority. Although we had committees for years they haven't helped because they never had teeth. He made a major mistake when, after a long meeting discussing the price of a particular extension lead, he refused to allow the decision; and it was such a minor issue. If he had let it stand, it would have given us confidence and shown his good intent. No one ever took the committee seriously after that.

Fourth, the continued presence of the directors, and particularly Dixon, allowd them to exercise the informal power accrued from years of control – knowledge, expertise, self-confidence and the deference their status invoked. Dixon's actions weakened the committee; for example, he actively supported the grading grievance of the two managers, thus undermining the committee's authority. Yet, at the same assembly meeting, Dixon urged the committee to remember that 'It's your profit now, you can decide what to do with it', while berating them for not doing what *he* told them to do! He pointed to various anomalies in the grading of staff, criticized the committee's inaction, and bemoaned how 'this company has been badly managed on a day-to-day basis'. Very quickly, those younger proponents of organizational change recognized that 'Many people don't see that there has been any change, for having Dixon around means people assume he is still running things.'

By using the monthly meeting and committee as the basis of the co-operative constitution, the workforce continued to view these structures as powerless and irrelevant creations of Dixon. Even though the workforce did acquire some extra powers, they lacked the authority or will to exercise them. The hand of Dixon was still seen behind every action: he seemed incapable of relinquishing control and continued to employ a wide variety of informal strategies to secure this end.

Control over the work process

Dixon envisaged no alteration to the organization of work: a dual-control system would see the co-operative structure operating alongside the existing managerial hierarchy (Paton and Lockett 1978). The directors were still in key managerial posts where they had access to information, contacts with other businesses, and control over their departments. Similarly, area managers still exercised authority over their assistants. The retention of the management hierarchy meant that the workforce were unable to detect any difference in their day-to-day work.

Dixon had developed a paternalistic form of managerial control similar to the simple control described by Edwards (1979) as typifying early capitalist firms and those on the periphery of the modern economy. The simple management hierarchy utilized unsophisticated mechanisms of control that relied on informal, unstructured methods largely based on Dixon's personal charisma, rather than on a set of rational bureaucratic rules. For example, the wage system was complex and irrational, with workers on different wage rates for the same job, or length of service, according to some past whim of Dixon. This paternalistic system depended on the immobility of labour resulting from the non-transferability of skills, the early socialization of school leavers, and the constant propagation of unitary values by which Dixon tried to produce a workforce that could be trusted to work with minimal supervision.

The emphasis on consensual control suited the nature of work at Topline where many workers had considerable freedom and discretion in their daily job because they worked 'in the field', making service, maintenance, and sales visits to customers. This gave them considerable autonomy over the planning and organization of their own day: they could choose when to make visits, when to use the workshop and, virtually, when to work. This autonomy was cherished; even the assistants who had the most tedious maintenance calls and heaviest workloads appreciated not being 'deskbound'. The main methods of control were to count the call cards completed after each customer visit and to review the monthly area figures. Both methods were ineffective: the first was widely abused and the second was unable to isolate individual performance.

However, the market in office equipment was undergoing a transformation that had profound implications for business strategy, internal conflict, and the nature and organization of work. The profusion of new products on the market – microelectronic typewriters, word processors, screen printers – led the new management teams to begin restructuring the company, away from its traditional emphasis on back-up service, towards a more aggressive sales and marketing strategy that could compete with the discount suppliers now entering the market. The 'old guard's' Luddite opposition to the new technology reflected a vain hope this threat would somehow go away, and they were severely frightened by the ability of younger staff to grasp the new concepts and skills. Not surprisingly, the new managerial elite chose to reorganize the company to best utilize their own skills and expose the limitations of the older managers, many of whom were later sacked or demoted. But the complaints of the 'old guard' did represent a legitimate concern about the way reorganization reduced the individual autonomy of most staff by making them more directly accountable for their performance to management: sales were concentrated on a few key staff with greater rewards for success and sanctions for failure, while the tasks of the majority became increasingly mundane.

Thus there was a move away from the informal consensual system of control under Dixon, to a more coercive, rule-based system under a new management elite. It was a transformation necessitated by the pending withdrawal of Dixon as paternal figurehead and made possible by the changes to the product market and the instability arising from the unsuccessful transition to worker ownership. So, although the workforce acquired no greater control, the conversion did generate a shift in control to a new management team, albeit in a manner unintended by Dixon. But in co-operative terms, because the workforce were unable to participate in decision-making and experience no more autonomy in their daily work, they were unable to ascribe any significance to the experiment. Perhaps, if they had secured a meaningful taste of control, the workers might have reacted more positively to the conversion. But there was also the dimension of organizational culture.

Organizational culture

In recent years, the study of corporate cultures has been popular amongst students of organizational behaviour (Deal and Kennedy 1982: Peters and Waterman 1982). The case of Topline reveals the importance of the extant organizational culture in defining and shaping any attempt to change an organization into a co-operative. Change is obviously located in a historical context, 'the particular network of people, place and circumstance present at the moment of the co-operative's inception are likely to be reflected in its structures, processes and pattern of development' (Gherardi and Masiero 1987: 326). Understanding the organizational culture of Topline contributes to an explanation of three related features of this experiment – why the co-operative meant so little to the workforce, why there were several definitions of co-operation, and why the conversion had a minimal effect on the behaviour of the workforce.

First, to understand why the co-operative meant so little to the workforce it is important to recognize that for many years Dixon had striven to construct a particular organizational culture, largely through processes of character formation. In trying to translate individual drive into collective purpose and commitment, entrepreneurs do more than create the formal organizational structures, they are also: 'Creators of symbols, ideologies, language, beliefs, rituals and myths, aspects of the more cultural and expressive components of organizational life' (Pettigrew 1979: 574). Thus Selznick (1957) argued that values are embodied in organizational structures by statements of mission, programmes of activity, selective recruitment, and socialization: the organization is a historical product representing the success of the leader in generating a 'distinctive competence' for members to define and accept. Clark (1972) pointed to the bonding role of sagas in giving purpose to organizational activity and creating unity; a tactic that is particularly effective in new organizations where the culture can be built top-down. It is argued that Dixon attempted to create a distinctive organizational culture through similar symbolic means.

Dixon adopted a paternalistic style that sought to imbue the workforce with unitary values emphasizing the need for individual effort for the collective benefit of the company and its employees. The catchphrase 'Topline Thinking' was drummed into all new recruits and constantly referred to in meetings and documents. Dixon had always promised the workforce that their loyalty would be rewarded by some kind of stake or share in the company. To reinforce this message he frequently repeated the 'cathedral' metaphor. Cathedrals were built, brick by brick, as a labour of love over many years. Similarly, he argued, the successful company, with high wages, good conditions, and job security, could gradually evolve. The socialization of young workers through the training scheme was reinforced by the system of financial participation: the annual bonus based on profits was a tangible reward for good productivity. Dixon stressed this link in the regular discussion of monthly annual figures and his idiosyncratic notion, 'The Pound Earned'; a concept that few people could understand, but one that he employed with some success in establishing the relationship between effort, profits, and financial reward. The company motto urged the need for fairness: 'To our customers and suppliers. To and between ourselves.' Thus Dixon used his legitimized authority to build symbolic constructs that attempted to frame and define the organizational reality for his workforce.

The co-operative was imposed on the workforce so the employees had little knowledge of co-operation apart from what Dixon told them. This enabled him to present the co-operative plan in a form congruent with the picture of reality he had already painted, locating the co-operative in existing stocks-of-knowledge that sustained the organizational culture of Topline. He selected and emphasized those 'co-operative' values that replicated the unitarist values already operating at Topline – notably individual effort for the collective benefit, commitment and profit-sharing.

Ironically, this resulted in the workforce's being unable to detect any real differences between the old form and the new co-operative.

Second, however, the existence of a variety of definitions of co-operatives indicates that not everyone accepted this ideal cultural form. For a cultural form is not built in a vacuum, it is located in a context involving employees, product, market, and so on (Pettigrew 1979). The management of meaning is an interactive process: as 'boss' Dixon was certainly able to generate: 'A point of reference, against which a feeling of organization and direction can emerge' (Smircich and Morgan 1982: 258). But symbols can be interpreted in more than one way and the acceptance of unitarist attitudes was not unanimous. Dixon used the 'cathedral' metaphor to exhort individual hard work and short-term sacrifice for the long-term collective benefit, but some employees interpreted it differently. One 'old guard' manager observed: 'Cathedrals were built as labours of love, but now they are hollow structures, no one goes there. The same could happen here. The younger members live for today, they don't care about getting involved in running the company.' He believed that the cathedral saga should promise him, as a senior manager, a stake in the company, but younger members should not yet receive a share. In contrast, a younger manager criticized the notion of sacrifice implied by the cathedral saga: 'That's rubbish. If we make money from selling new technology, then we can pay ourselves well now: it's up to us to do it.' He rejected the metaphor for justifying the cushy seniority-by-length-of-service principle which he believed encouraged laziness by older 'time-servers' and penalized the harder-working younger staff.

Dixon was never completely successful in socializing all the workforce, although the consensus was that, in recent years, staff had developed less positive attitudes towards the company. This was probably because the recession had deflated profits, so making financial rewards no better than those paid by competitors. Morale was lowered further by feelings of job insecurity. Thus the baseline of a paternalistic system – that the instrumental needs of wages and job security are provided for – was under some threat, with predictable consequences for worker attitudes and behaviour.

Third, despite Dixon's repeated exhortations that 'they were on their own now', it was not surprising that employees were unwilling to change behaviour after the conversion by, for example, assuming responsibility, dropping their second job, or training in new technology. Why should they, when the co-operative appeared no different from what went before and they were becoming increasingly disenchanted with working at Topline?

But this was not simply a result of the breakdown of the paternalistic culture for, despite the qualifications expressed above, this culture was still strong and it acted as a constraint on organizational change. Topline

335

was characterized by a strong subordinate trait that is common in paternalistic cultures. For example, the directors had always taken the key decisions:

> The culture, once established, prescribes for its creators and inheritors certain ways of believing, thinking, and acting which in some circumstances can prevent meaningful interaction and induce a condition of learned helplessness – that is a psychological state in which people are unable to conceptualize their problems in such a way as to be able to resolve them.
>
> (Bate 1984: 44)

So it was not surprising that the committee and the assembly proved incapable of effective decision-making. This learned helplessness afflicted all staff: the fact that the old guard were so used to Dixon's telling them what to do partly explains why they could not come to terms with learning new business and technological skills. The presence of the directors meant that deferential habits continued; directors were still called 'Mr' and the upstairs office area remained foreign territory for non-management staff. When conflict or indecision arose – over the wage grievance and the corruption incident – the natural response was still to turn to Dixon.

But because organizational culture is an evolving process in continual flux, it should not be regarded simply as a constraint on change. Indeed, although the culture helped prevent the workforce from taking an active, participative role in the co-operative structure, paradoxically the culture also gave the opportunity for two relatively dynamic individuals to seize power with minimal resistance – a development that led to a fundamental change in the organizational culture. Clearly, the concept of organizational culture is an important means of explaining the nature and extent of change in Topline.

Discussion

The experience of Topline Typewriters illustrates two general points about the study of co-operatives. First, organizational change is not achieved by simply transferring ownership and rewriting the formal control structures of a company. The reality is far more complex; yet politicians and policy-makers often seem unaware of this point. Hence, second, the co-operative literature must adopt a broader perspective that analyses the form of individual co-operatives to ask in what way they differ, if at all, from what came before. The approach adopted here focuses on the processes of meaning formation, a broader concept of control, and the influence of the organizational culture.

The meaning that the members attributed to the experiment was, in short, very little! Despite the existence of several, contrasting definitions of the conversion situation, few people held a clear view of what Dixon was trying to achieve. But several people were aware that co-operatives elsewhere could be 'different', as illustrated by observations on Dixon's intervention:

> In a co-operative the workforce should decide everything, but what ever the trustees decide goes – so to my mind we're not a co-op yet.

> I liked the committee but now it's been banned hasn't it? I don't think that's right. How can you ban a committee in a co-op when it's been elected by its members? It's still Mr Dixon who runs the show.

These comments from non-managerial members suggest a critical disjunction: such definitions of co-operation were not applied to Topline because co-operatives were something that other people were doing – they did not see Topline in these terms. No one regarded 'co-operation' at Topline as implying fundamental change: after all, managers still gave orders, the views of non-members were largely ignored, workers had little say, the day-to-day job was no different, and Dixon clearly still 'ran the show'. Only when Dixon intervened was this commonsense understanding briefly disturbed, prompting some members to reflect that he could not have acted in this way if Topline was a true co-operative. However, this disruption to their thinking-as-usual was not permanent; even if members had wished to act on this feeling, there was little to nurture this oppositional line, now that the co-operative structures were in abeyance.

It is of significance that the co-operative was the result of a top-down initiative by Dixon. It was Dixon's 'baby'; he conceived and designed it to his own specifications, without involving the workforce in this creative process. This issue of ownership and authorship is important; people will possess a feeling of ownership for what they create, but the Topline workforce had no part in constructing the plan and, consequently, despite having a share in ownership, they displayed little understanding or attachment to the co-operative. Significantly, there was no struggle involved in forming the co-operative and this has proven critical elsewhere (Bate and Carter 1986), nor the involvement of an external stakeholder such as a Co-operative Development Agency to help nurture 'co-operative ideas and processes.'

The definitions of the situation were influenced by the workers' experience of the systems of control within the organization. The workforce acquired minimal formal control over organizational decisions and it was constrained by various informal control processes. The evidence suggests that the members were unable to detect any benefit from the conversion without perceiving or experiencing control. Nor did Dixon's scheme attempt any reorganization of the work process that would reduce the managerial hierarchy, provide more information, or enhance job discretion for the non-managerial staff. Wider technological and product market developments brought new demands but, although the company had to adapt to these changes, the way in which it did was open to negotiation. The new managerial elite made the strategic choice (Child 1972) to interpret product market changes in a way that reduced job autonomy, made skills and individuals redundant, and resulted in a more coercive, rule-bound system of control. Would a 'co-operative' have chosen differently – perhaps by maintaining the emphasis on service back-up and defending individual job autonomy? In essence, the continuing absence of control sustained a powerlessness that prevented the workforce from conceptualizing a different way of organizing themselves.

Last, because Dixon expressed his plans in terms of the extant organizational culture and based the co-operative constitution on institutions that had fallen into disrepute, there was a strong sense of *déjà vu*. People asked: what was different? what was new? Dixon was telling the same stories, repeating the same platitudes, urging the same behaviour, so that people reacted to the conversion in the same way they did before – some positive, others negative; some believing, others disbelieving. Furthermore, because the paternalist culture engendered subordinate and dependent attitudes and behaviour, the workforce was unable or unwilling to adopt a positive response to the possibility of developing a co-operative form. Dixon's definition of the situation failed to become a collective definition; staff did not adopt Dixon's co-operative idea, they held a variety of individual definitions of the situation, and they felt no inclination to change their views. Dixon's plan for orderly transition failed. Without this social construction there was no common vision or will among the workforce that could counter either Dixon's intervention or the ascendency of the new managerial elite.

Future research on the nature of co-operative organizational forms would benefit from the adoption of a broader analytical perspective that builds on ideas generated by other disciplines and which are beginning to permeate the co-operative literature. Topline itself also provides a fascinating story. Although this particular experiment proved a failure – judged by its impact on individual attitudes and behaviour, and the nature of the new organizational structures and processes – this chapter should not be read as warning against converting an existing organization to a co-operative. Rather it highlights the different problems raised by this particular route to worker ownership. One can speculate about criteria for improving the likelihood of 'success'. For example, a bottom-up approach in which the workforce articulates a desire for a co-operative and plans the transition may prove more effective. This may be enhanced if there is a consensus concerning the aims of a co-operative, whatever these may be – to operate democratically, to make a specific product, to create more jobs, or to earn the members bigger profits!

However, Topline also highlights the contradiction between the unitarist vision of Dixon and the democratic co-operative. Although the 'ideal-type' co-operative is unitarist because shared ownership and control should remove all capital/labour conflict, the unitarism of Dixon aimed to remove the manifestation of conflict without changing the underlying structures and processes of control. His top-down, non-consultative imposition of co-operation was hardly conducive to nurturing a democratic environment. Dixon was a 'benevolent dictator', in the Robert Owen mould, the father of the co-operative movement, who shared a style and approach to co-operation that generated similar frustrations when workers did not behave in the way he intended. Topline serves as a warning about this particular type of conversion – where an owner has a clear vision of a co-operative and the means to achieve this end – which confronts the familiar reforming paradox that authoritarian means are an inappropriate way of obtaining democratic, participative ends.

Notes

1 'Topline Typewriters' and 'George Dixon' are not the true names of the company or the individual concerned.
2 The term 'conversion' is used to refer to the handover of power by Dixon and the word 'co-operative' is used throughout the analysis, despite the fact the company never legally passed completely into worker ownership.

References

Abell, P. (1979) 'Hierarchy and democratic authority', in T. Burns *et al.* (eds.) *Work and Power*, London: Sage.

Bate, P. (1984) 'The impact of organizational culture on approaches to organizational problem-solving', *Organizational Studies*, 5, 1, 43–66.

Bate, P. and Carter, N. (1986) 'The future for producers co-operatives', *Industrial Relations Journal*, 17, 1, 57–70.

Batstone, E. (1983) 'Organization and orientation: a life cycle model of French co-operatives', *Economic and Industrial Democracy*, 4, 139–61.

Carter, N. (1988) 'Control, consciousness and change: a study of the development processes of a worker co-operative', unpublished PhD thesis, University of Bath.

Child, J. (1972) 'Organization structure, environment and performance: the role of strategic choice', *Sociology*, 6, 1–22.

Clark, B. (1972) 'The organizational saga in higher education', *Administrative Science Quarterly*, 17, 178–84.

Clarke, T. (1984) 'Alternative models of co-operative production', *Economic and Industrial Production*, 5, 97–129.

Coates, K. (1976) *The New Worker Co-operatives*, Nottingham: Spokesman.

Cornforth, C. (1986) 'Worker co-operatives: reformulating the degeneration thesis', paper presented at 11th World Congress of Sociology.

Cosyns, J. and Loveridge, R. (1981) 'The role of leadership in the genesis of producer co-operatives', Working Paper 217, University of Aston Management Centre.

Deal, T. and Kennedy, P. (1982) *Corporate Cultures*, Reading, Mass: Addison-Wesley.

Edwards, R. (1979) *Contested Terrain*, London: Heinemann.

Gherardi, S. and Masiero, A. (1987) 'The impact of organizational culture in life-cycle and decision-making processes in newborn co-operatives', *Economic and Industrial Democracy*, 8, 323–47.

Jones, D. (1975) 'British producer co-operatives and the views of the Webbs on participation and ability to survive', *Annals of Public and Co-operative Economy*, 46, 23–44.

Oakeshott, R. (1978) *The Case for Workers Co-operatives*, London: Routledge & Kegan Paul.

Oliver, N. and Thomas, A. (1990), see chapter 19 of this volume.

Paton, R. and Lockett, M. (1978) *Fairblow Dynamics Ltd: Participation and Common Ownership*, Milton Keynes: Open University Press.

Peters T. and Waterman, R. (1982) *In Search of Excellence*, New York: Harper & Row.

Pettigrew, A. (1979) 'On studying organizational cultures', *Administrative Science Quarterly*, 24, 570–81.

Rothschild-Whitt, J. (1979) 'The collectivist organization: an alternative to rational-bureaucratic models', *American Sociological Review*, 44, 509–27.

Russell, R. (1985) *Sharing Ownership in the Workplace*, Albany: State University of New York Press.

Selznick, P. (1957) *Leadership in Administration*, New York: Harper & Row.

Smircich, L. and Morgan, G. (1982) 'Leadership: the management of meaning', *Journal of Applied Behavioural Science*, 18, 3, 257–73.

Wajcman, J. (1983) *Women in Control*, Milton Keynes: Open University Press.

Webb, S. and Webb, B. (1914) 'Co-operative production and profit-sharing', *New Statesman Special Supplement*, 14 February.

Chapter nineteen

Ownership, commitment, and control: the case of producer co-operatives

Nick Oliver and Alan Thomas

Introduction

In the last decade there has been a surge of interest in worker co-operatives in the UK and many other countries. This interest spans many shades of social, political, and economic opinion – the case for co-operatives has been argued on many premises including social justice, business efficiency, human growth, and, at the level of the economy, job-creating by means that minimize the risk of capital flight.

Although some aspects of co-operative functioning have received extensive research attention, a crucial element which has hitherto received scant attention is the issue of organizational control of member behaviour.

Co-operatives are interesting in terms of control for two reasons. First, they frequently embody a set of beliefs and values that are antagonistic to traditional systems of organizational control. This antagonism is manifested in a number of ways, examples being a dislike of hierarchies (and hence concentrations) of authority, a rejection of a highly fragmented or rigid division of labour and a resistance to the formality of rules and procedures. Rothschild and Whitt (1986: 22) go so far as to say that 'The prime goal of collectivist organization is escape from the Weberian imperatives of domination and hierarchical administration.'

However, Rothschild and Whitt recognize that this goal is not always achieved and detail nine conditions under which collectivist organization can flourish. These conditions are a provisional orientation; mutual and self-criticism; limits to size and internal growth; homogeneity of membership; the existence of an internal support base; diffusion of knowledge and technology; oppositional services and values; a supportive professional base; a social-movement orientation and economic marginality.

The second reason for interest in co-operatives from the viewpoint of theories about organizational control is more specific. It has been suggested that vesting ownership and control of an organization in the hands of those who work in it creates the conditions for a marked

341

increase in labour efficiency. Abell (1983) has summarized the reasons behind this argument. As the worker members of a co-operative are its owners and ultimate controllers, residual benefits accrue solely to them, thereby creating a 'community of interests' within the firm. This may serve to increase efficiency by enhanced member motivation; a reduction in the need for supervision; a reduction in the incidence of internally competitive behaviour; an increase in the probability of workers' contributing constructive ideas, and an increase in 'altruistic' concern about the welfare of the co-operative and its members, a condition heavily dependent on the solidarity and commitment of the members.

The arguments for increased efficiency assume increased motivation and commitment. There may, of course, also be constraints on efficiency arising from economic or other factors. For example, undercapitalization or lack of skills may reduce labour efficiency both directly and indirectly through low wages and poor working conditions, both undermining the development of commitment in the first place and negating its effects if it does develop.

In combination, the ideas of Abell and Rothschild and Whitt pose some interesting questions about control in co-operatives. Can co-operatives resist the bureaucratic imperative? How feasible is it for mechanisms of control 'external' to individuals such as rules and hierarchical supervision to be replaced by 'internal' mechanisms such as member commitment? Are conditions such as those suggested by Rothschild and Whitt necessary before such 'internal' control mechanisms are workable? To explore these questions we shall first present a framework for analysing control in organizations in general, and then use this framework to explore control and commitment in three different types of producer co-operatives.

Authority, control and commitment

The issue of control reveals more ambiguities for co-operatives than perhaps any other. Being a member of a co-operative is often described in terms of 'individual freedom', 'an absence of bosses', and so on. Membership of an organization typically entails an exchange – the benefits of membership are exchanged for contributions to the organization. Inevitably individuals are constrained by organizational directives to some degree. Control of individuals is thus central to purposeful collective action of any description.

Control can be exercised in a number of ways, some of which are less intrusive than others. A typology which specifically considers the issue of compliance in organizations has been put forward by Etzioni (1961). Etzioni argues that organizations have essentially three means of eliciting appropriate behaviour from their members. These are:

calculative means, in which rewards are offered in return for the desired behaviour – rewards may be material or symbolic; co-ercive means, where particular behaviour is secured under threat; normative or moral means, in which member behaviour is shaped not by the prospect of threat or reward, but by appeal to a shared set of values or implicit rules concerning what is 'right' or 'wrong' behaviour. This last means has been described as cultural control (Child 1985).

The means of control used by an organization is reflected in different psychological states or 'contracts' (Kotter 1973) on the part of its members. Organizational members are likely to respond to the first strategy by developing an instrumental attitude to their activities, to the second with alienation, and to the third with commitment, or at least automatic compliance to directives on the grounds that compliance is the 'right' response to legitimate demands.

Cultural control is currently attracting a great deal of interest among academics and practitioners alike. Ever since Peters and Waterman (1982) claimed a link between strong organization culture and business success, many organizations have sought to create the conditions in which committed members pour their energies into their employing organization, guided by values which are 'clearly ordered, deeply held and widely shared'.

When one considers the arguments in support of co-operatives reproduced in the introduction of this paper, it is apparent that co-operatives' potential for creating such commitment is assumed. Thus the primary type of control expected in co-operatives is 'normative' or cultural control.

Following Peters and Waterman, a number of writers have documented the conditions which create and sustain a 'strong' culture. These include:

1 A shared set of over-arching or superordinate goals, a sense of mission.
2 Minimal internal divisions. This condition may be supported in a number of ways, including comprehensive systems of communication (avoiding internal barriers to communication which may permit sub- or counter-cultures to form); rotation of staff between different functional areas; generous benefits; small units; single status terms and conditions; and a consultative management style. Such conditions support normative control by creating a homogeneous social system.
3 Selective recruitment and intensive socialization of new members. This helps maintain another aspect of homogeneity, in the makeup of the workforce.
4 Structures and systems which make individual behaviour public, hence encouraging easy monitoring of behaviour.

Homogeneity is perhaps one of the most important elements of normative control. If organizational members are similar (at least in certain key respects), then the potential variations in individual behaviour which the organization's control mechanisms must 'tame' will be smaller and the control mechanisms that much milder. The control an organization exerts over its members may only be experienced as an intrusion when it conflicts with what the individual would do if left to his or her own devices. A homogeneous workforce whose norms and values coincide with those of the organization is less likely to have to be 'brought into line' by external control mechanisms than a heterogeneous workforce, some of whose members may not share the aims and objectives of the organization. Superficially co-operatives possess a number of features corresponding to the conditions above.

However, it is clearly not automatic for a co-operative to possess a 'community of interests' and a 'strong' culture. In fact the conditions suggested by Rothschild and Whitt for successful collectivist organization bear remarkable similarities to the conditions given by Peters and Waterman for sustaining a 'strong' culture in any organization. There are some differences, notably that the collective requires oppositional values and a social movement orientation, whereas Peters and Waterman argue that any set of over-arching goals will suffice. Also Rothschild and Whitt give some conditions that do not correspond to anything in Peters and Waterman, namely, provisional orientation, supportive professional base, and economic marginality.

The types of control exercised in producer co-operatives comprise the main theme explored by this chapter. What types of control do co-operatives use to direct member behaviour? Do co-operatives use 'normative' or 'cultural' control as has commonly been assumed? Does the mere fact of being a producer co-operative provide the necessary conditions for normative control?

Answers to these questions are sought at two levels. First, organizational conditions are considered in terms of dominant control strategies. We assume that a successful normative control can be recognized by a low level of overt conflict; ease of acceptance of organizational directives; with appeals to common interest or to guiding values being the usual means for gaining compliance. Second, individual attitudes and orientations are analysed. At this level, we look for a high level of commitment on the part of organizational members; identification with the organization as a whole; members acting supportively towards the organization for its own sake.

This approach assumes that the control strategy used by an organization and the attitudes of individual members are reciprocally dependent. Thus the type of control in use will influence whether members are instrumental, alientated from, or committed to the organization. Similarly, it is accepted that people do not enter organizations as 'blank slates', but bring expectations and orientations with them. Member orientations may thus significantly determine which control strategies are desirable or feasible.

Each of our three main examples is quite different in terms of the circumstances of its foundation. We examine a small 'new start' co-operative; an established business given away to its employees by its benevolent owner; and a large 'rescue' co-operative. The three cases differ also in terms of the dominant motivation behind their formation: the first started with 'alternativist' ideals; the second through paternalism; the third guided by pragmatic considerations of job saving. We will see below the importance of these differences in terms of how feasible it proved in each case to promote common goals or a sense of mission. In each case we describe some of the organizational conditions pertinent to the issue of control, and then consider the response of co-operative members to the experience of co-operative working.

Recycles Ltd

Recycles is a small co-operative which began trading in 1977 and is engaged in the business of cycle sales, hire, and repairs. At the time of writing seven people work there. A full account of the co-operative's history is available elsewhere (Oliver 1987).

Organizational conditions

The co-operative began as a small back-street cycle-repair shop. It was soon recognized that this operation did not generate sufficient income to sustain the business, so the co-operative moved into cycle hire and retailing. After six years the co-operative was generally regarded as the leading retailer of specialist bicycles and equipment in Scotland. In the course of this development the co-operative changed from a predominantly alternative-movement orientation to one centred around the specialist cycling market. The co-operative currently has seven members, each of whom work a four-day week, though the business is open six days a week. Wage levels, although average for the cycle trade, are considerably less than most of the co-operative's members could have earned elsewhere; most have a high level of educational qualifications.

There are two discernible levels of authority at Recycles: the individual and the collective. The collective comprises the total membership of the co-operative and is typically represented by a meeting of all the co-operative's members. It is this body which has ultimate decision-making power in the co-operative. Obviously not all decisions are taken by the general meeting, but those recognized as important generally are. For less important ones individuals have the authority to act without reference to the general meeting, thus giving a second level of authority, the individual level.

General meetings function both as arenas for information exchange, and as the ultimate source of authority. There are three such types of meetings: weekly business meetings (two hours in duration); six weekly 'horizon' meetings (a whole evening in duration); and ad hoc meetings to cover special issues.

Collective control over individuals largely occurs informally; instances of individuals overstepping the bounds of their authority are rare. The members of the co-operative have developed a shared sense of what is an acceptable decision to make individually and which decisions require collective endorsement. It is possible for members (sometimes knowingly) to overstep the bounds of their authority. One example of this is an occasion on which the person responsible for shopfitting purchased several hundred pounds' worth of display material without the approval of the rest of the co-operative. This was seen by some as a major overstepping of authority and this message was conveyed both overtly and covertly at meetings for some months afterwards.

In terms of the types of control mechanisms described previously, the evidence points to cultural control. Acceptance of responsibility is high, and members' behaviour shows every sign of being governed by a shared view of what is appropriate or expected, with minimal external pressure. In balancing business and democratic demands, Recycles has adopted a degree of specialization, with some delegation and formalization in terms of procedures, record books, and so on. Ironically, for a business of its size, the co-operative is in some ways considerably more 'bureaucratic' than an equivalent traditional business.

Individual responses

All Recycles' members reported a high degree of job satisfaction, particularly when compared to other jobs that they had held. However, on a standard scale measuring organizational commitment the members did not score significantly more highly than the population average. On the same scale some three years previously significantly higher than average scores had been obtained. Although the ideological fervour because the business was a co-operative had declined over time, this decline had not diminished 'committed' behaviour. If anything, as a businesslike ethos replaced the initial 'alternative' ethos, business performance improved.

Discussion

The predominant mechanism by which the collective entity exerts control over individual members appears to be normative or cultural. A number of factors appear to be playing a role here. These are: the small size of the group, which is conducive to member involvement and group cohesion; common comprehension of all aspects of the various jobs and the techniques involved by all members, leading to easy communication and possibilities for rotating between functions; a homogeneous membership; encouraged by the economic marginality of the co-operative.

In terms of homogeneity an interesting shift is discernible during Recycles' development. In the early days homogeneity was promoted (albeit unconsciously) by the recruitment of pro-co-op people, often friends or friends of friends in the Edinburgh alternative community. Following the departures of a number of people recruited in this way, whose competence as mechanics had turned out to be extremely limited, the recruitment policy shifted towards recruiting people who were cycling enthusiasts first and foremost. Although this shift occurred for business reasons, it permitted one means of gaining people's intrinsic interest and commitment (bicycles) to substitute for another – the co-operative ideal.

The economic marginality of the co-operative, particularly in its early days, meant that there was little scope for dissension over goals – most actions were constrained by the logic of survival. As two members of the co-operative commented:

> In the first three years the long-term aims of the co-operative were so specific you could write them on a postcard.

> When the co-operative is poor and struggling there is very little dissent about what the goal is – the goal is to keep going.

As the business gained financial soundness, the scope for dissension could have increased, although this has not occurred. One explanation may be that continued, though less acute, marginality has continued to constrain options open to the co-operative and hence conflict about those options. A second possibility is that the interest and enthusiasm for bicycles on the part of the members provides an energizing and uniting effect. The shift in recruitment emphasis away from specifically pro-co-op people which could have led to a degeneration of democracy in the co-operative paradoxically seems to have improved it. Although wages remained low, the new emphasis meant people with higher levels of skills and knowledge about bicycles were employed. An intrinsic interest (assisted by a self-selection process engendered by the low wages) in the business remained, and the higher skill levels helped create more organizational elbow room – which in turn supported the democratic process.

Scott Bader Ltd

Scott Bader is a common ownership company engaged in the manufacturing, retailing, and distribution of resins products. The company has a manufacturing site with about 250 staff and a retailing and distribution subsidiary with about 100 staff. At the time this research was conducted, the manufacturing site had been under common ownership for about thirty years, having been given to its employees by its benevolent owner in the 1950s.

Organizational conditions

The manufacturing company is located in rural Northamptonshire. The local labour culture may be characterized as paternalistic, with little tradition of adversarial industrial relations. The company's assets are held in trust by a holding company. Individuals have no financial stake in the company; were it to be dissolved, no individual would benefit. The majority of any surplus in a given year is ploughed back into the business, the remainder being divided equally between a bonus to the employees and donations to charities nominated by the membership.

There are two systems of control in the company. There is a conventional management hierarchy to handle the routine co-ordination and control of the company's operations. Differentials are compressed; the constitution states that the ratio of highest to lowest salary shall not exceed 7:1. In addition to the conventional management structure, there is a complex representative system, which largely (though not wholly) handles policy issues. Elected representatives sit on the company board along with senior management. The company is divided into fourteen constituencies, each of which elects a representative to sit on the major representative body, known as the Community Council. Two Council members sit on the company board; it must approve the appointment and removal of all other directors. It is responsible for approving the remuneration of the directors and discusses and makes recommendations to the Board of matters of company policy. It has the power to veto executive decisions. Ultimately decisions are made on the basis of one person, one vote, either in general meetings or via ballots, although this procedure is generally only used in special circumstances.

After eighteen months' service employees are eligible to become members of the Commonwealth. Only Commonwealth members are able to vote in any of the elections and ballots, or stand in a representative capacity. Approximately 90 per cent of the workforce are members. To gain membership, they are required to show a basic understanding of (and sympathy with) the organization's philosophy and principles. These are laid down in a document detailing company objectives and a code of practice for members and include the statement that 'The basic purpose of the company is to render the best possible service as a corporate body to our fellow men.'

Items in the code of practice reflect this sentiment; the language is couched in terms of the company as a community with four tasks: economic, technical, social, and political. Management is by consent – the managerial role is seen as one of a 'catalyst of common effort'. Members are required to show a corresponding sense of responsibility mainfested by 'a desire to attend meetings and to participate in the affairs of our community'. The code of practice also states that the company shall not manufacture any products used in 'weapons of war' and shall make every effort to avoid damage to the natural environment.

About a sixth of the workforce are trade union members, mainly in the TGWU and ASTMS. However, wages and conditions are not negotiated with trade unions; the Community Council is the vehicle of representation for both issues of remuneration and grievances.

All members enjoy single-status terms and conditions; there is no system of 'clocking on' for anyone. The compressed differentials means that wages for lower grades of worker are high relative to comparable jobs outside the co-operative, about the same for middle management, and somewhat lower for senior managers.

Member responses

There has been little overt conflict since the introduction of common-ownership. Wage negotiations with trade unions were abandoned during the mid-1950s. Since then the Community Council has served as the representative body endorsing decisions on wage rates. The language used within Scott Bader reflects a perception of the organization's being the members' company, with a corresponding acceptance of actions which are in 'the company's' interest. This is not to say that there have not been differences of opinion. A decision to close down a section of the plant and relocate the workers elsewhere led to an angry reaction from the members of that section, but the closure went ahead virtually unhindered. Differences of opinion have tended to focus on the extent to which commercial decisions conflicted with the constitution; there was very little explicit questioning of the constitution *per se*.

In terms of commitment, on a standard commitment scale, the membership at Scott Bader showed significantly higher scores than the population as a whole. This significantly higher score held when the potentially confounding effects of skill level and gender were taken into account. The members of the co-operative also showed significantly higher scores on measures of involvement and loyalty.

In terms of satisfaction 73 per cent of respondents indicated that they were satisfied with their jobs. The features which elicited the highest satisfaction were the friendly atmosphere in the company, features of their immediate jobs (degree of control, variety, and skills utilization), the convenience of the site for home, and the high product quality. Slightly more than half the respondents felt that they put more effort into their work at Scott Bader than they would in a conventional company.

Members were asked a variety of questions about the company's objectives and their participation in the democratic machinery. The vast majority (92 per cent) claimed to be familiar with the company's objectives; of these 17 per cent report 'strong agreement' with them, 68 per cent 'agreement' with the others being either indifferent or in mild disagreement with them. Participation in the company's affairs was high. Approximately a third of respondents had served on the Community Council at some time during their employment with the company.

The SRL episode

The harmony enjoyed by the company received a jolt in 1982 when Scott Bader acquired Synthetic Resins (SRL) of Speke, Liverpool. SRL had been owned by Unilever and had contracted from employing 545 people in 1974 to 220 by 1982. Prior to the Scott Bader takeover, there were a further 100 redundancies (allegedly at Scott Bader's insistence), which reduced the workforce to 125.

SRL operated a closed shop with five unions on site; USDAW, ASTMS, EETPU, AEUW, and the GMB. There were many antagonisms in the company; between white- and blue-collar workers, the skilled and the unskilled, management, and unions. There were also inter-union tensions. Most of the workforce welcomed the Scott Bader takeover, as a number of the other companies interested were suspected to be asset-strippers. However, a labour research document on Scott Bader was circulated among the workforce and caused some concern. The craft workers feared skill dilution as a consequence of more flexible working; others feared that traditional trade-union rights would be undermined by a company where wage rates were not determined by negotiation between management and unions. In a ballot 34 out of 36 craft workers indicated they would prefer redundancy to working for Scott Bader.

This suspicious reception augured badly for the future. An account by McMonnies (1985) describes poor communication, confusion, and misunderstanding between the two organizations. The unions at SRL understood neither Scott Bader's intentions nor how they operated; Scott Bader did little to inform them of either. Differences came to a head in 1983; the Community Council agreed to forgo a pay rise and this was communicated to SRL. Unions at SRL interpreted this as a refusal to negotiate and worked to rule; under this pressure the Scott Bader Board made a pay offer of 1.9 per cent, plus a further 1.1 per cent for increased flexibility. This was accepted, after threats by Scott Bader to close SRL down. The issue re-emerged later in the year when it was decided (on the basis of a narrow majority in a ballot of all Commonwealth members) to exclude SRL staff from the annual bonus.

In 1985 Scott Bader closed SRL down.

Discussion

Scott Bader displays a number of features supportive of cultural control. The company is based on a clearly articulated set of principles which are both bold, unusual, and in a sense 'superordinate'. Membership of the Commonwealth has to be applied for and can be (and is) witheld if there is evidence of inappropriate attitudes and behaviour. Communication is open and fairly intense, although in recent years increasing concern has been voiced about what is seen as autocratic behaviour on the part of the executive team. Considerable effort is devoted to fostering a sense of community, a condition backed up by single-status facilities and generous benefits. The business is in a rural location with a paternalist local labour culture. Moroever it is the main employer in its area and is seen as 'a good company to work for'.

In terms of member responses, commitment is significantly greater than population norms at Scott Bader. Agreement with the philosophy on which the company is based is high, and this is reflected by a high usage of the democratic machinery. This suggests that member acceptance of organizational directives is given willingly rather than extracted under duress.

This contrasts markedly with the reaction of SRL employees to Scott Bader following the takeover. SRL was sited in a declining region where there was a tradition of mobile (multi-national) capital; McMonnies reports one SRL craft worker as remarking: 'I've been made redundant so many times it doesn't matter to me any more.'

Under these conditions, it is perhaps understandable that, as an outside company moving in, Scott Bader did not in many respects appear significantly different to other companies moving in (and out) of Merseyside. Where Scott Bader was perceived as different was antagonistic to SRL's workforce in that collective bargaining – the central tenet in terms of management–workforce relations – was not recognized by Scott Bader. Effectively two powerful and incommensurate sets of values collided; when coupled with SRL's substantial internal divisions this negated any possibility of normative control.

Kirkby Manufacturing and Engineering Ltd (KME)

KME was one of three large rescue co-operatives set up with the support of Tony Benn when he was Secretary of State for Industry in 1974–5. The factory was a large, unionized workplace with a history of changes in management and in product, poor profitability and takeovers, big plans followed by rationalizations, and a high level of union activism.

In January 1972 there was the first of two factory occupations. AUEW Senior Steward Jack Spriggs issued an ultimatum to the managers:

> In 1963 there were 2,500 people who worked here and every time a product was sold off and you made money you made redundancies. Now we have a workforce of 700 – well, we've had enough. We're giving you formal notice now, in our own little way – we've got no papers – but as from today *you're* redundant.

Despite an agreement to save jobs, by 1974 there had been another change in ownership and the announcement that the factory would have to close. The second occupation – this time a work-in – lasted two weeks during July 1974. Tony Benn then pushed through the idea of setting up the Kirkby factory and workforce as a co-operative. Despite government grant aid the co-operative was underfunded from its inception.

KME inherited a strange combination of products: radiators, engineering products, and soft drinks. Previous expansions had left the expectation of reasonably good wages and conditions, though these had already been considerably eroded before the co-operative took over. The underfunding was exacerbated by difficulties in obtaining good credit terms. The co-operative was never profitable, although about 750 jobs were sustained relatively cheaply for almost five years. KME was forced to close in 1979.

Organizational conditions

The worker co-operative at Kirkby was in a sense foisted on to a workforce whose militant action was directed simply at saving as many jobs as possible. The idea of 'workers' control' was current at the time, but there was no clear model translating this into how to run a large and complex organization, and there was no idealistic element within the workforce in favour of co-operation as such.

KME's only democratic tradition in the workplace was that of trade unionism, and six unions were present in some strength. In addition to the traditional forms of unionism, there were elements of the new grassroots shop-stewards movement, derived from the euphoric episodes of the two occupations. Of the three democratic organs established or mooted to oversee democratic working in the co-operative, two thus came directly from existing union structures. At the top of the new structure, the two convenors became directors; at the middle management level the joint Shop Stewards Committee assumed new powers. Eccles (1981) points out that both convenors and stewards were caught in dual roles, where they kept the traditional union role of representing workers' interests via collective bargaining at the same time as taking on new roles of 'guardianship' of the enterprise. Between these two levels there was to have been a third democratic organ, a Works Council, with Council members elected on a ballot, including candidates from management. In the words of an ex-employee manager:

> The Council lasted three months. [The elected General Manager] even asked if he could chair meetings. We asked Jack Spriggs if it could meet once a month; he said 'It says in the constitution once every six weeks and I think that's too often.' . . . We were serious; we wanted to run that factory.

Despite the efforts of activists on the Council to get it involved in company matters, it never achieved legitimacy, and after a phase in which Jack Spriggs himself chaired the Council, any influence it may have had withered away. It was possible to discredit it on the basis that the way it was elected under-represented the shopfloor unions, but the real point was that, as an independently elected body, it presented a challenge to both established union and management structures.

The long-standing union structures based their legitimacy on upholding defensive attitudes on the part of their members. Members' individual interests could conflict with the interests of the business as a whole, and the interests of different sections of the membership certainly conflicted – despite the new fact of being a co-operative. There was never enough economic success to create the 'slack' that might have simultaneously satisfied all interests. Several business advisers suggested closing the soft-drinks section. Though the least profitable, it had shown great solidarity during the occupations. This clear demonstration of the basic conflict persisting between workers' interests and the company's commercial interests was not lost on the workers themselves. In the words of two of them:

> I could never see workers on the shop floor saying that, in the interests of the firm, 150 people are going to have to go up the road. It's going to have to be Jesus Christ to get that over to them.

> [I'm still] . . . militant! But you couldn't fight against yourself. It's like looking at yourself in the mirror and cracking yourself on the chin, sort of thing.

Sectional interests were still strong. On one occasion seven tool setters refused an instruction to move from skilled to semi-skilled work – they saw it as more important to uphold their status than to be flexible for

353

the good of the co-operative. They were actually sacked, but not before a confusing dispute, with a mass-meeting vote apparently overturned by the management with the support of the Director-Convenors, and four stewards resigning. On another occasion there was a strike when maintenance workers who refused to be reallocated to other work were threatened with dismissal.

The Director-Convenors were in a difficult position. They were effectively in top management positions, but their authority rested on their ability to protect jobs, and the jobs of everyone – even of 'free-riders must be protected equally. Despite all these difficulties, the co-operative did get a great deal of commitment and effort out of its ordinary workers, particularly at first. According to one manager:

> When the co-op started Jack asked for more radiators . . . [The radiator workers] found a better way of doing it. They condensed the relaxation time. Spriggs asked the welders for more and they had the worst job and they gave more.

However, there was a limit to the extra effort forthcoming without extra material rewards. Stewards were in a particularly difficult position in combining the traditional role of representing members' interests with the new one of being essentially part of middle management. One younger steward commented:

> Our role changed from that of a conventional shop steward to that of a boss – cajoling the workers to do the job . . . We had no consultation over the big decisions concerning plant, finance or products. But when there was a touchy situation and things were getting a bit hairy then the shop stewards were called in to deal with the people and quieten the shopfloor.

However, stress, ill health, disillusion, and, in some cases, promotion caused very high turnover among stewards. This and the lack of alternative independent democratic organs led control to be increasingly concentrated in the hands of the Directors-Convenor. They preserved unity and directed a company that performed as a co-operative at least as well as it had under private management.

Individual responses

KME's workforce was more or less a cross-section of the ordinary working population, a long way from the self-selected homogeneity of Recycles. The majority retained a fairly passive, utilitarian attitude to work. However, they were mostly prepared to work hard and give extra for the co-operative, as in the case described above. Unfortunately, conditions of work remained poor, though there were some compensations: 'The best thing was it was not really strict. It was like meeting all your sisters – a home from home.'

There were also a number of 'activists', including stewards and others – individuals wanting to show that the co-operative ideal could work, wanting to share power and use it responsibly, prepared to put not only effort but a great deal of themselves into the co-operative. Most of these became disillusioned, though some did achieve things they couldn't otherwise have got – status, training, or just a wider view than their own job. Unfortunately, within the working situation at KME, particularly with its lack of commercial success, there was not the scope for all the different rewards the various activists were looking for.

Discussion

Unlike the previous two cases, co-operation clearly failed at KME – jobs were maintained for several years relatively cheaply. There was in a way an attempt at normative control – exhortation, 'cajoling', and the need for solidarity in support of the leadership were used on top of conventional management control methods – but this too failed in that workers, after a period of complying with exhortations to produce extra, reverted to instrumental and defensive attitudes. Once the co-operative promise failed to deliver, it was also unable to continue to bring out positive responses.

The conditions for normative control were mostly absent. There was no agreed goal or ideals beyond the pragmatic saving of jobs. Internal divisions were exacerbated by lack of communication channels, very different technologies and skill levels between different workers in different parts of the factory, and poor working conditions. The workforce was not homogenous, and there was no selective recruitment – indeed, it was almost a point of honour to try to protect the jobs of all equally. Finally, although to some extent there was increased openness, there were no systems in place to ensure fairness.

What was perhaps even more disappointing was that there was apparently no real attempt to promote any of the conditions that might have assisted the maintenance or development of a 'community of interests' – no promotion of common ideals; only a small reduction in status differentials; no attempt at consultation, 'intensive socialization', or developing good systems of internal communication.

There are job-saving co-operatives that have been more successful (Bate and Carter 1986; Thomas and Thornley 1988). These are generally cases of smaller co-operative businesses rising out of the ashes of failed conventional organizations. They are more likely to have at least partly self-selected membership, and to have more in common in terms of technology and skills, by comparison to a large rescue like KME. They may in some cases be able to set up on the basis of clearly agreed values in addition to pure job-saving, such as the maintenance of skills or of local quality service. Nevertheless, the difficulties encountered by KME are probably indicative of the kind of problems to be overcome at such co-operatives.

Discussion and conclusions

Co-operatives, like other organizations, exert control over their members. In the three examples looked at in detail, and in many others reported elsewhere (Cornforth *et al.* 1988; Mellor *et al.* 1988; Thomas and Thornley 1988), there is a clear attempt to utilize mechanisms or normative or cultural control. However, in most cases, although these may be the dominant mechanisms, material-reward structures also play a part, even if only at the level of ensuring a minimum standard of living relative to each member's individual changing needs and opportunities. In two of our cases, normative control seemed to work well; in the third (KME), it did not.

Thus, in co-operatives as elsewhere, normative control requires certain conditions if it is to operate successfully. Such conditions include a homogeneity of membership; small(ish) size; face-to-face interaction; an absence of sources of internal division, and so on.

However, we can go further and differentiate between cases. First of all, there are co-operatives that are attempting more than this in that their ideals include collective working. Many 'alternative' co-operatives, including Recycles, are like this at least in their early years. It is clear that this is a much more difficult undertaking and probably requires the kind of additional conditions suggested by Rothschild and Whitt; a supportive professional base; not just common goals but oppositional values (collectivism may itself be perceived as such) and a social movement orientation; a provisional orientation (and possibly economic marginality also).

Three main reasons appear to limit the possibilities for such an extreme undertaking. First, the size has to be really small and the homogeneity condition pretty fiercely applied, to maintain full collective working. Second, few people are prepared to accept the personal material sacrifice implied – indeed, this is why 'provisional orientation' (and 'economic marginality') figure in the list of conditions. At Recycles, as at other alternative co-operatives, material considerations became more important for members as time went on and the co-operative became a permanent business rather than the project of a few ex-students – though normative control remained dominant. Third, collectivism does not seem to be sufficient in itself to be the guiding value for any but a few exceptional individuals. Values which are more external to the business, and which at the same time allow identification between the job itself, the business, and its external goals, seem to offer the best possibility. Thus, a belief in promoting bicycles and good quality service to the biking community, though not oppositional, seems to unify and generate the 'community of interests' required in a more sustainable fashion.

A second model is where the conditions for normative control may be partly met, but continuing effort is needed to maintain them. This applies in larger or growing alternative co-operatives, in cases like Scott Bader, and in certain more successful rescue co-operatives. Here, it is certainly extremely useful to realize that ownership structure in itself does not appear to be the answer. By attending to features described previously, large traditional businesses have normatively controlled their workforces. Strategies to achieve this include careful selection and socialization of new members, systems for monitoring behaviour and performance, and open and intensive communication. These things do not just happen automatically because of the fact of being a co-operative. More generally, the 'over-arching goals' of a co-operative have to be constantly debated and promoted, rather than its being assumed that new recruits can absorb them 'by osmosis'.

The third model may be regarded as a failure but is potentially of importance. In cases such as large rescues, some conversions, or takeovers (KME and the Scott Bader takeover of SRL are both good examples), the workforce is clearly not homogeneous and nor is the internal organization conducive to normative control. In such cases it should be clearly recognized that a complete switch to normative control methods will not work well. A transition would have to be planned, with perhaps a fairly long period in which elements of conventional material-reward structures persist alongside new cultural elements. There is no reason, however, why a worker co-operative should not be run with a hierarchical control system even though it is owned by its workers.

What of the question of whether the fact of being a co-operative makes any difference at all? It certainly makes no automatic difference. However, it may be argued that in many cases in conventional capitalist organizations there is in fact a basic conflict of interest that no amount of appealing to artificial company-mission statements can overcome. Although strategies of cultural control have been shown to work in traditional businesses, they may be more appropriate in a co-operative, where the residual profits as well as the direct rewards of labour accrue to the workers.

One has to be cautious about this propositon for two reasons. First, it could be that real control lies outside the individual co-operative, for example, with large firms that employ the small firms or co-operatives as subcontractors, or with the market in a more general sense. This seriously limits the possibilities, though this is an aspect of organizational control in co-operatives hardly touched on in this paper. Secondly, the basic conflict of interest referred to above persists in co-operatives, though it takes the form of an internalized conflict between the short-term interest of individual workers and the longer-term interests of the business as a whole. Finally, there is a reluctance to see control of any kind as relevant to co-operatives, since co-operatives may be set up in specific opposition to traditional forms of organizational control – and there may be no awareness of other possibilities.

References

Abell, P. (1983) 'The viability of industrial producer c-operation', in Crouch, C. and Heller F. (eds.) *International Yearbook of Organizational Democracy*, pp. 73–103. London: Wiley.

Bate, P. and Carter, N. (1986) 'The producers' co-operative; its status and potential as an alternative form of organisation', *Industrial Relations Journal* 17, 1.

Cornforth, C., Thomas, A., Lewis, J. and Spear, S. (1988) *Developing Successful Worker Co-operatives*, London: Sage.

Child, J. (1985) *Organization: A Guide to Problems and Practice*, London: Harper and Row.

Eccles, A. (1981) *Under New Management*, London: Pan.

Etzioni, A. (1961) *A Comparative Analysis of Complex Organisations*, New York: Free Press.

Kotter, J. (1973) 'The psychological contract: managing the joining up process', *California Management Review*, 15, 3, 91–9.

McMonnies, D. (1985) 'The Scott Bader – Synthetic Resins Saga' *Employee Relations* 7, 2, 20–5.

Mellor, M., Hannah, J. and Stirling, J. (1988) *Worker Co-operatives in Theory and Practice*, Milton Keynes: Open University Press.

Oliver, N. (1987) *The Evolution of Recycles Ltd*, Milton Keynes: Co-operatives Research Unit, Open University.

Peters, T. and Waterman, R. (1982) *In Search of Excellence*, New York: Harper Row.

Rothschild, J. and Whitt, A. (1986) *The Co-operative Workplace*, Cambridge: Cambridge University Press.

Thomas, A. and Thornley, J. (1988) Co-ops to the Rescue, London: Industrial Common Ownership Movement co-publications.

Index

Abbreviations are consistent with those used in the text.

Printed in the United States
by Baker & Taylor Publisher Services

TO : ....

FROM : ....

TODAY'S DATE : ....

Visit our website at skyhorsepublishing.com

10 9 8 7 6 5 4 3 2 1

Editorial by Sam Hutchinson
Design and illustration by Vicky Barker

ISBN: 978-1-63158-716-0

Printed in China

My MOMMY and ME

A KEEPSAKE ACTIVITY BOOK

WRITTEN BY
SAM HUTCHINSON

ILLUSTRATED BY
VICKY BARKER

FOR
YOUNG
READERS

This is my mommy!

STICK PHOTO
IN HERE!

Her first name is ....

She is .... years old.

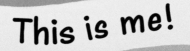

This is me!

STICK PHOTO
IN HERE!

My first name is ....

I am .... years old.

My mommy's full name is

....

Her date of birth is

....

She was born in

....

She has .... siblings

Was your mommy born where you live now?
Look up her place of birth on a map
... even if it is only a few streets away!

My full name is

....

My date of birth is

....

I was born in

....

I have .... siblings

Do you know where your name comes from?
Who chose it? Does it have a special meaning?
Design a badge all about your name.

My mommy's height is

....

Her hair color is

....

Her hair length is

....

Her eye color is

....

Draw a picture of your mommy!

My height is

....

My mommy is .... taller than me

My hair color is   My hair length is

....

My eye color is

....

Do you look similar to your mommy?
Do you have the same hair color?
How about your mommy's mommy
(your grandparent!). Do they look similar?

Draw a picture of yourself!
Make sure to sign your drawing,
like a famous artist.

The school my mommy went to is called

....

It is in

....

Her favorite lesson was

Her least favorite lesson was

....

Did your mommy do any activities at school or after school? Write about them here.

....

....

....

....

Ask your mommy if she has any photos or certificates you can see.

My school is called

....

It is in

....

My favorite
lesson is

My least favorite
lesson is

....

Do you do any activities at school or after school?
Are they similar to the activities your mommy did?
Write about a time that your mommy helped you
with something at school or after school.

....

....

....

....

During the school day,
when I am at school
or learning at home,
my mommy does

....

....

....

Stick a photo or
draw a picture here

Stick a photo or
draw a picture here

When mommy was my age
she dreamed of being a

....

....

....

When I am my mommy's age I want to be doing ...

My mommy's favorite color is

....

My mommy's favorite
piece of clothing is

....

Design a T-shirt
that you think
your mommy
will love!

My favorite color is

....

My favorite piece
of clothing is

....

Design a piece of clothing that
shows you and you mommy together!

Tell a funny story or draw a comic strip that will make your mommy laugh!

My mommy's favorite song is

....

The name of the band or the singer is

....

The song first came out in

....

My mommy loves this song because

....

....

....

My favorite song is

....

The name of the band or the singer is

....

The song first came out in

....

I love this song because

....

....

....

For breakfast, my mommy likes to eat

....

For lunch, my mommy likes to eat

....

For dinner, my mommy likes to eat

....

Her favorite food is   Her least favorite food is

....

She can cook .... really well!

Draw a picture here

For breakfast, I like to eat

For lunch, I like to eat

For dinner, I like to eat

My favorite food is   My least favorite food is

I can cook .... really well!

Draw a picture here

Using three different colors, circle words that describe you in one color, words that describe your mommy in another color and, in a third color, circle words that describe you both.

Kind

Funny

Silly

Serious

Outgoing

Fun

Clean

Confident

Friendly

Private

Quiet

Energetic

Caring

Calm

Thoughtful

My perfect day with my mommy would involve:

In the morning,

....

....

....

At lunchtime,

....

....

....

In the afternoon,

....

....

....

In the evening,

....

....

....

Draw you and your mommy together at the end of a happy day together! You can stick in a photograph if you prefer.

My mommy travels around by

....

Draw a picture of your mommy and her
favorite mode of transportation.

When I am my mommy's age,
I will travel around in my

....

Draw a picture of your futuristic
mode of transport!

My mommy's favorite hobbies include:

....

....

....

....

....

STICK PHOTO
IN HERE!

My favorite hobbies include:

....

....

....

....

....

One thing we love to do together is:

....

One thing we would like to do together in the future is:

....

Finish writing this poem about your mommy!

I know my mommy loves me
She says it every day ...

....

....

....

....

....

....

....

....